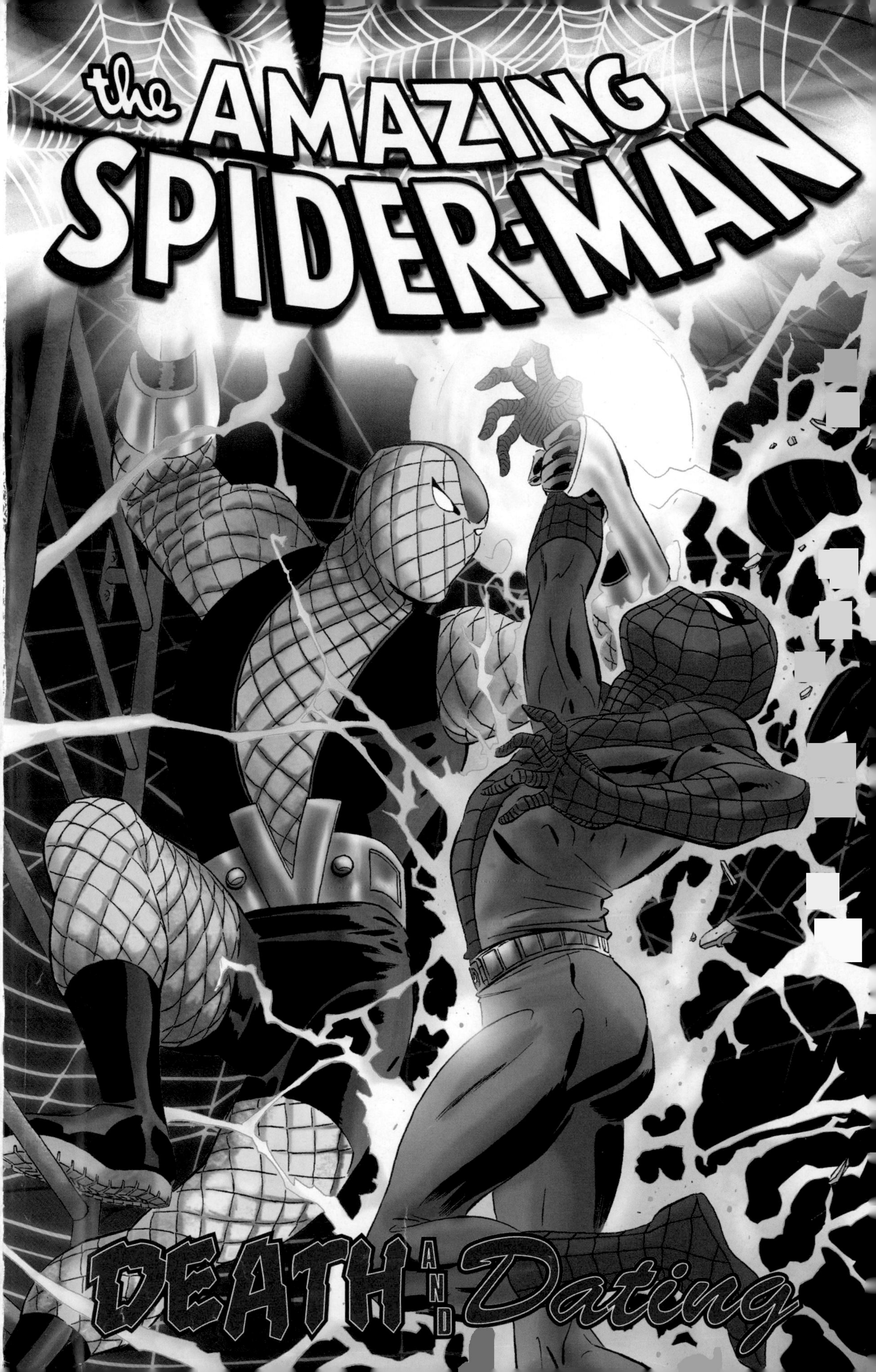
the AMAZING
SPIDER-MAN
DEATH AND Dating

the AMAZING SPIDER-MAN
DEATH AND Dating

SPIDER-MAN: DEATH AND DATING. Contains material originally published in magazine form as AMAZING SPIDER-MAN #578-583 and 2008 ANNUAL. First printing 2009. Hardcover ISBN# 978-0-7851-3394-0. Softcover ISBN# 978-0-7851-3418-3. Published by MARVEL PUBLISHING, INC., a subsidiary of MARVEL ENTERTAINMENT, INC. OFFICE OF PUBLICATION: 417 5th Avenue, New York, NY 10016. Copyright © 2009 Marvel Characters, Inc. All rights reserved. Hardcover: $24.99 per copy in the U.S. (GST #R127032852). Softcover: $19.99 per copy in the U.S. (GST #R127032852). Canadian Agreement #40668537. All characters featured in this issue and the distinctive names and likenesses thereof, and all related indicia are trademarks of Marvel Characters, Inc. No similarity between any of the names, characters, persons, and/or institutions in this magazine with those of any living or dead person or institution is intended, and any such similarity which may exist is purely coincidental. Printed in the U.S.A. ALAN FINE, CEO Marvel Toys & Publishing Divisions and CMO Marvel Characters, Inc.; JIM SUKOLOWSKI, Chief Operating Officer; DAVID GABRIEL, SVP of Publishing Sales & Circulation; DAVID BOGART, SVP of Business Affairs & Talent Management; MICHAEL PASCIULLO, VP Merchandising & Communications; JIM O'KEEFE, VP of Operations & Logistics; DAN CARR, Executive Director of Publishing Technology; JUSTIN F. GABRIE, Director of Publishing & Editorial Operations; SUSAN CRESPI, Editorial Operations Manager; ALEX MORALES, Publishing Operations Manager; STAN LEE, Chairman Emeritus. For information regarding advertising in Marvel Comics or on Marvel.com, please contact Mitch Dane, Advertising Director, at mdane@marvel.com. For Marvel subscription inquiries, please call 800-217-9158.

10 9 8 7 6 5 4 3 2 1

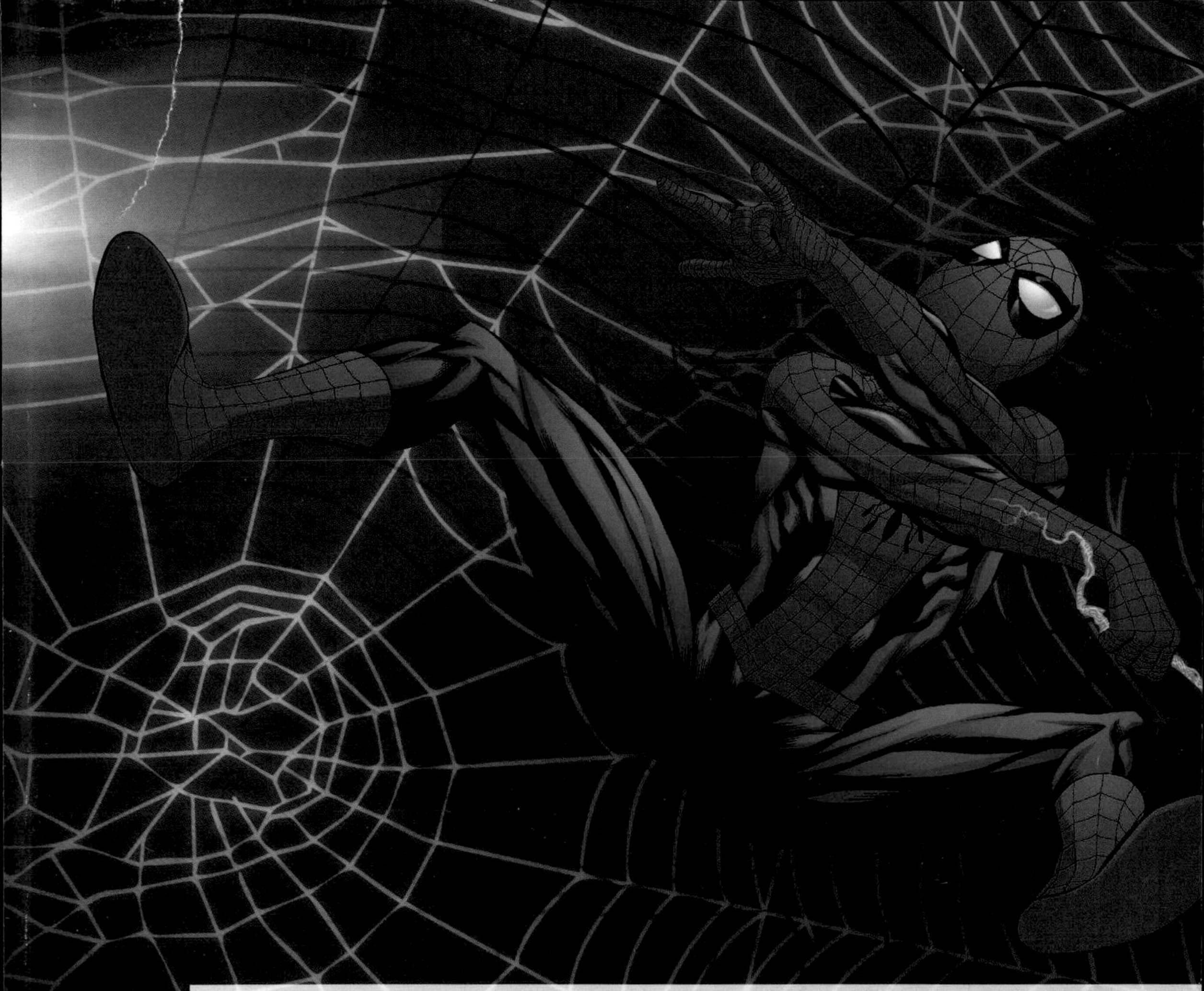

Letters: **VC'S CORY PETIT** with
JOE CARAMAGNA (Issue #578) & **CHRIS ELIOPOULOS** (Issue #578)
Spidey's Braintrust: **BOB GALE**,
MARC GUGGENHEIM & **DAN SLOTT**
Assistant Editor: **TOM BRENNAN**
Editor: **STEPHEN WACKER**
Executive Editor: **TOM BREVOORT**

Collection Editor: **JENNIFER GRÜNWALD**
Editorial Assistant: **ALEX STARBUCK**
Assistant Editors: **CORY LEVINE** & **JOHN DENNING**
Editor, Special Projects: **MARK D. BEAZLEY**
Senior Editor, Special Projects: **JEFF YOUNGQUIST**
Senior Vice President of Sales: **DAVID GABRIEL**

Editor in Chief: **JOE QUESADA**
Publisher: **DAN BUCKLEY**
Executive Producer: **ALAN FINE**

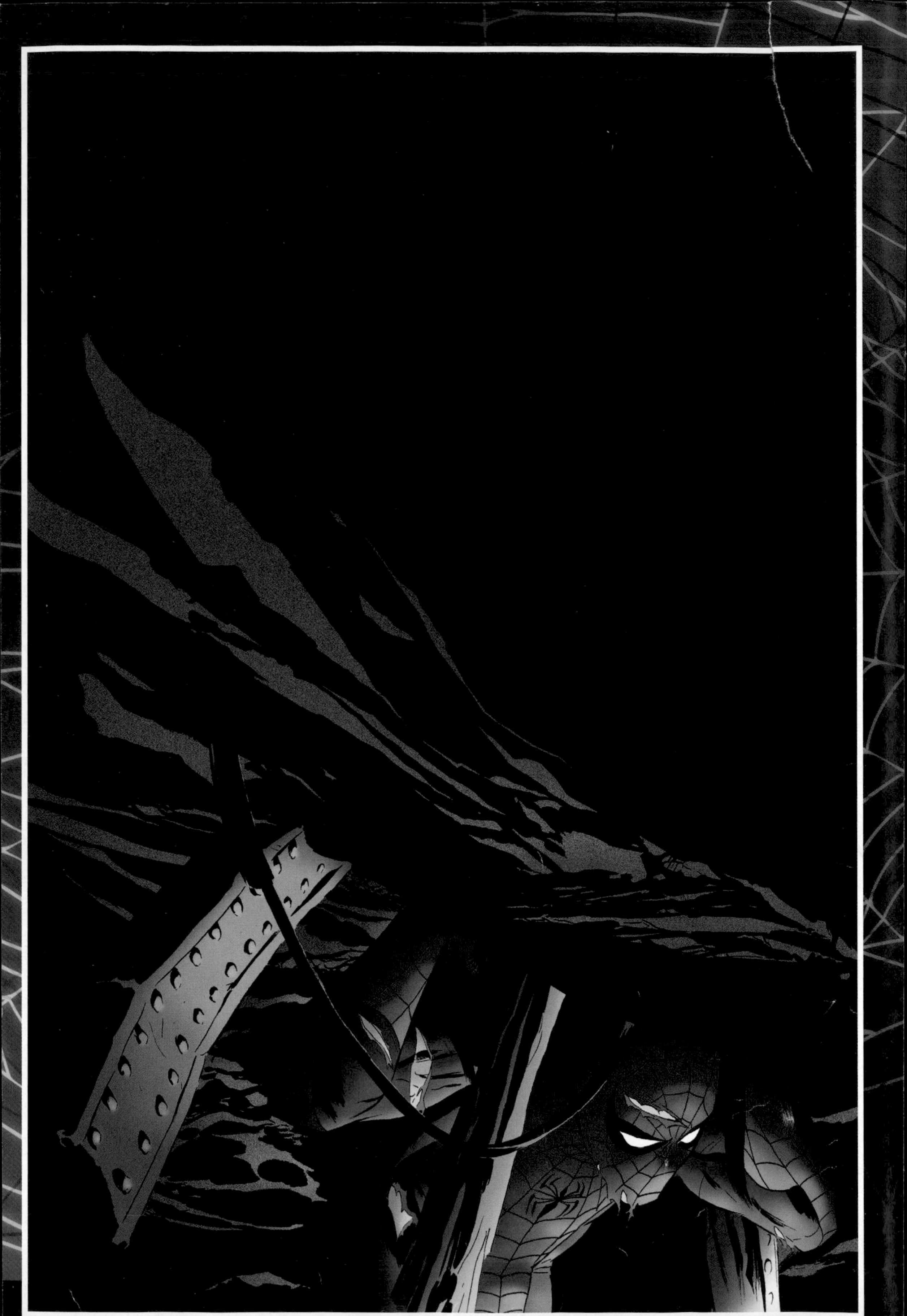

AMAZING SPIDER-MAN #578

THE DB! FOR EVERY BRAND *NEWS* DAY[illegible]

THE DB

NOVEMBER 19, 2008 • WEDNESDAY

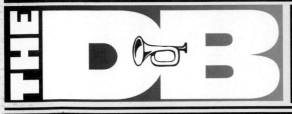

WHO'S THE TOUGHER CANDIDATE ON CRIME? RANDALL CROWNE PUBLICLY DERIDES KARNELLI FAMILY'S CONNECTION TO GIACOMO MOB TRIAL, FORMER D.A. BILL HOLLISTER "WON'T COMMENT IN RESPECT TO THE PROCESS!" MORE ON PAGE L68

CRIME & PUNISHERS

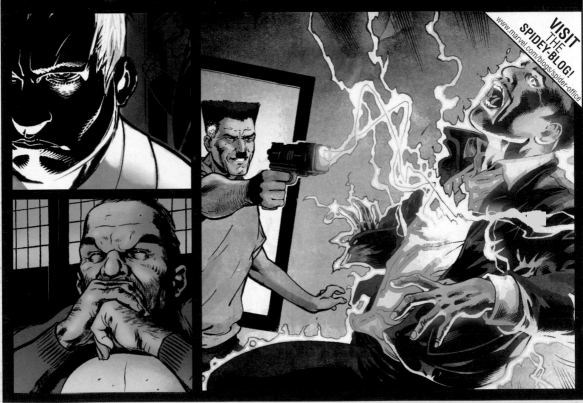

VISIT
THE
SPIDEY-BLOG!
www.marvel.com/blogs/spider-office

A recent revival of superhuman forces in the criminal underworld has Spider-Man on high alert. First, Hammerhead received a power upgrade and position within Mr. Negative's burgeoning criminal organization. Then Pete found himself aligned with the Punisher, of all people, to stop old Avenger's foe Moses Magnum from an arms deal that would put ordinary mobsters on a super-powered level. Factor in Spidey's tacit alliance with super-villain bet-taker extraordinaire, The Bookie (whose shoddy investigation of the Spider-Tracer killings left him on the business end of a stun gun, courtesy of Spider-Foe and deposed Daily Bugle publisher, J. Jonah Jameson), and you get the feeling that when it rains for Spider-Man, it pours…

POLICE [illegible] SPIDER-[illegible]A[illegible] TO RECE[illegible] MURDE[illegible]!

EXCLUSIVE TO T[illegible]E DB!

In off-the-record conversations with DB staffers, police have confirmed that Spider-Man is the key suspect in the string of recent murders that has shocked this city. Although police have been reluctant to discuss the specifics of the murders, so-called "Spider Tracers" have definitely been found on each victim, leaving no doubt as to the involvement of Spider-Man. Spider-Man is already wanted for violations of…

CONTINUED ON A2

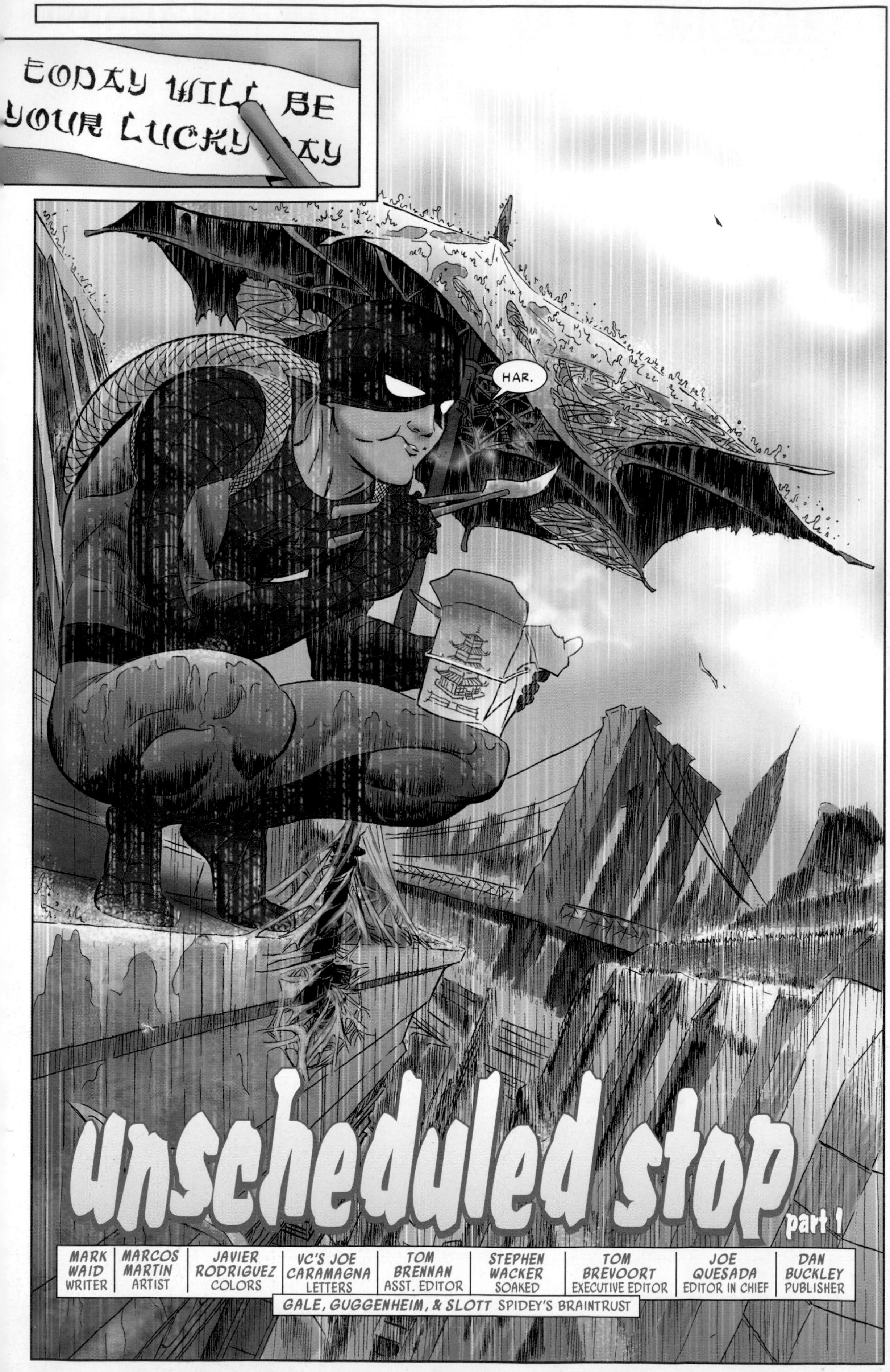

TODAY WILL BE YOUR LUCKY DAY
HAR.
unscheduled stop part 1
MARK WAID WRITER
MARCOS MARTIN ARTIST
JAVIER RODRIGUEZ COLORS
VC'S JOE CARAMAGNA LETTERS
TOM BRENNAN ASST. EDITOR
STEPHEN WACKER SOAKED
TOM BREVOORT EXECUTIVE EDITOR
JOE QUESADA EDITOR IN CHIEF
DAN BUCKLEY PUBLISHER
GALE, GUGGENHEIM, & SLOTT SPIDEY'S BRAINTRUST

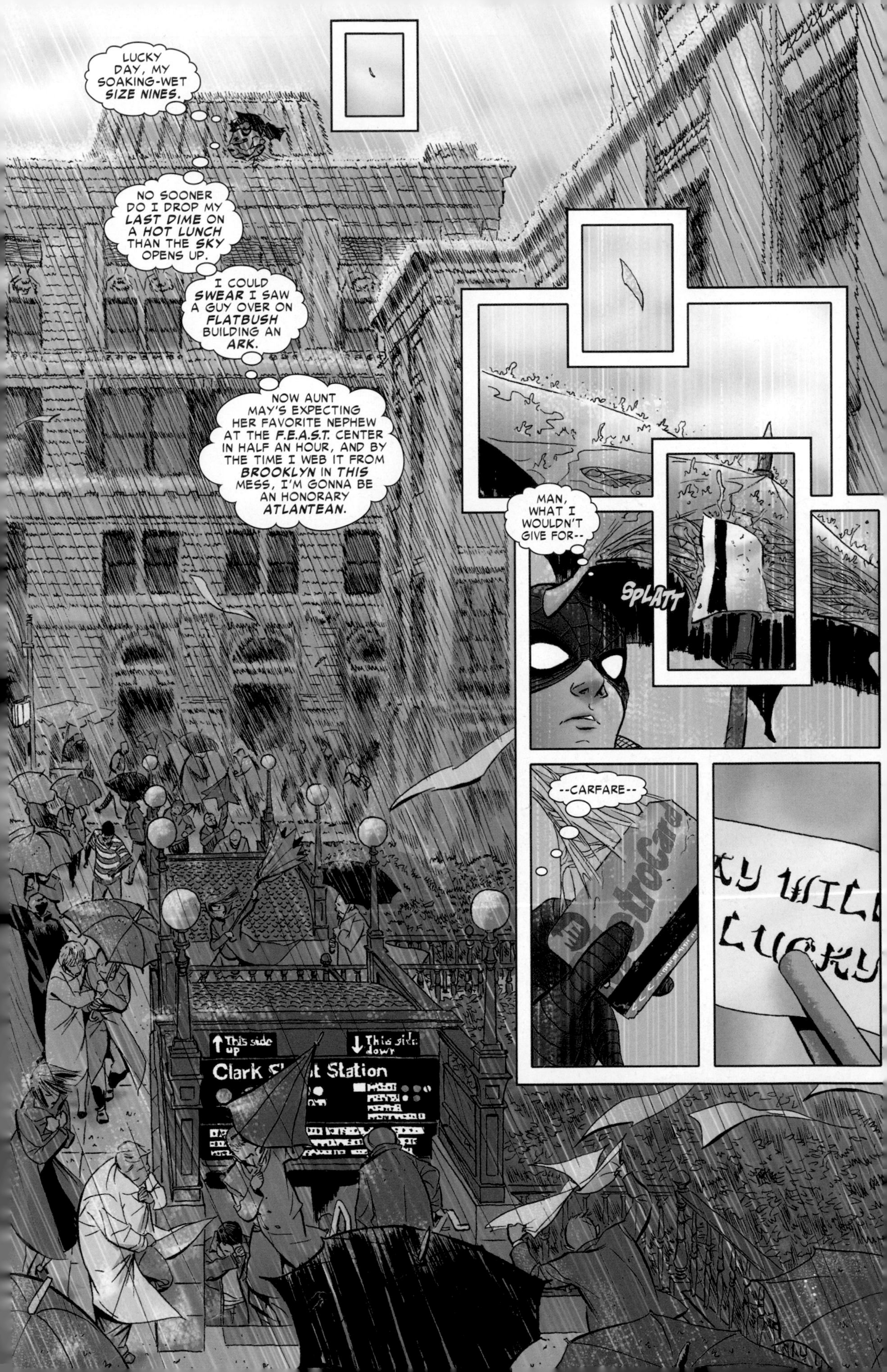

LUCKY DAY, MY SOAKING-WET SIZE NINES.
NO SOONER DO I DROP MY LAST DIME ON A HOT LUNCH THAN THE SKY OPENS UP.
I COULD SWEAR I SAW A GUY OVER ON FLATBUSH BUILDING AN ARK.
NOW AUNT MAY'S EXPECTING HER FAVORITE NEPHEW AT THE F.E.A.S.T. CENTER IN HALF AN HOUR, AND BY THE TIME I WEB IT FROM BROOKLYN IN THIS MESS, I'M GONNA BE AN HONORARY ATLANTEAN.
This side up
This side down
Station
MAN, WHAT I WOULDN'T GIVE FOR--
SPLATT
--CARFARE--
LUCKY

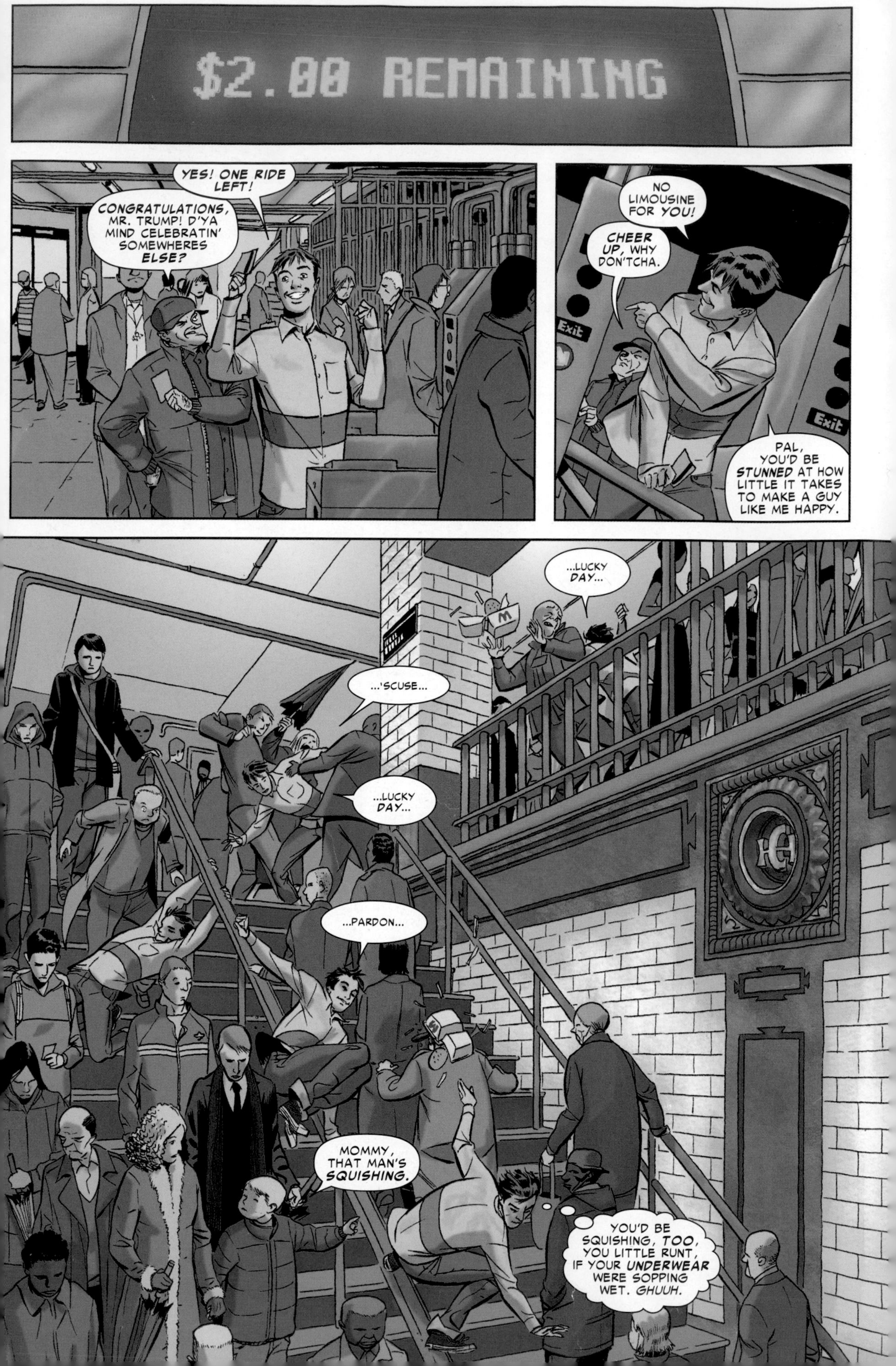
$2.00 REMAINING
YES! ONE RIDE LEFT!
CONGRATULATIONS, MR. TRUMP! D'YA MIND CELEBRATIN' SOMEWHERES ELSE?
NO LIMOUSINE FOR YOU!
CHEER UP, WHY DON'TCHA.
PAL, YOU'D BE STUNNED AT HOW LITTLE IT TAKES TO MAKE A GUY LIKE ME HAPPY.
...LUCKY DAY...
...'SCUSE...
...LUCKY DAY...
...PARDON...
MOMMY, THAT MAN'S SQUISHING.
YOU'D BE SQUISHING, TOO, YOU LITTLE RUNT, IF YOUR UNDERWEAR WERE SOPPING WET. GHUUH.

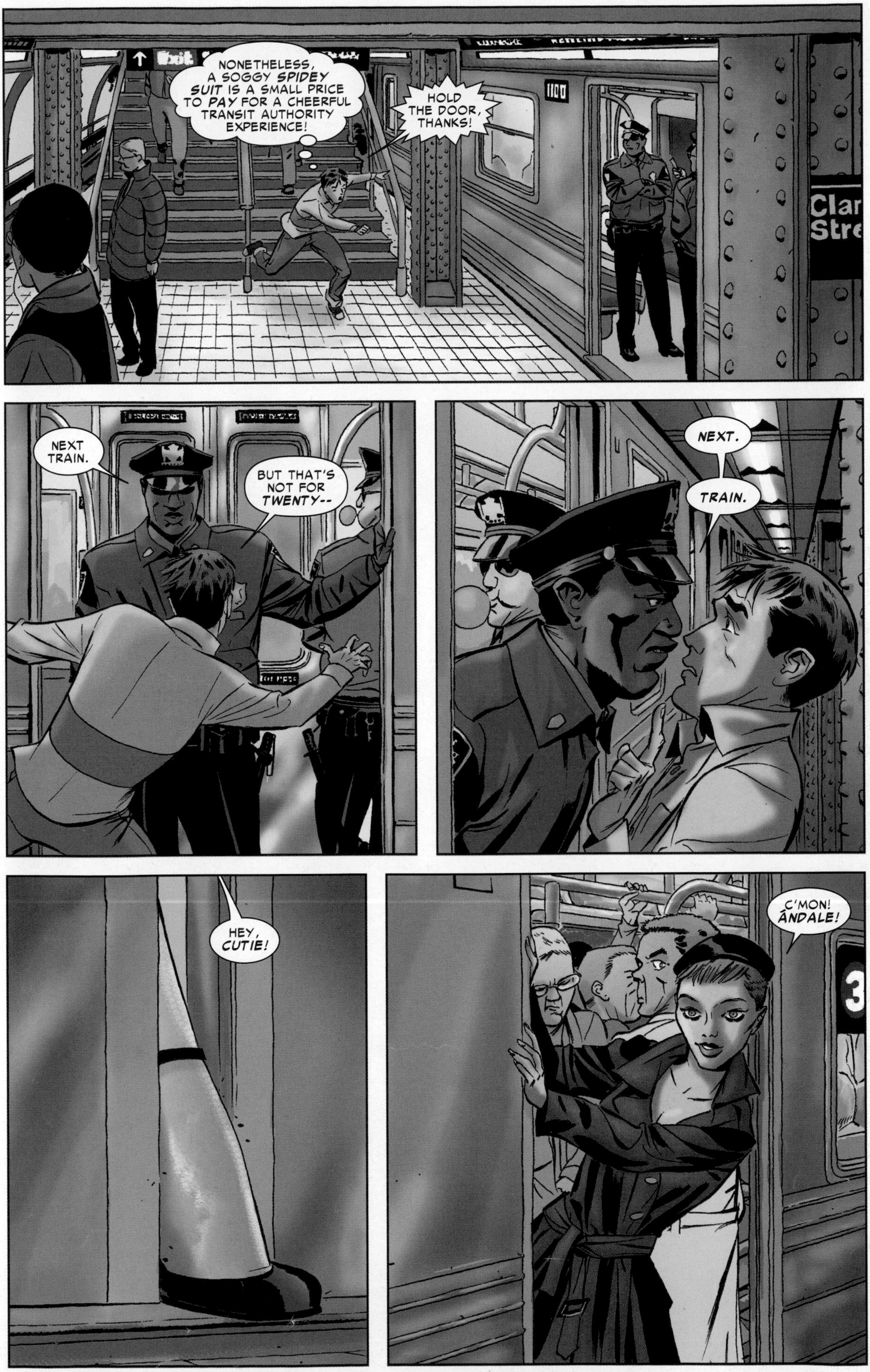

NONETHELESS, A SOGGY SPIDEY SUIT IS A SMALL PRICE TO PAY FOR A CHEERFUL TRANSIT AUTHORITY EXPERIENCE!
HOLD THE DOOR, THANKS!
Clar
Stre
NEXT TRAIN.
BUT THAT'S NOT FOR TWENTY--
NEXT.
TRAIN.
HEY, CUTIE!
C'MON! ÁNDALE!

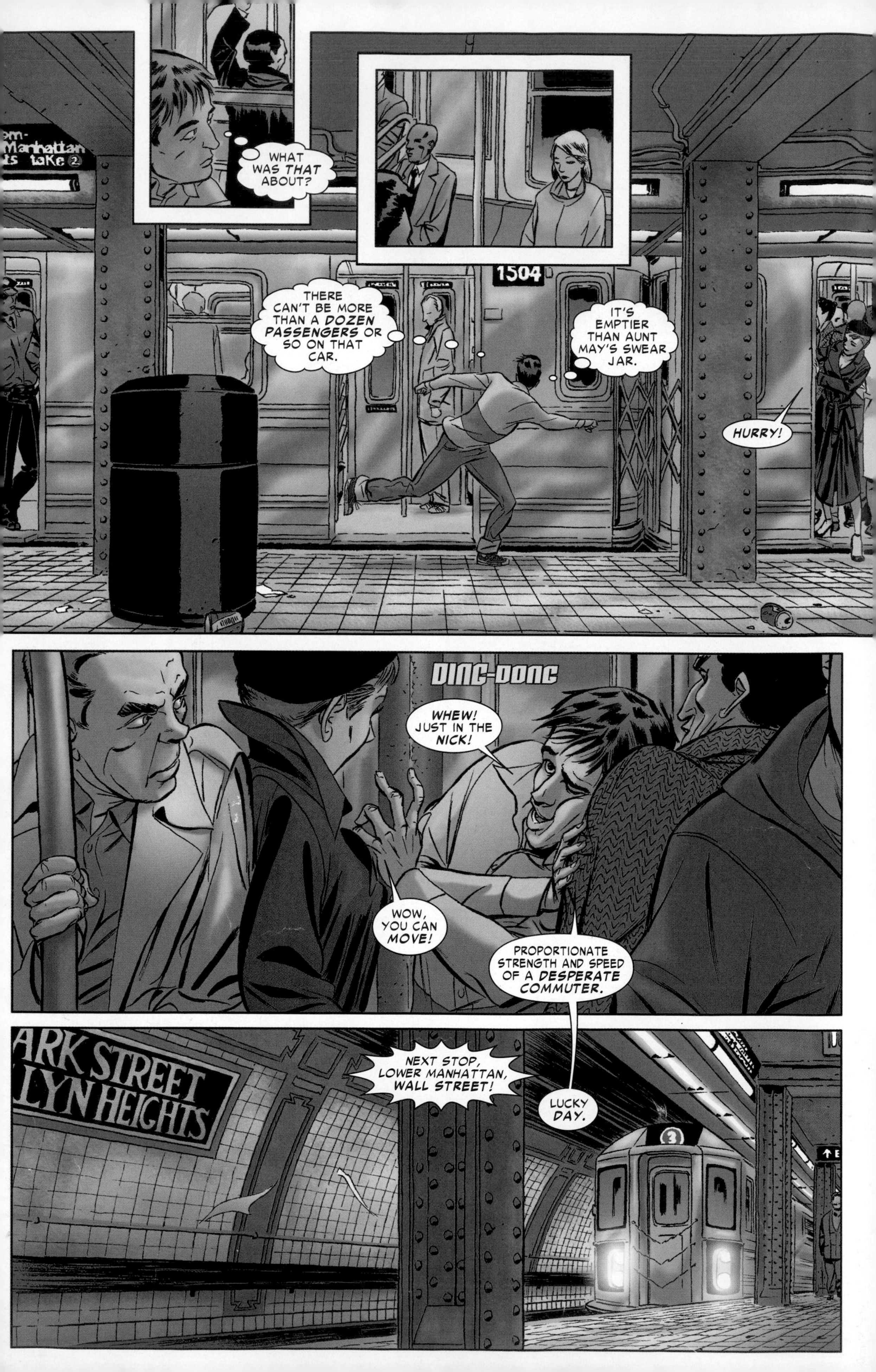

...em-
...Manhattan
...ts take 2
WHAT WAS THAT ABOUT?
1504
THERE CAN'T BE MORE THAN A DOZEN PASSENGERS OR SO ON THAT CAR.
IT'S EMPTIER THAN AUNT MAY'S SWEAR JAR.
HURRY!
DING-DONG
WHEW! JUST IN THE NICK!
WOW, YOU CAN MOVE!
PROPORTIONATE STRENGTH AND SPEED OF A DESPERATE COMMUTER.
ARK STREET
LYN HEIGHTS
NEXT STOP, LOWER MANHATTAN, WALL STREET!
LUCKY DAY.
3

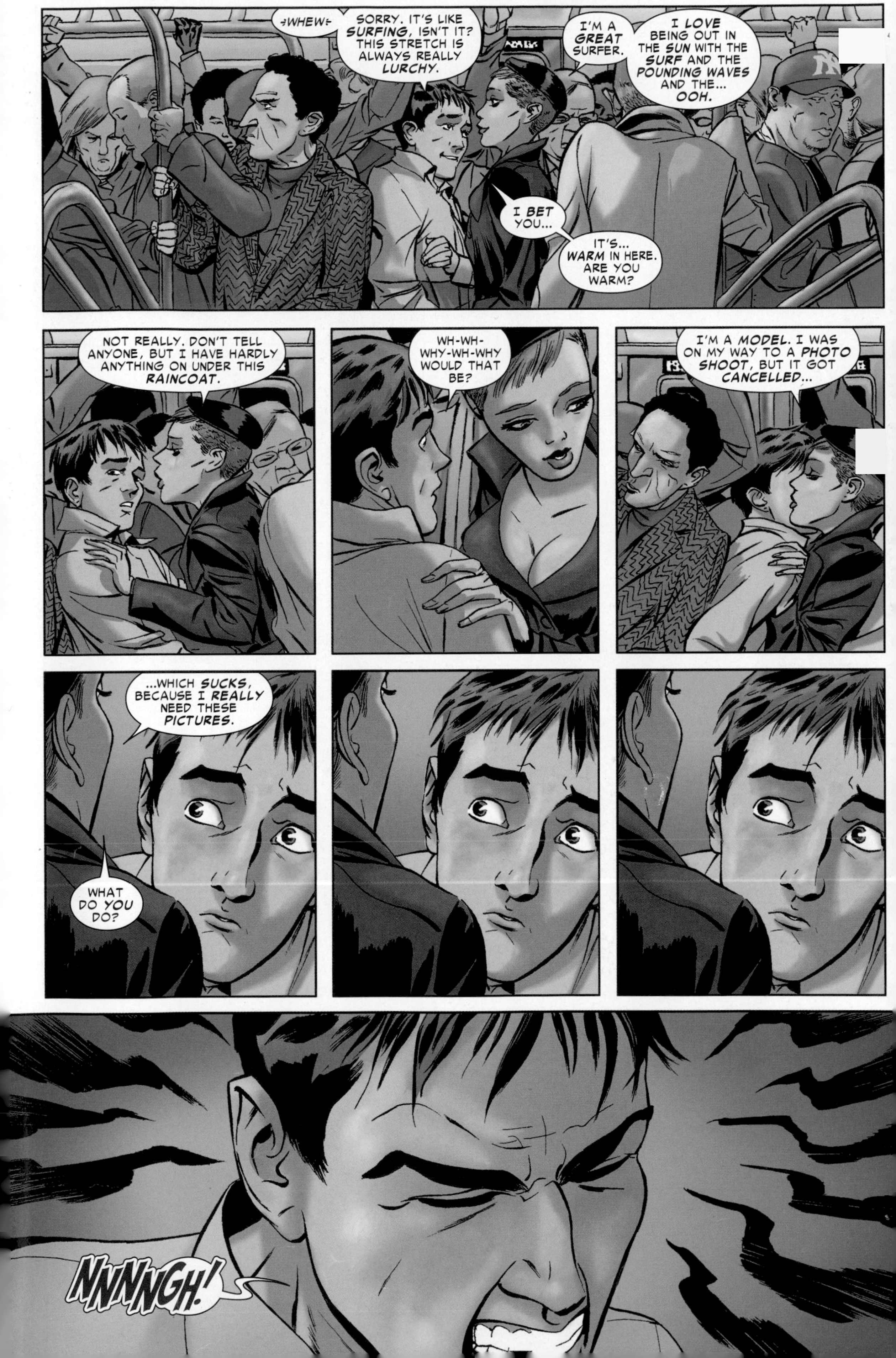

-WHEW-
SORRY. IT'S LIKE SURFING, ISN'T IT? THIS STRETCH IS ALWAYS REALLY LURCHY.
I'M A GREAT SURFER.
I LOVE BEING OUT IN THE SUN WITH THE SURF AND THE POUNDING WAVES AND THE... OOH.
I BET YOU...
IT'S... WARM IN HERE. ARE YOU WARM?
NOT REALLY. DON'T TELL ANYONE, BUT I HAVE HARDLY ANYTHING ON UNDER THIS RAINCOAT.
WH-WH-WHY-WH-WHY WOULD THAT BE?
I'M A MODEL. I WAS ON MY WAY TO A PHOTO SHOOT, BUT IT GOT CANCELLED...
...WHICH SUCKS, BECAUSE I REALLY NEED THESE PICTURES.
WHAT DO YOU DO?
NNNNGH!

YOU OKAY, DOLLFACE?

NOT WITH MY *SPIDER-SENSE* GOING OFF LIKE A *FIRE ALARM*, NO!

I CAN'T EVEN TELL WHERE THE *DANGER'S* COMING FROM--NOT SARDINE-CRAMMED INTO THIS *CROWD!*

WAIT--

--SOMETHING ABOUT THAT *REAR CAR*--!

'SCUSE ME! COMIN' THROUGH!

WHATEVER, LOSER.

ONE SIDE, FOLKS!

HEY!

WATCH IT, YOU JERK!

OW!

PLEASE-- YOU DON'T *UNDERSTAND!* I'M TRYING NOT TO *HURT* ANYONE--!

DON'T YOU THREATEN MY BOY!

THAT'S NOT WHAT I--

FOR GOD'S SAKE, LET ME THROUGH!

FINE!

ALMOST THERE...

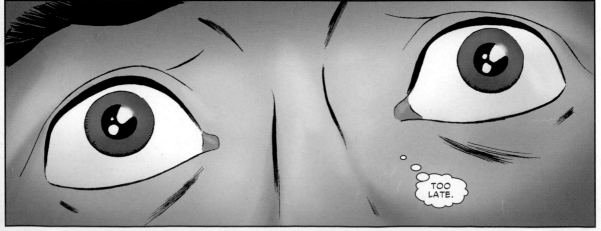

TOO LATE.

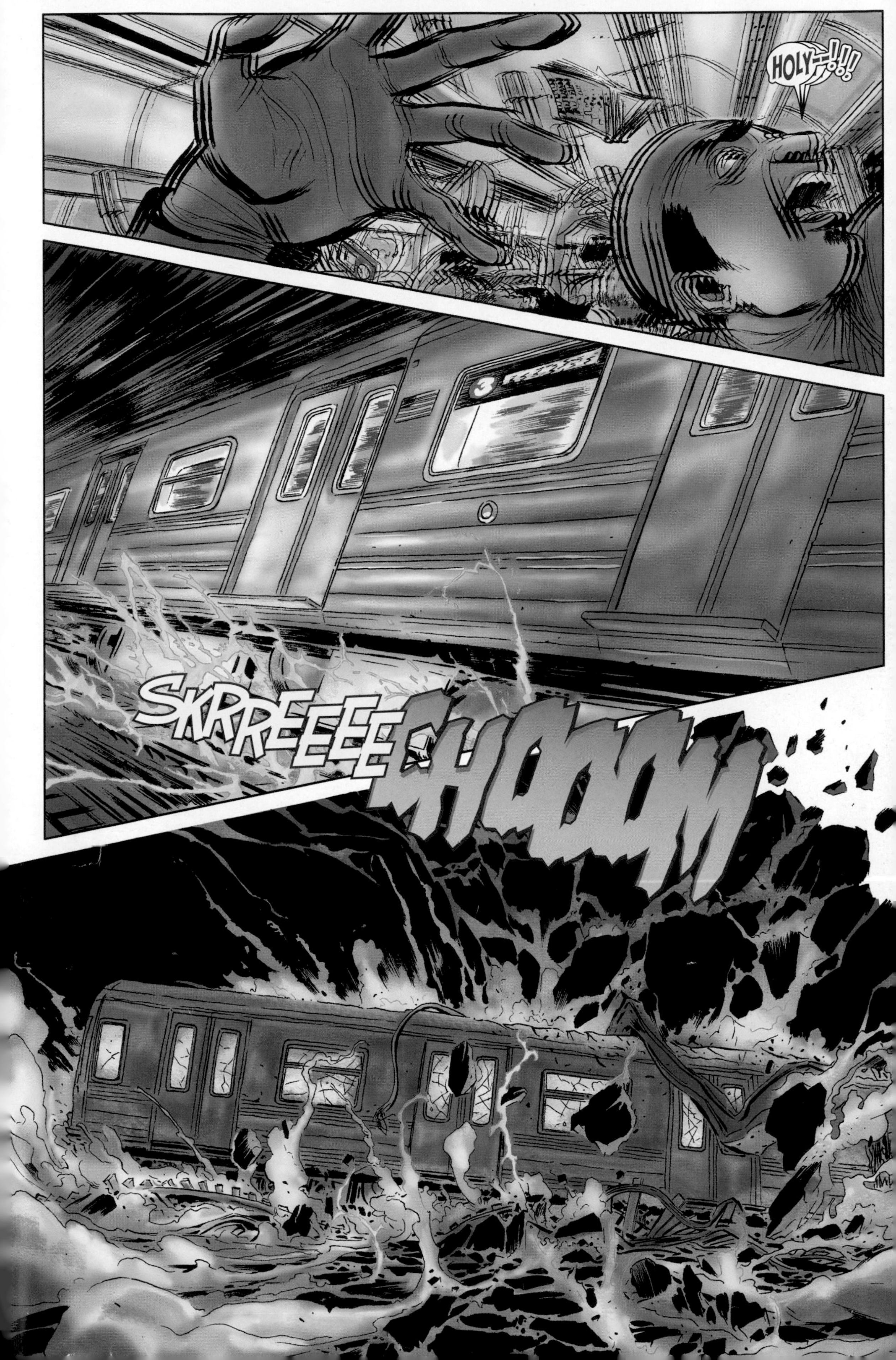
HOLY--!!!
SKRREEEEE
CHOOOM

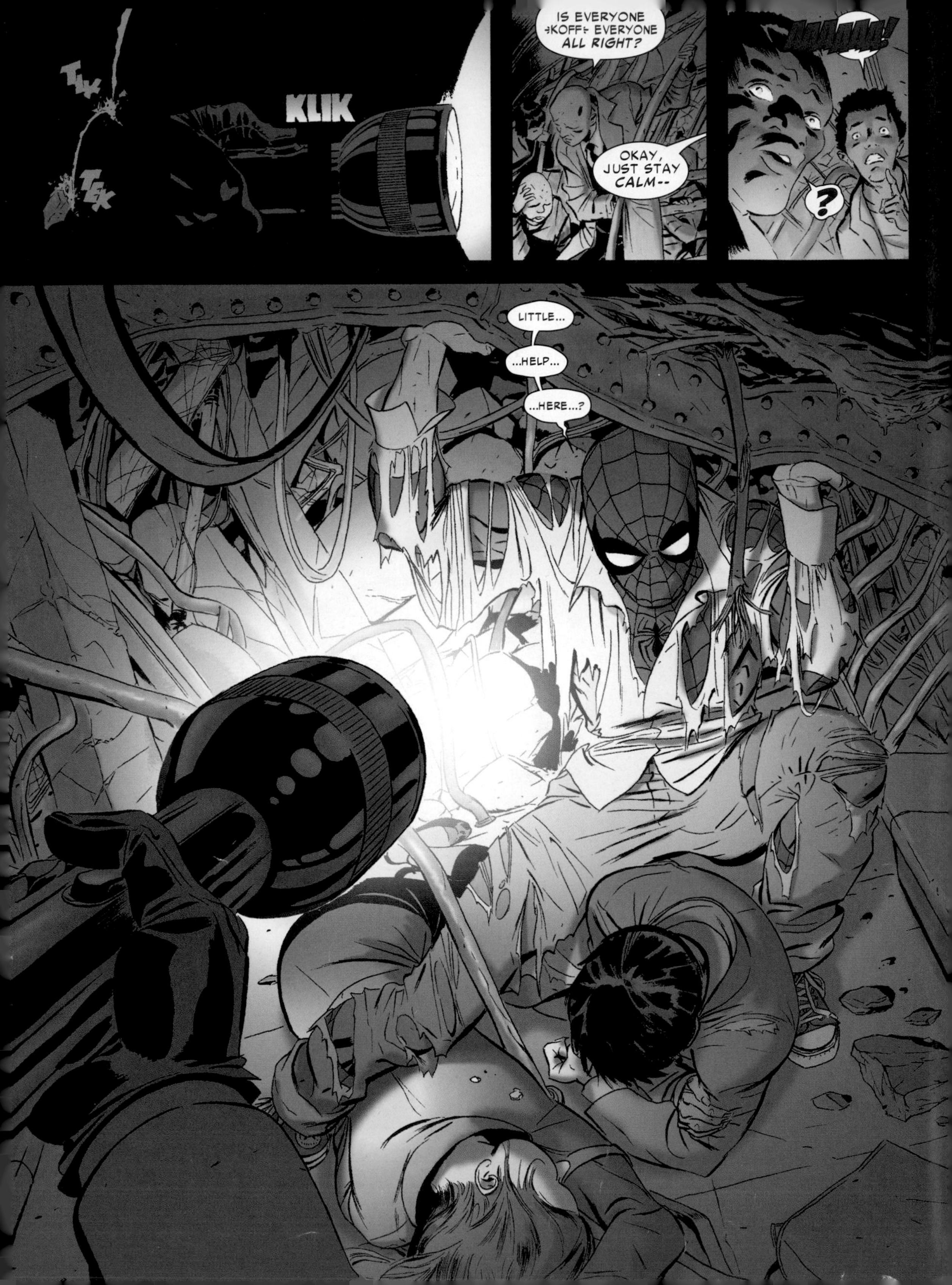
TEK
TEK
KLIK
IS EVERYONE -KOFF- EVERYONE ALL RIGHT?
OKAY, JUST STAY CALM--
?
LITTLE...
...HELP...
...HERE...?

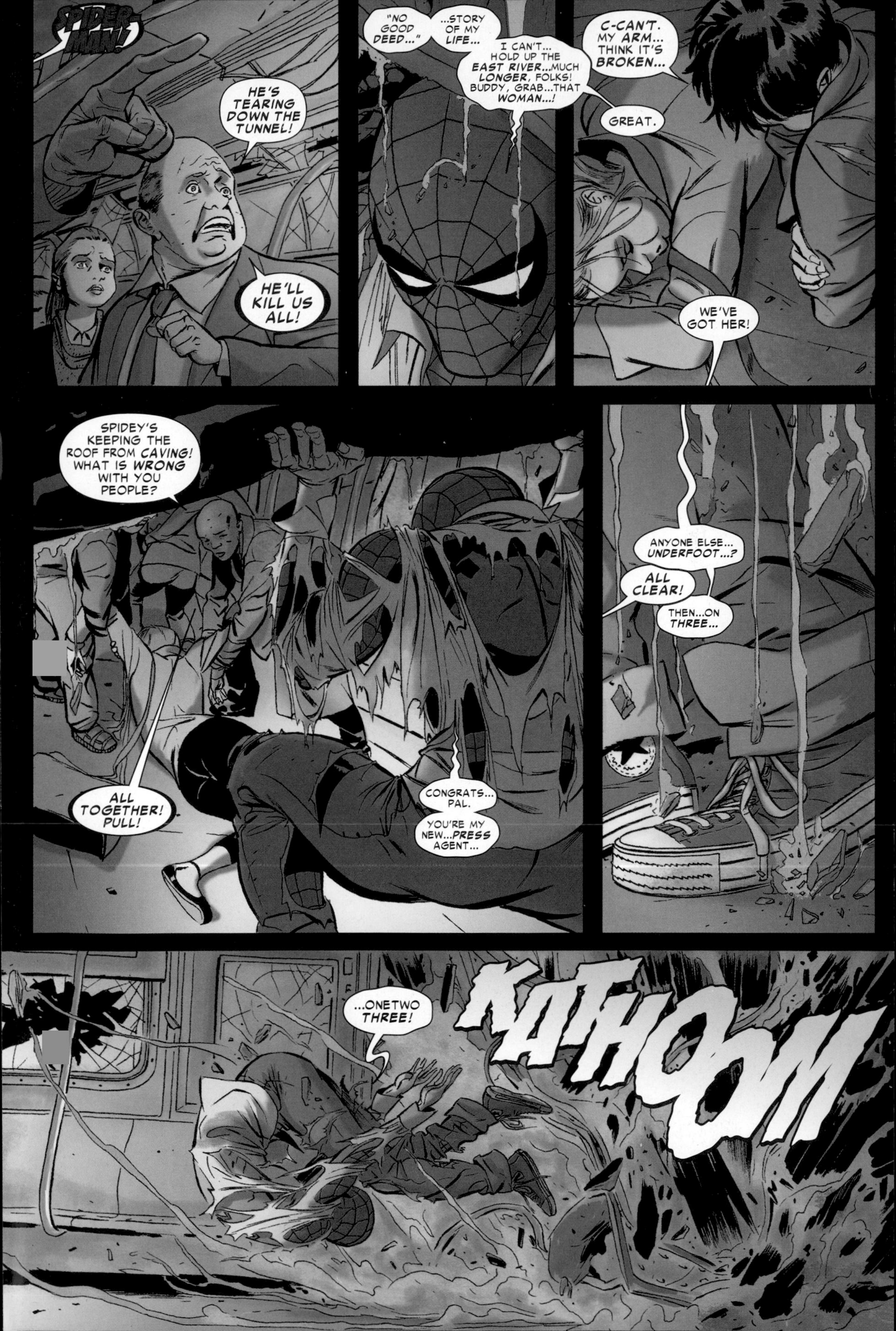
SPIDER-MAN!
HE'S TEARING DOWN THE TUNNEL!
HE'LL KILL US ALL!
"NO GOOD DEED..."
...STORY OF MY LIFE...
I CAN'T... HOLD UP THE EAST RIVER...MUCH LONGER, FOLKS! BUDDY, GRAB...THAT WOMAN...!
C-CAN'T. MY ARM... THINK IT'S BROKEN...
GREAT.
WE'VE GOT HER!
SPIDEY'S KEEPING THE ROOF FROM CAVING! WHAT IS WRONG WITH YOU PEOPLE?
ALL TOGETHER! PULL!
CONGRATS... PAL.
YOU'RE MY NEW...PRESS AGENT...
ANYONE ELSE... UNDERFOOT...?
ALL CLEAR!
THEN...ON THREE...
...ONETWO THREE!
KATHOOM

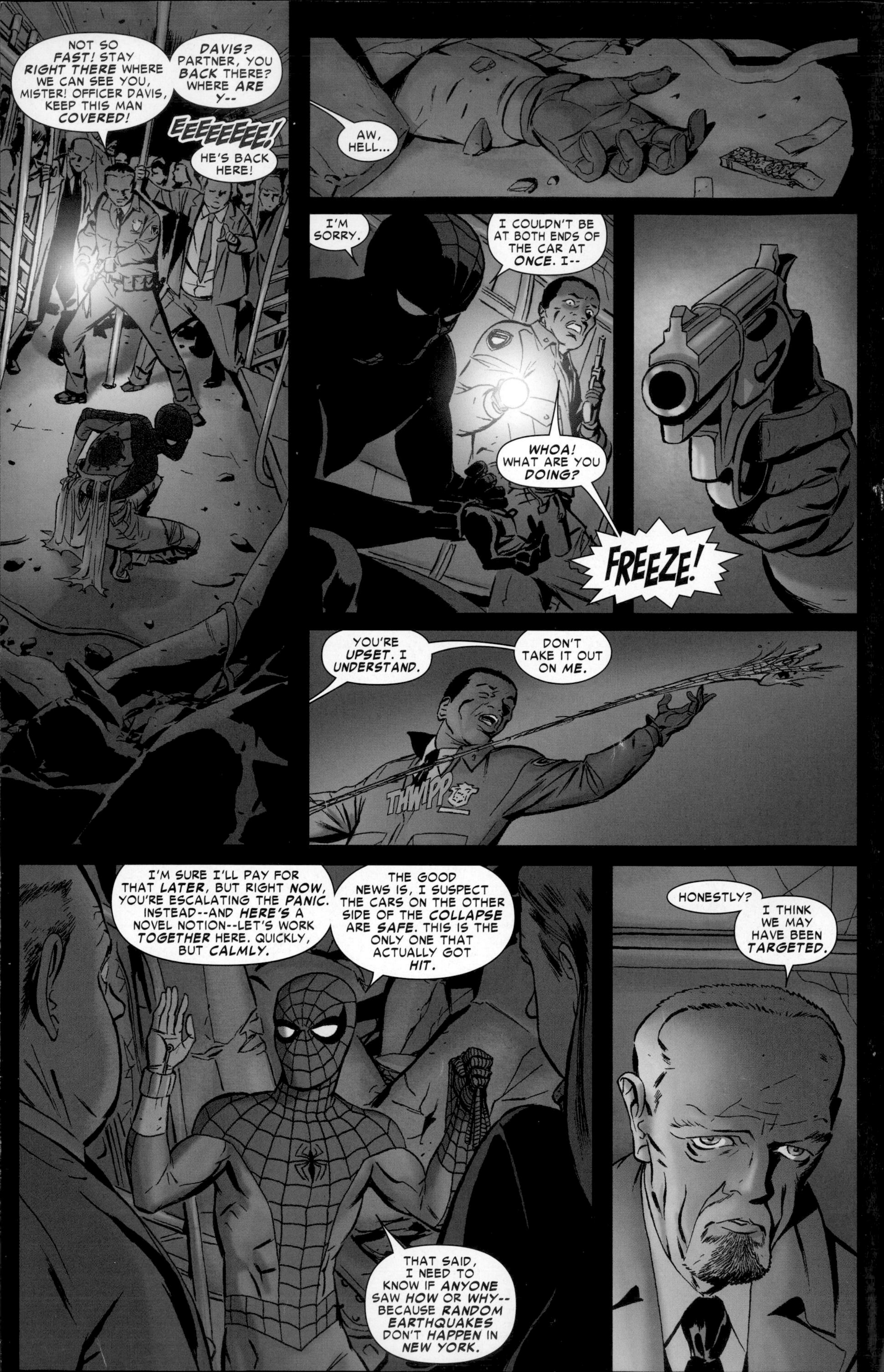
NOT SO FAST! STAY RIGHT THERE WHERE WE CAN SEE YOU, MISTER! OFFICER DAVIS, KEEP THIS MAN COVERED!
DAVIS? PARTNER, YOU BACK THERE? WHERE ARE Y--
EEEEEEEE!
HE'S BACK HERE!
AW, HELL...
I'M SORRY.
I COULDN'T BE AT BOTH ENDS OF THE CAR AT ONCE. I--
WHOA! WHAT ARE YOU DOING?
FREEZE!
YOU'RE UPSET. I UNDERSTAND.
DON'T TAKE IT OUT ON ME.
THWIPP
I'M SURE I'LL PAY FOR THAT LATER, BUT RIGHT NOW, YOU'RE ESCALATING THE PANIC. INSTEAD--AND HERE'S A NOVEL NOTION--LET'S WORK TOGETHER HERE. QUICKLY, BUT CALMLY.
THE GOOD NEWS IS, I SUSPECT THE CARS ON THE OTHER SIDE OF THE COLLAPSE ARE SAFE. THIS IS THE ONLY ONE THAT ACTUALLY GOT HIT.
THAT SAID, I NEED TO KNOW IF ANYONE SAW HOW OR WHY-- BECAUSE RANDOM EARTHQUAKES DON'T HAPPEN IN NEW YORK.
HONESTLY?
I THINK WE MAY HAVE BEEN TARGETED.

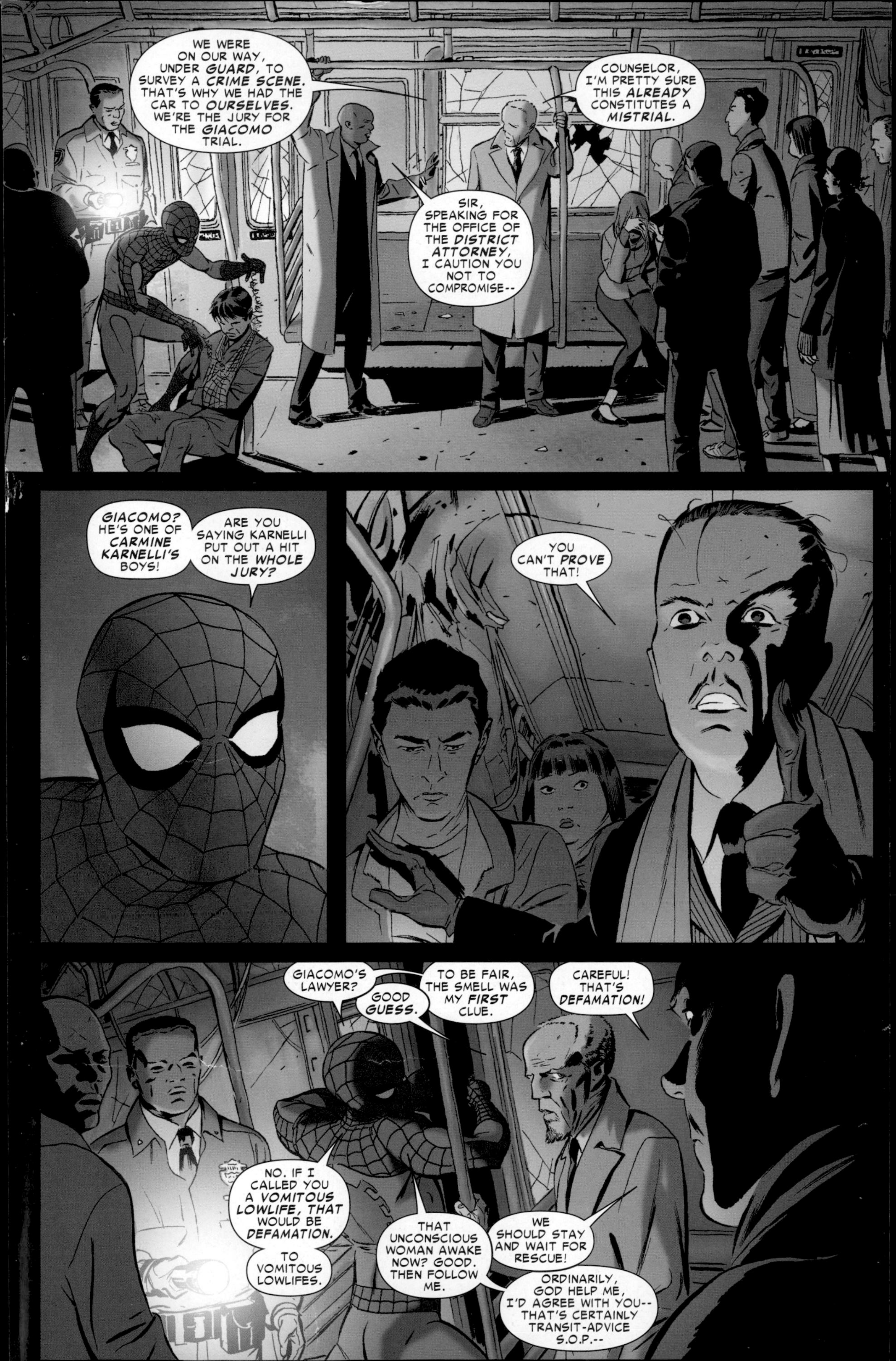
WE WERE ON OUR WAY, UNDER GUARD, TO SURVEY A CRIME SCENE. THAT'S WHY WE HAD THE CAR TO OURSELVES. WE'RE THE JURY FOR THE GIACOMO TRIAL.
COUNSELOR, I'M PRETTY SURE THIS ALREADY CONSTITUTES A MISTRIAL.
SIR, SPEAKING FOR THE OFFICE OF THE DISTRICT ATTORNEY, I CAUTION YOU NOT TO COMPROMISE--
GIACOMO? HE'S ONE OF CARMINE KARNELLI'S BOYS!
ARE YOU SAYING KARNELLI PUT OUT A HIT ON THE WHOLE JURY?
YOU CAN'T PROVE THAT!
GIACOMO'S LAWYER?
GOOD GUESS.
TO BE FAIR, THE SMELL WAS MY FIRST CLUE.
CAREFUL! THAT'S DEFAMATION!
NO. IF I CALLED YOU A VOMITOUS LOWLIFE, THAT WOULD BE DEFAMATION.
TO VOMITOUS LOWLIFES.
THAT UNCONSCIOUS WOMAN AWAKE NOW? GOOD. THEN FOLLOW ME.
WE SHOULD STAY AND WAIT FOR RESCUE!
ORDINARILY, GOD HELP ME, I'D AGREE WITH YOU-- THAT'S CERTAINLY TRANSIT-ADVICE S.O.P.--

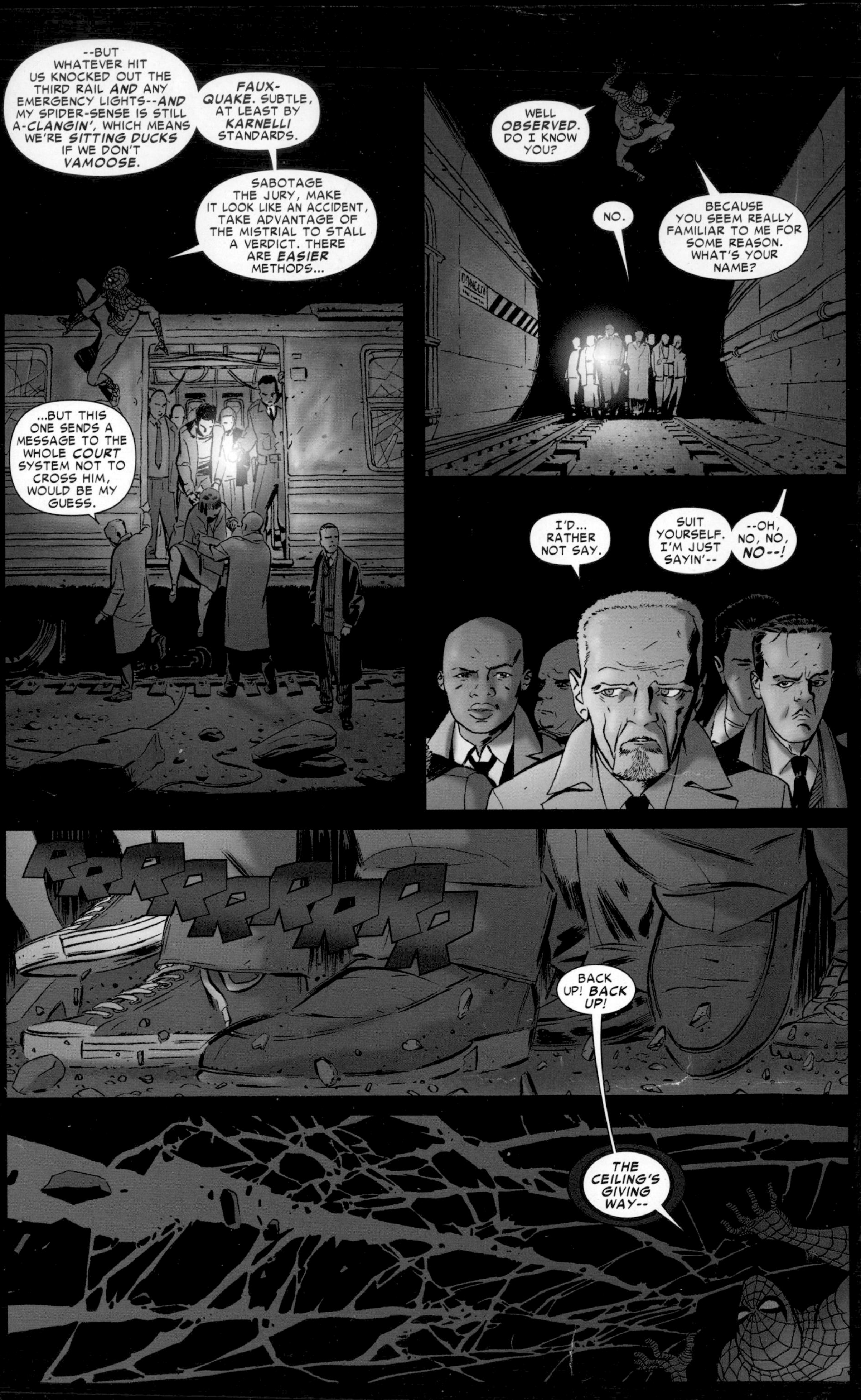
--BUT WHATEVER HIT US KNOCKED OUT THE THIRD RAIL AND ANY EMERGENCY LIGHTS--AND MY SPIDER-SENSE IS STILL A-CLANGIN', WHICH MEANS WE'RE SITTING DUCKS IF WE DON'T VAMOOSE.
FAUX-QUAKE. SUBTLE, AT LEAST BY KARNELLI STANDARDS.
SABOTAGE THE JURY, MAKE IT LOOK LIKE AN ACCIDENT, TAKE ADVANTAGE OF THE MISTRIAL TO STALL A VERDICT. THERE ARE EASIER METHODS...
...BUT THIS ONE SENDS A MESSAGE TO THE WHOLE COURT SYSTEM NOT TO CROSS HIM, WOULD BE MY GUESS.
WELL OBSERVED. DO I KNOW YOU?
NO.
BECAUSE YOU SEEM REALLY FAMILIAR TO ME FOR SOME REASON. WHAT'S YOUR NAME?
I'D... RATHER NOT SAY.
SUIT YOURSELF. I'M JUST SAYIN'--
--OH, NO, NO, NO--!
RRRRRRRRR
BACK UP! BACK UP!
THE CEILING'S GIVING WAY--

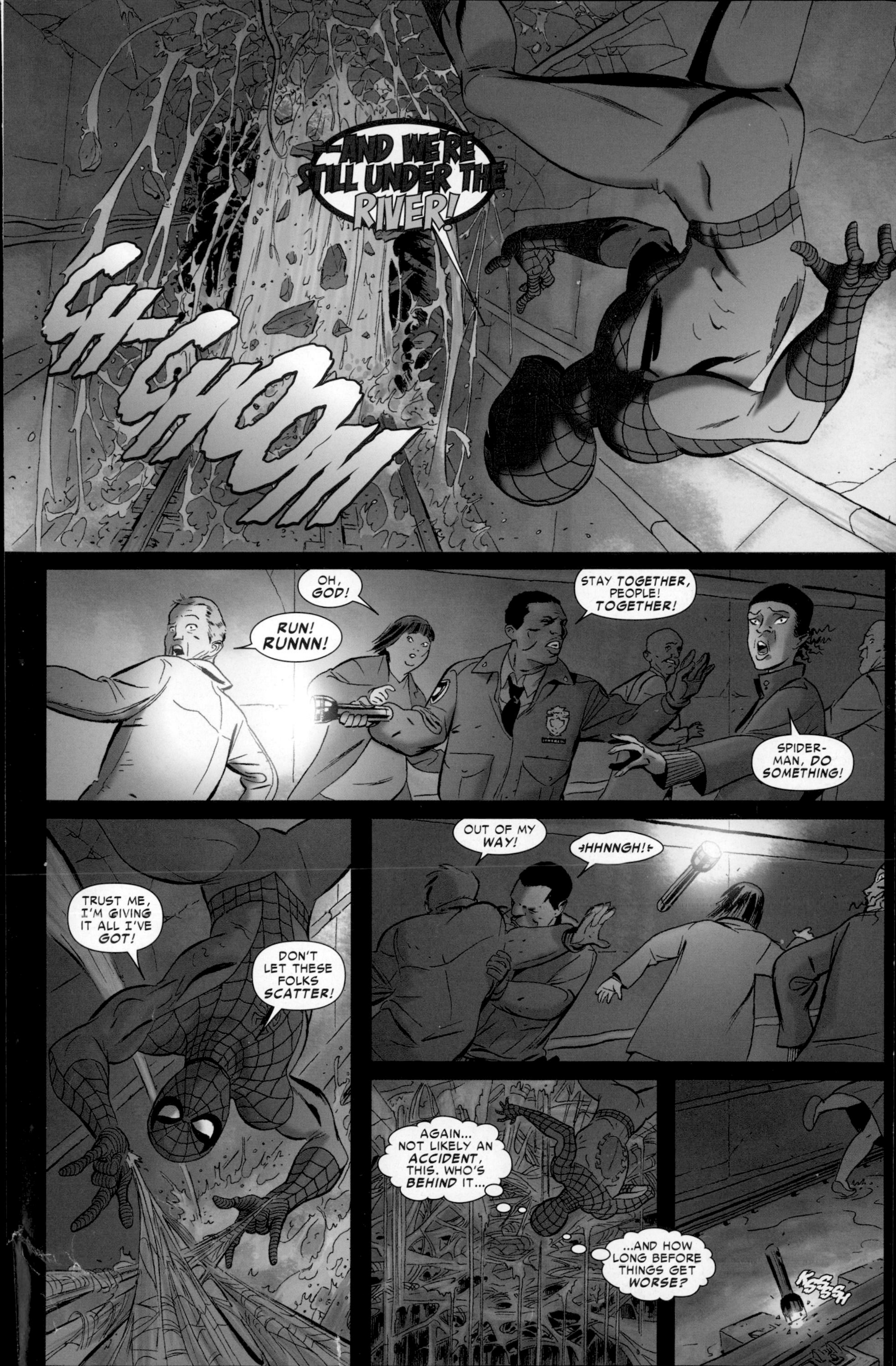

--AND WE'RE STILL UNDER THE RIVER!
GH-GHOOM
OH, GOD!
RUN! RUNNN!
STAY TOGETHER, PEOPLE! TOGETHER!
SPIDER-MAN, DO SOMETHING!
TRUST ME, I'M GIVING IT ALL I'VE GOT!
DON'T LET THESE FOLKS SCATTER!
OUT OF MY WAY!
HHNNGH!
AGAIN... NOT LIKELY AN ACCIDENT, THIS. WHO'S BEHIND IT...
...AND HOW LONG BEFORE THINGS GET WORSE?
KSSSH

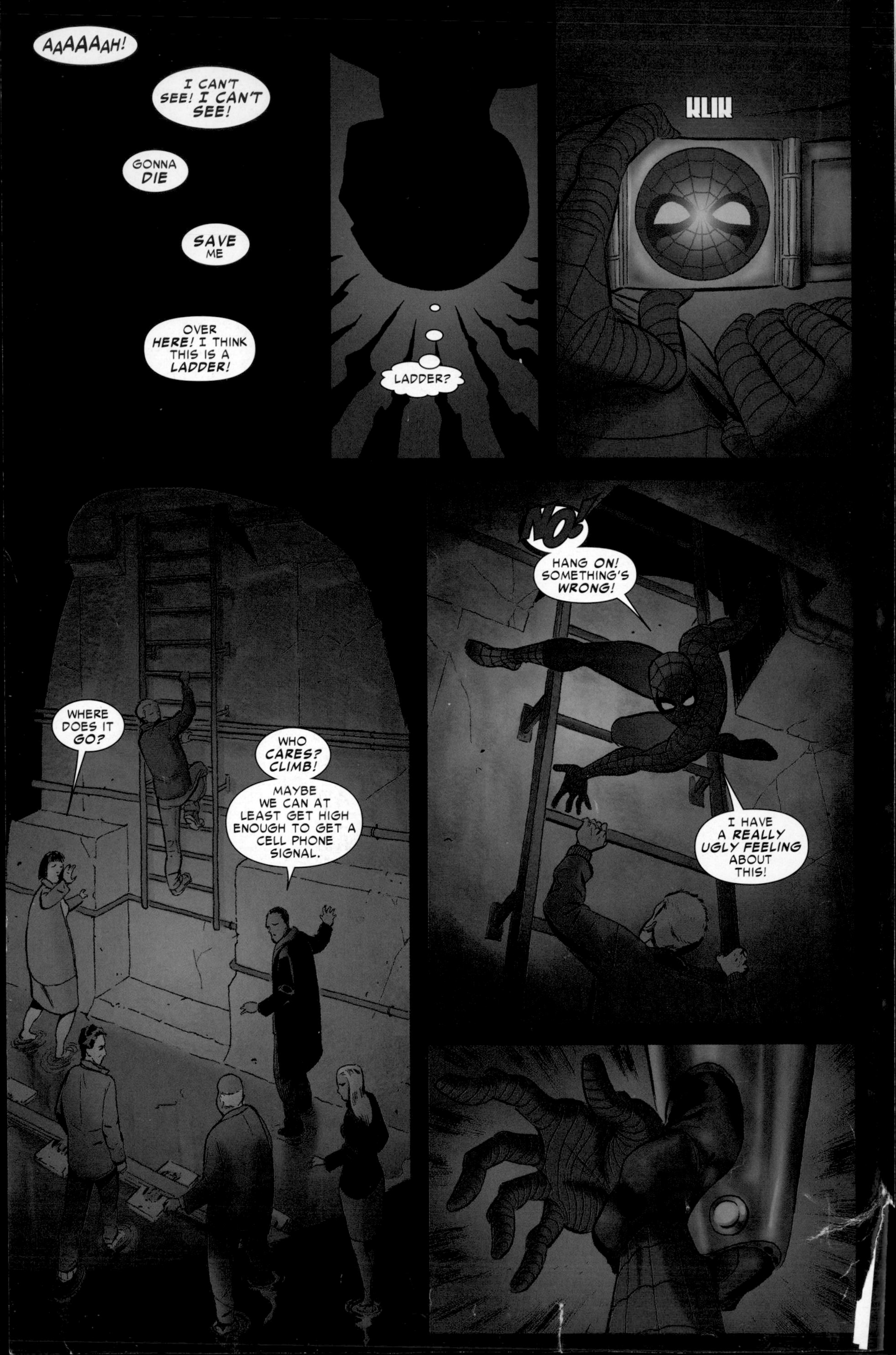
AAAAAAH!
I CAN'T SEE! I CAN'T SEE!
GONNA DIE
SAVE ME
OVER HERE! I THINK THIS IS A LADDER!
LADDER?
KLIK
WHERE DOES IT GO?
WHO CARES? CLIMB!
MAYBE WE CAN AT LEAST GET HIGH ENOUGH TO GET A CELL PHONE SIGNAL.
NO!
HANG ON! SOMETHING'S WRONG!
I HAVE A REALLY UGLY FEELING ABOUT THIS!

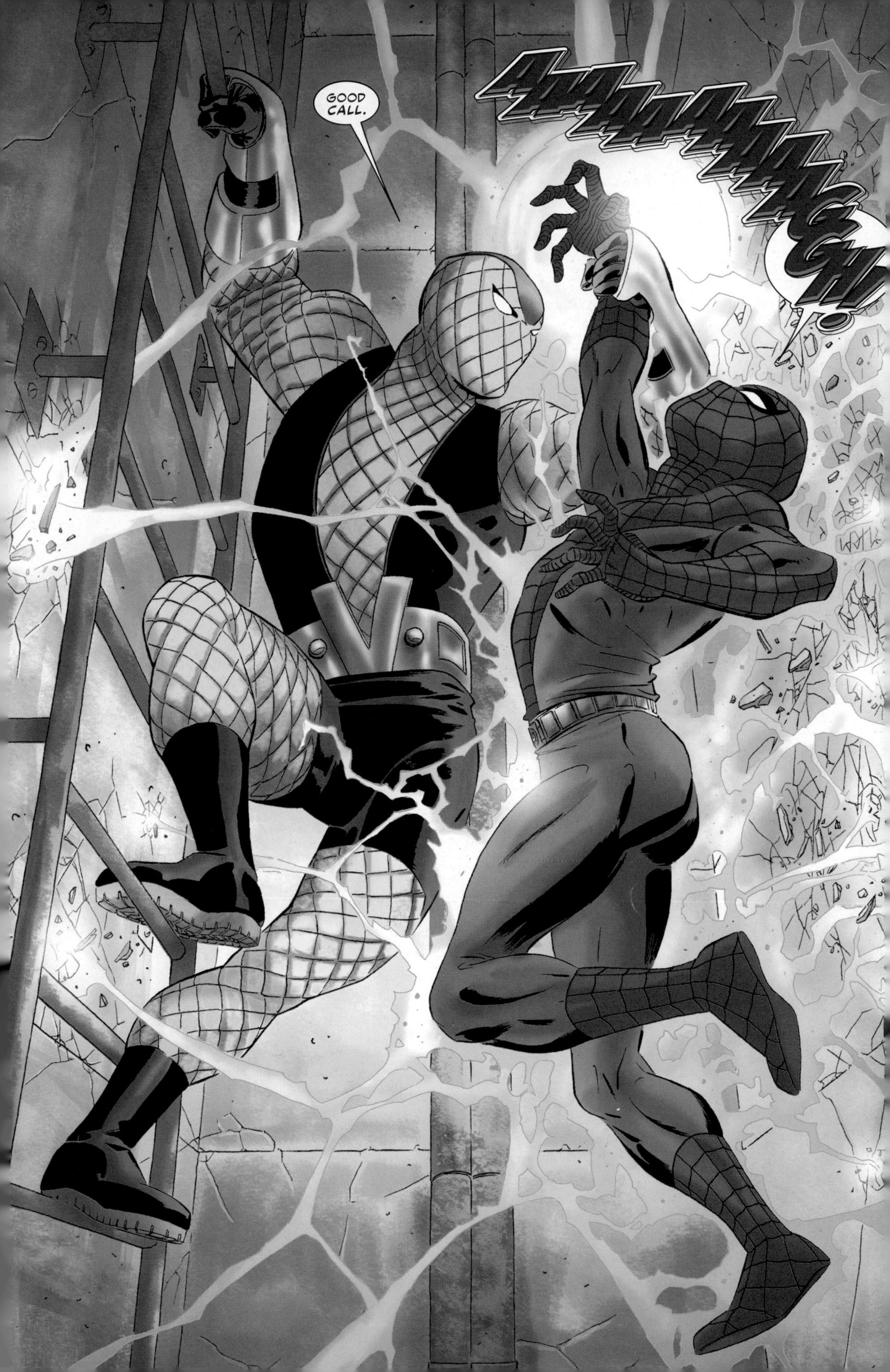
GOOD CALL.
AAAAAAAAAGH!

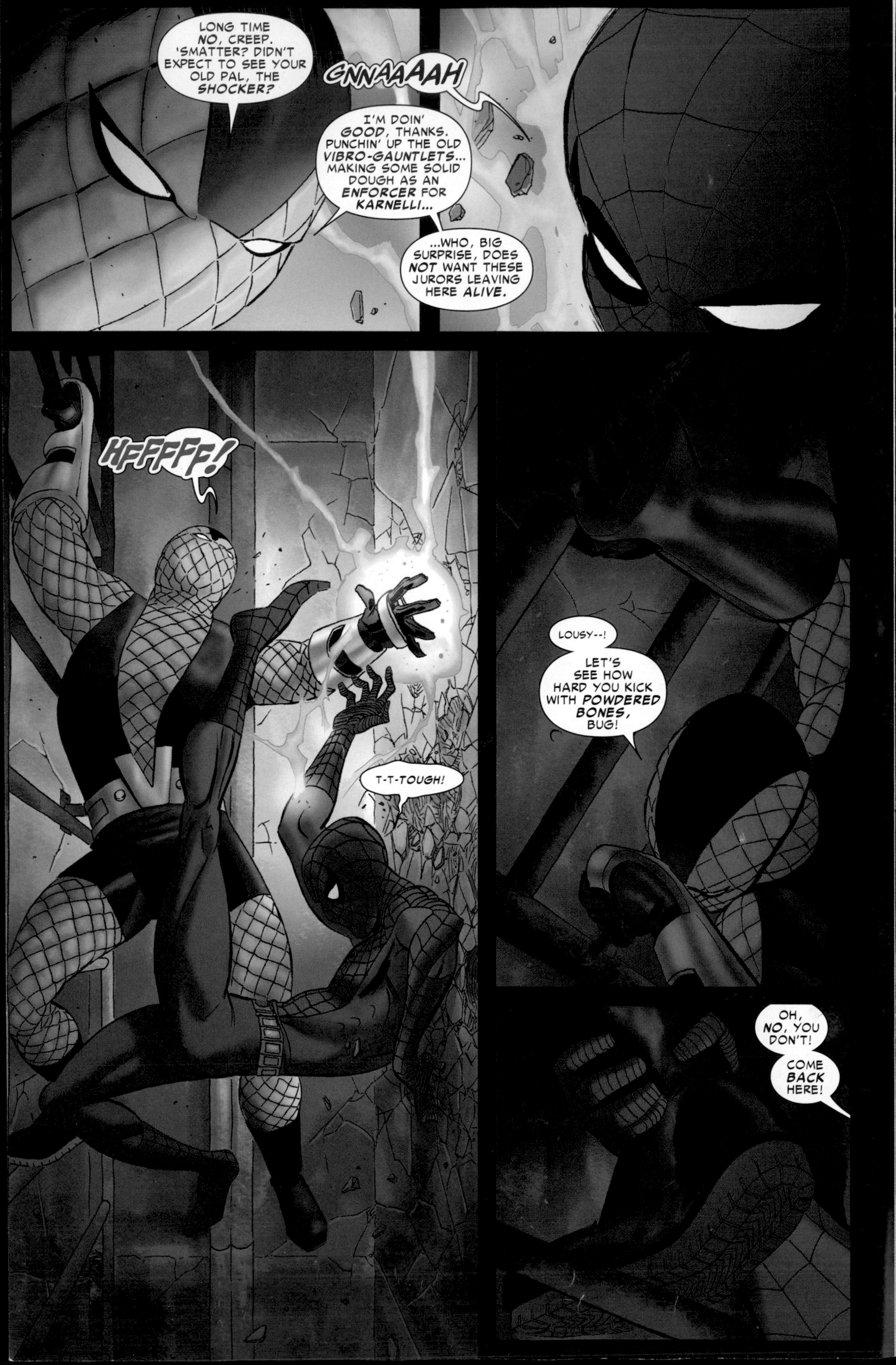
LONG TIME NO, CREEP. 'SMATTER? DIDN'T EXPECT TO SEE YOUR OLD PAL, THE SHOCKER?
GNNAAAAH
I'M DOIN' GOOD, THANKS. PUNCHIN' UP THE OLD VIBRO-GAUNTLETS... MAKING SOME SOLID DOUGH AS AN ENFORCER FOR KARNELLI...
...WHO, BIG SURPRISE, DOES NOT WANT THESE JURORS LEAVING HERE ALIVE.
HFFFFF!
T-T-TOUGH!
LOUSY--!
LET'S SEE HOW HARD YOU KICK WITH POWDERED BONES, BUG!
OH, NO, YOU DON'T!
COME BACK HERE!

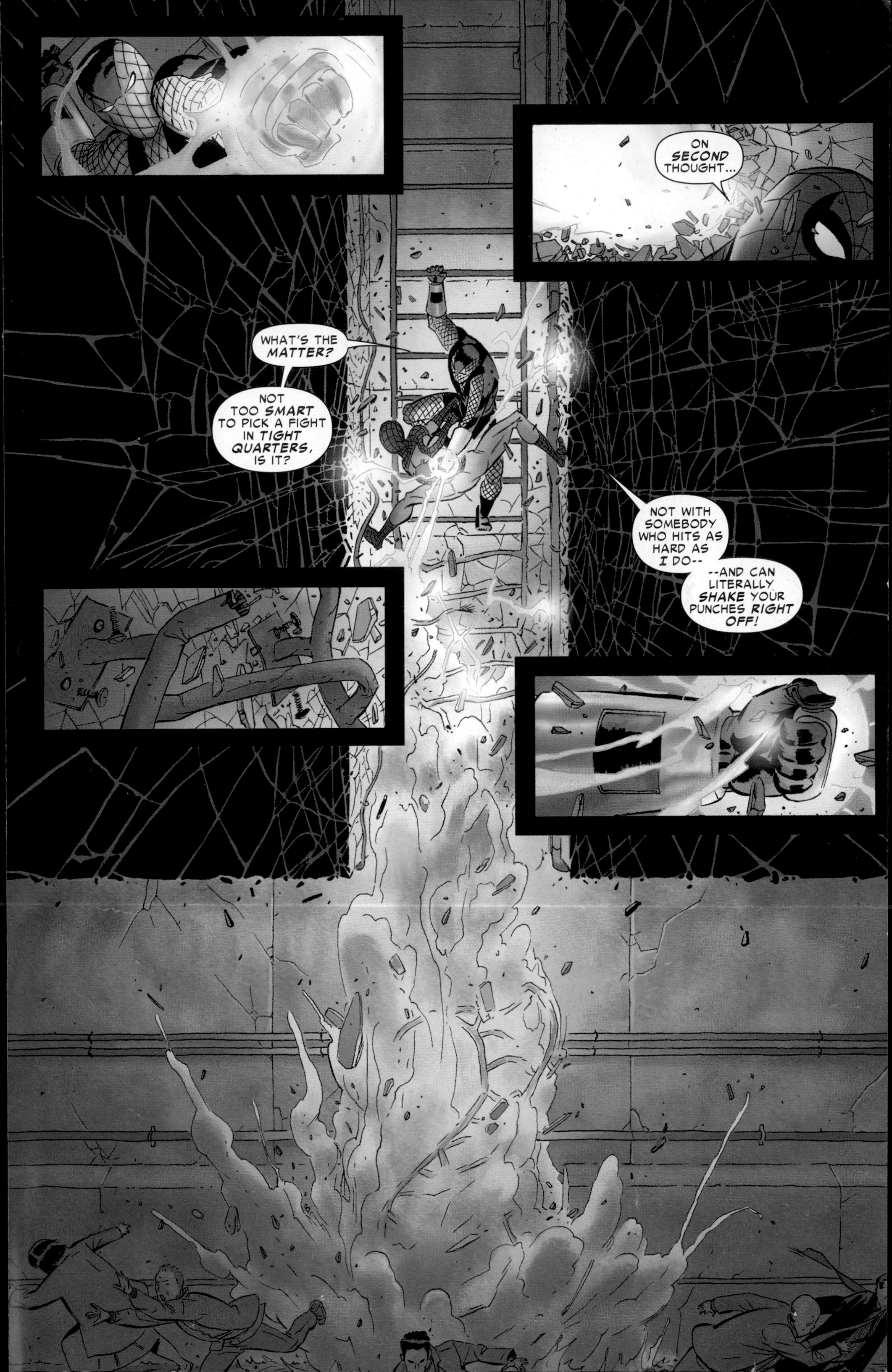
ON SECOND THOUGHT...
WHAT'S THE MATTER?
NOT TOO SMART TO PICK A FIGHT IN TIGHT QUARTERS, IS IT?
NOT WITH SOMEBODY WHO HITS AS HARD AS I DO--
--AND CAN LITERALLY SHAKE YOUR PUNCHES RIGHT OFF!

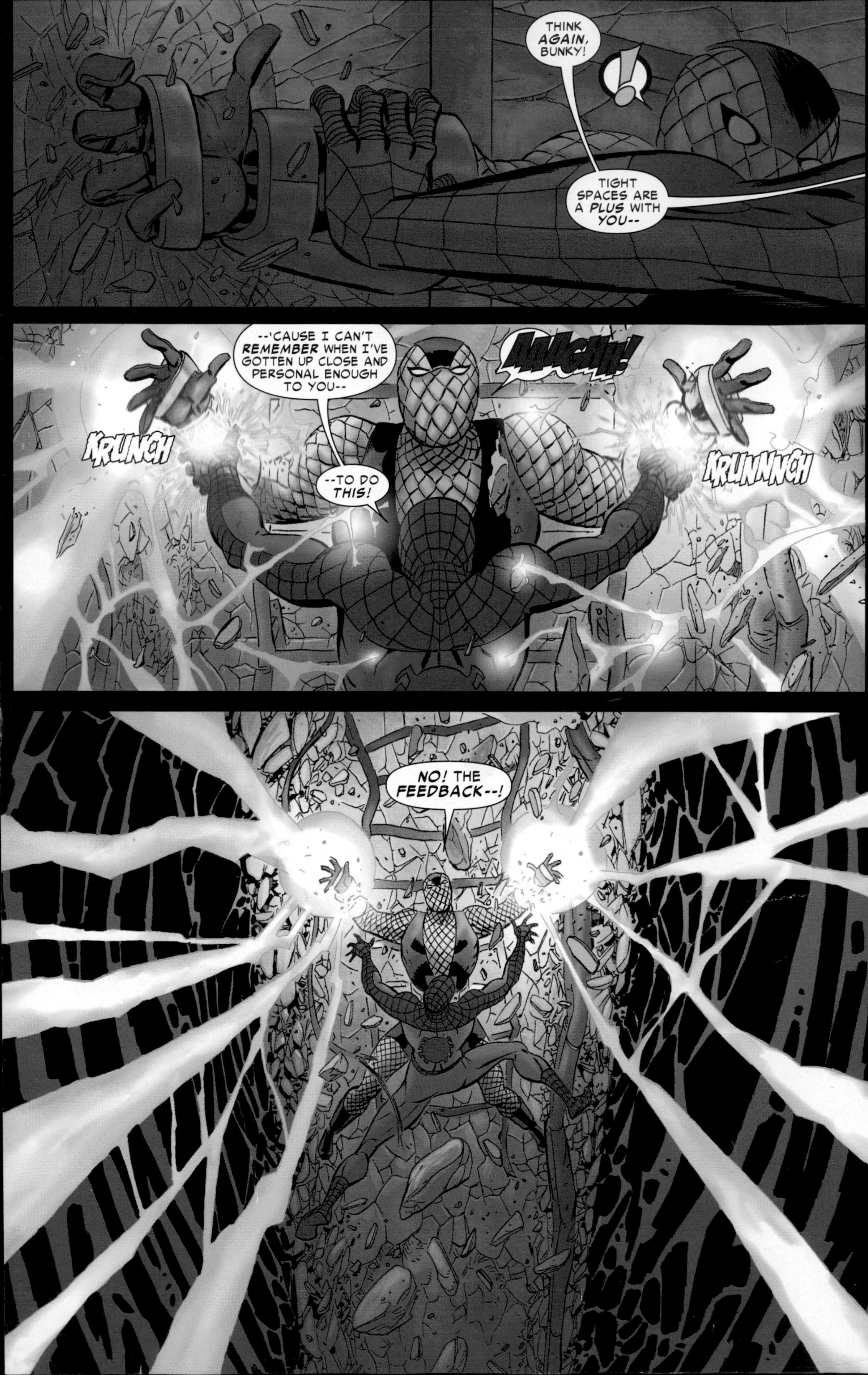
THINK AGAIN, BUNKY!
!
TIGHT SPACES ARE A PLUS WITH YOU--
--'CAUSE I CAN'T REMEMBER WHEN I'VE GOTTEN UP CLOSE AND PERSONAL ENOUGH TO YOU--
AAAGHH!
KRUNCH
--TO DO THIS!
KRUNNNCH
NO! THE FEEDBACK--!

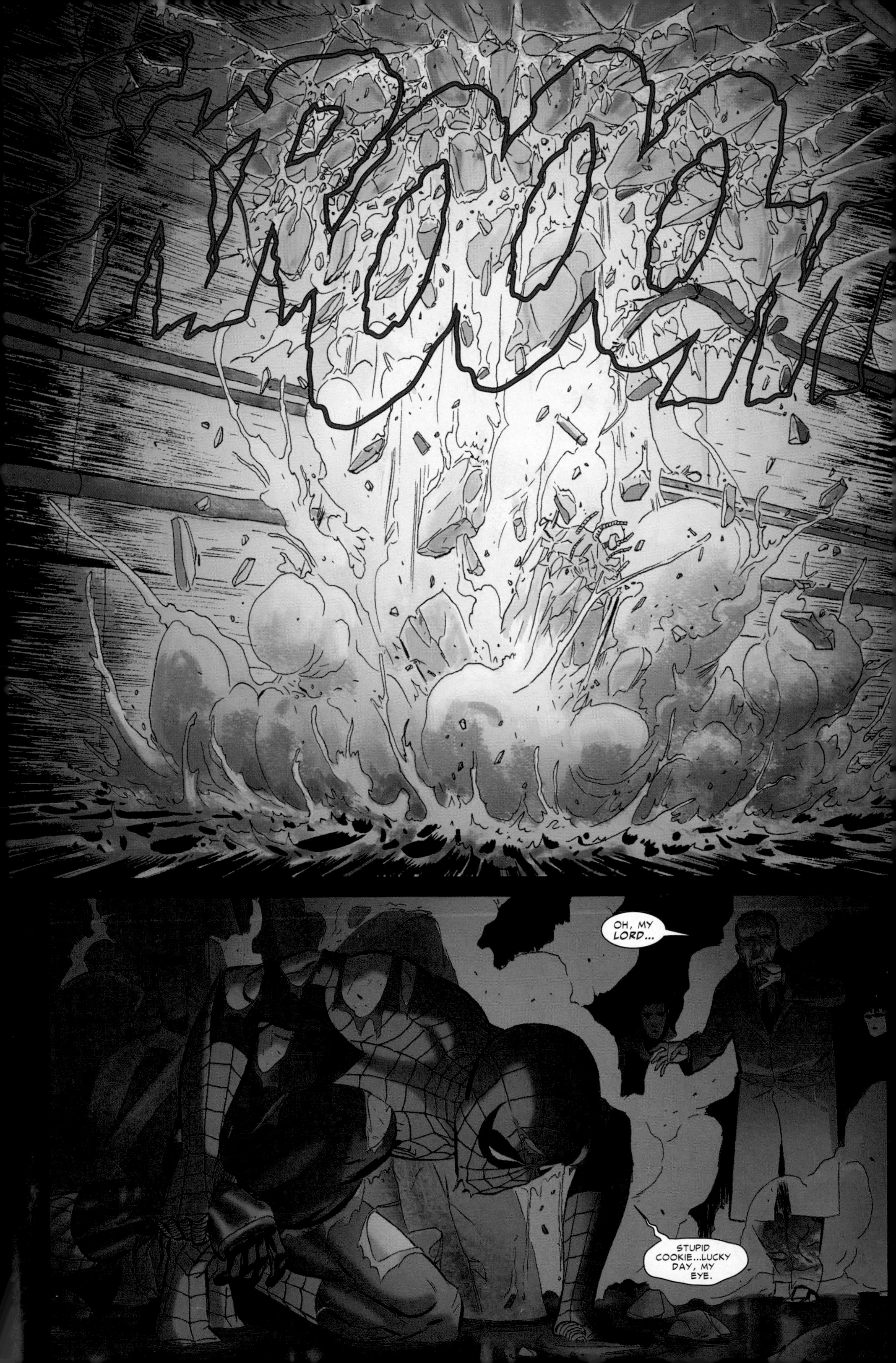
OH, MY LORD...
STUPID COOKIE...LUCKY DAY, MY EYE.

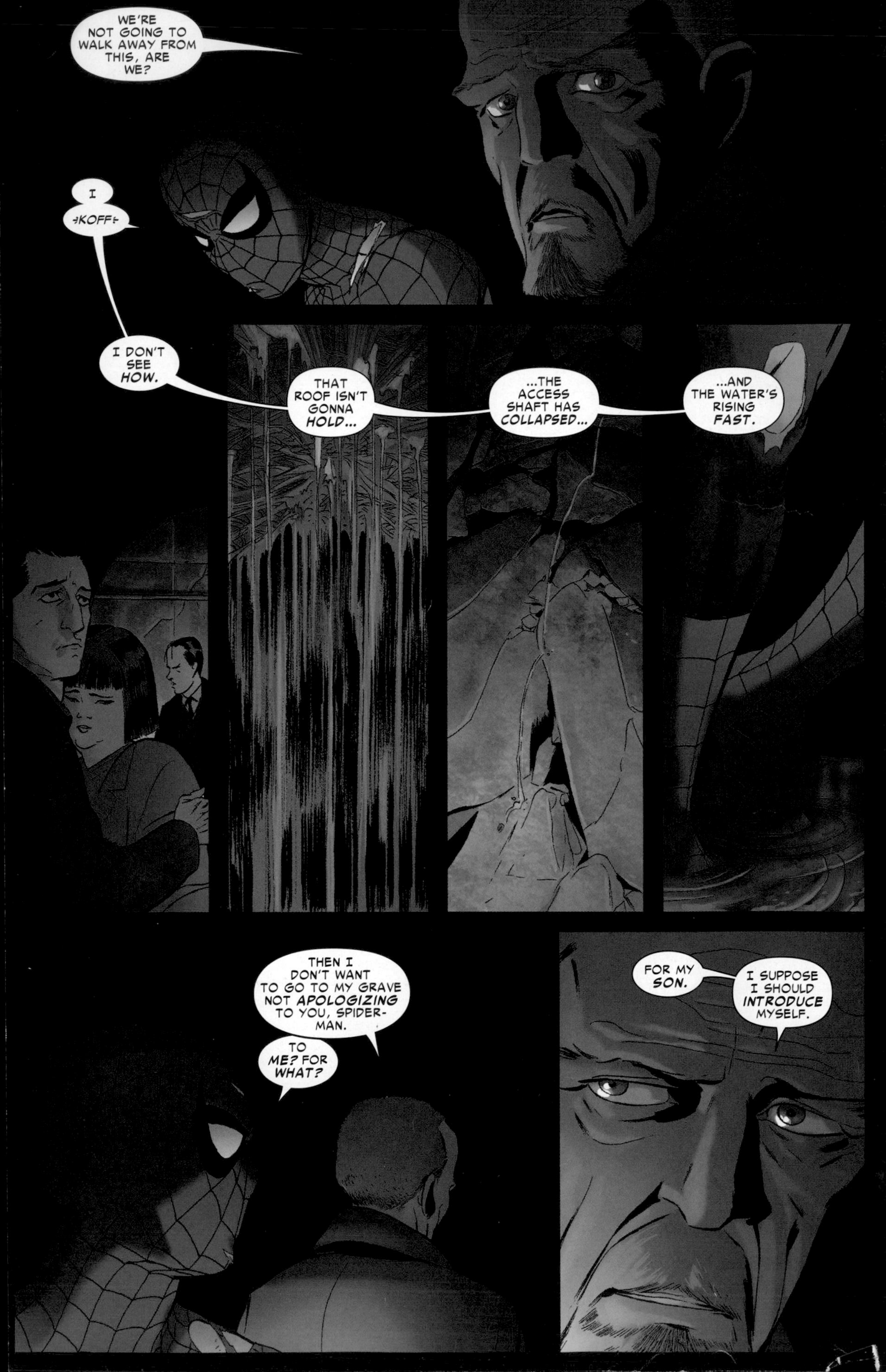

WE'RE NOT GOING TO WALK AWAY FROM THIS, ARE WE?
I
=KOFF=
I DON'T SEE HOW.
THAT ROOF ISN'T GONNA HOLD...
...THE ACCESS SHAFT HAS COLLAPSED...
...AND THE WATER'S RISING FAST.
THEN I DON'T WANT TO GO TO MY GRAVE NOT APOLOGIZING TO YOU, SPIDER-MAN.
TO ME? FOR WHAT?
FOR MY SON.
I SUPPOSE I SHOULD INTRODUCE MYSELF.

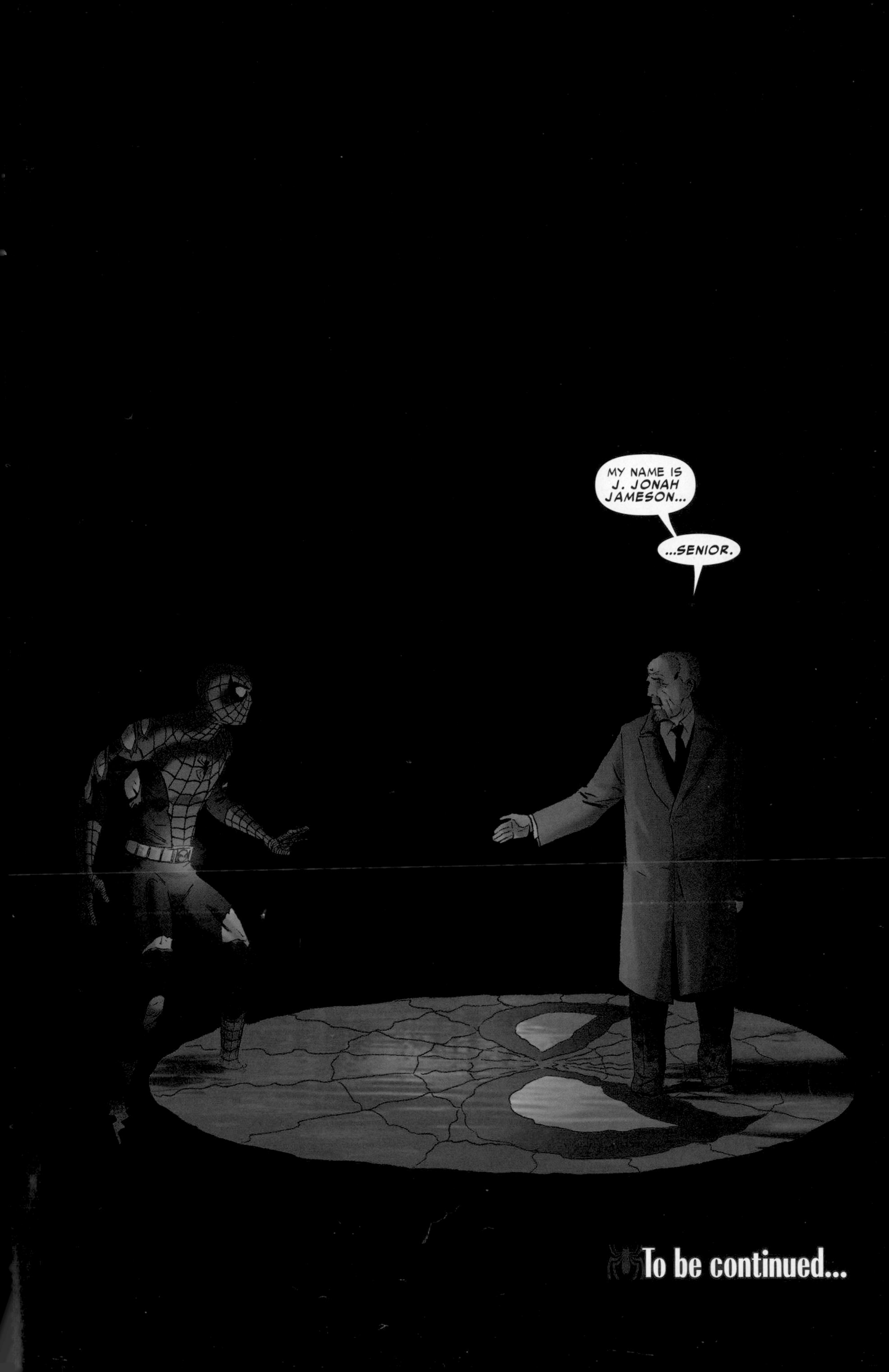
MY NAME IS J. JONAH JAMESON...
...SENIOR.
To be continued...

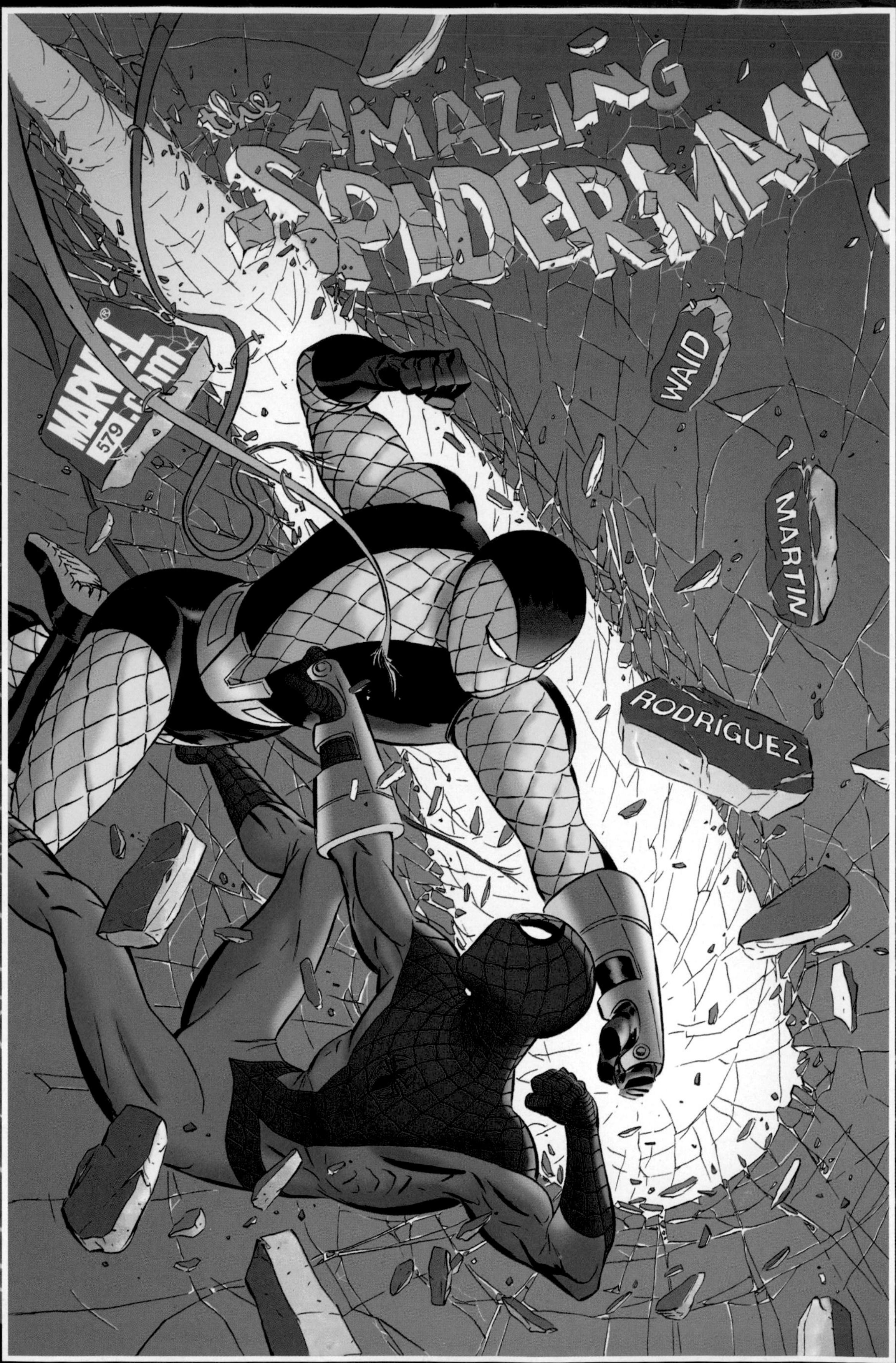
the AMAZING SPIDER-MAN®
MARVEL® .com
579
WAID
MARTIN
RODRÍGUEZ

TCH.

The F.E.A.S.T. Center.

WHAT'S IRKIN', MIZ PARKER?

OH, IT'S MY NEPHEW, PETER. HE PROMISED HE'D BE HERE BEFORE NOON.

IZZE COMIN' FROM BROOKLYN? MIGHT NOT BE HIS FAULT HE'S LATE...

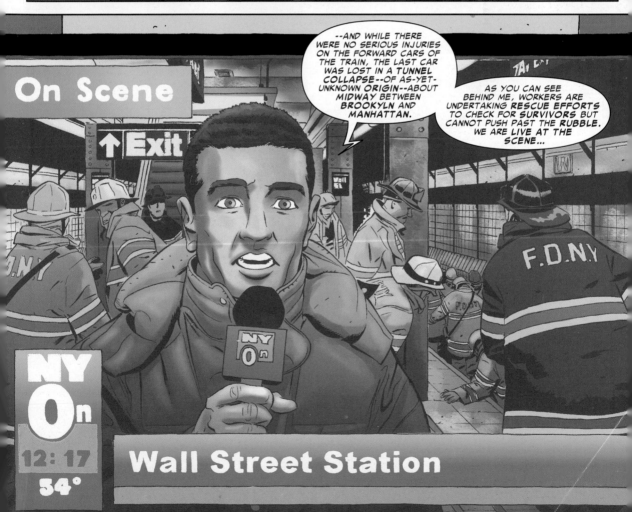

--AND WHILE THERE WERE NO SERIOUS INJURIES ON THE FORWARD CARS OF THE TRAIN, THE LAST CAR WAS LOST IN A TUNNEL COLLAPSE--OF AS-YET-UNKNOWN ORIGIN--ABOUT MIDWAY BETWEEN BROOKYLN AND MANHATTAN.

AS YOU CAN SEE BEHIND ME, WORKERS ARE UNDERTAKING RESCUE EFFORTS TO CHECK FOR SURVIVORS BUT CANNOT PUSH PAST THE RUBBLE. WE ARE LIVE AT THE SCENE...

On Scene

↑ Exit

F.D.N.Y

NY On

12:17

54°

Wall Street Station

ZONY

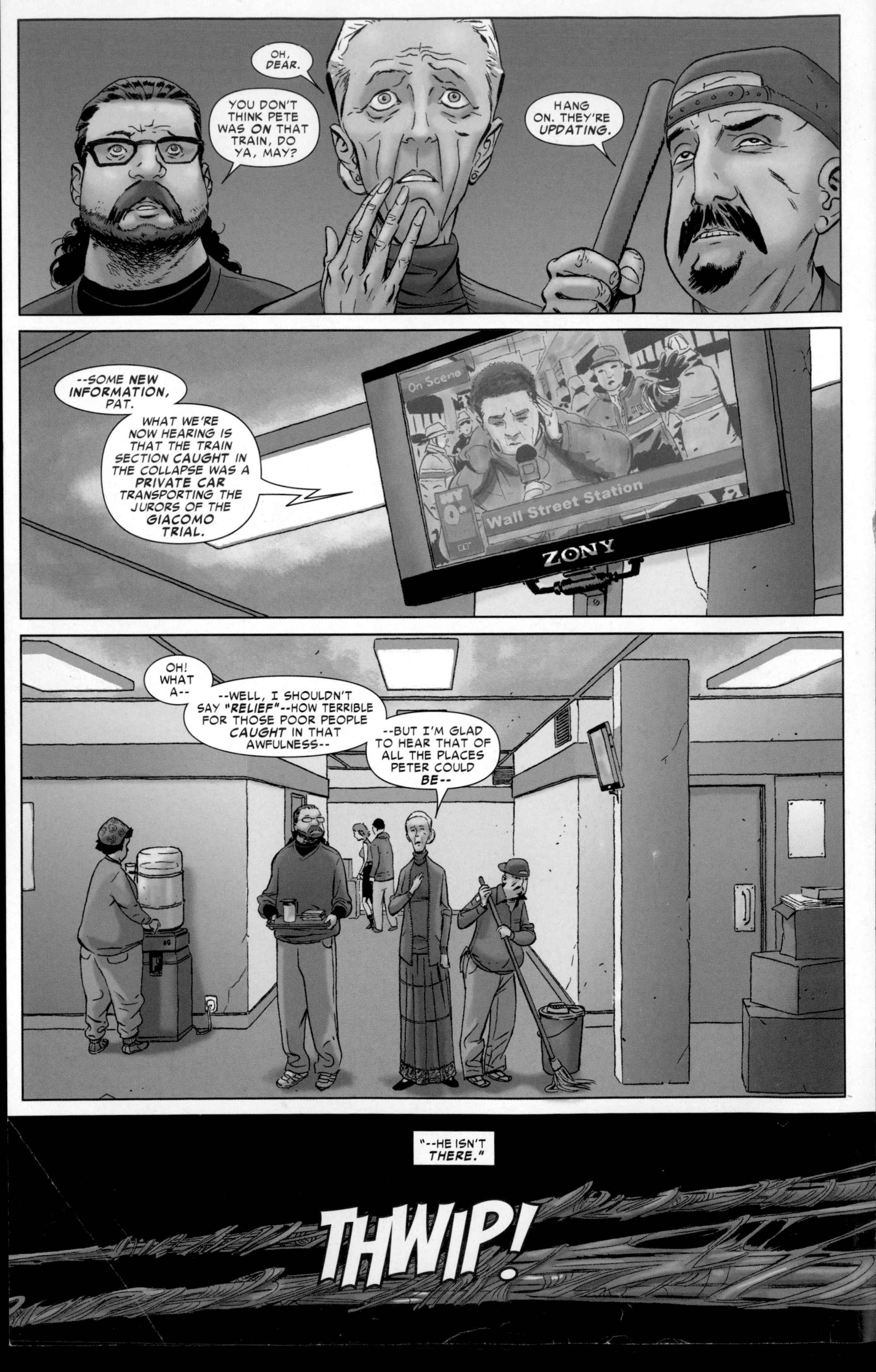
OH, DEAR.
YOU DON'T THINK PETE WAS ON THAT TRAIN, DO YA, MAY?
HANG ON. THEY'RE UPDATING.
--SOME NEW INFORMATION, PAT.
WHAT WE'RE NOW HEARING IS THAT THE TRAIN SECTION CAUGHT IN THE COLLAPSE WAS A PRIVATE CAR TRANSPORTING THE JURORS OF THE GIACOMO TRIAL.
On Scene
Wall Street Station
ZONY
OH! WHAT A--
--WELL, I SHOULDN'T SAY "RELIEF"--HOW TERRIBLE FOR THOSE POOR PEOPLE CAUGHT IN THAT AWFULNESS--
--BUT I'M GLAD TO HEAR THAT OF ALL THE PLACES PETER COULD BE--
"--HE ISN'T THERE."
THWIP!

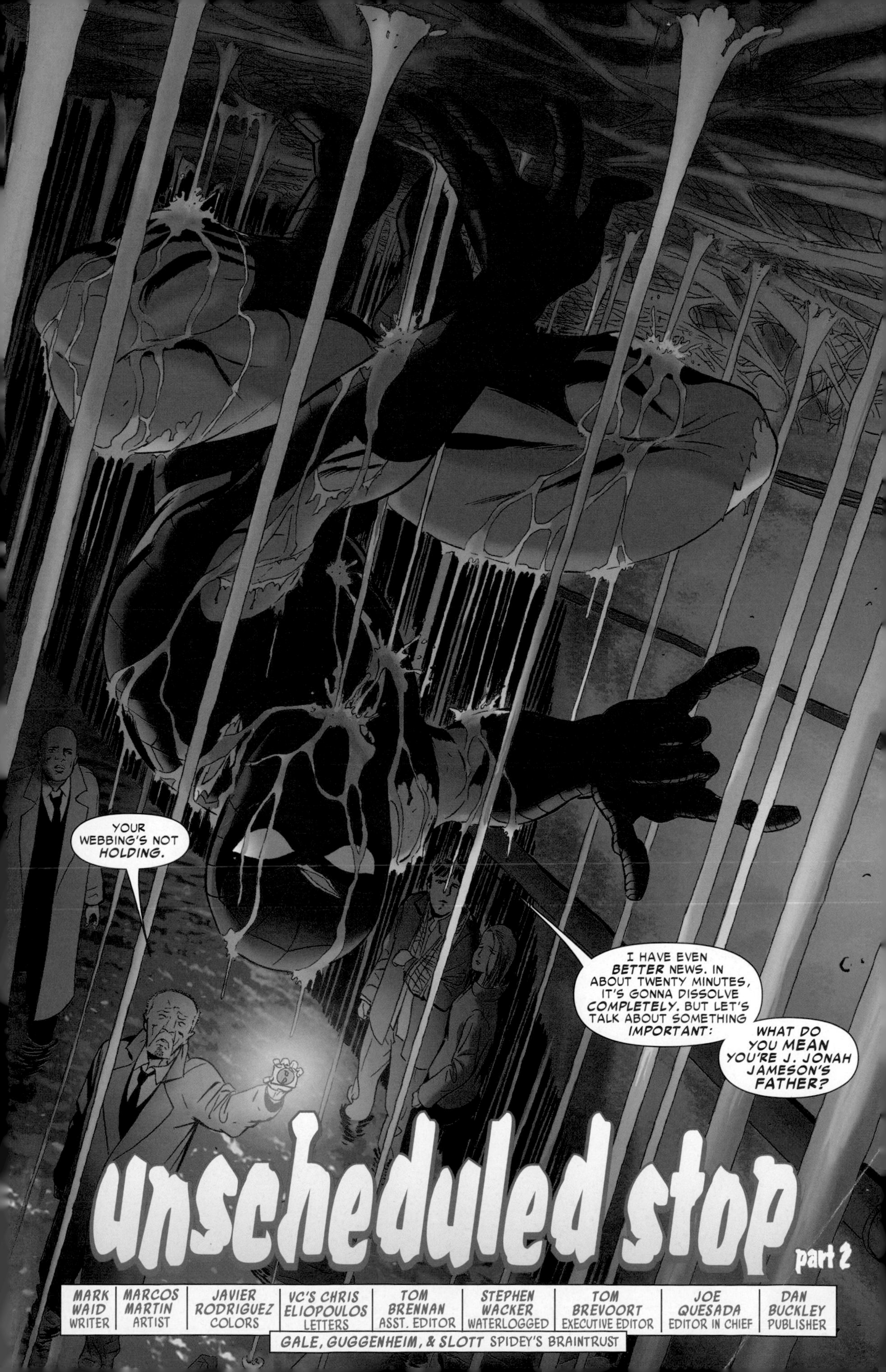
YOUR WEBBING'S NOT HOLDING.
I HAVE EVEN BETTER NEWS. IN ABOUT TWENTY MINUTES, IT'S GONNA DISSOLVE COMPLETELY. BUT LET'S TALK ABOUT SOMETHING IMPORTANT:
WHAT DO YOU MEAN YOU'RE J. JONAH JAMESON'S FATHER?
unscheduled stop part 2
MARK WAID WRITER
MARCOS MARTIN ARTIST
JAVIER RODRIGUEZ COLORS
VC'S CHRIS ELIOPOULOS LETTERS
TOM BRENNAN ASST. EDITOR
STEPHEN WACKER WATERLOGGED
TOM BREVOORT EXECUTIVE EDITOR
JOE QUESADA EDITOR IN CHIEF
DAN BUCKLEY PUBLISHER
GALE, GUGGENHEIM, & SLOTT SPIDEY'S BRAINTRUST

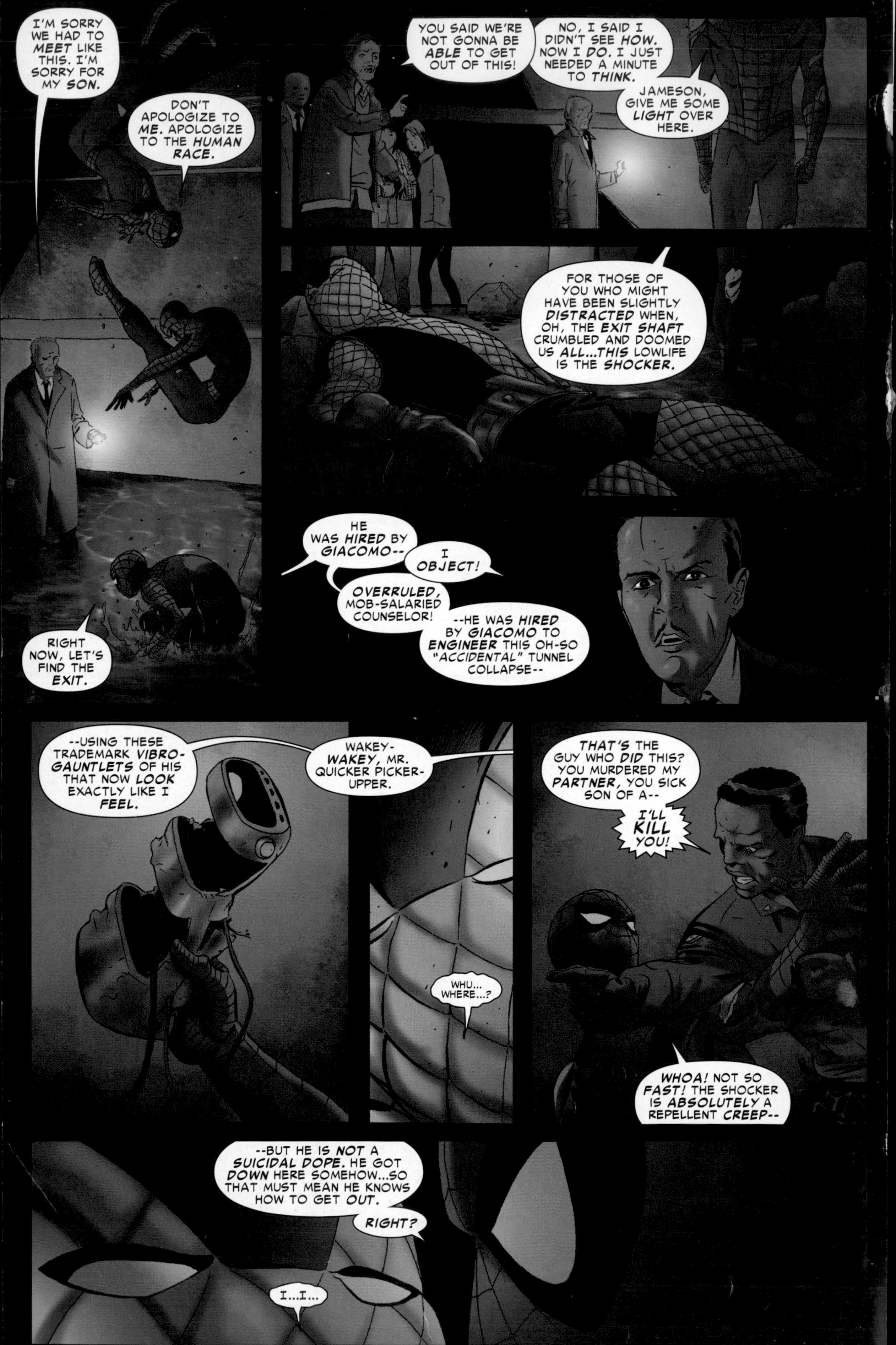

I'M SORRY WE HAD TO MEET LIKE THIS. I'M SORRY FOR MY SON.
DON'T APOLOGIZE TO ME. APOLOGIZE TO THE HUMAN RACE.
RIGHT NOW, LET'S FIND THE EXIT.
YOU SAID WE'RE NOT GONNA BE ABLE TO GET OUT OF THIS!
NO, I SAID I DIDN'T SEE HOW. NOW I DO. I JUST NEEDED A MINUTE TO THINK.
JAMESON, GIVE ME SOME LIGHT OVER HERE.
FOR THOSE OF YOU WHO MIGHT HAVE BEEN SLIGHTLY DISTRACTED WHEN, OH, THE EXIT SHAFT CRUMBLED AND DOOMED US ALL...THIS LOWLIFE IS THE SHOCKER.
HE WAS HIRED BY GIACOMO--
I OBJECT!
OVERRULED, MOB-SALARIED COUNSELOR!
--HE WAS HIRED BY GIACOMO TO ENGINEER THIS OH-SO "ACCIDENTAL" TUNNEL COLLAPSE--
--USING THESE TRADEMARK VIBRO-GAUNTLETS OF HIS THAT NOW LOOK EXACTLY LIKE I FEEL.
WAKEY-WAKEY, MR. QUICKER PICKER-UPPER.
WHU... WHERE...?
THAT'S THE GUY WHO DID THIS? YOU MURDERED MY PARTNER, YOU SICK SON OF A--
I'LL KILL YOU!
WHOA! NOT SO FAST! THE SHOCKER IS ABSOLUTELY A REPELLENT CREEP--
--BUT HE IS NOT A SUICIDAL DOPE. HE GOT DOWN HERE SOMEHOW...SO THAT MUST MEAN HE KNOWS HOW TO GET OUT.
RIGHT?
I...I...

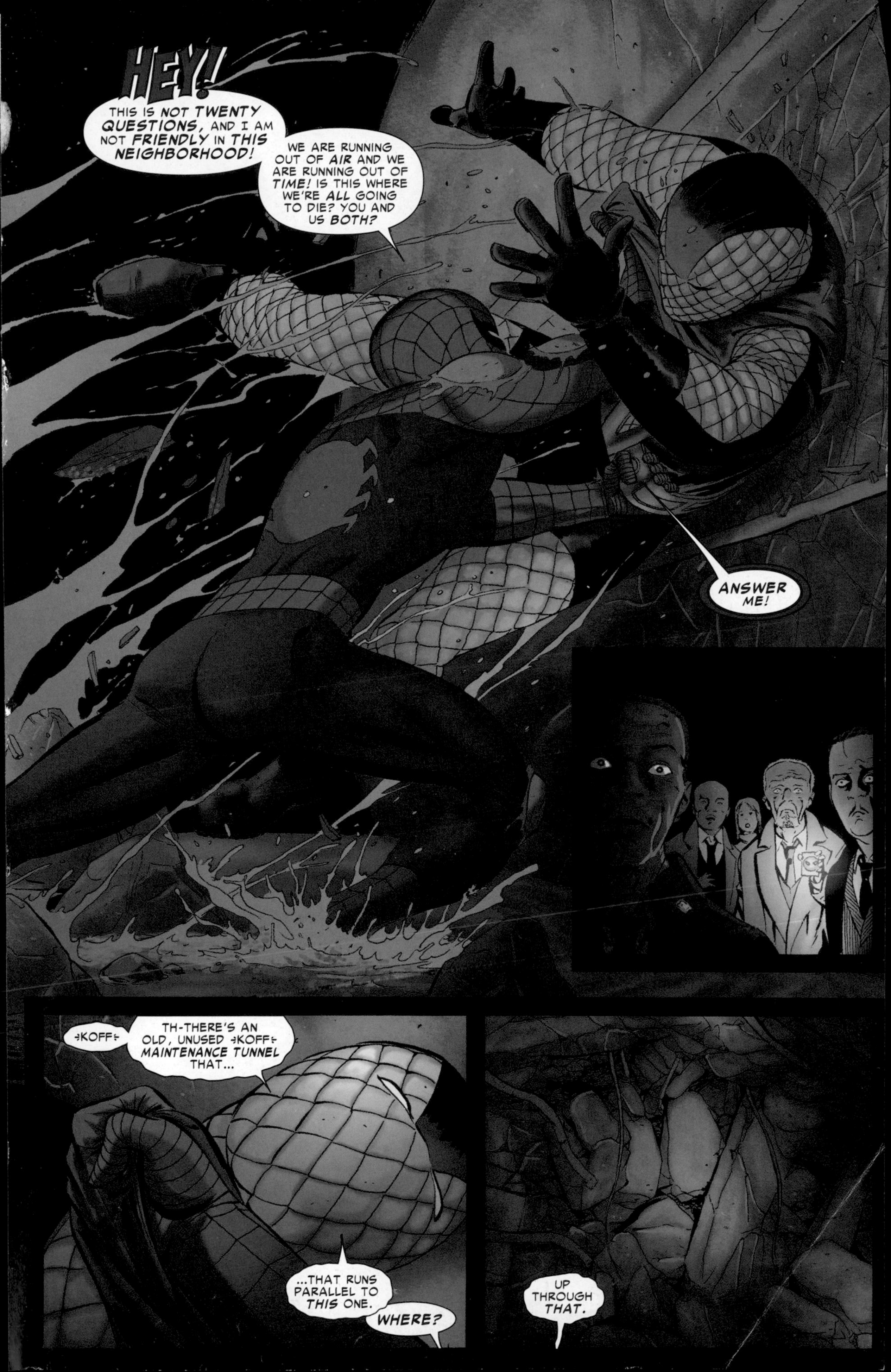
HEY!
THIS IS NOT TWENTY QUESTIONS, AND I AM NOT FRIENDLY IN THIS NEIGHBORHOOD!
WE ARE RUNNING OUT OF AIR AND WE ARE RUNNING OUT OF TIME! IS THIS WHERE WE'RE ALL GOING TO DIE? YOU AND US BOTH?
ANSWER ME!
-KOFF-
TH-THERE'S AN OLD, UNUSED -KOFF- MAINTENANCE TUNNEL THAT...
...THAT RUNS PARALLEL TO THIS ONE.
WHERE?
UP THROUGH THAT.

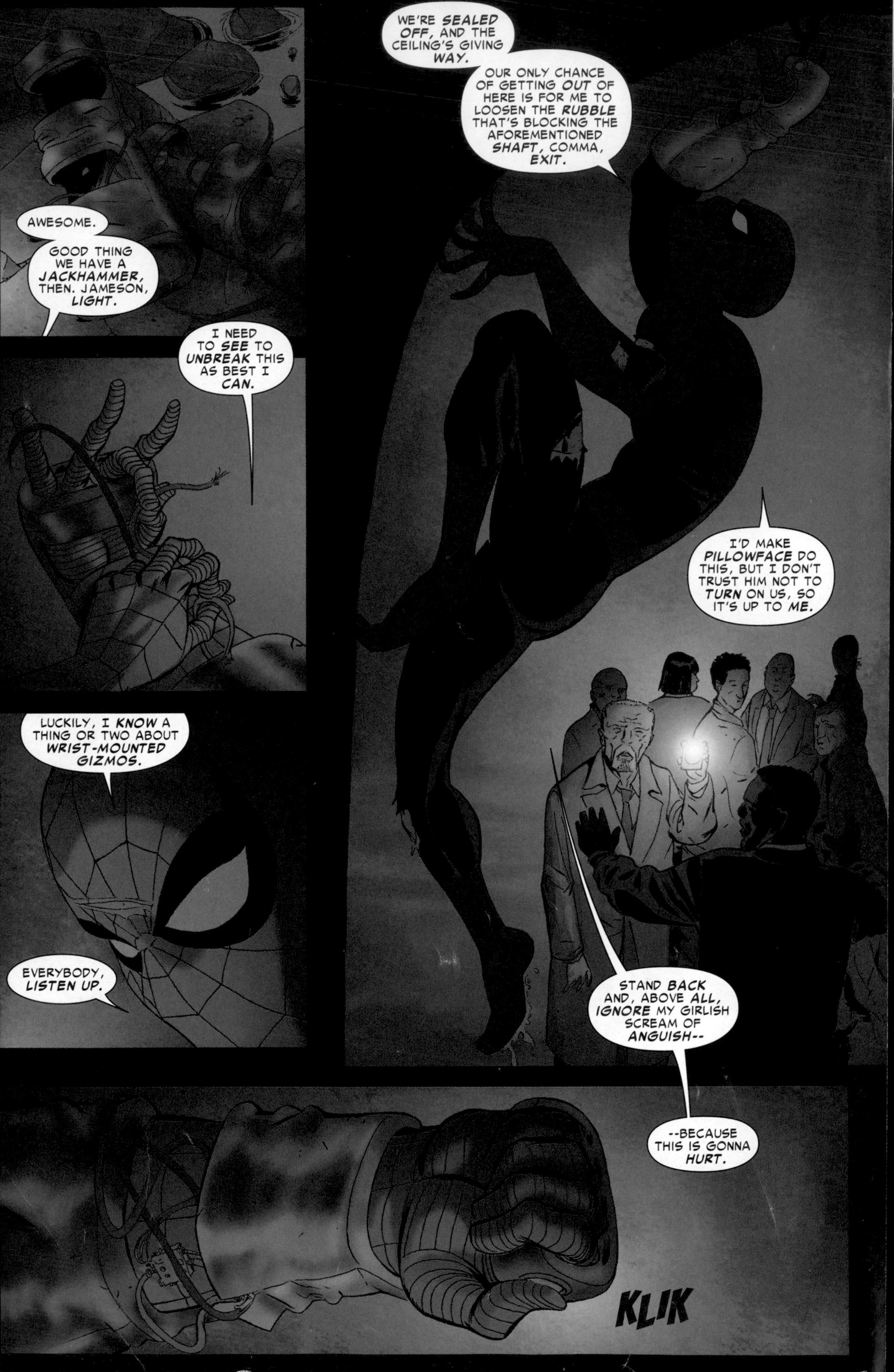

AWESOME.
GOOD THING WE HAVE A JACKHAMMER, THEN. JAMESON, LIGHT.
I NEED TO SEE TO UNBREAK THIS AS BEST I CAN.
LUCKILY, I KNOW A THING OR TWO ABOUT WRIST-MOUNTED GIZMOS.
EVERYBODY, LISTEN UP.
WE'RE SEALED OFF, AND THE CEILING'S GIVING WAY.
OUR ONLY CHANCE OF GETTING OUT OF HERE IS FOR ME TO LOOSEN THE RUBBLE THAT'S BLOCKING THE AFOREMENTIONED SHAFT, COMMA, EXIT.
I'D MAKE PILLOWFACE DO THIS, BUT I DON'T TRUST HIM NOT TO TURN ON US, SO IT'S UP TO ME.
STAND BACK AND, ABOVE ALL, IGNORE MY GIRLISH SCREAM OF ANGUISH--
--BECAUSE THIS IS GONNA HURT.
KLIK

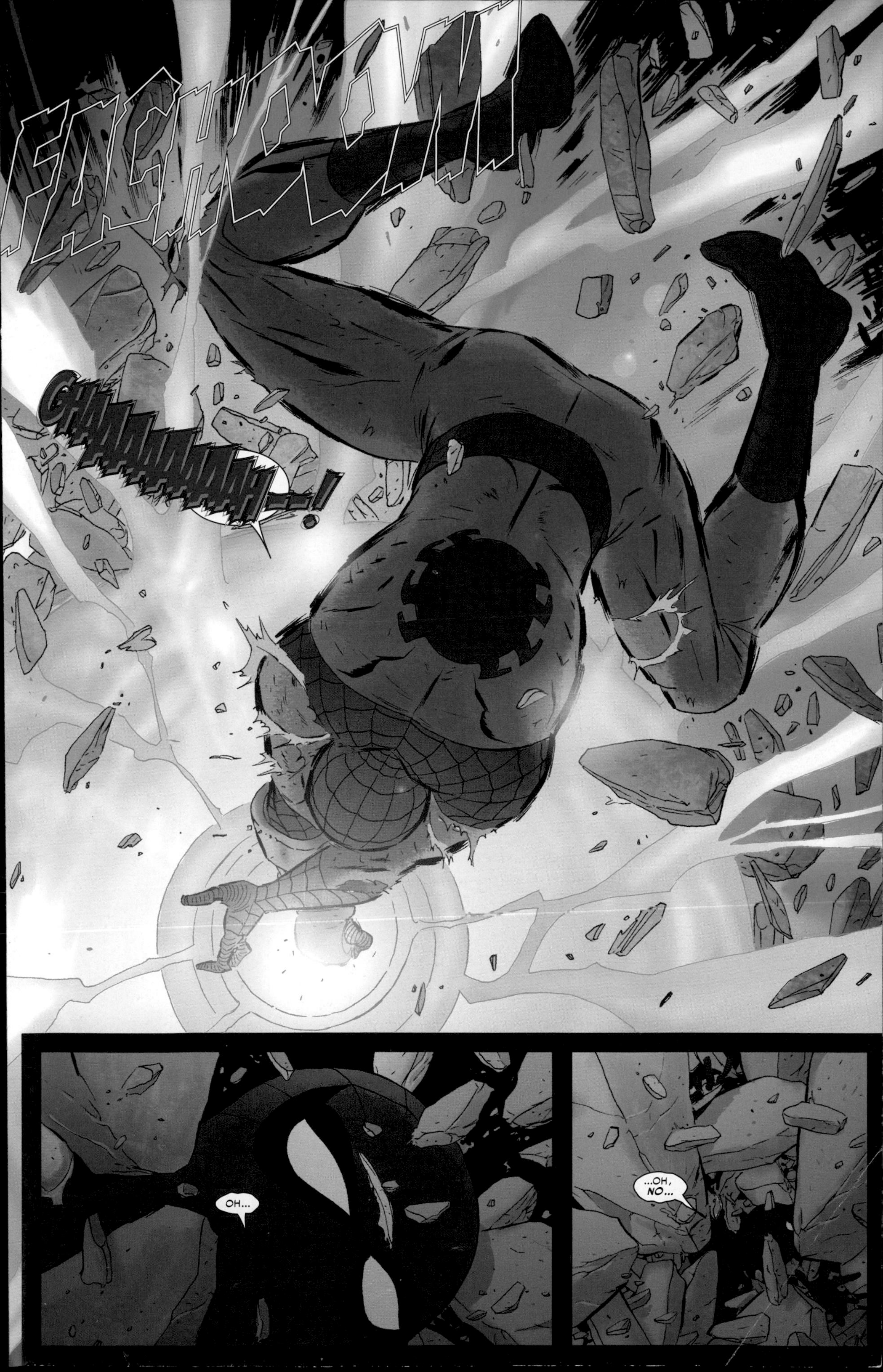
OH...
...OH, NO...

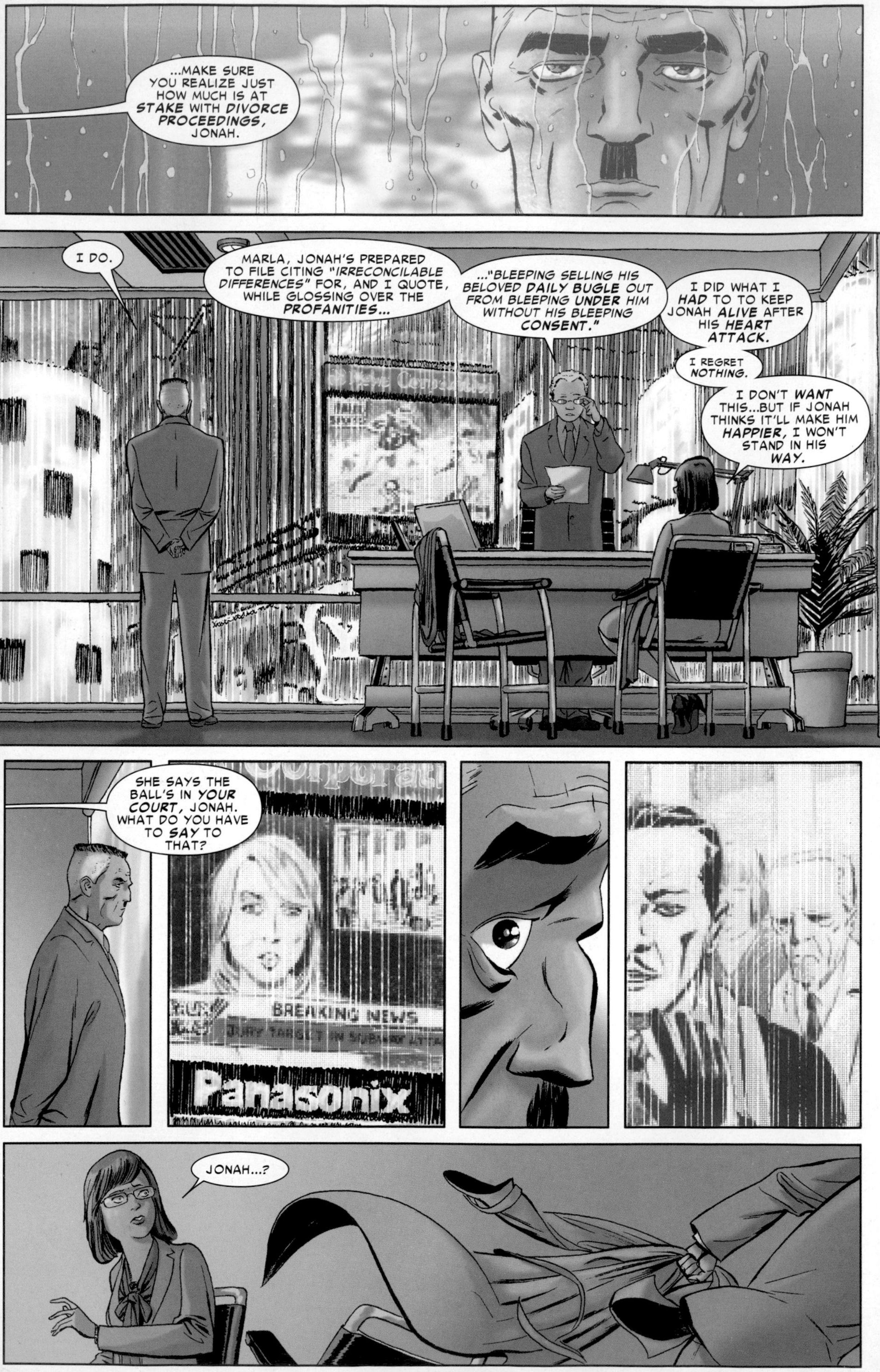
...MAKE SURE YOU REALIZE JUST HOW MUCH IS AT STAKE WITH DIVORCE PROCEEDINGS, JONAH.
I DO.
MARLA, JONAH'S PREPARED TO FILE CITING "IRRECONCILABLE DIFFERENCES" FOR, AND I QUOTE, WHILE GLOSSING OVER THE PROFANITIES...
..."BLEEPING SELLING HIS BELOVED DAILY BUGLE OUT FROM BLEEPING UNDER HIM WITHOUT HIS BLEEPING CONSENT."
I DID WHAT I HAD TO TO KEEP JONAH ALIVE AFTER HIS HEART ATTACK.
I REGRET NOTHING.
I DON'T WANT THIS...BUT IF JONAH THINKS IT'LL MAKE HIM HAPPIER, I WON'T STAND IN HIS WAY.
SHE SAYS THE BALL'S IN YOUR COURT, JONAH. WHAT DO YOU HAVE TO SAY TO THAT?
BREAKING NEWS
Panasonix
JONAH...?

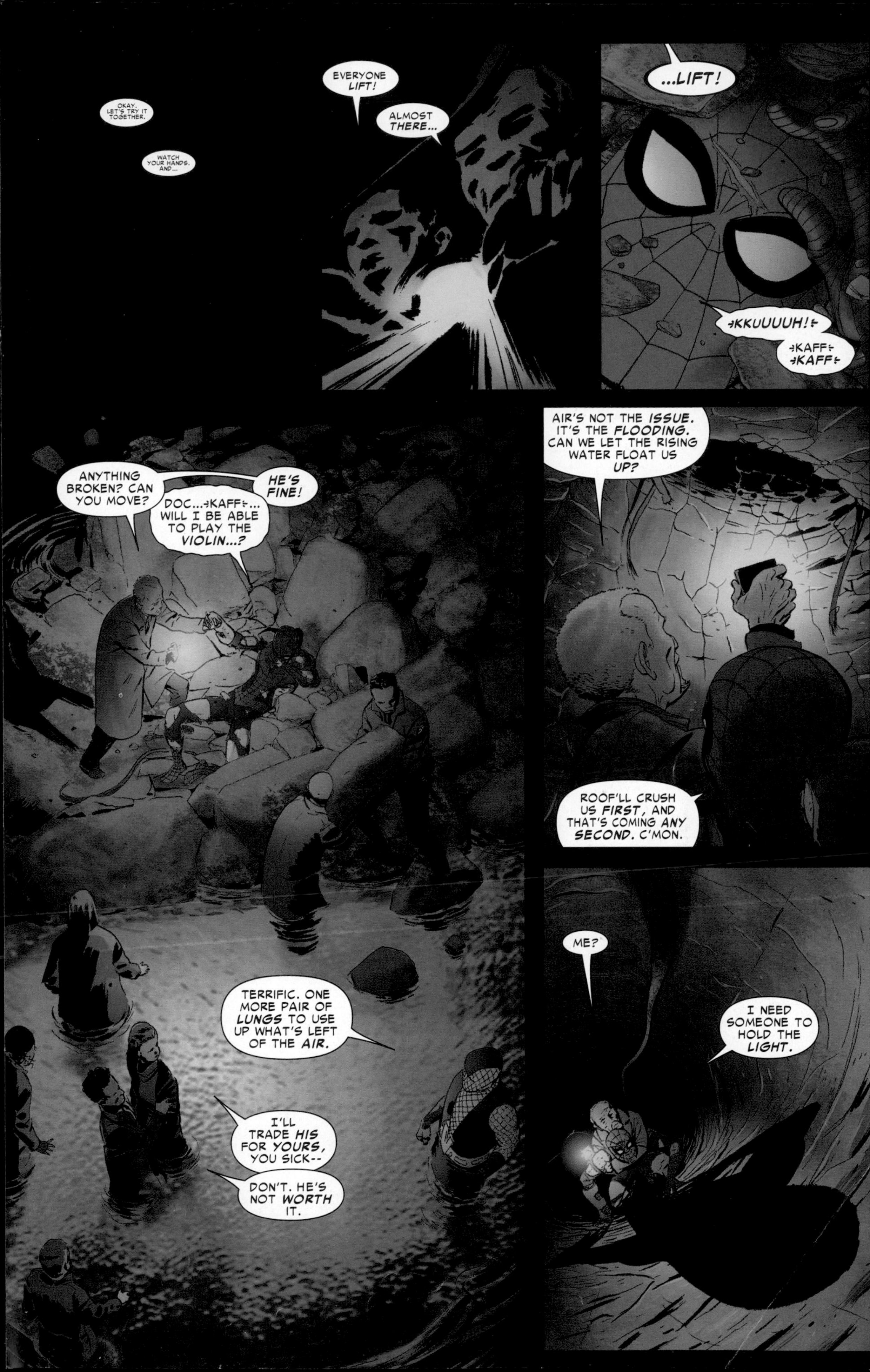
OKAY. LET'S TRY IT TOGETHER.
WATCH YOUR HANDS. AND...
EVERYONE LIFT!
ALMOST THERE...
...LIFT!
KKUUUUH!
KAFF KAFF
ANYTHING BROKEN? CAN YOU MOVE?
HE'S FINE!
DOC...KAFF... WILL I BE ABLE TO PLAY THE VIOLIN...?
TERRIFIC. ONE MORE PAIR OF LUNGS TO USE UP WHAT'S LEFT OF THE AIR.
I'LL TRADE HIS FOR YOURS, YOU SICK--
DON'T. HE'S NOT WORTH IT.
AIR'S NOT THE ISSUE. IT'S THE FLOODING. CAN WE LET THE RISING WATER FLOAT US UP?
ROOF'LL CRUSH US FIRST, AND THAT'S COMING ANY SECOND. C'MON.
ME?
I NEED SOMEONE TO HOLD THE LIGHT.

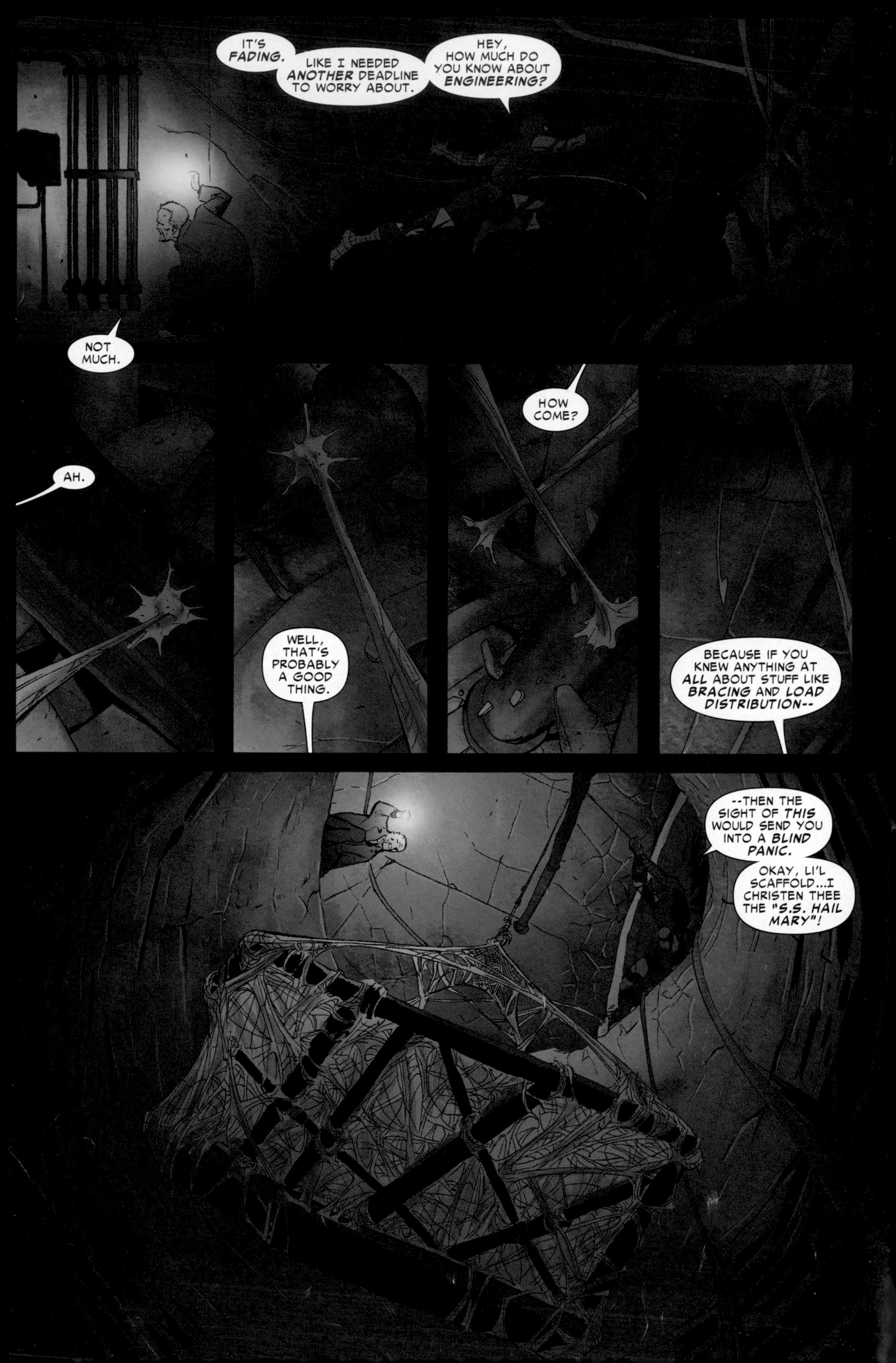
IT'S FADING.
LIKE I NEEDED ANOTHER DEADLINE TO WORRY ABOUT.
HEY, HOW MUCH DO YOU KNOW ABOUT ENGINEERING?
NOT MUCH.
AH.
WELL, THAT'S PROBABLY A GOOD THING.
HOW COME?
BECAUSE IF YOU KNEW ANYTHING AT ALL ABOUT STUFF LIKE BRACING AND LOAD DISTRIBUTION--
--THEN THE SIGHT OF THIS WOULD SEND YOU INTO A BLIND PANIC.
OKAY, LI'L SCAFFOLD...I CHRISTEN THEE THE "S.S. HAIL MARY"!

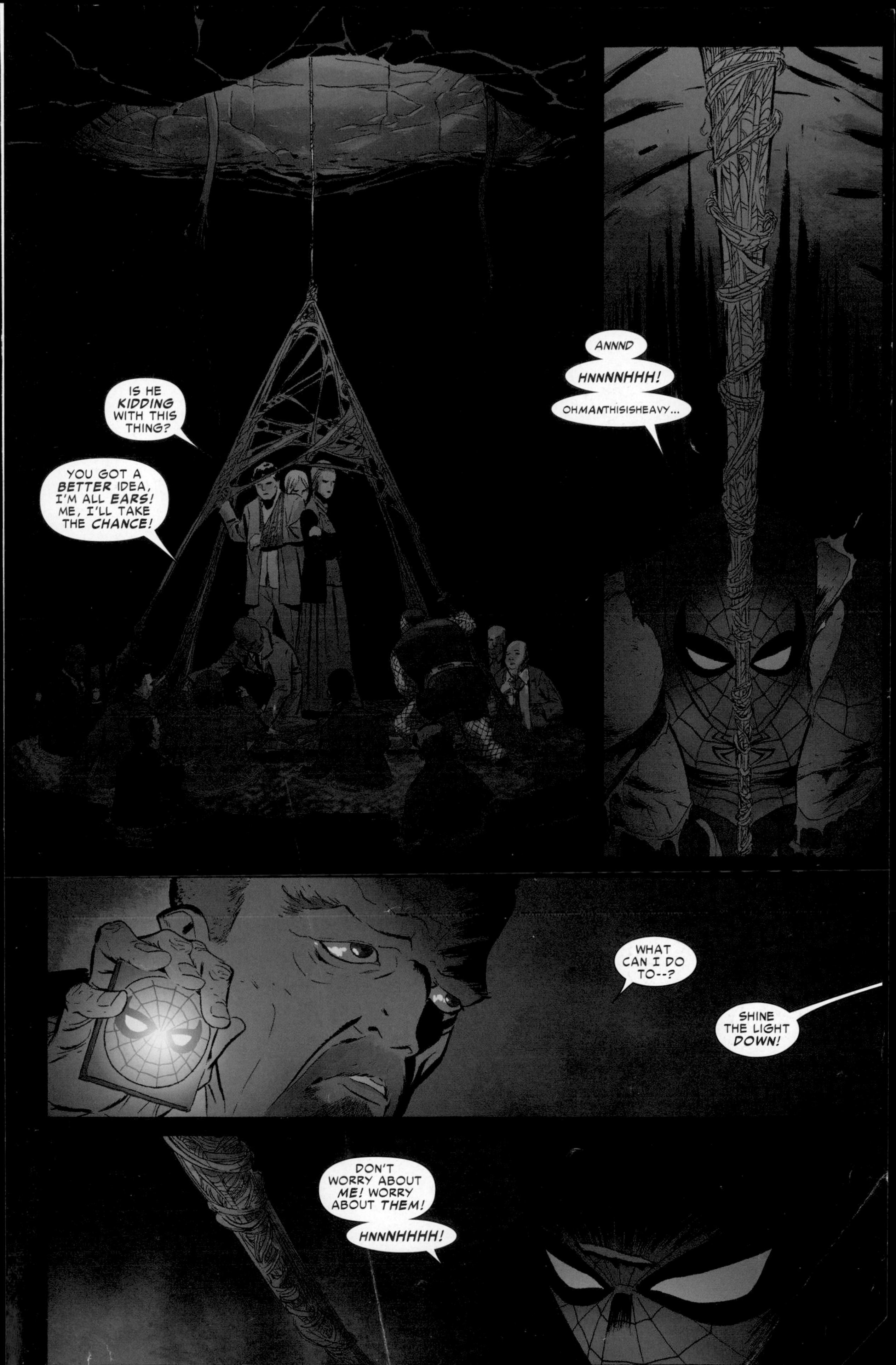
IS HE KIDDING WITH THIS THING?
YOU GOT A BETTER IDEA, I'M ALL EARS! ME, I'LL TAKE THE CHANCE!
ANNND
HNNNNHHH!
OHMANTHISISHEAVY...
WHAT CAN I DO TO--?
SHINE THE LIGHT DOWN!
DON'T WORRY ABOUT ME! WORRY ABOUT THEM!
HNNNHHHH!

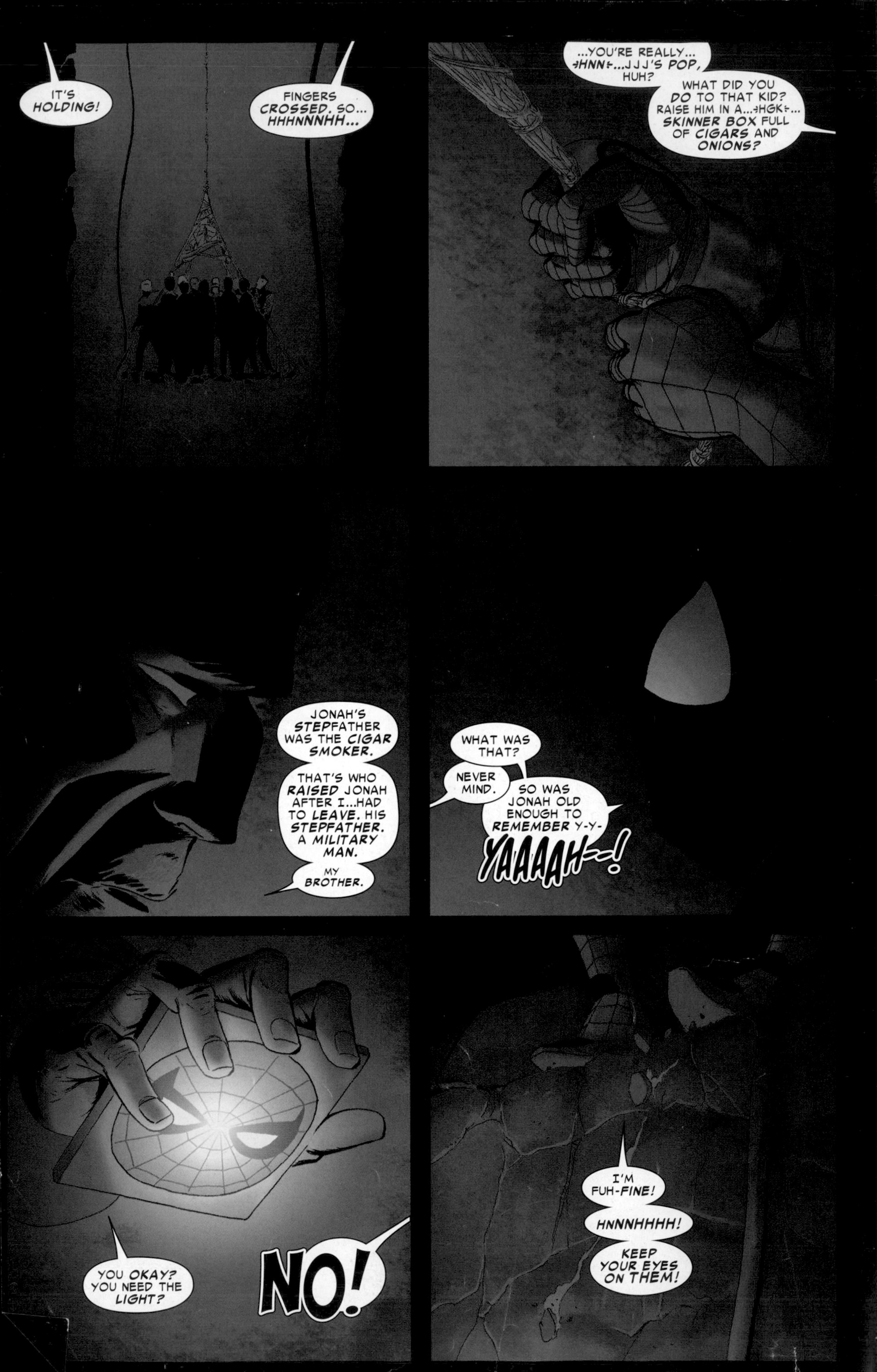
IT'S HOLDING!
FINGERS CROSSED. SO... HHHNNNHH...
...YOU'RE REALLY... ƎHNNƐ...JJJ'S POP, HUH?
WHAT DID YOU DO TO THAT KID? RAISE HIM IN A...ƎHGKƐ... SKINNER BOX FULL OF CIGARS AND ONIONS?
JONAH'S STEPFATHER WAS THE CIGAR SMOKER.
THAT'S WHO RAISED JONAH AFTER I...HAD TO LEAVE. HIS STEPFATHER. A MILITARY MAN.
MY BROTHER.
WHAT WAS THAT?
NEVER MIND.
SO WAS JONAH OLD ENOUGH TO REMEMBER Y-Y-
YAAAAH--!
YOU OKAY? YOU NEED THE LIGHT?
NO!
I'M FUH-FINE!
HNNNHHHH!
KEEP YOUR EYES ON THEM!

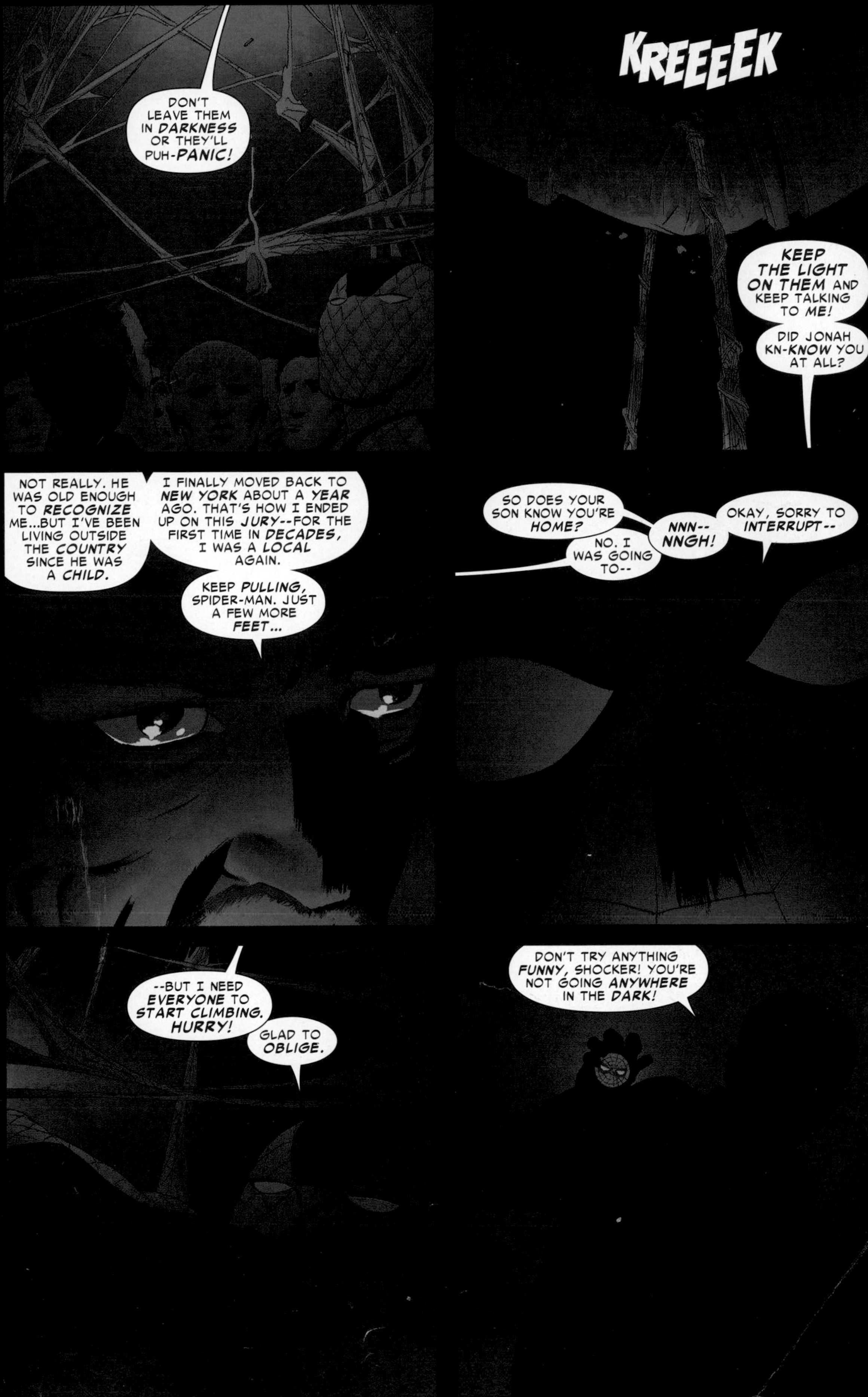
DON'T LEAVE THEM IN DARKNESS OR THEY'LL PUH-PANIC!
KREEEEK
KEEP THE LIGHT ON THEM AND KEEP TALKING TO ME!
DID JONAH KN-KNOW YOU AT ALL?
NOT REALLY. HE WAS OLD ENOUGH TO RECOGNIZE ME...BUT I'VE BEEN LIVING OUTSIDE THE COUNTRY SINCE HE WAS A CHILD.
I FINALLY MOVED BACK TO NEW YORK ABOUT A YEAR AGO. THAT'S HOW I ENDED UP ON THIS JURY--FOR THE FIRST TIME IN DECADES, I WAS A LOCAL AGAIN.
KEEP PULLING, SPIDER-MAN. JUST A FEW MORE FEET...
SO DOES YOUR SON KNOW YOU'RE HOME?
NO. I WAS GOING TO--
NNN-- NNGH!
OKAY, SORRY TO INTERRUPT--
--BUT I NEED EVERYONE TO START CLIMBING. HURRY!
GLAD TO OBLIGE.
DON'T TRY ANYTHING FUNNY, SHOCKER! YOU'RE NOT GOING ANYWHERE IN THE DARK!

RELAX, OLD MAN! I REMEMBER SEEIN' A TOOLBOX UP HERE SOMEWHERE, AND--
HURRY!
KLIK
AH-HA!
YOW.
MY GOD...
I SAID HURRY!

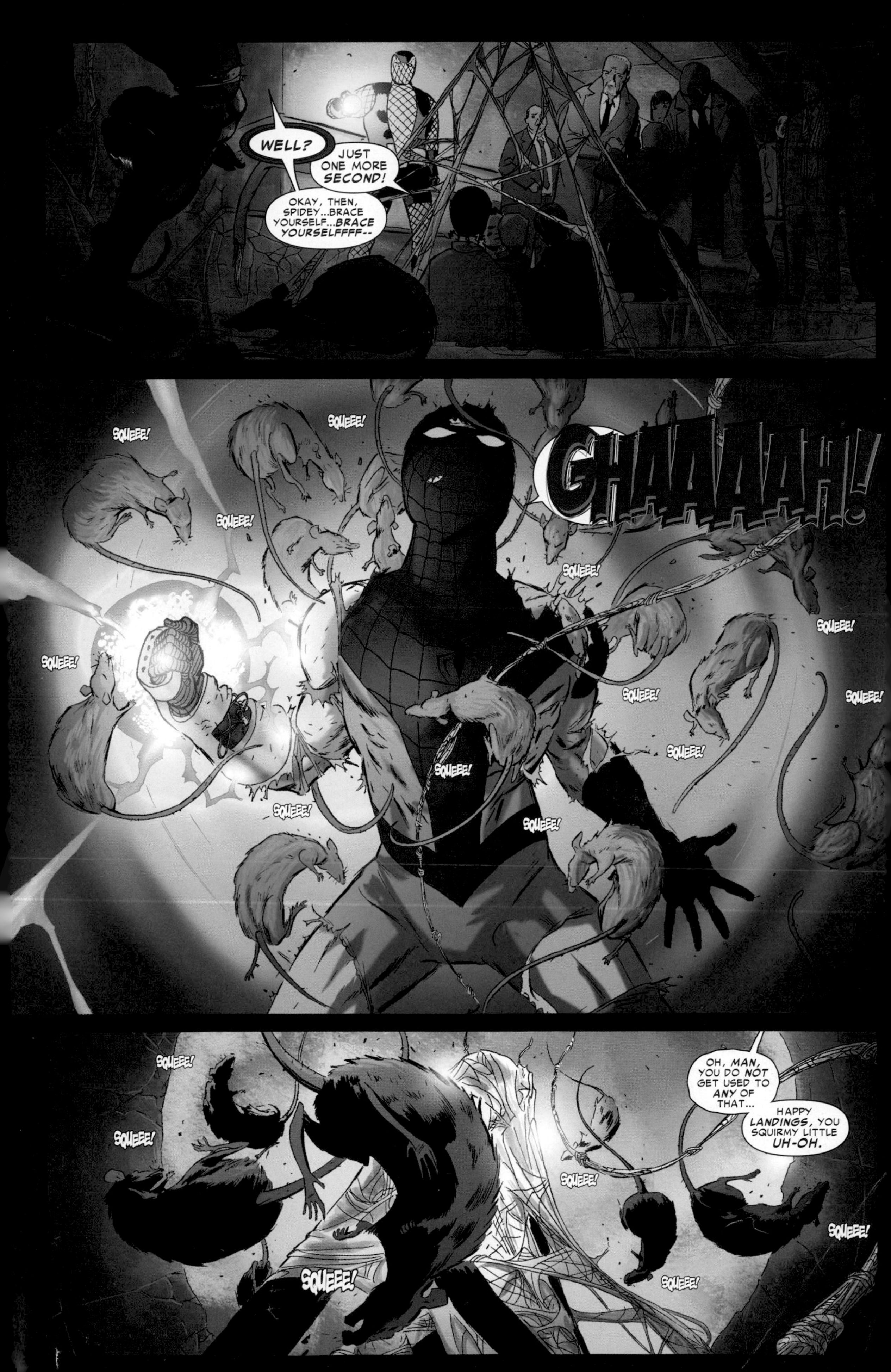
WELL?
JUST ONE MORE SECOND!
OKAY, THEN, SPIDEY...BRACE YOURSELF...BRACE YOURSELFFFF--
GHAAAAH!
SQUEEE!
SQUEEE!
SQUEEE!
SQUEEE!
SQUEEE!
SQUEEE!
SQUEEE!
SQUEEE!
SQUEEE!
SQUEEE!
SQUEEE!
SQUEEE!
SQUEEE!
OH, MAN, YOU DO NOT GET USED TO ANY OF THAT...
HAPPY LANDINGS, YOU SQUIRMY LITTLE UH-OH.
SQUEEE!
SQUEEE!
SQUEEE!
SQUEEE!
SQUEEE!
SQUEEE!

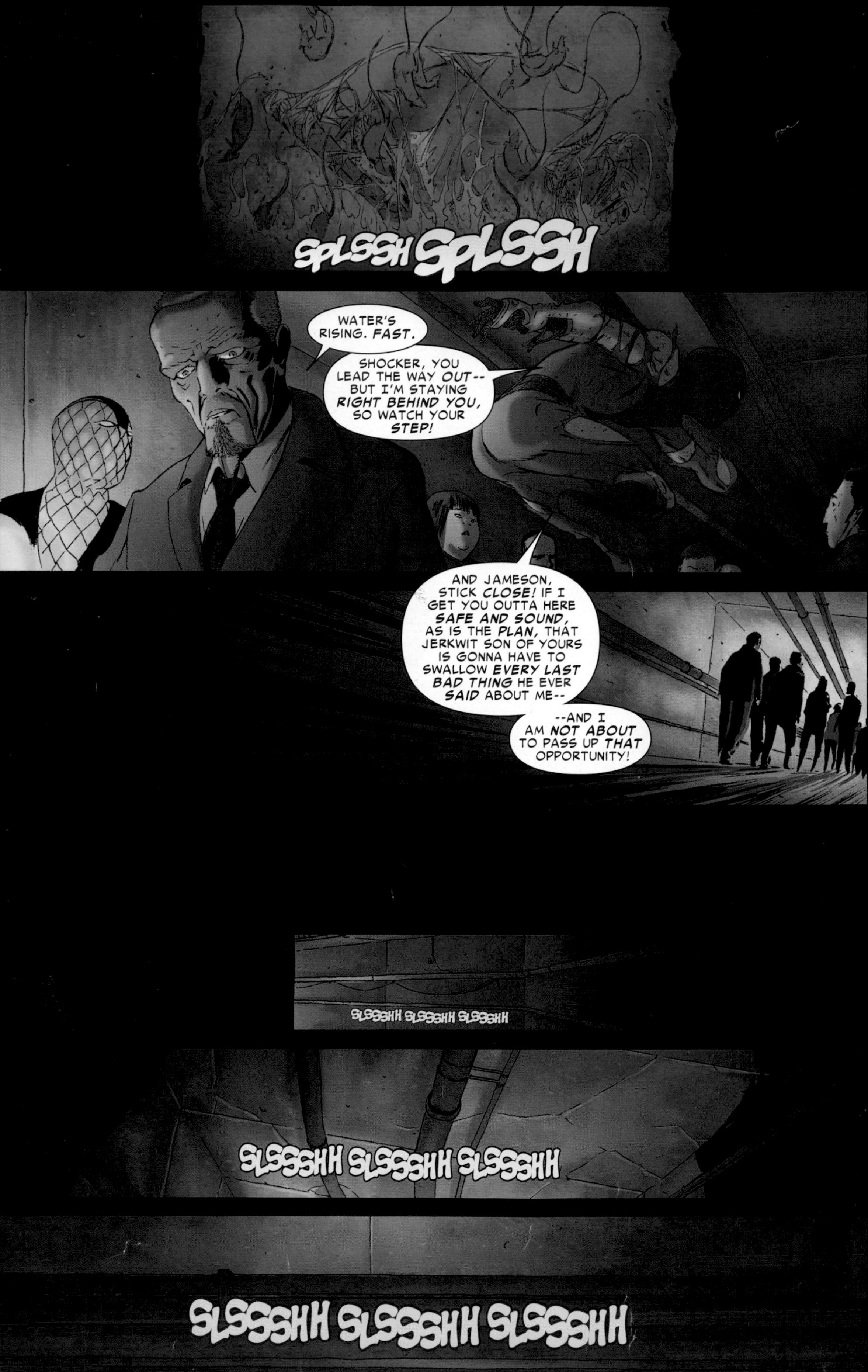
SPLSSH SPLSSH
WATER'S RISING. FAST.
SHOCKER, YOU LEAD THE WAY OUT-- BUT I'M STAYING RIGHT BEHIND YOU, SO WATCH YOUR STEP!
AND JAMESON, STICK CLOSE! IF I GET YOU OUTTA HERE SAFE AND SOUND, AS IS THE PLAN, THAT JERKWIT SON OF YOURS IS GONNA HAVE TO SWALLOW EVERY LAST BAD THING HE EVER SAID ABOUT ME--
--AND I AM NOT ABOUT TO PASS UP THAT OPPORTUNITY!
SLSSSHH SLSSSHH SLSSSHH
SLSSSHH SLSSSHH SLSSSHH
SLSSSHH SLSSSHH SLSSSHH

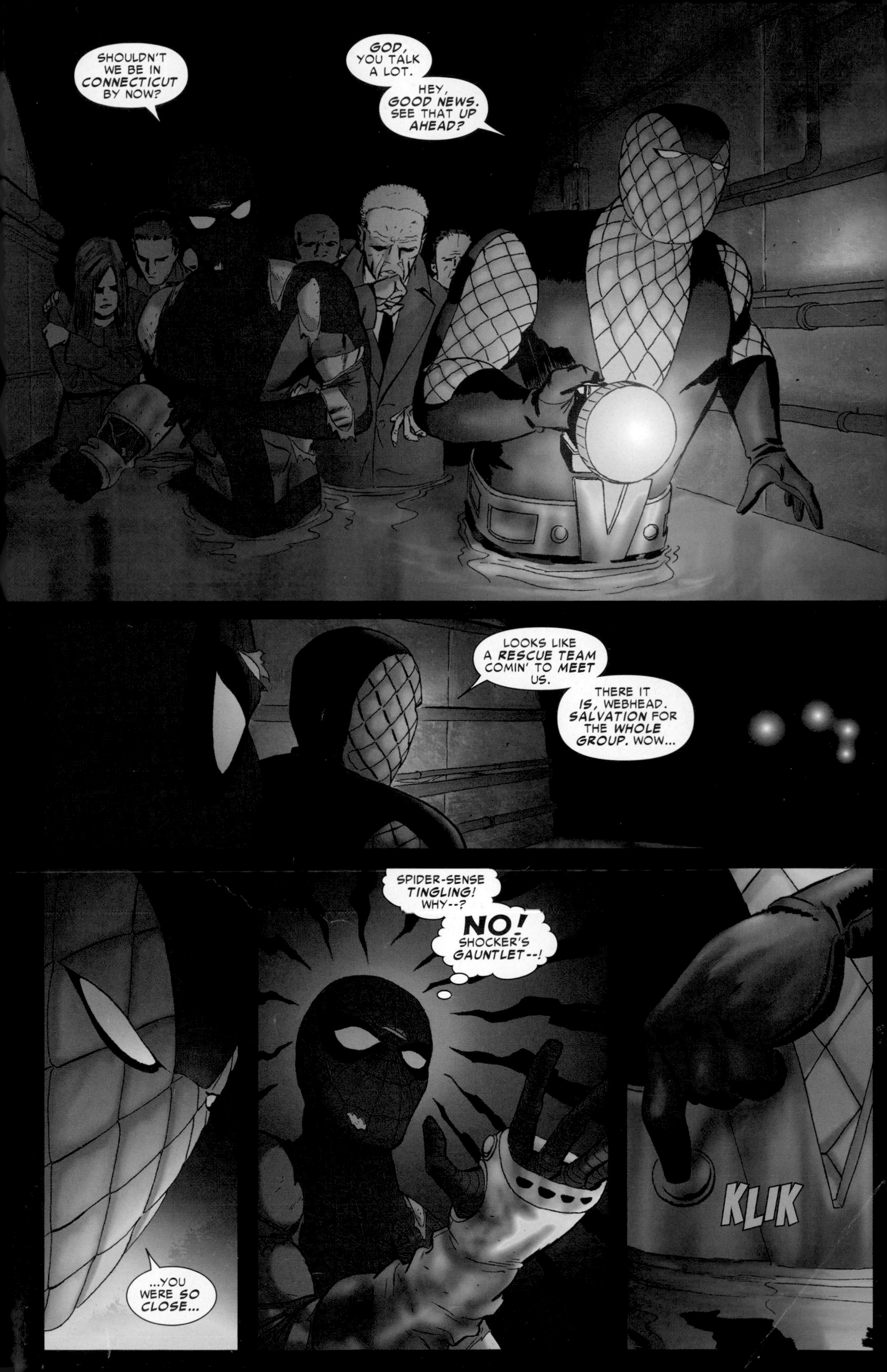
SHOULDN'T WE BE IN CONNECTICUT BY NOW?
GOD, YOU TALK A LOT.
HEY, GOOD NEWS. SEE THAT UP AHEAD?
LOOKS LIKE A RESCUE TEAM COMIN' TO MEET US.
THERE IT IS, WEBHEAD. SALVATION FOR THE WHOLE GROUP. WOW...
...YOU WERE SO CLOSE...
SPIDER-SENSE TINGLING! WHY--?
NO! SHOCKER'S GAUNTLET--!
KLIK

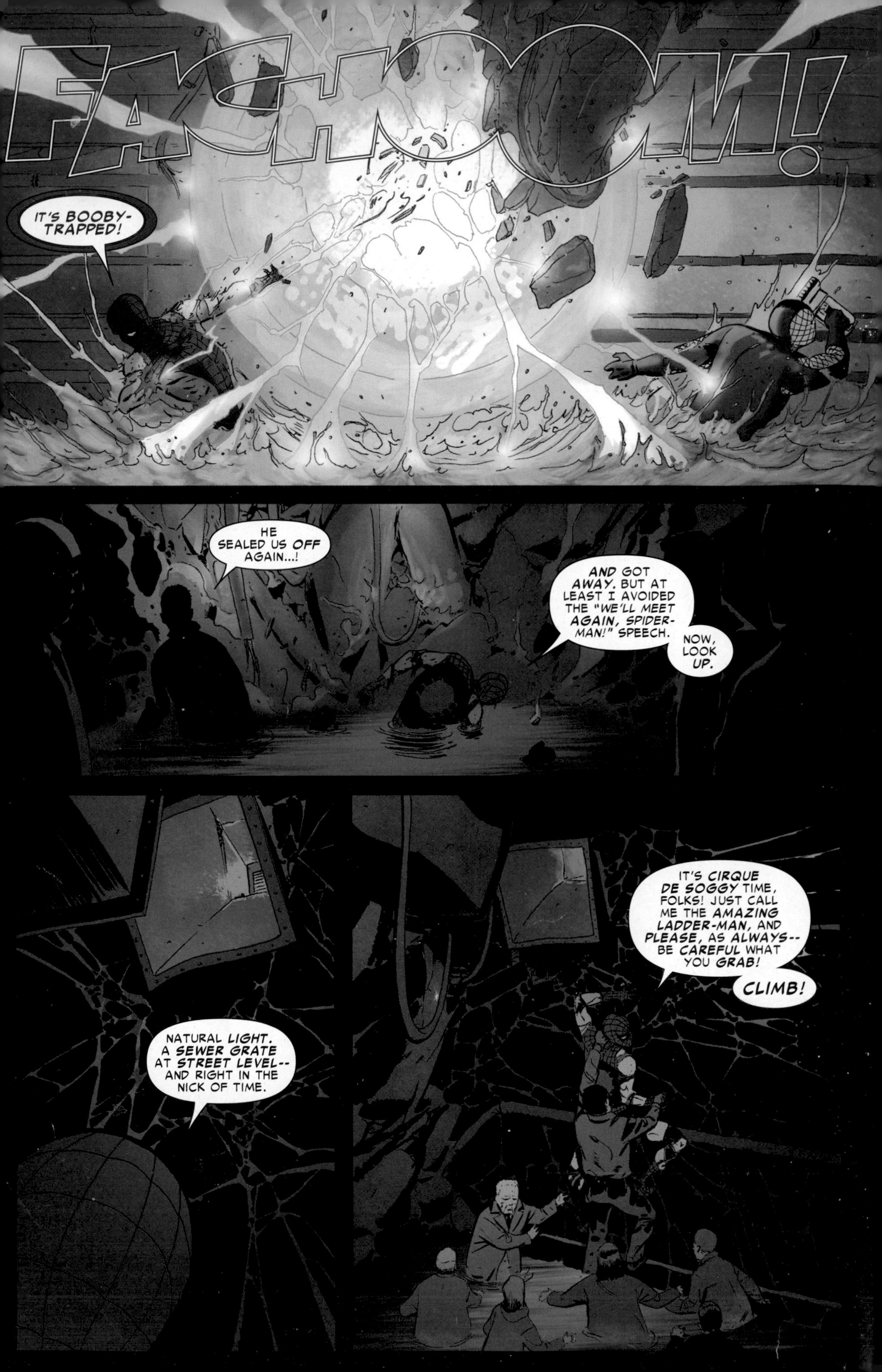
FACHOOM!
IT'S BOOBY-TRAPPED!
HE SEALED US OFF AGAIN...!
AND GOT AWAY. BUT AT LEAST I AVOIDED THE "WE'LL MEET AGAIN, SPIDER-MAN!" SPEECH.
NOW, LOOK UP.
NATURAL LIGHT. A SEWER GRATE AT STREET LEVEL-- AND RIGHT IN THE NICK OF TIME.
IT'S CIRQUE DE SOGGY TIME, FOLKS! JUST CALL ME THE AMAZING LADDER-MAN, AND PLEASE, AS ALWAYS-- BE CAREFUL WHAT YOU GRAB!
CLIMB!

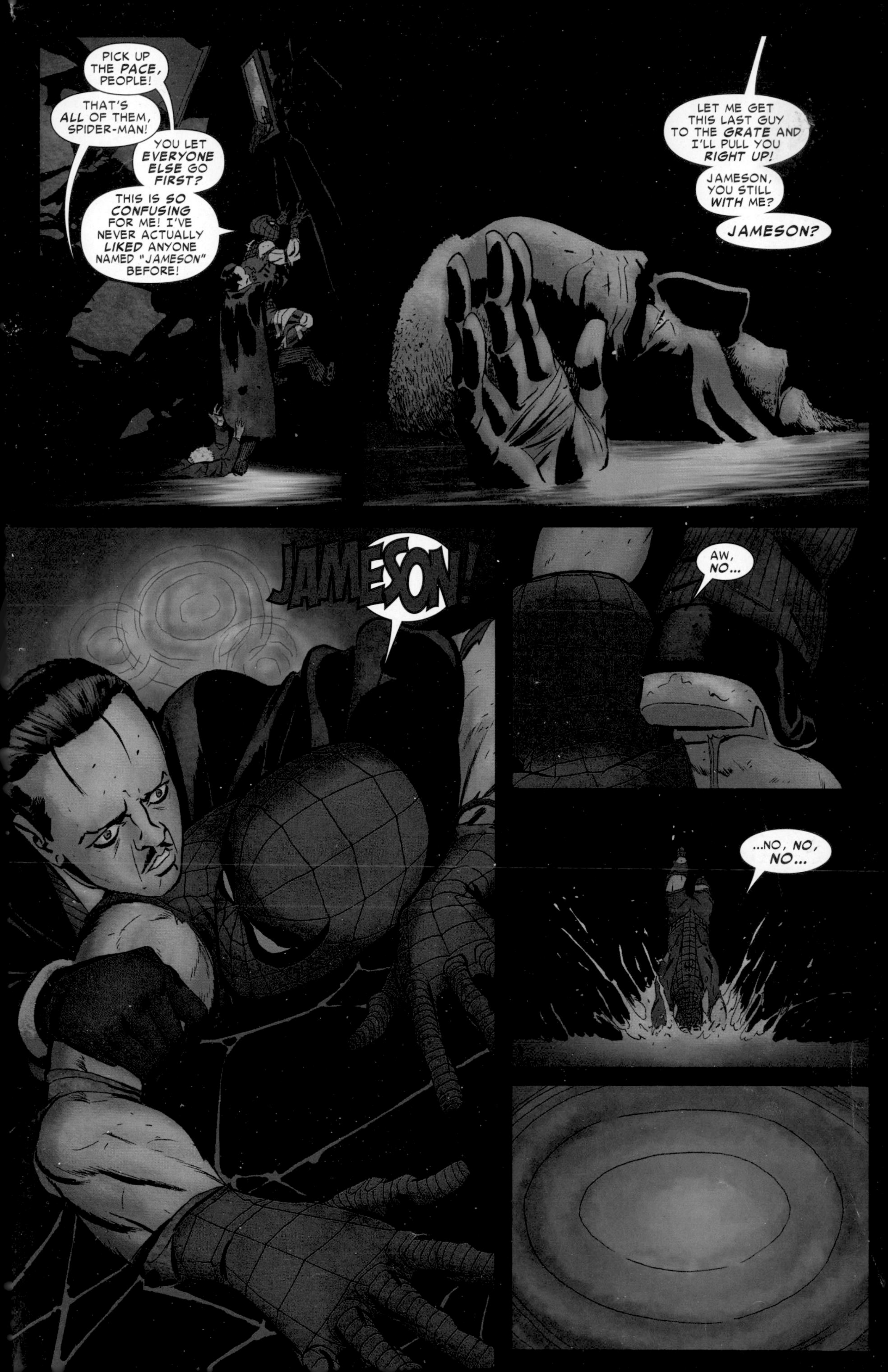
PICK UP THE PACE, PEOPLE!
THAT'S ALL OF THEM, SPIDER-MAN!
YOU LET EVERYONE ELSE GO FIRST?
THIS IS SO CONFUSING FOR ME! I'VE NEVER ACTUALLY LIKED ANYONE NAMED "JAMESON" BEFORE!
LET ME GET THIS LAST GUY TO THE GRATE AND I'LL PULL YOU RIGHT UP!
JAMESON, YOU STILL WITH ME?
JAMESON?
JAMESON!
AW, NO...
...NO, NO, NO...

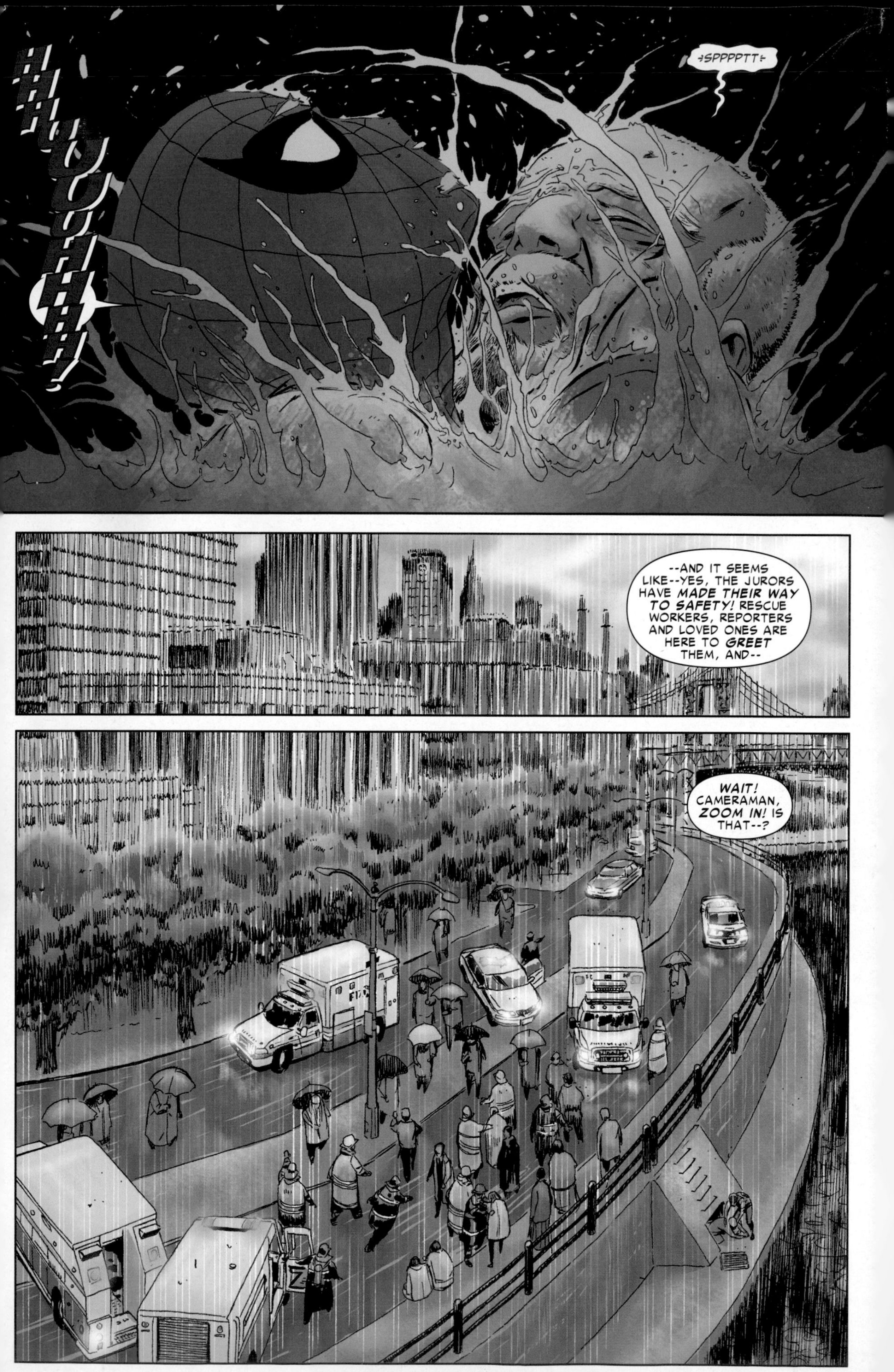
HHUUUHHHH!
SPPPPTT
--AND IT SEEMS LIKE--YES, THE JURORS HAVE MADE THEIR WAY TO SAFETY! RESCUE WORKERS, REPORTERS AND LOVED ONES ARE HERE TO GREET THEM, AND--
WAIT! CAMERAMAN, ZOOM IN! IS THAT--?

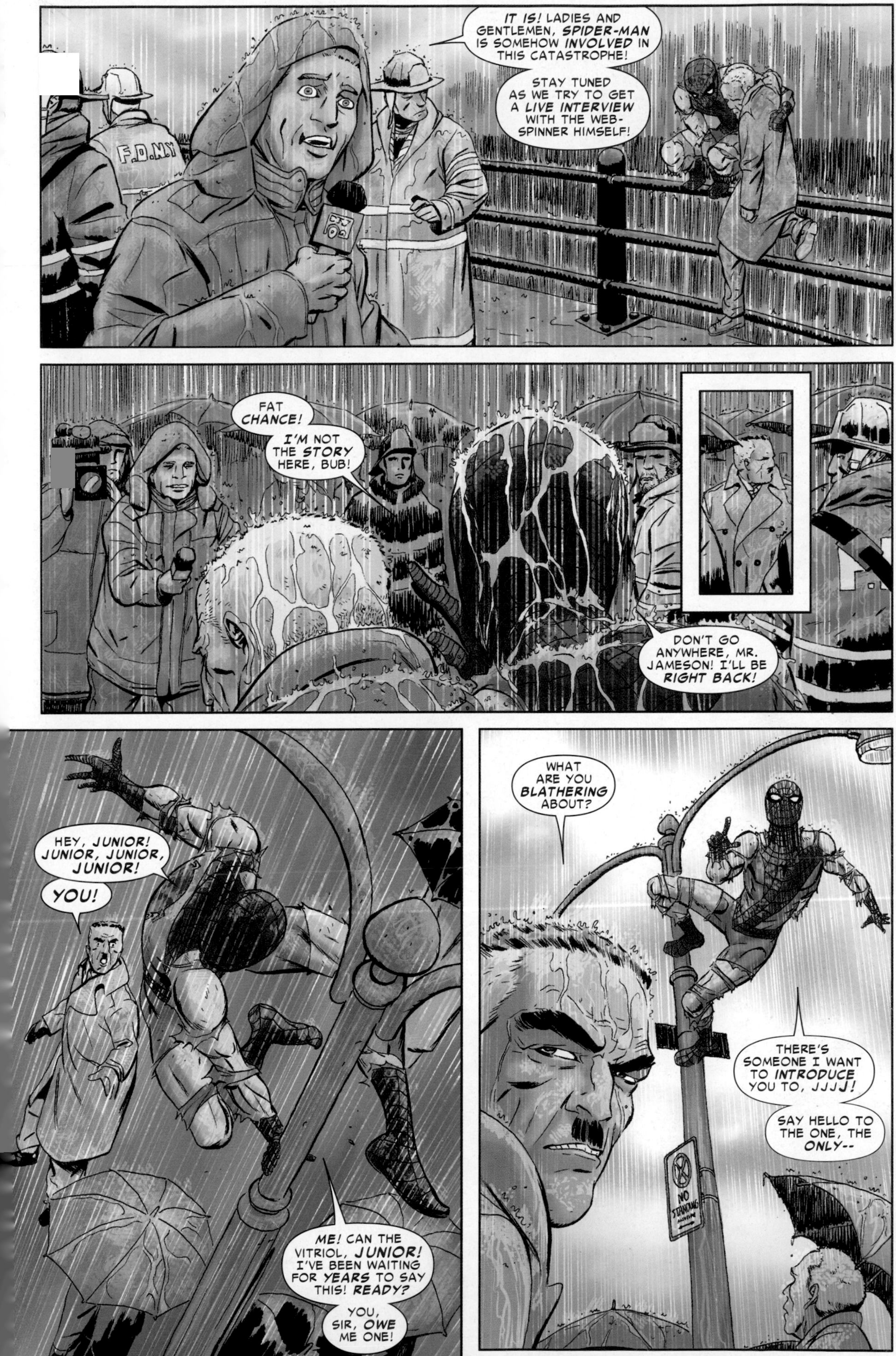
IT IS! LADIES AND GENTLEMEN, SPIDER-MAN IS SOMEHOW INVOLVED IN THIS CATASTROPHE!
STAY TUNED AS WE TRY TO GET A LIVE INTERVIEW WITH THE WEB-SPINNER HIMSELF!
F.D.N.Y
FAT CHANCE!
I'M NOT THE STORY HERE, BUB!
DON'T GO ANYWHERE, MR. JAMESON! I'LL BE RIGHT BACK!
HEY, JUNIOR! JUNIOR, JUNIOR, JUNIOR!
YOU!
ME! CAN THE VITRIOL, JUNIOR! I'VE BEEN WAITING FOR YEARS TO SAY THIS! READY?
YOU, SIR, OWE ME ONE!
WHAT ARE YOU BLATHERING ABOUT?
THERE'S SOMEONE I WANT TO INTRODUCE YOU TO, JJJJ!
SAY HELLO TO THE ONE, THE ONLY--
NO STANDING

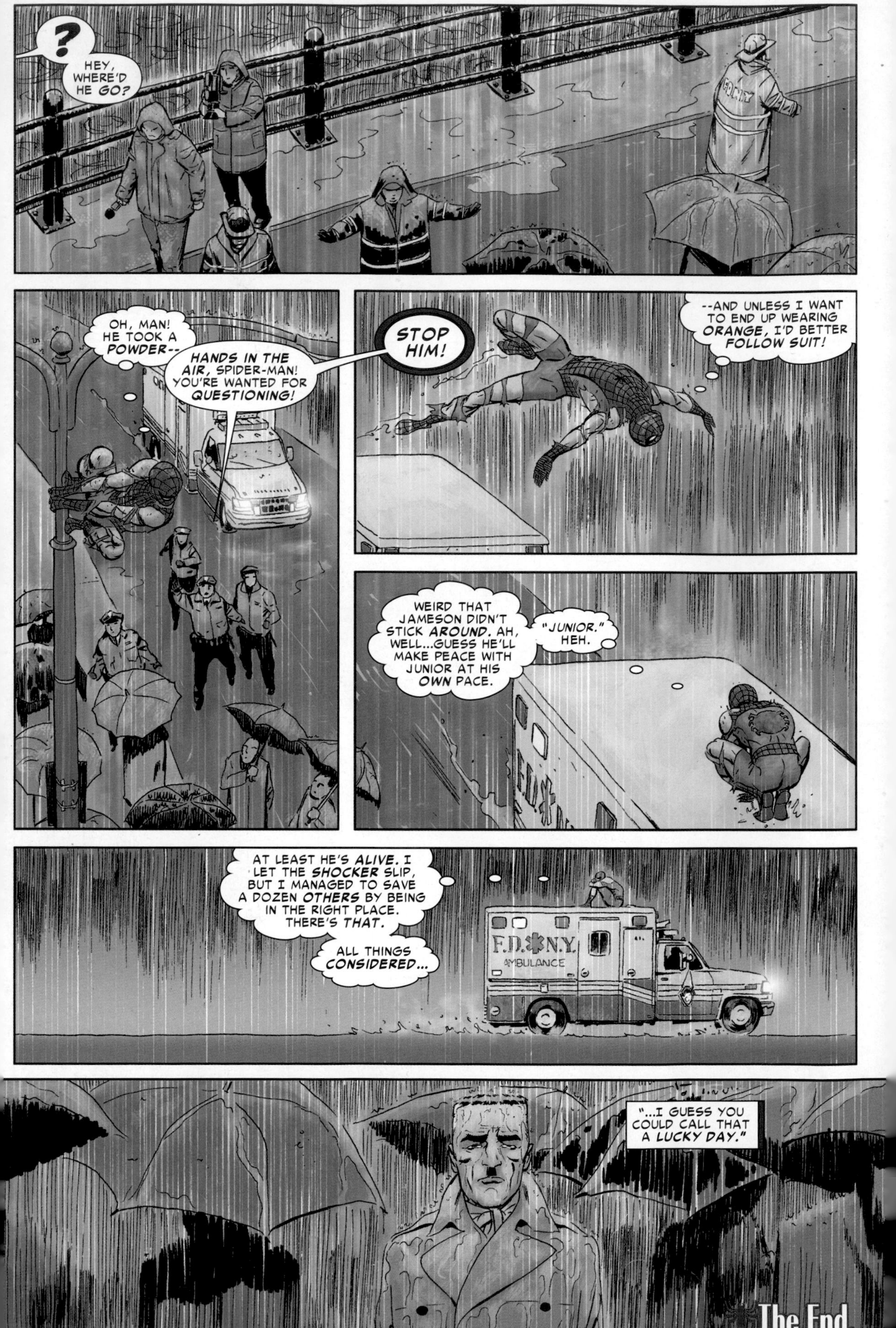
?
HEY, WHERE'D HE GO?
OH, MAN! HE TOOK A POWDER--
HANDS IN THE AIR, SPIDER-MAN! YOU'RE WANTED FOR QUESTIONING!
STOP HIM!
--AND UNLESS I WANT TO END UP WEARING ORANGE, I'D BETTER FOLLOW SUIT!
WEIRD THAT JAMESON DIDN'T STICK AROUND. AH, WELL...GUESS HE'LL MAKE PEACE WITH JUNIOR AT HIS OWN PACE.
"JUNIOR." HEH.
AT LEAST HE'S ALIVE. I LET THE SHOCKER SLIP, BUT I MANAGED TO SAVE A DOZEN OTHERS BY BEING IN THE RIGHT PLACE. THERE'S THAT.
ALL THINGS CONSIDERED...
F.D.N.Y.
AMBULANCE
"...I GUESS YOU COULD CALL THAT A LUCKY DAY."
The End.

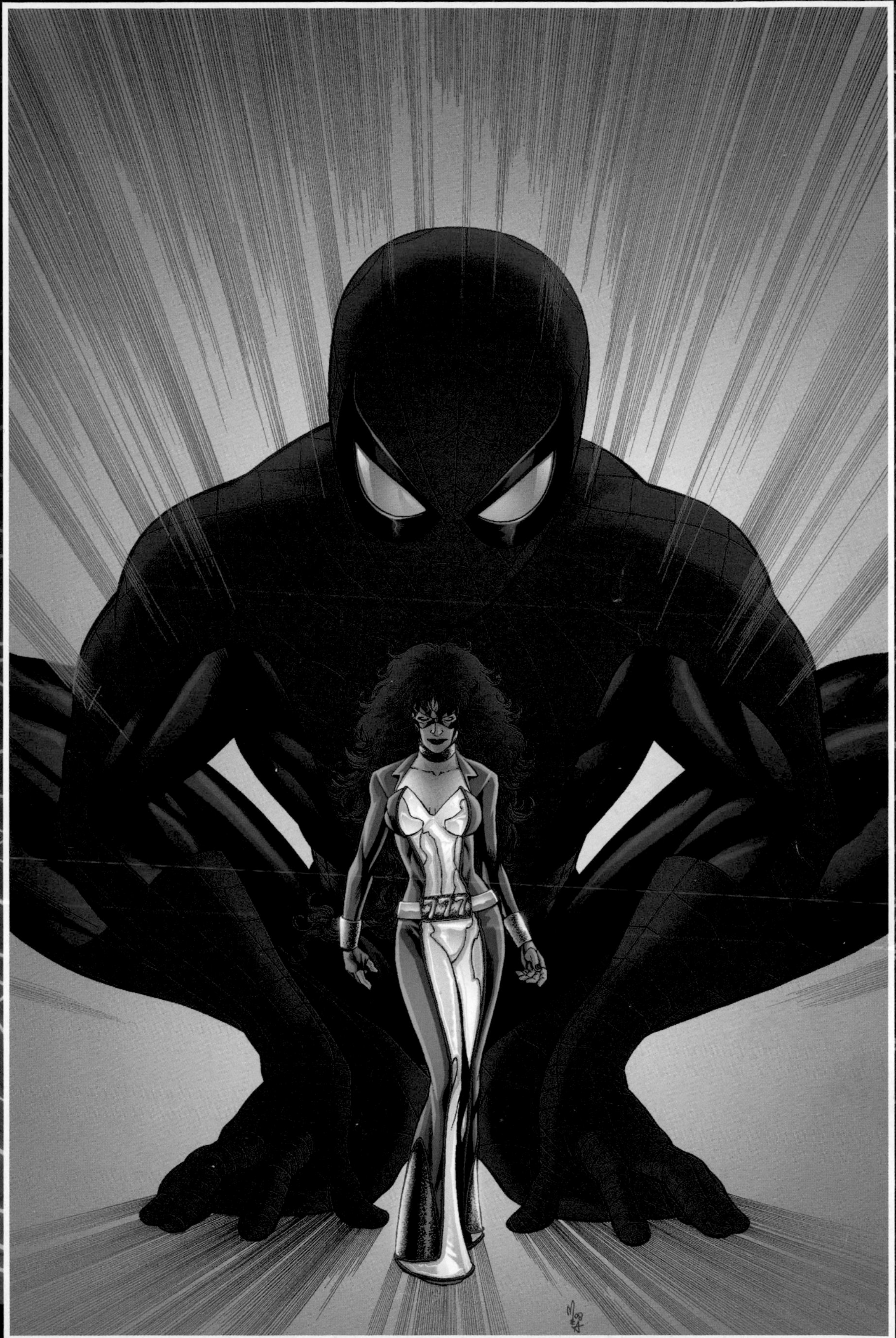

THE DB! SPECIAL EDITION!

THE DB

BILL HOLLISTER: SUPER-VILLAIN SUPPORTER? "WILD" BILL WAS ON THE SAME BOARD OF ADVISORS FOR HAIDORFER/JAMMET DEFENSE TECHNOLOGY COMMITTEE AS DR. OTTO OCTAVIUS. WHY IS THE MAYORAL CANDIDATE HIDING HIS SUPER-VILLAIN FRIENDS? SEE PAGE P23

OCTOBER 29, 2008 • WEDNESDAY

WHO IS JACKPOT?

VISIT THE SPIDEY-BLOG!
www.marvel.com/blogs/spider-office

Jackpot, a mysterious new hero assigned by the Initiative to monitor New York City's street level crimes, has frequently crossed paths with the Amazing Spider-Man. She's tough and resourceful, but green at the job, clearly needing a little more experience. At the first debate for Mayor between businessman Randall Crowne and then-council-woman Lisa Parfrey, Jackpot's brash behavior left Parfrey dead at the hands of Menace. But she's gotten over her hump, recently playing a small but pivotal role in defending New York during the Skrull invasion. She's also closed in on proving the criminal activity of billionaire Walter Declun. As her fame grows, everyone, even Spidey, can't help but ask: who is Jackpot really?

POLICE TIE SPIDER-MAN TO RECENT MURDERS!

EXCLUSIVE TO THE DB!

In off-the-record conversations with DB staffers, police have confirmed that Spider-Man is the key suspect in the string of recent murders that has shocked this city. Although police have been reluctant to discuss the specifics of the murders, so-called "Spider Tracers" have definitely been found on each victim, leaving no doubt as to the involvement of Spider-Man. Spider-Man is already wanted for violations of...

CONTINUED ON A2

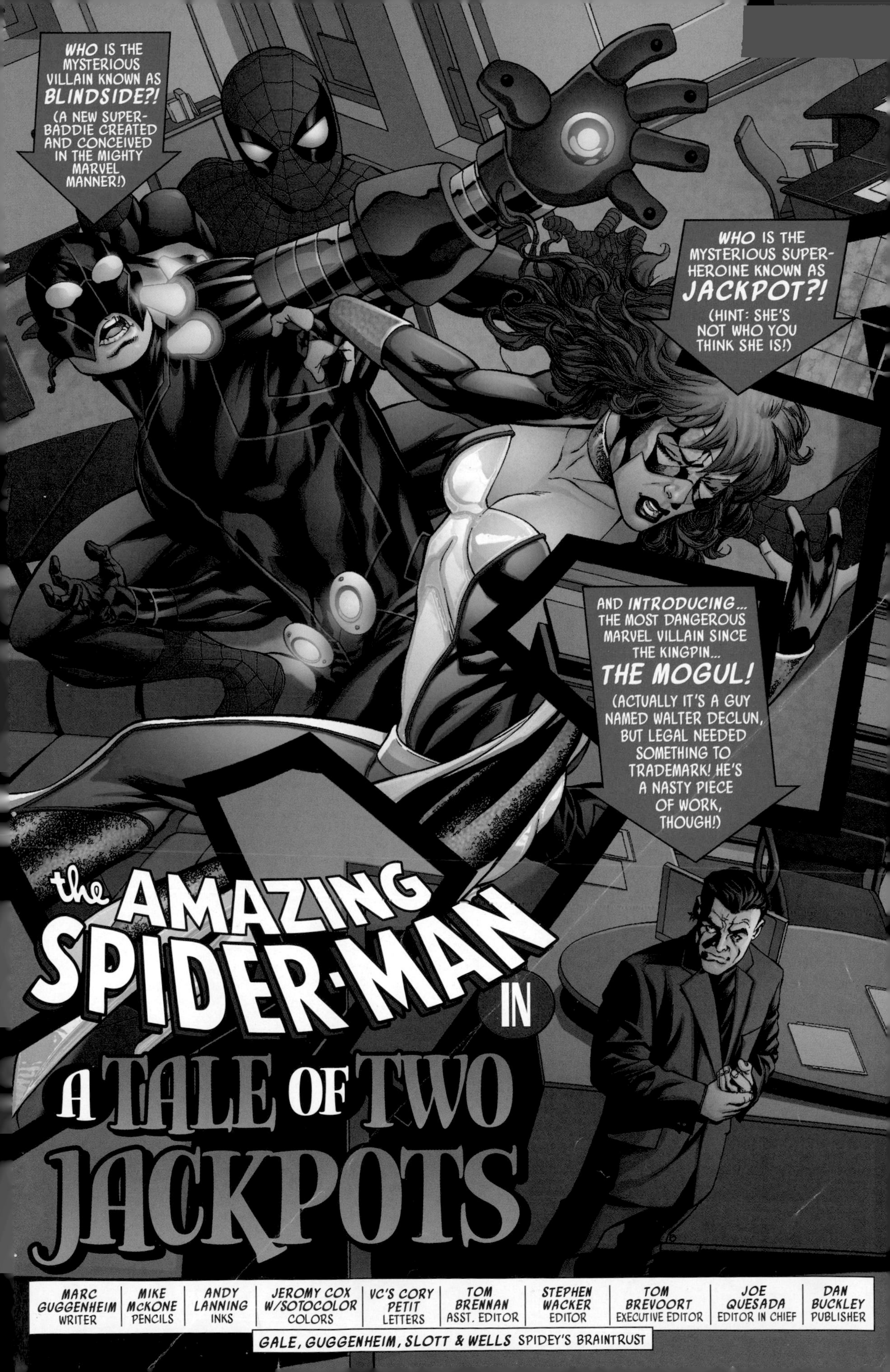
WHO IS THE MYSTERIOUS VILLAIN KNOWN AS BLINDSIDE?! (A NEW SUPER-BADDIE CREATED AND CONCEIVED IN THE MIGHTY MARVEL MANNER!)
WHO IS THE MYSTERIOUS SUPER-HEROINE KNOWN AS JACKPOT?! (HINT: SHE'S NOT WHO YOU THINK SHE IS!)
AND INTRODUCING... THE MOST DANGEROUS MARVEL VILLAIN SINCE THE KINGPIN... THE MOGUL! (ACTUALLY IT'S A GUY NAMED WALTER DECLUN, BUT LEGAL NEEDED SOMETHING TO TRADEMARK! HE'S A NASTY PIECE OF WORK, THOUGH!)
the AMAZING SPIDER-MAN IN
A TALE OF TWO JACKPOTS
MARC GUGGENHEIM WRITER
MIKE McKONE PENCILS
ANDY LANNING INKS
JEROMY COX W/SOTOCOLOR COLORS
VC'S CORY PETIT LETTERS
TOM BRENNAN ASST. EDITOR
STEPHEN WACKER EDITOR
TOM BREVOORT EXECUTIVE EDITOR
JOE QUESADA EDITOR IN CHIEF
DAN BUCKLEY PUBLISHER
GALE, GUGGENHEIM, SLOTT & WELLS SPIDEY'S BRAINTRUST

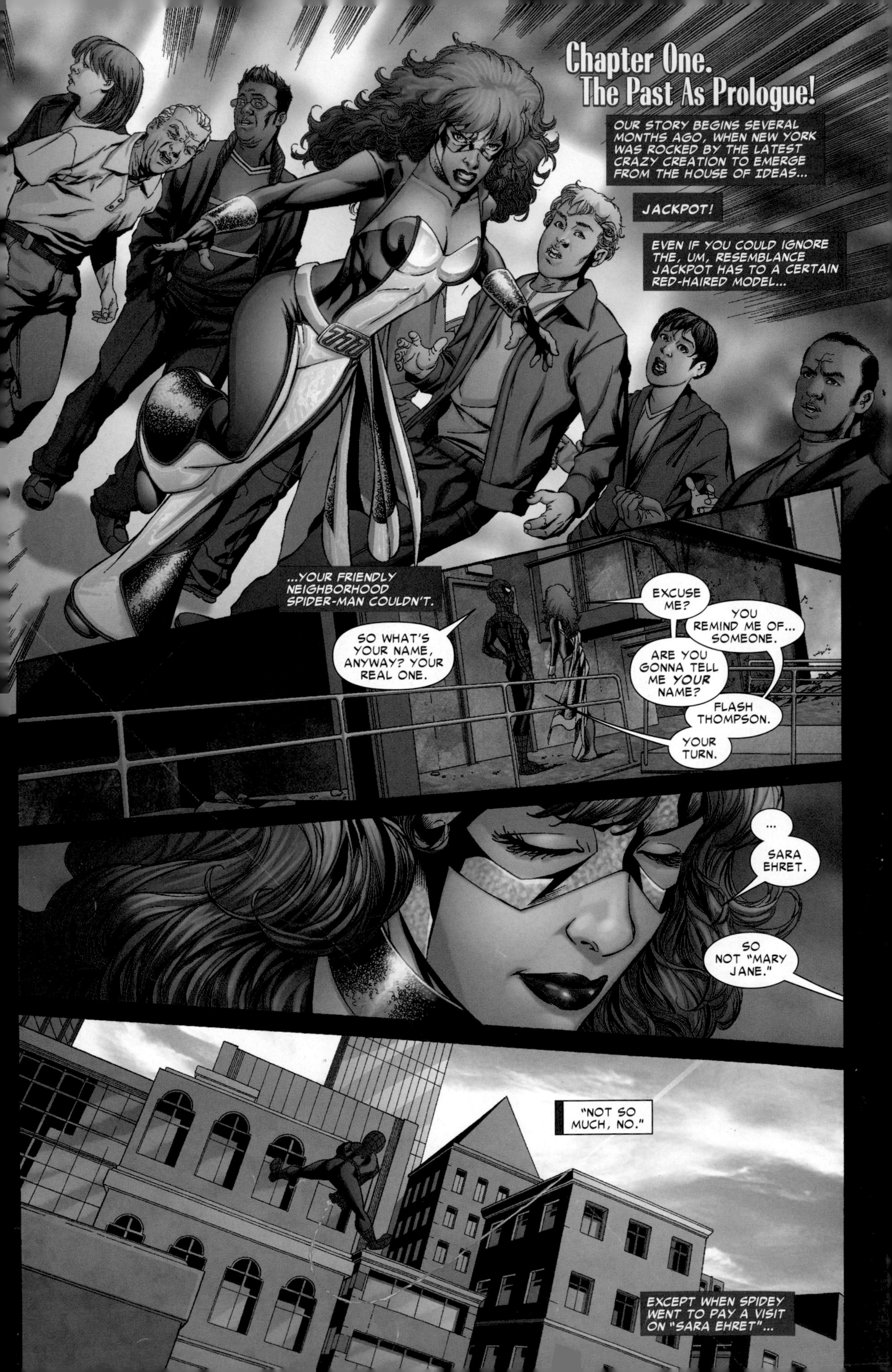
Chapter One.
The Past As Prologue!
OUR STORY BEGINS SEVERAL MONTHS AGO, WHEN NEW YORK WAS ROCKED BY THE LATEST CRAZY CREATION TO EMERGE FROM THE HOUSE OF IDEAS...
JACKPOT!
EVEN IF YOU COULD IGNORE THE, UM, RESEMBLANCE JACKPOT HAS TO A CERTAIN RED-HAIRED MODEL...
...YOUR FRIENDLY NEIGHBORHOOD SPIDER-MAN COULDN'T.
SO WHAT'S YOUR NAME, ANYWAY? YOUR REAL ONE.
EXCUSE ME?
YOU REMIND ME OF... SOMEONE.
ARE YOU GONNA TELL ME YOUR NAME?
FLASH THOMPSON.
YOUR TURN.
...
SARA EHRET.
SO NOT "MARY JANE."
"NOT SO MUCH, NO."
EXCEPT WHEN SPIDEY WENT TO PAY A VISIT ON "SARA EHRET"...

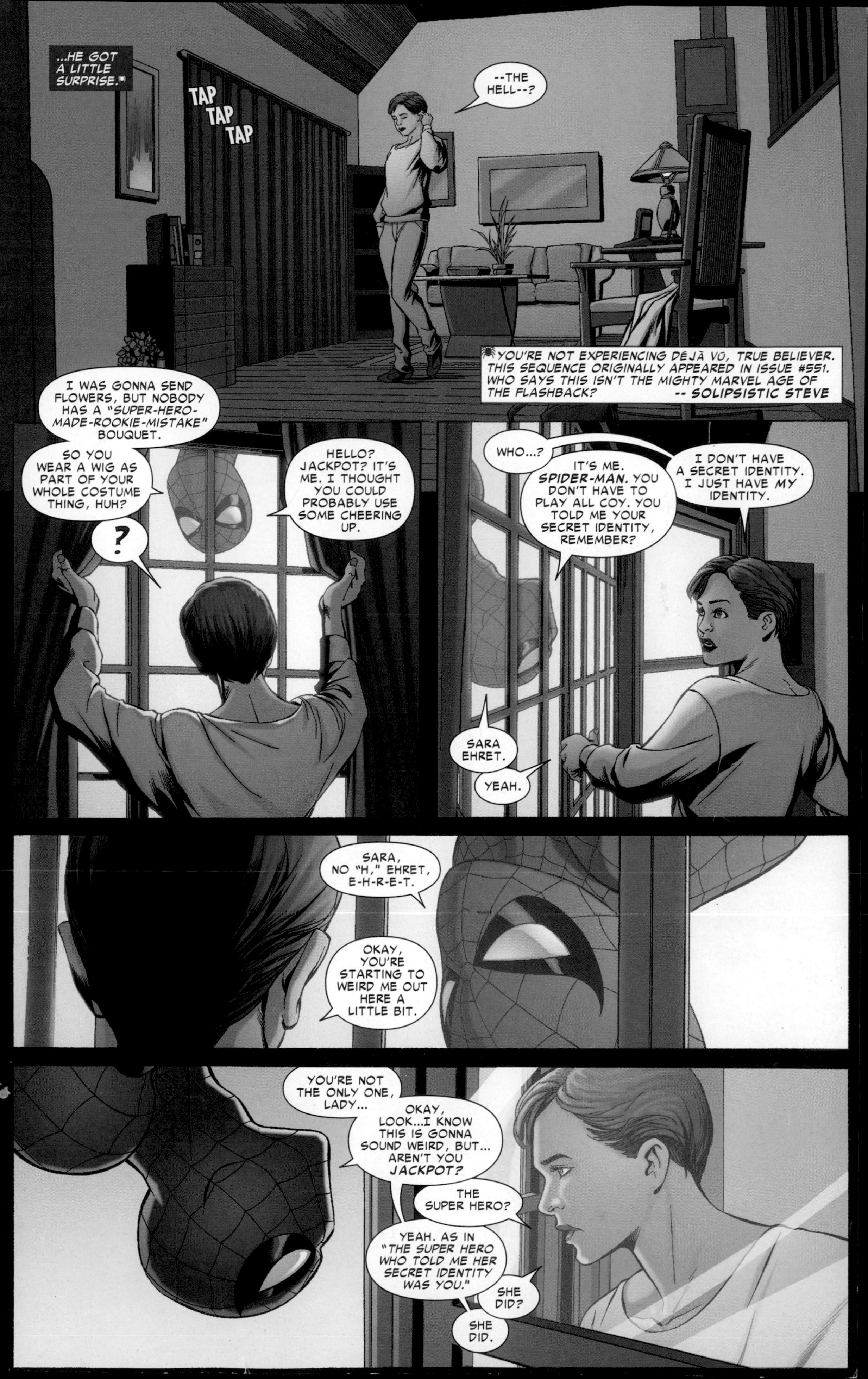
...HE GOT A LITTLE SURPRISE.*
TAP TAP TAP
--THE HELL--?
*YOU'RE NOT EXPERIENCING DÉJÀ VU, TRUE BELIEVER. THIS SEQUENCE ORIGINALLY APPEARED IN ISSUE #551. WHO SAYS THIS ISN'T THE MIGHTY MARVEL AGE OF THE FLASHBACK? -- SOLIPSISTIC STEVE
HELLO? JACKPOT? IT'S ME. I THOUGHT YOU COULD PROBABLY USE SOME CHEERING UP.
I WAS GONNA SEND FLOWERS, BUT NOBODY HAS A "SUPER-HERO-MADE-ROOKIE-MISTAKE" BOUQUET.
SO YOU WEAR A WIG AS PART OF YOUR WHOLE COSTUME THING, HUH?
?
WHO...?
IT'S ME. SPIDER-MAN. YOU DON'T HAVE TO PLAY ALL COY. YOU TOLD ME YOUR SECRET IDENTITY, REMEMBER?
I DON'T HAVE A SECRET IDENTITY. I JUST HAVE MY IDENTITY.
SARA EHRET.
YEAH.
SARA, NO "H," EHRET, E-H-R-E-T.
OKAY, YOU'RE STARTING TO WEIRD ME OUT HERE A LITTLE BIT.
YOU'RE NOT THE ONLY ONE, LADY...
OKAY, LOOK...I KNOW THIS IS GONNA SOUND WEIRD, BUT... AREN'T YOU JACKPOT?
THE SUPER HERO?
YEAH. AS IN "THE SUPER HERO WHO TOLD ME HER SECRET IDENTITY WAS YOU."
SHE DID?
SHE DID.

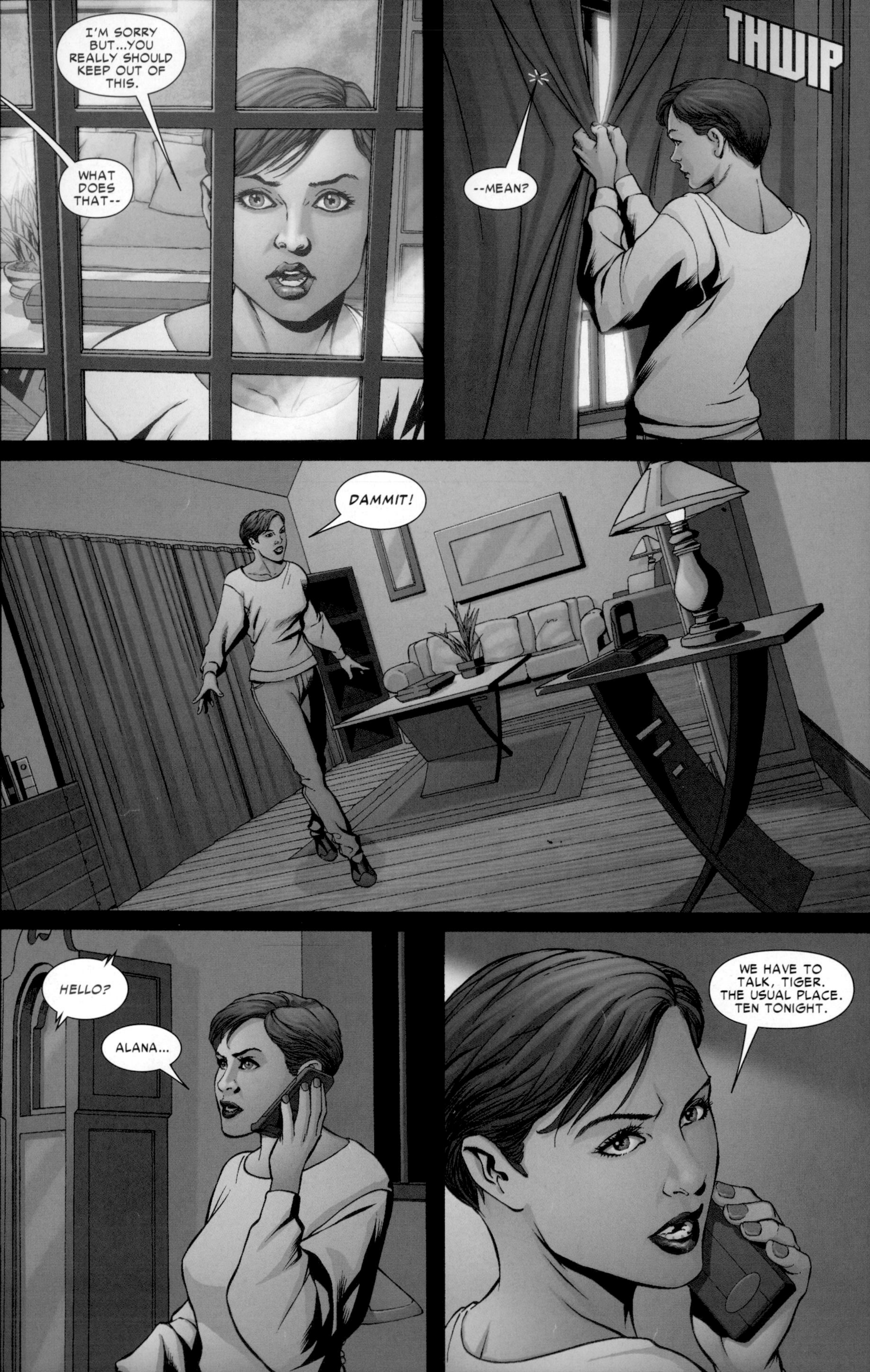
I'M SORRY BUT...YOU REALLY SHOULD KEEP OUT OF THIS.
WHAT DOES THAT--
THWIP
--MEAN?
DAMMIT!
HELLO?
ALANA...
WE HAVE TO TALK, TIGER. THE USUAL PLACE. TEN TONIGHT.

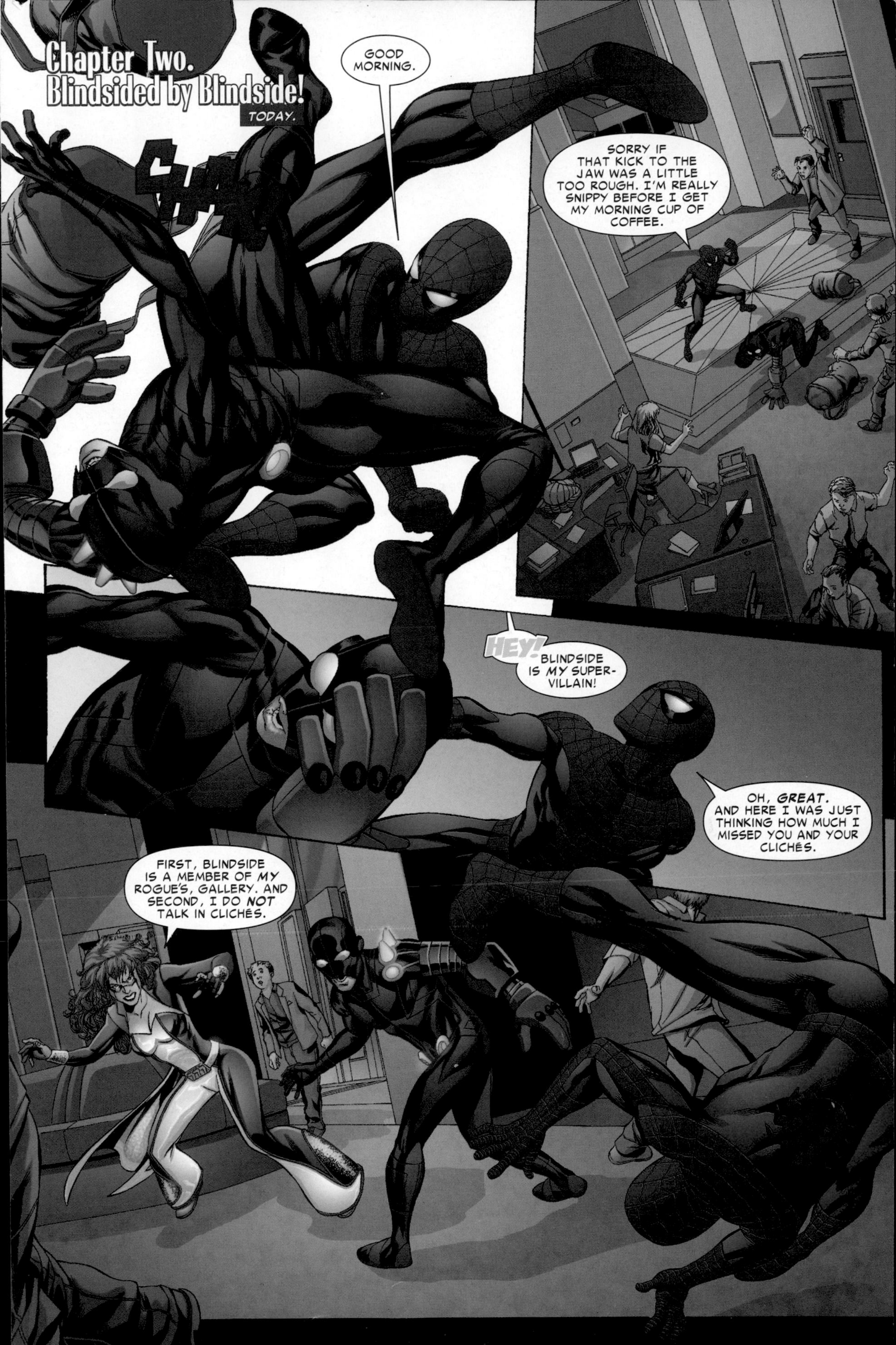
Chapter Two.
Blindsided by Blindside!
TODAY.
GOOD MORNING.
SORRY IF THAT KICK TO THE JAW WAS A LITTLE TOO ROUGH. I'M REALLY SNIPPY BEFORE I GET MY MORNING CUP OF COFFEE.
HEY! BLINDSIDE IS MY SUPER-VILLAIN!
OH, GREAT. AND HERE I WAS JUST THINKING HOW MUCH I MISSED YOU AND YOUR CLICHÉS.
FIRST, BLINDSIDE IS A MEMBER OF MY ROGUE'S, GALLERY. AND SECOND, I DO NOT TALK IN CLICHÉS.

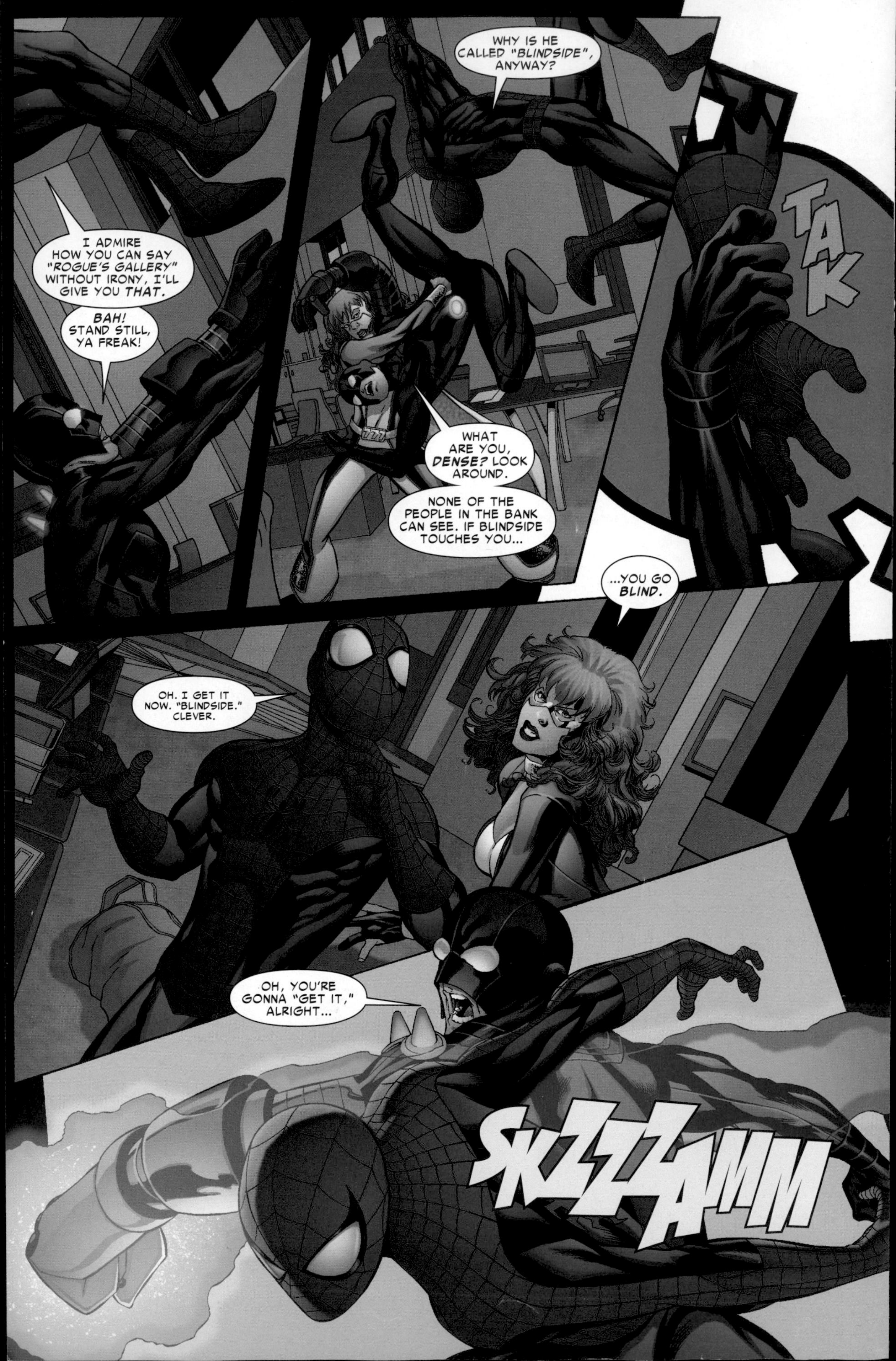

I ADMIRE HOW YOU CAN SAY "ROGUE'S GALLERY" WITHOUT IRONY, I'LL GIVE YOU THAT.
BAH! STAND STILL, YA FREAK!
WHY IS HE CALLED "BLINDSIDE", ANYWAY?
WHAT ARE YOU, DENSE? LOOK AROUND.
NONE OF THE PEOPLE IN THE BANK CAN SEE. IF BLINDSIDE TOUCHES YOU...
TAK
...YOU GO BLIND.
OH. I GET IT NOW. "BLINDSIDE." CLEVER.
OH, YOU'RE GONNA "GET IT," ALRIGHT...
SKZZZAMM

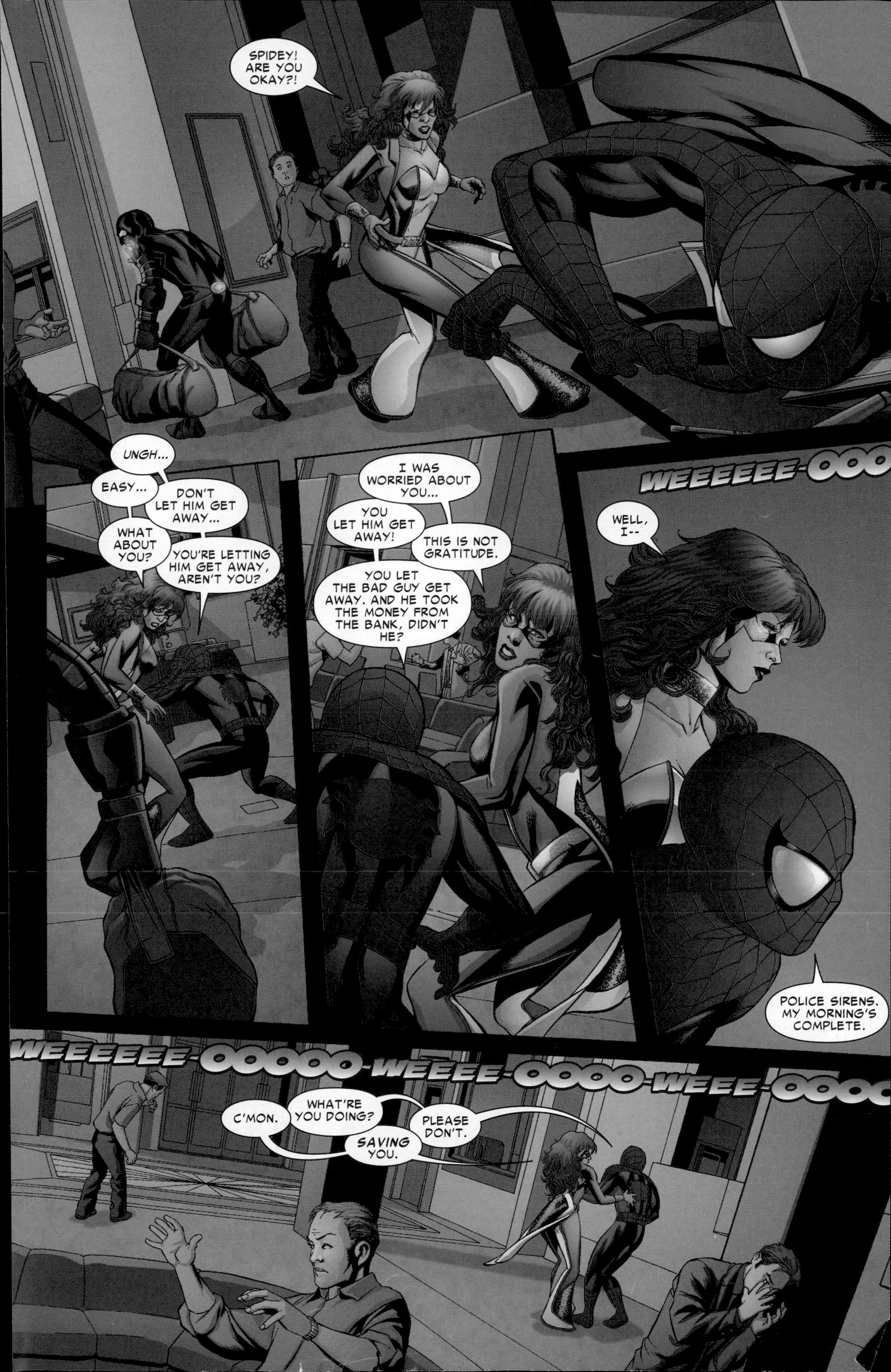
SPIDEY! ARE YOU OKAY?!
UNGH...
EASY...
DON'T LET HIM GET AWAY...
WHAT ABOUT YOU?
YOU'RE LETTING HIM GET AWAY, AREN'T YOU?
I WAS WORRIED ABOUT YOU...
YOU LET HIM GET AWAY!
THIS IS NOT GRATITUDE.
YOU LET THE BAD GUY GET AWAY. AND HE TOOK THE MONEY FROM THE BANK, DIDN'T HE?
WEEEEEE-OOO
WELL, I--
POLICE SIRENS. MY MORNING'S COMPLETE.
WEEEEEE-OOOOO-WEEEE-OOOO-WEEE-OOOO
C'MON.
WHAT'RE YOU DOING?
SAVING YOU.
PLEASE DON'T.

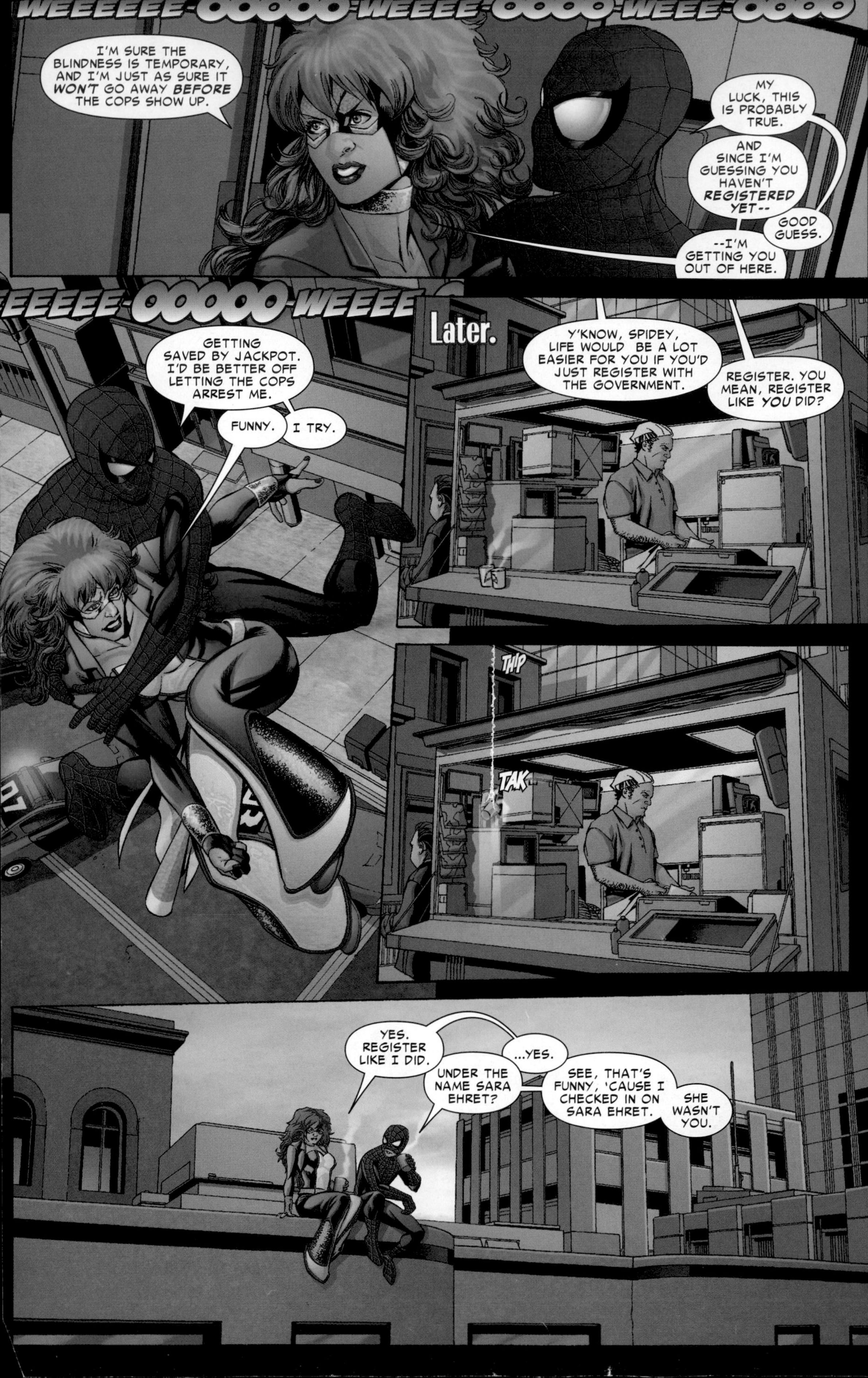
WEEEEEE-OOOOO-WEEEE-OOOO-WEEE-OOOO
I'M SURE THE BLINDNESS IS TEMPORARY, AND I'M JUST AS SURE IT WON'T GO AWAY BEFORE THE COPS SHOW UP.
MY LUCK, THIS IS PROBABLY TRUE.
AND SINCE I'M GUESSING YOU HAVEN'T REGISTERED YET--
GOOD GUESS.
--I'M GETTING YOU OUT OF HERE.
EEEEEE-OOOOO-WEEEE
GETTING SAVED BY JACKPOT. I'D BE BETTER OFF LETTING THE COPS ARREST ME.
FUNNY.
I TRY.
Later.
Y'KNOW, SPIDEY, LIFE WOULD BE A LOT EASIER FOR YOU IF YOU'D JUST REGISTER WITH THE GOVERNMENT.
REGISTER. YOU MEAN, REGISTER LIKE YOU DID?
THIP
TAK
YES. REGISTER LIKE I DID.
...YES.
UNDER THE NAME SARA EHRET?
SEE, THAT'S FUNNY, 'CAUSE I CHECKED IN ON SARA EHRET.
SHE WASN'T YOU.

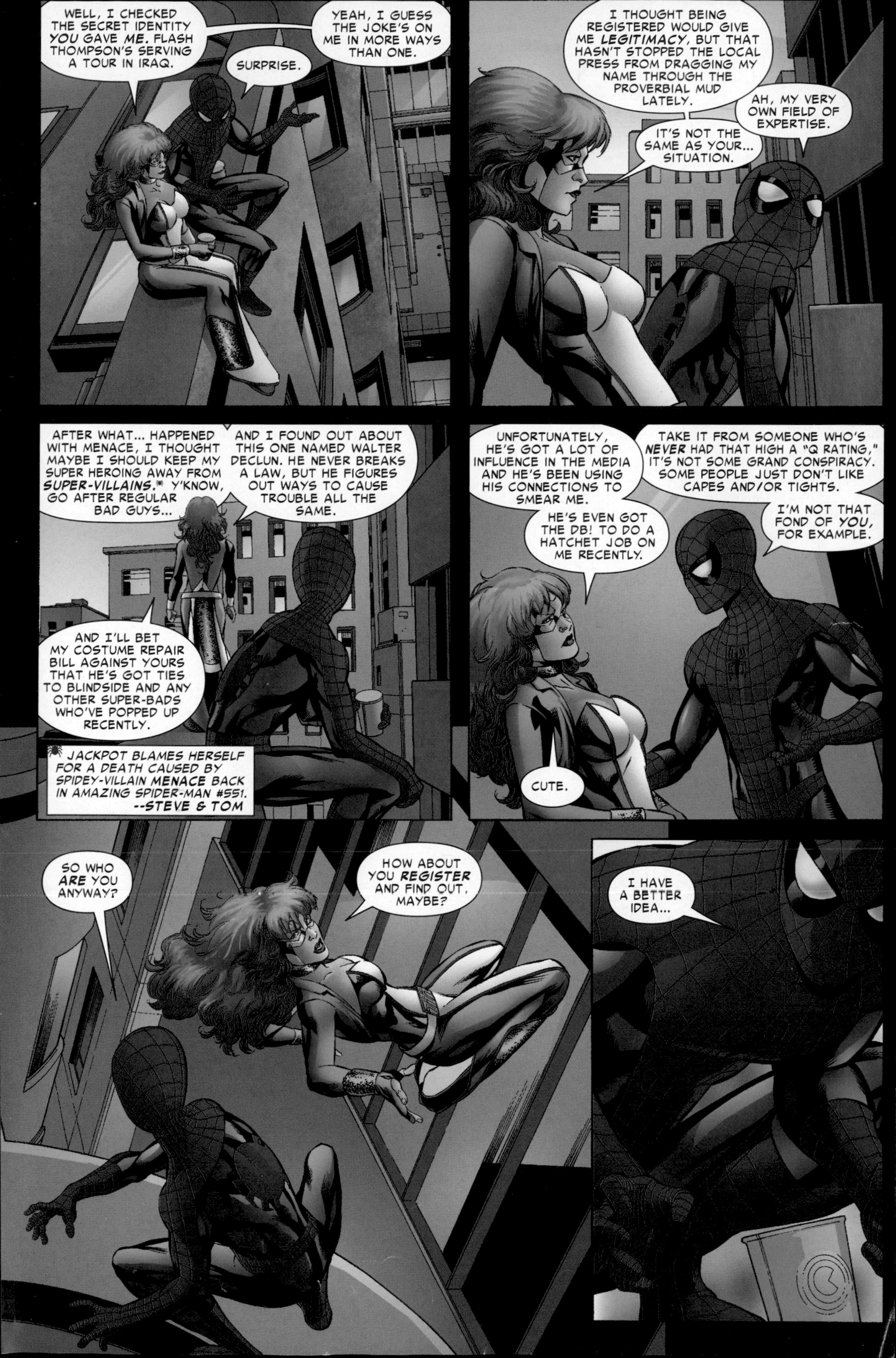
WELL, I CHECKED THE SECRET IDENTITY YOU GAVE ME. FLASH THOMPSON'S SERVING A TOUR IN IRAQ.
SURPRISE.
YEAH, I GUESS THE JOKE'S ON ME IN MORE WAYS THAN ONE.
I THOUGHT BEING REGISTERED WOULD GIVE ME LEGITIMACY, BUT THAT HASN'T STOPPED THE LOCAL PRESS FROM DRAGGING MY NAME THROUGH THE PROVERBIAL MUD LATELY.
AH, MY VERY OWN FIELD OF EXPERTISE.
IT'S NOT THE SAME AS YOUR... SITUATION.
AFTER WHAT... HAPPENED WITH MENACE, I THOUGHT MAYBE I SHOULD KEEP MY SUPER HEROING AWAY FROM SUPER-VILLAINS.* Y'KNOW, GO AFTER REGULAR BAD GUYS...
AND I FOUND OUT ABOUT THIS ONE NAMED WALTER DECLUN. HE NEVER BREAKS A LAW, BUT HE FIGURES OUT WAYS TO CAUSE TROUBLE ALL THE SAME.
AND I'LL BET MY COSTUME REPAIR BILL AGAINST YOURS THAT HE'S GOT TIES TO BLINDSIDE AND ANY OTHER SUPER-BADS WHO'VE POPPED UP RECENTLY.
*JACKPOT BLAMES HERSELF FOR A DEATH CAUSED BY SPIDEY-VILLAIN MENACE BACK IN AMAZING SPIDER-MAN #551. --STEVE & TOM
UNFORTUNATELY, HE'S GOT A LOT OF INFLUENCE IN THE MEDIA AND HE'S BEEN USING HIS CONNECTIONS TO SMEAR ME.
HE'S EVEN GOT THE DB! TO DO A HATCHET JOB ON ME RECENTLY.
TAKE IT FROM SOMEONE WHO'S NEVER HAD THAT HIGH A "Q RATING," IT'S NOT SOME GRAND CONSPIRACY. SOME PEOPLE JUST DON'T LIKE CAPES AND/OR TIGHTS.
I'M NOT THAT FOND OF YOU, FOR EXAMPLE.
CUTE.
SO WHO ARE YOU ANYWAY?
HOW ABOUT YOU REGISTER AND FIND OUT, MAYBE?
I HAVE A BETTER IDEA...

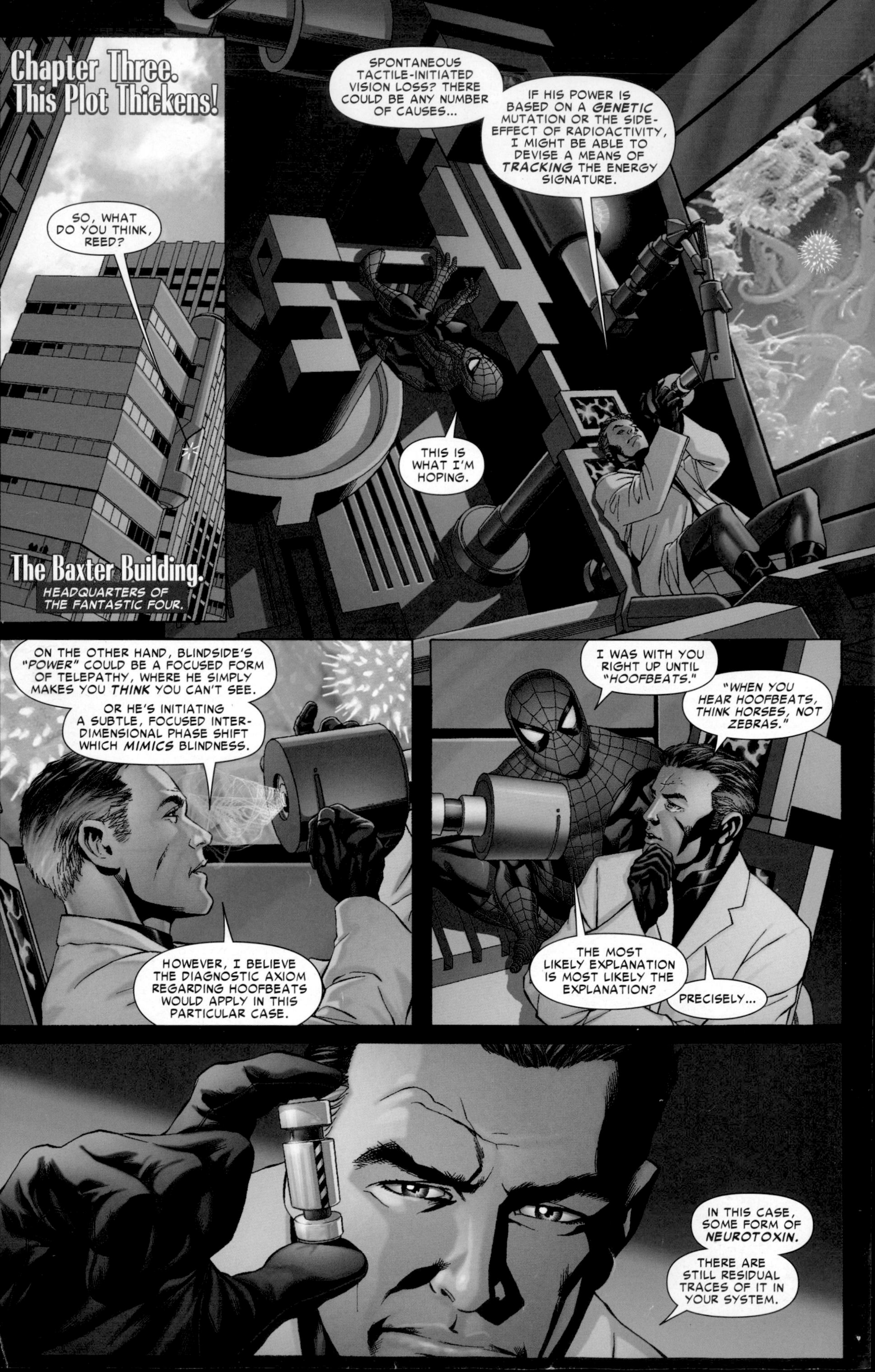
Chapter Three. This Plot Thickens!
SO, WHAT DO YOU THINK, REED?
SPONTANEOUS TACTILE-INITIATED VISION LOSS? THERE COULD BE ANY NUMBER OF CAUSES...
IF HIS POWER IS BASED ON A GENETIC MUTATION OR THE SIDE-EFFECT OF RADIOACTIVITY, I MIGHT BE ABLE TO DEVISE A MEANS OF TRACKING THE ENERGY SIGNATURE.
THIS IS WHAT I'M HOPING.
The Baxter Building.
HEADQUARTERS OF THE FANTASTIC FOUR.
ON THE OTHER HAND, BLINDSIDE'S "POWER" COULD BE A FOCUSED FORM OF TELEPATHY, WHERE HE SIMPLY MAKES YOU THINK YOU CAN'T SEE.
OR HE'S INITIATING A SUBTLE, FOCUSED INTER-DIMENSIONAL PHASE SHIFT WHICH MIMICS BLINDNESS.
HOWEVER, I BELIEVE THE DIAGNOSTIC AXIOM REGARDING HOOFBEATS WOULD APPLY IN THIS PARTICULAR CASE.
I WAS WITH YOU RIGHT UP UNTIL "HOOFBEATS."
"WHEN YOU HEAR HOOFBEATS, THINK HORSES, NOT ZEBRAS."
THE MOST LIKELY EXPLANATION IS MOST LIKELY THE EXPLANATION?
PRECISELY...
IN THIS CASE, SOME FORM OF NEUROTOXIN.
THERE ARE STILL RESIDUAL TRACES OF IT IN YOUR SYSTEM.

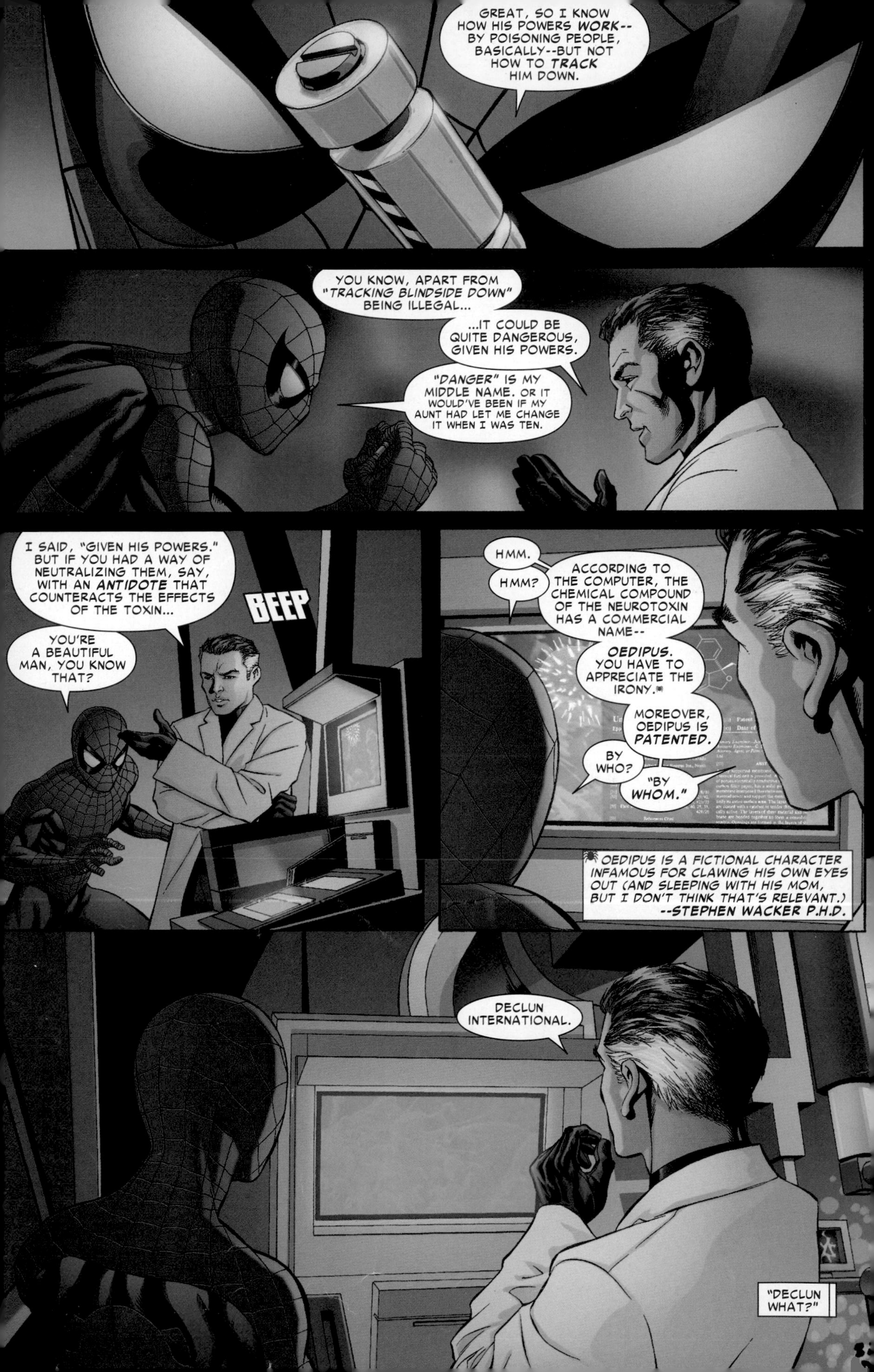
GREAT, SO I KNOW HOW HIS POWERS WORK-- BY POISONING PEOPLE, BASICALLY--BUT NOT HOW TO TRACK HIM DOWN.
YOU KNOW, APART FROM "TRACKING BLINDSIDE DOWN" BEING ILLEGAL...
...IT COULD BE QUITE DANGEROUS, GIVEN HIS POWERS.
"DANGER" IS MY MIDDLE NAME. OR IT WOULD'VE BEEN IF MY AUNT HAD LET ME CHANGE IT WHEN I WAS TEN.
I SAID, "GIVEN HIS POWERS." BUT IF YOU HAD A WAY OF NEUTRALIZING THEM, SAY, WITH AN ANTIDOTE THAT COUNTERACTS THE EFFECTS OF THE TOXIN...
BEEP
YOU'RE A BEAUTIFUL MAN, YOU KNOW THAT?
HMM.
HMM?
ACCORDING TO THE COMPUTER, THE CHEMICAL COMPOUND OF THE NEUROTOXIN HAS A COMMERCIAL NAME--
OEDIPUS. YOU HAVE TO APPRECIATE THE IRONY.
MOREOVER, OEDIPUS IS PATENTED.
BY WHO?
"BY WHOM."
OEDIPUS IS A FICTIONAL CHARACTER INFAMOUS FOR CLAWING HIS OWN EYES OUT (AND SLEEPING WITH HIS MOM, BUT I DON'T THINK THAT'S RELEVANT.) --STEPHEN WACKER P.H.D.
DECLUN INTERNATIONAL.
"DECLUN WHAT?"

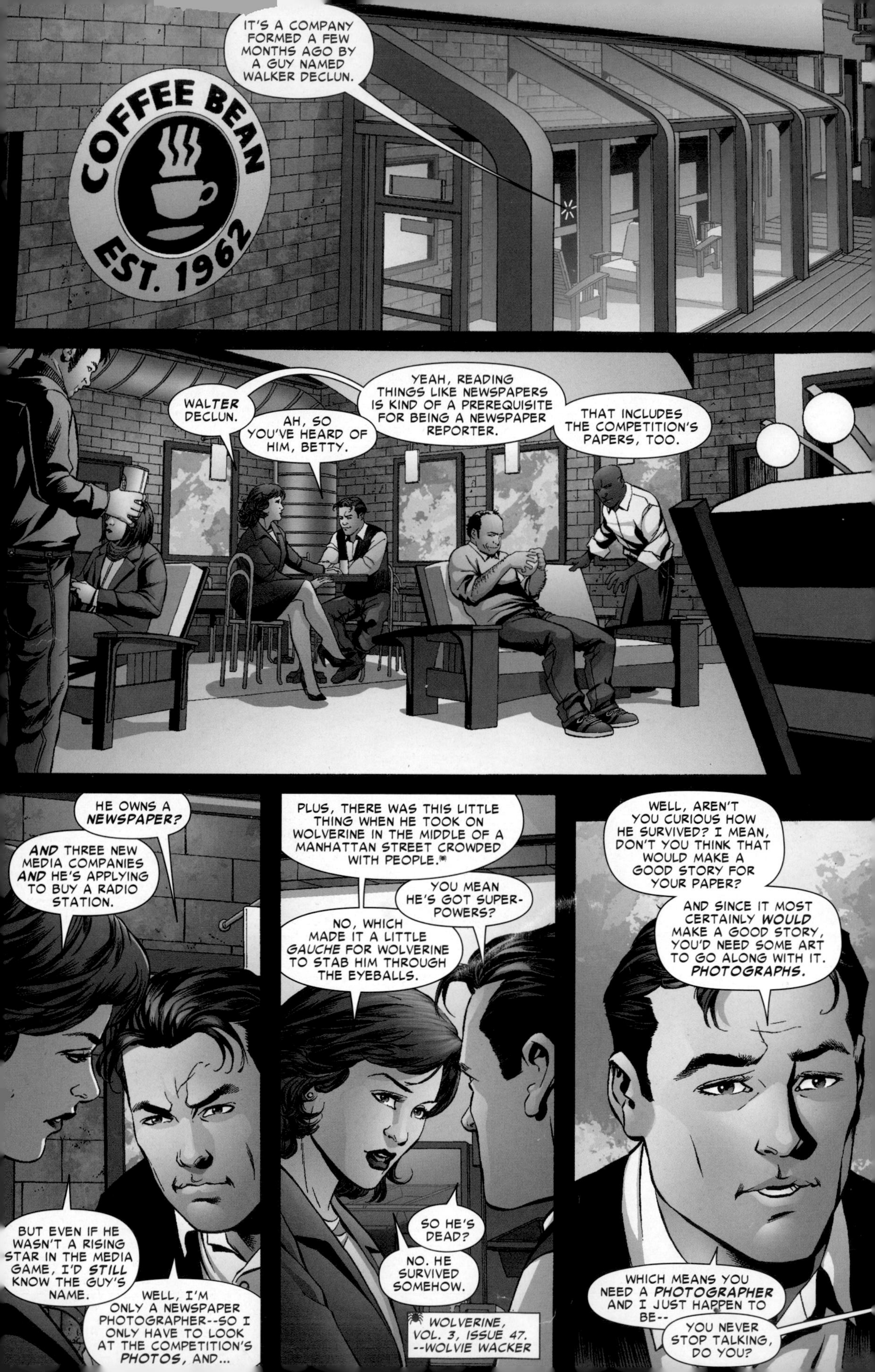

COFFEE BEAN EST. 1962
IT'S A COMPANY FORMED A FEW MONTHS AGO BY A GUY NAMED WALKER DECLUN.
WALTER DECLUN.
AH, SO YOU'VE HEARD OF HIM, BETTY.
YEAH, READING THINGS LIKE NEWSPAPERS IS KIND OF A PREREQUISITE FOR BEING A NEWSPAPER REPORTER.
THAT INCLUDES THE COMPETITION'S PAPERS, TOO.
HE OWNS A *NEWSPAPER?*
AND THREE NEW MEDIA COMPANIES *AND* HE'S APPLYING TO BUY A RADIO STATION.
BUT EVEN IF HE WASN'T A RISING STAR IN THE MEDIA GAME, I'D *STILL* KNOW THE GUY'S NAME.
WELL, I'M ONLY A NEWSPAPER PHOTOGRAPHER--SO I ONLY HAVE TO LOOK AT THE COMPETITION'S *PHOTOS*, AND...
PLUS, THERE WAS THIS LITTLE THING WHEN HE TOOK ON WOLVERINE IN THE MIDDLE OF A MANHATTAN STREET CROWDED WITH PEOPLE.*
YOU MEAN HE'S GOT SUPER-POWERS?
NO, WHICH MADE IT A LITTLE *GAUCHE* FOR WOLVERINE TO STAB HIM THROUGH THE EYEBALLS.
SO HE'S DEAD?
NO. HE SURVIVED SOMEHOW.
WOLVERINE, VOL. 3, ISSUE 47. --WOLVIE WACKER
WELL, AREN'T YOU CURIOUS HOW HE SURVIVED? I MEAN, DON'T YOU THINK THAT WOULD MAKE A GOOD STORY FOR YOUR PAPER?
AND SINCE IT MOST CERTAINLY *WOULD* MAKE A GOOD STORY, YOU'D NEED SOME ART TO GO ALONG WITH IT. *PHOTOGRAPHS.*
WHICH MEANS YOU NEED A *PHOTOGRAPHER* AND I JUST HAPPEN TO BE--
YOU NEVER STOP TALKING, DO YOU?

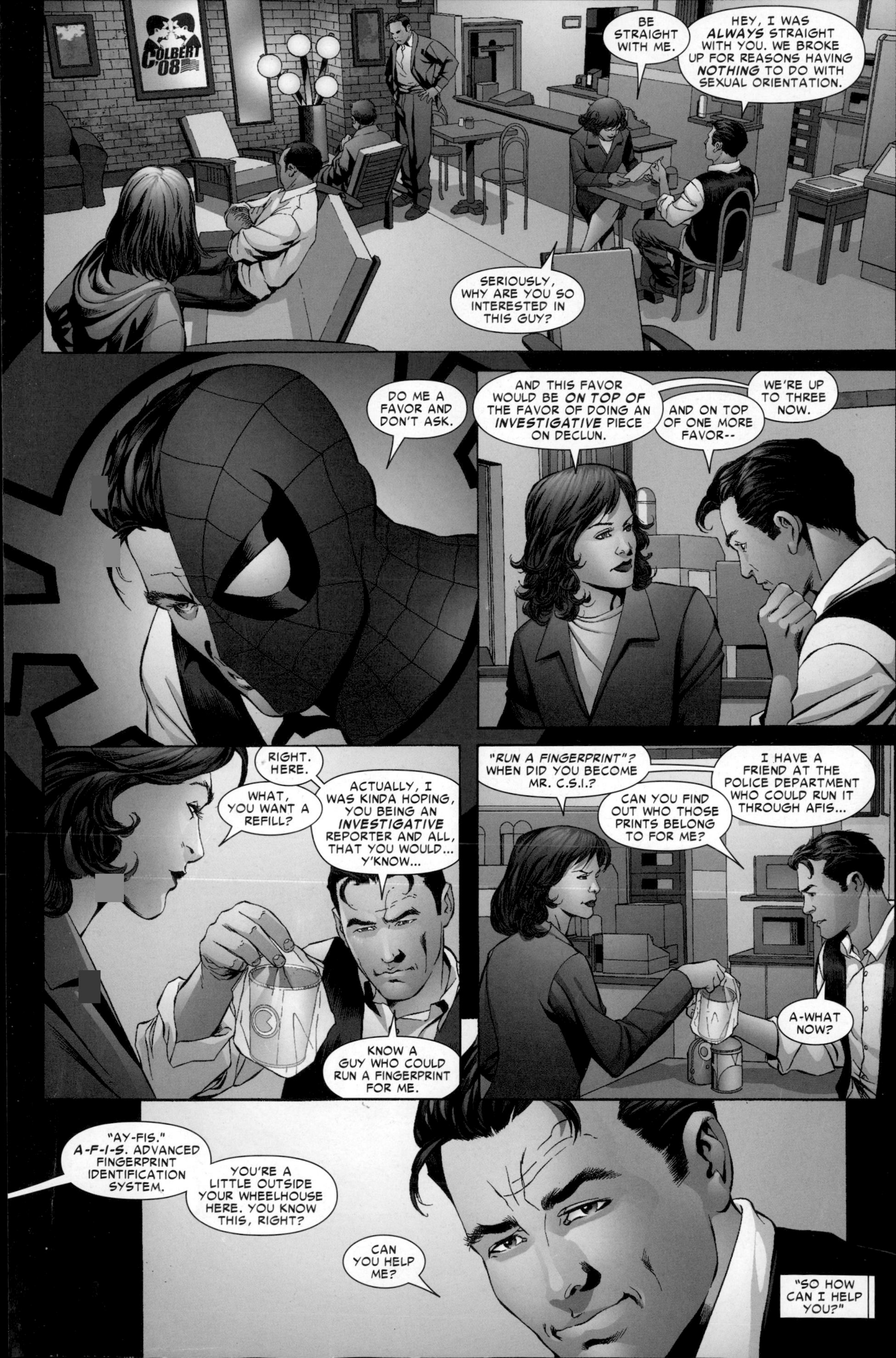
COLBERT '08
BE STRAIGHT WITH ME.
HEY, I WAS *ALWAYS* STRAIGHT WITH YOU. WE BROKE UP FOR REASONS HAVING *NOTHING* TO DO WITH SEXUAL ORIENTATION.
SERIOUSLY, WHY ARE YOU SO INTERESTED IN THIS GUY?
DO ME A FAVOR AND DON'T ASK.
AND THIS FAVOR WOULD BE *ON TOP OF* THE FAVOR OF DOING AN *INVESTIGATIVE* PIECE ON DECLUN.
AND ON TOP OF ONE MORE FAVOR--
WE'RE UP TO THREE NOW.
RIGHT. HERE.
WHAT, YOU WANT A REFILL?
ACTUALLY, I WAS KINDA HOPING, YOU BEING AN *INVESTIGATIVE* REPORTER AND ALL, THAT YOU WOULD... Y'KNOW...
KNOW A GUY WHO COULD RUN A FINGERPRINT FOR ME.
"RUN A FINGERPRINT"? WHEN DID YOU BECOME MR. C.S.I.?
I HAVE A FRIEND AT THE POLICE DEPARTMENT WHO COULD RUN IT THROUGH AFIS...
CAN YOU FIND OUT WHO THOSE PRINTS BELONG TO FOR ME?
A-WHAT NOW?
"AY-FIS." *A-F-I-S.* ADVANCED FINGERPRINT IDENTIFICATION SYSTEM.
YOU'RE A LITTLE OUTSIDE YOUR WHEELHOUSE HERE. YOU KNOW THIS, RIGHT?
CAN YOU HELP ME?
"SO HOW CAN I HELP YOU?"

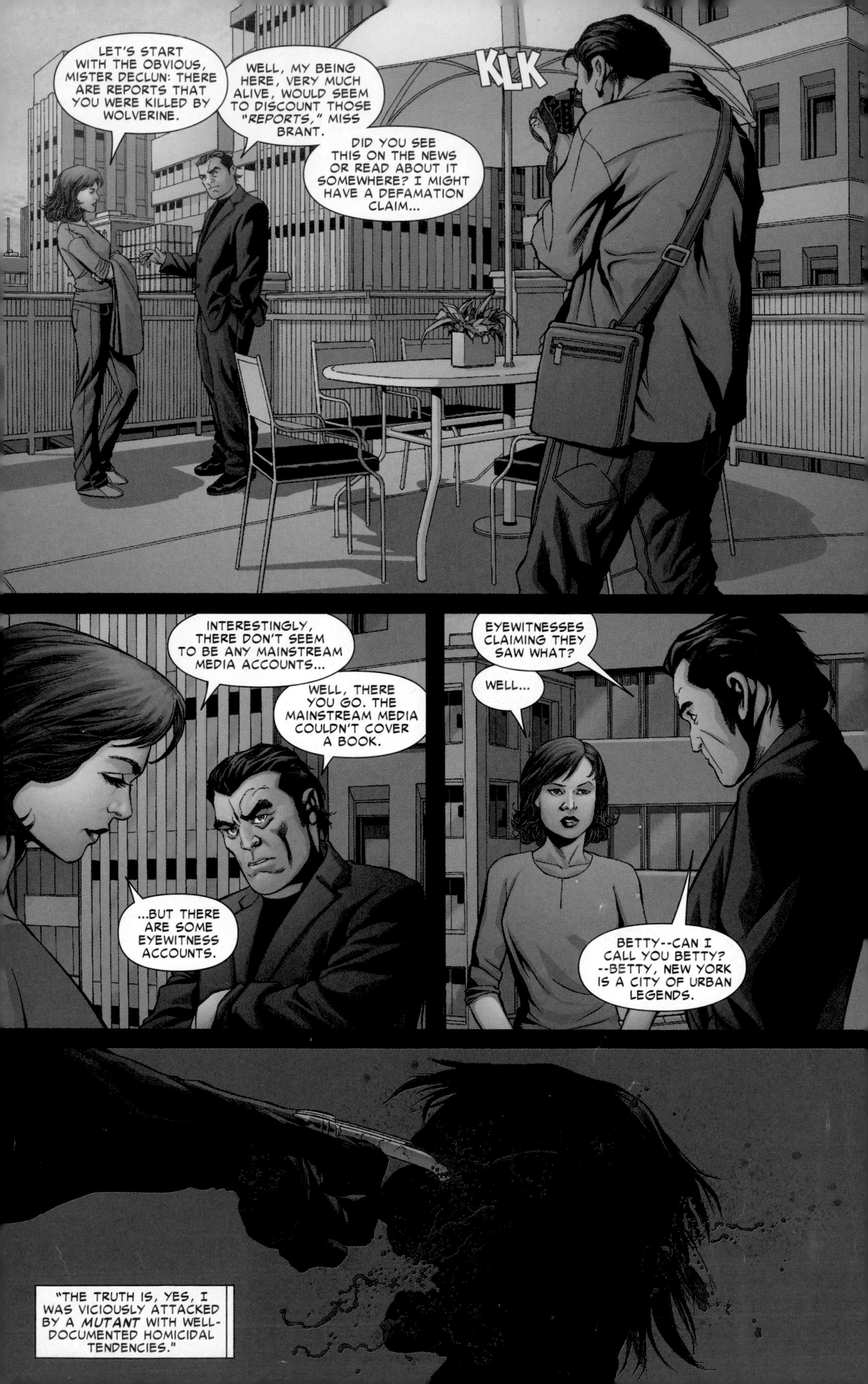

KLK
LET'S START WITH THE OBVIOUS, MISTER DECLUN: THERE ARE REPORTS THAT YOU WERE KILLED BY WOLVERINE.
WELL, MY BEING HERE, VERY MUCH ALIVE, WOULD SEEM TO DISCOUNT THOSE "REPORTS," MISS BRANT.
DID YOU SEE THIS ON THE NEWS OR READ ABOUT IT SOMEWHERE? I MIGHT HAVE A DEFAMATION CLAIM...
INTERESTINGLY, THERE DON'T SEEM TO BE ANY MAINSTREAM MEDIA ACCOUNTS...
WELL, THERE YOU GO. THE MAINSTREAM MEDIA COULDN'T COVER A BOOK.
...BUT THERE ARE SOME EYEWITNESS ACCOUNTS.
EYEWITNESSES CLAIMING THEY SAW WHAT?
WELL...
BETTY--CAN I CALL YOU BETTY? --BETTY, NEW YORK IS A CITY OF URBAN LEGENDS.
"THE TRUTH IS, YES, I WAS VICIOUSLY ATTACKED BY A MUTANT WITH WELL-DOCUMENTED HOMICIDAL TENDENCIES."

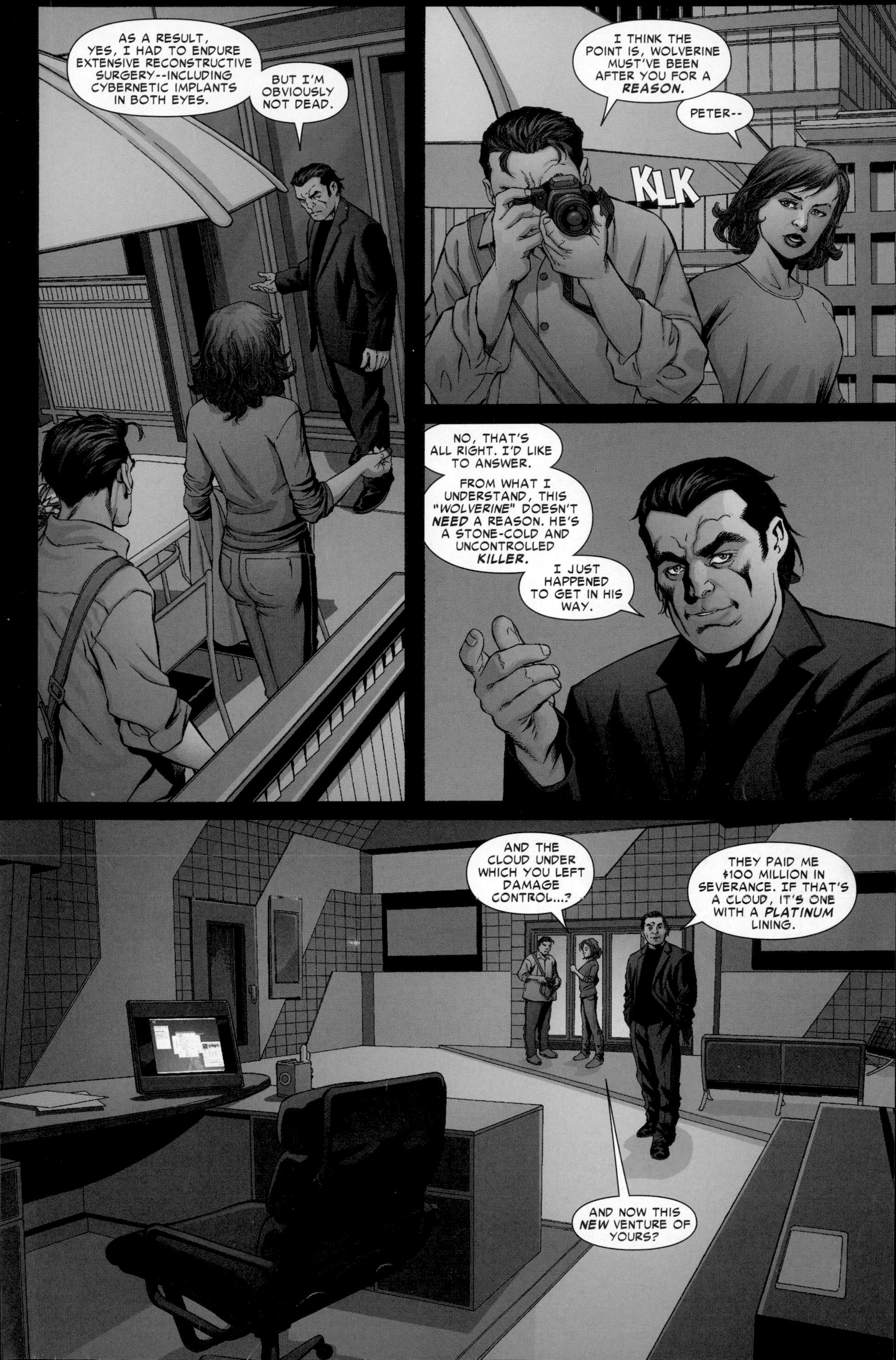
AS A RESULT, YES, I HAD TO ENDURE EXTENSIVE RECONSTRUCTIVE SURGERY--INCLUDING CYBERNETIC IMPLANTS IN BOTH EYES.
BUT I'M OBVIOUSLY NOT DEAD.
I THINK THE POINT IS, WOLVERINE MUST'VE BEEN AFTER YOU FOR A *REASON.*
PETER--
KLK
NO, THAT'S ALL RIGHT. I'D LIKE TO ANSWER.
FROM WHAT I UNDERSTAND, THIS "*WOLVERINE*" DOESN'T ***NEED*** A REASON. HE'S A STONE-COLD AND UNCONTROLLED ***KILLER.***
I JUST HAPPENED TO GET IN HIS WAY.
AND THE CLOUD UNDER WHICH YOU LEFT DAMAGE CONTROL...?
THEY PAID ME $100 MILLION IN SEVERANCE. IF THAT'S A CLOUD, IT'S ONE WITH A *PLATINUM* LINING.
AND NOW THIS ***NEW*** VENTURE OF YOURS?

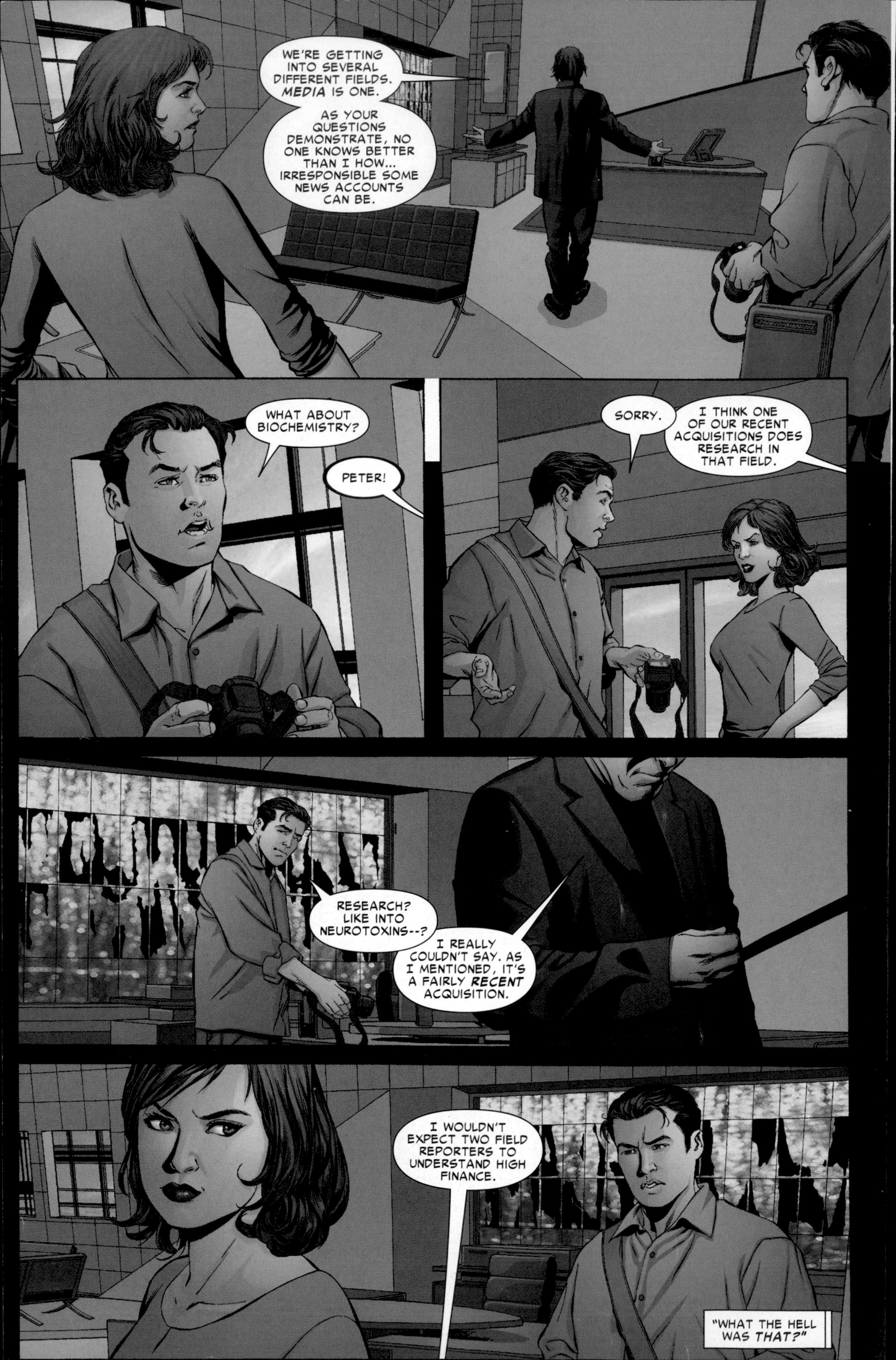

WE'RE GETTING INTO SEVERAL DIFFERENT FIELDS. *MEDIA* IS ONE.
AS YOUR QUESTIONS DEMONSTRATE, NO ONE KNOWS BETTER THAN I HOW... IRRESPONSIBLE SOME NEWS ACCOUNTS CAN BE.
WHAT ABOUT BIOCHEMISTRY?
PETER!
SORRY.
I THINK ONE OF OUR RECENT ACQUISITIONS DOES RESEARCH IN THAT FIELD.
RESEARCH? LIKE INTO NEUROTOXINS--?
I REALLY COULDN'T SAY. AS I MENTIONED, IT'S A FAIRLY *RECENT* ACQUISITION.
I WOULDN'T EXPECT TWO FIELD REPORTERS TO UNDERSTAND HIGH FINANCE.
"WHAT THE HELL WAS *THAT?*"

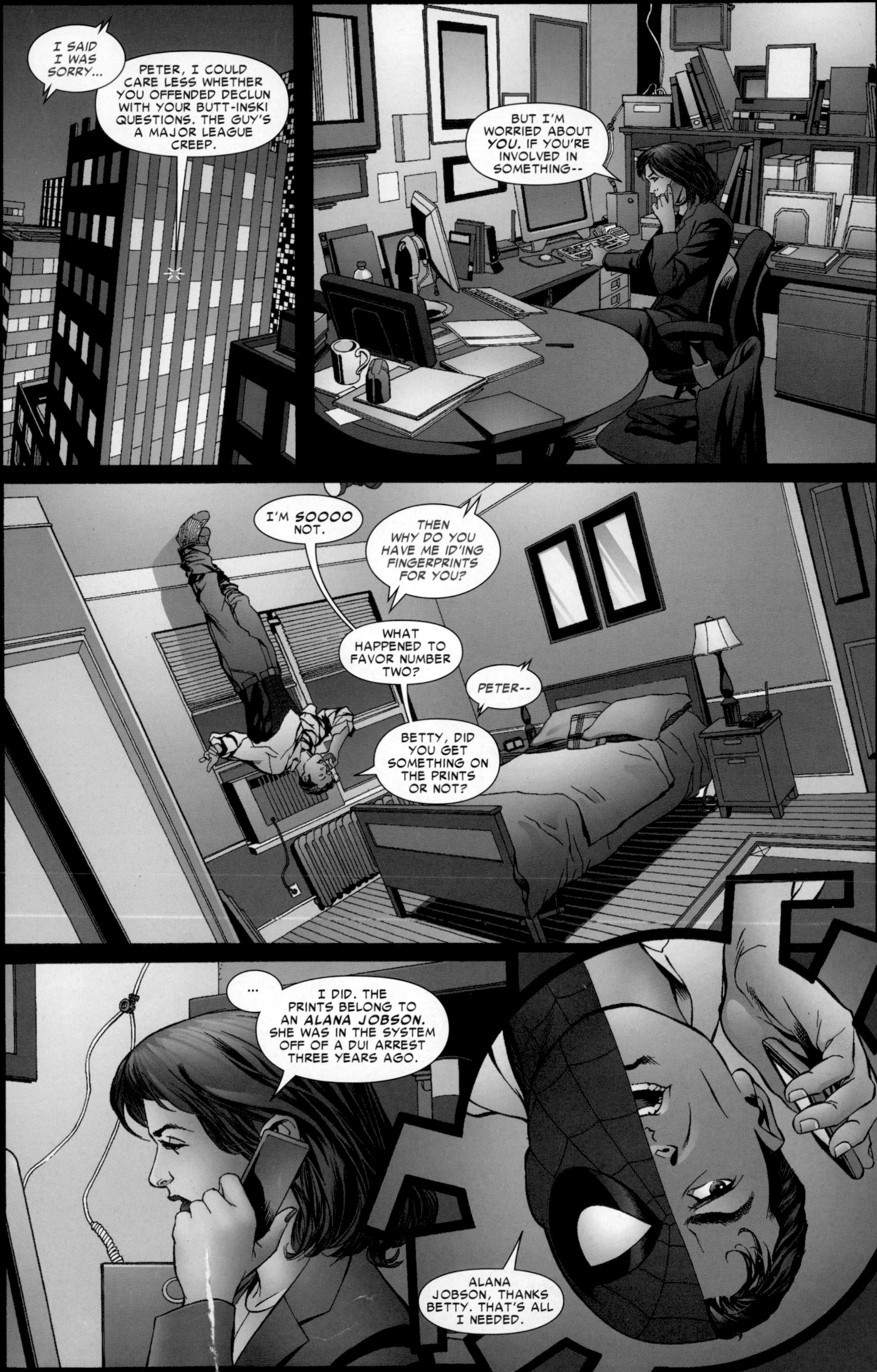
I SAID I WAS SORRY...
PETER, I COULD CARE LESS WHETHER YOU OFFENDED DECLUN WITH YOUR BUTT-INSKI QUESTIONS. THE GUY'S A MAJOR LEAGUE CREEP.
BUT I'M WORRIED ABOUT YOU. IF YOU'RE INVOLVED IN SOMETHING--
I'M SOOOO NOT.
THEN WHY DO YOU HAVE ME ID'ING FINGERPRINTS FOR YOU?
WHAT HAPPENED TO FAVOR NUMBER TWO?
PETER--
BETTY, DID YOU GET SOMETHING ON THE PRINTS OR NOT?
...
I DID. THE PRINTS BELONG TO AN ALANA JOBSON. SHE WAS IN THE SYSTEM OFF OF A DUI ARREST THREE YEARS AGO.
ALANA JOBSON, THANKS BETTY. THAT'S ALL I NEEDED.

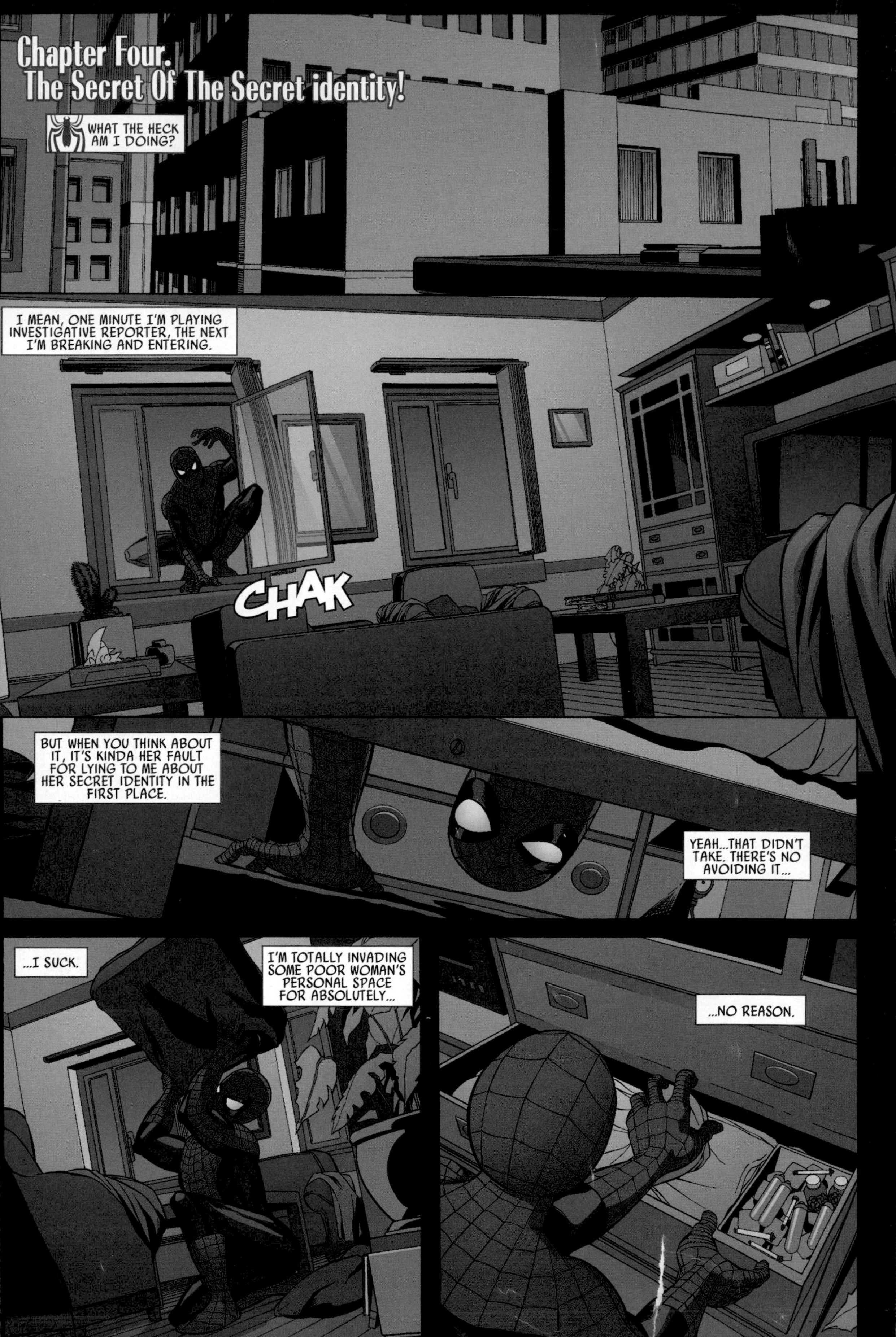

Chapter Four.
The Secret Of The Secret identity!
WHAT THE HECK AM I DOING?
I MEAN, ONE MINUTE I'M PLAYING INVESTIGATIVE REPORTER, THE NEXT I'M BREAKING AND ENTERING.
CHAK
BUT WHEN YOU THINK ABOUT IT, IT'S KINDA HER FAULT FOR LYING TO ME ABOUT HER SECRET IDENTITY IN THE FIRST PLACE.
YEAH...THAT DIDN'T TAKE. THERE'S NO AVOIDING IT...
...I SUCK.
I'M TOTALLY INVADING SOME POOR WOMAN'S PERSONAL SPACE FOR ABSOLUTELY...
...NO REASON.

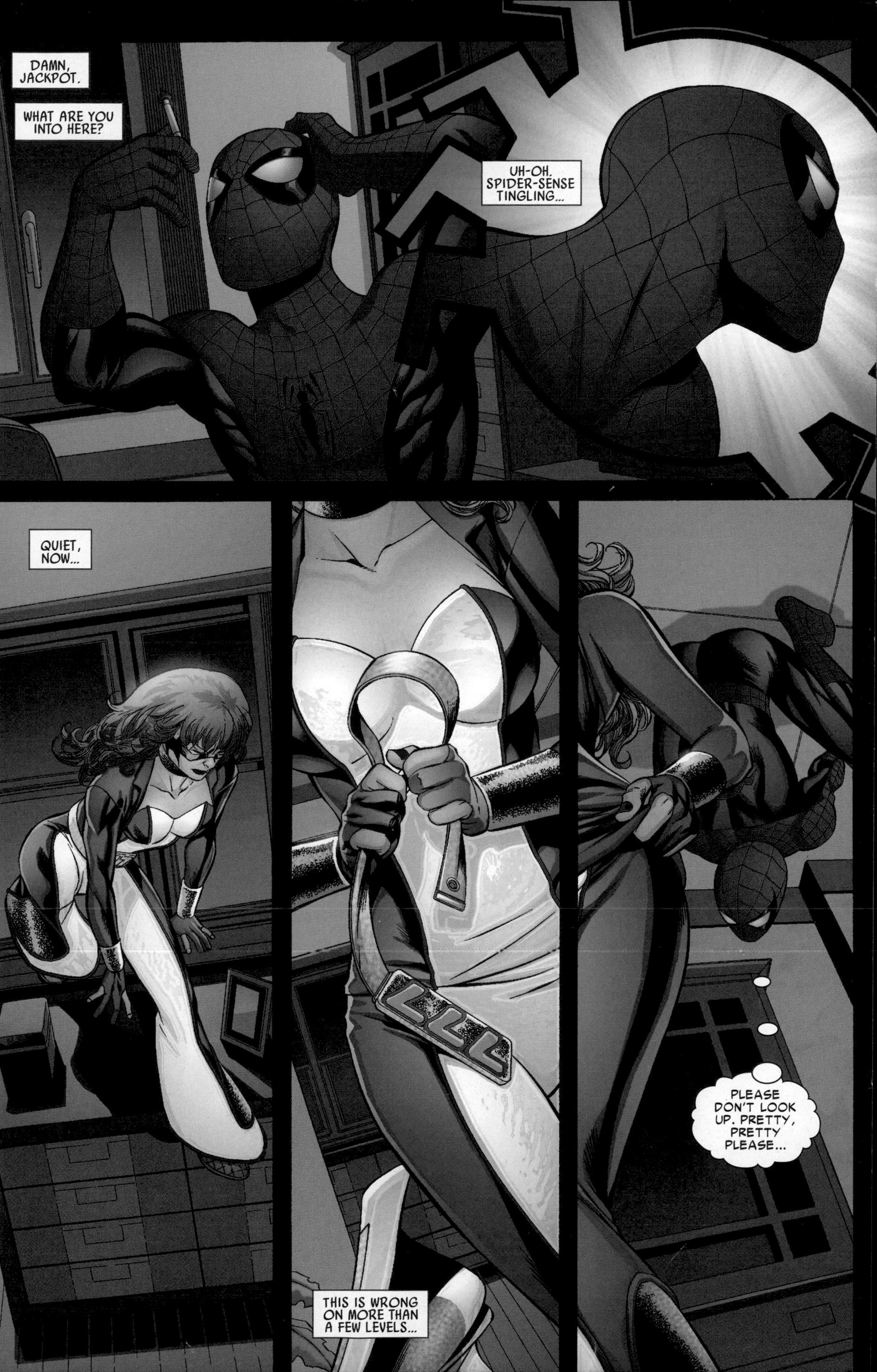
DAMN, JACKPOT.
WHAT ARE YOU INTO HERE?
UH-OH. SPIDER-SENSE TINGLING...
QUIET, NOW...
THIS IS WRONG ON MORE THAN A FEW LEVELS...
PLEASE DON'T LOOK UP. PRETTY, PRETTY PLEASE...

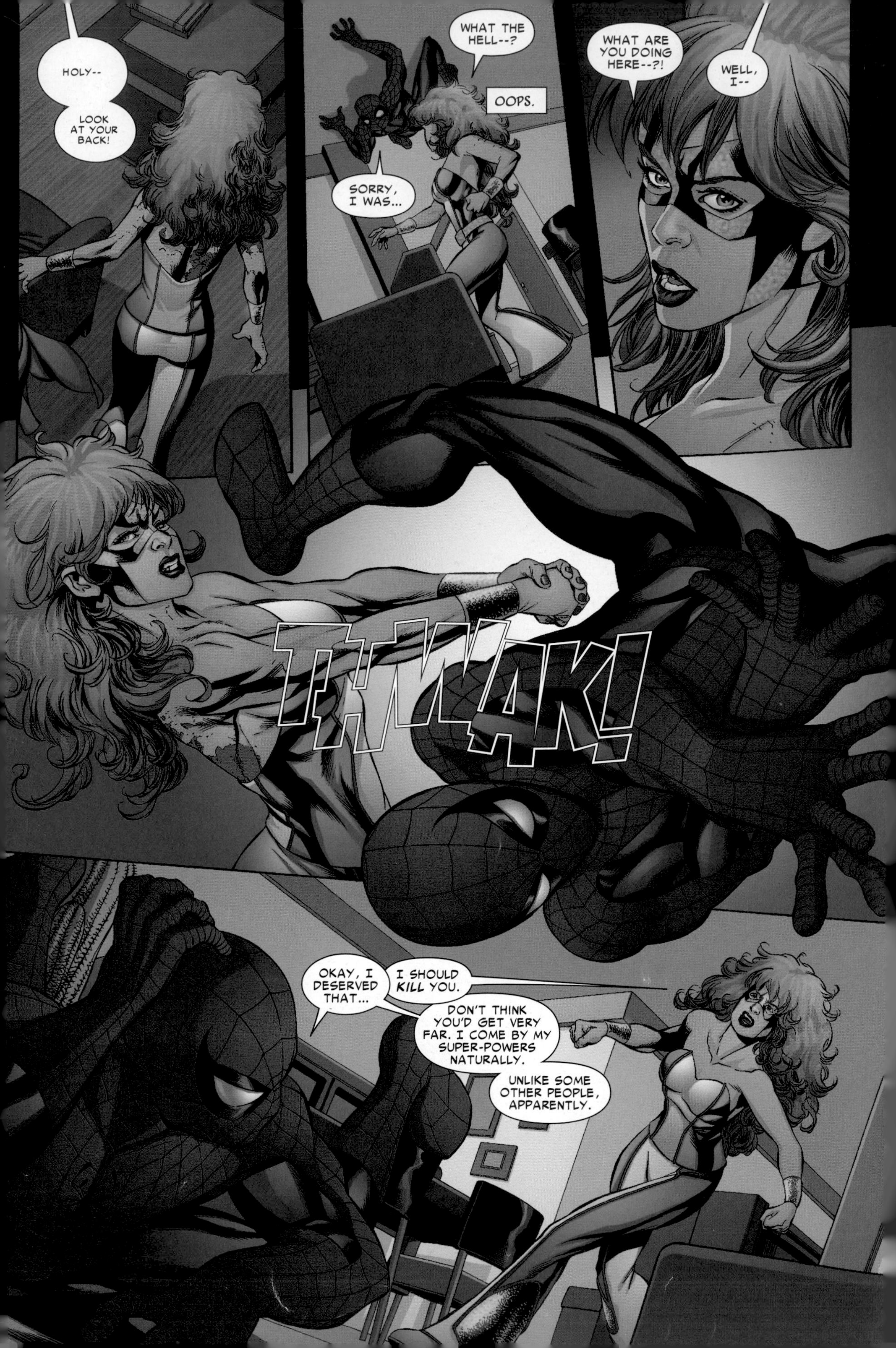
HOLY--
LOOK AT YOUR BACK!
WHAT THE HELL--?
SORRY, I WAS...
OOPS.
WHAT ARE YOU DOING HERE--?!
WELL, I--
THWAK!
OKAY, I DESERVED THAT...
I SHOULD KILL YOU.
DON'T THINK YOU'D GET VERY FAR. I COME BY MY SUPER-POWERS NATURALLY.
UNLIKE SOME OTHER PEOPLE, APPARENTLY.

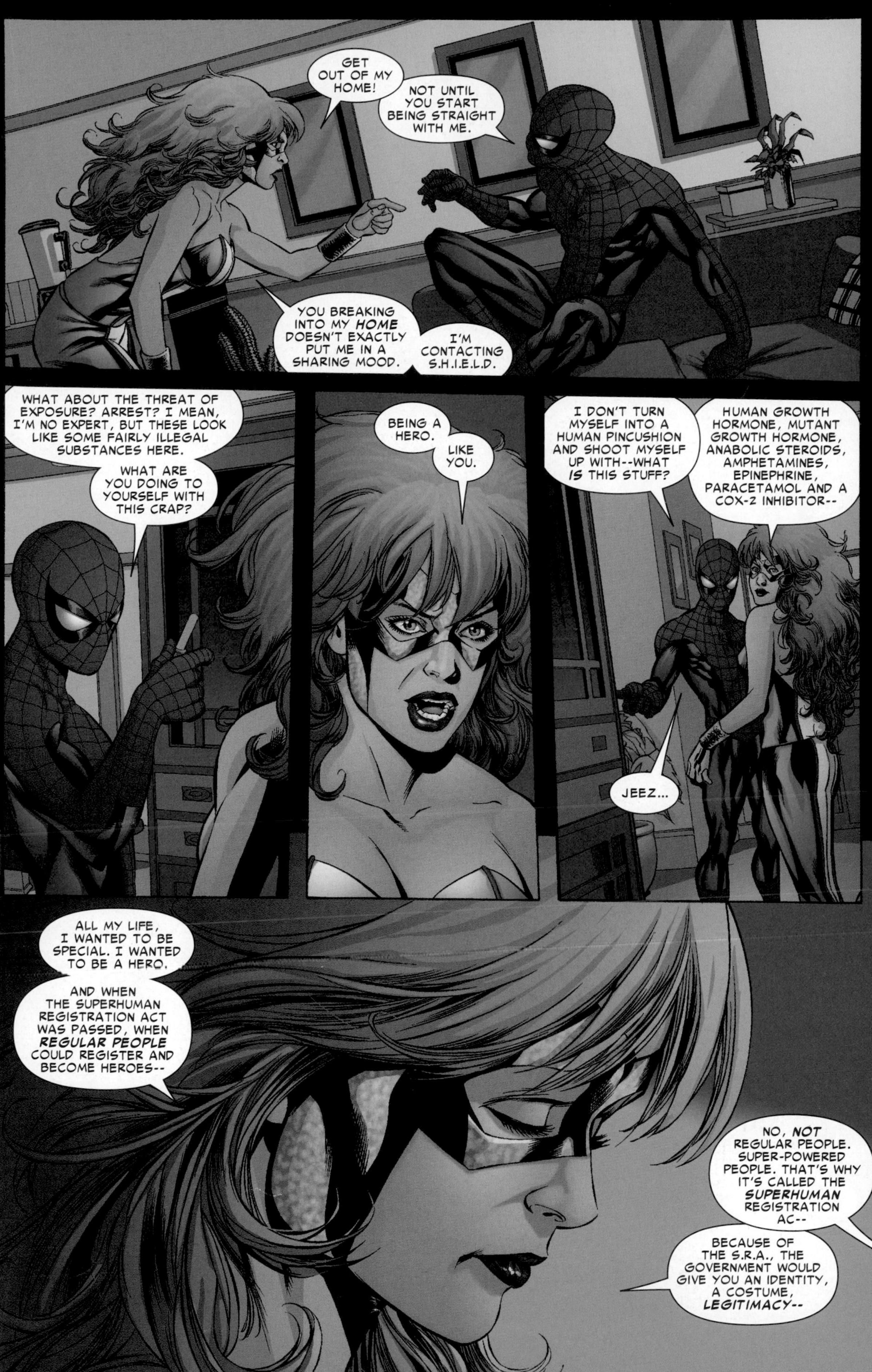
GET OUT OF MY HOME!
NOT UNTIL YOU START BEING STRAIGHT WITH ME.
YOU BREAKING INTO MY HOME DOESN'T EXACTLY PUT ME IN A SHARING MOOD.
I'M CONTACTING S.H.I.E.L.D.
WHAT ABOUT THE THREAT OF EXPOSURE? ARREST? I MEAN, I'M NO EXPERT, BUT THESE LOOK LIKE SOME FAIRLY ILLEGAL SUBSTANCES HERE.
WHAT ARE YOU DOING TO YOURSELF WITH THIS CRAP?
BEING A HERO.
LIKE YOU.
I DON'T TURN MYSELF INTO A HUMAN PINCUSHION AND SHOOT MYSELF UP WITH--WHAT IS THIS STUFF?
HUMAN GROWTH HORMONE, MUTANT GROWTH HORMONE, ANABOLIC STEROIDS, AMPHETAMINES, EPINEPHRINE, PARACETAMOL AND A COX-2 INHIBITOR--
JEEZ...
ALL MY LIFE, I WANTED TO BE SPECIAL. I WANTED TO BE A HERO.
AND WHEN THE SUPERHUMAN REGISTRATION ACT WAS PASSED, WHEN REGULAR PEOPLE COULD REGISTER AND BECOME HEROES--
NO, NOT REGULAR PEOPLE. SUPER-POWERED PEOPLE. THAT'S WHY IT'S CALLED THE SUPERHUMAN REGISTRATION AC--
BECAUSE OF THE S.R.A., THE GOVERNMENT WOULD GIVE YOU AN IDENTITY, A COSTUME, LEGITIMACY--

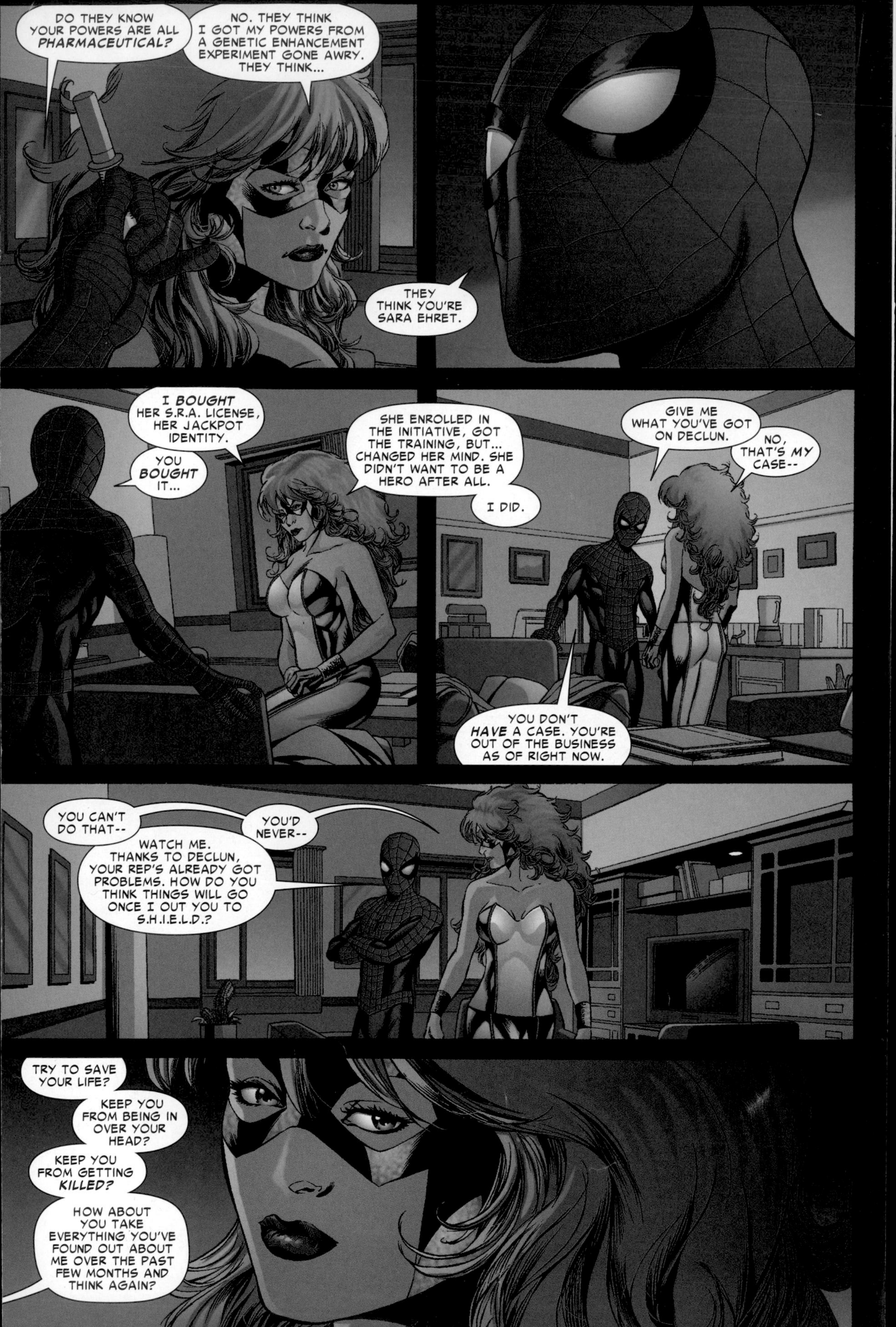
DO THEY KNOW YOUR POWERS ARE ALL *PHARMACEUTICAL?*
NO. THEY THINK I GOT MY POWERS FROM A GENETIC ENHANCEMENT EXPERIMENT GONE AWRY. THEY THINK...
THEY THINK YOU'RE SARA EHRET.
I *BOUGHT* HER S.R.A. LICENSE, HER JACKPOT IDENTITY.
YOU *BOUGHT* IT...
SHE ENROLLED IN THE INITIATIVE, GOT THE TRAINING, BUT... CHANGED HER MIND. SHE DIDN'T WANT TO BE A HERO AFTER ALL.
I DID.
GIVE ME WHAT YOU'VE GOT ON DECLUN.
NO, THAT'S *MY* CASE--
YOU DON'T *HAVE* A CASE. YOU'RE OUT OF THE BUSINESS AS OF RIGHT NOW.
YOU CAN'T DO THAT--
YOU'D NEVER--
WATCH ME. THANKS TO DECLUN, YOUR REP'S ALREADY GOT PROBLEMS. HOW DO YOU THINK THINGS WILL GO ONCE I OUT YOU TO S.H.I.E.L.D.?
TRY TO SAVE YOUR LIFE?
KEEP YOU FROM BEING IN OVER YOUR HEAD?
KEEP YOU FROM GETTING *KILLED?*
HOW ABOUT YOU TAKE EVERYTHING YOU'VE FOUND OUT ABOUT ME OVER THE PAST FEW MONTHS AND THINK AGAIN?

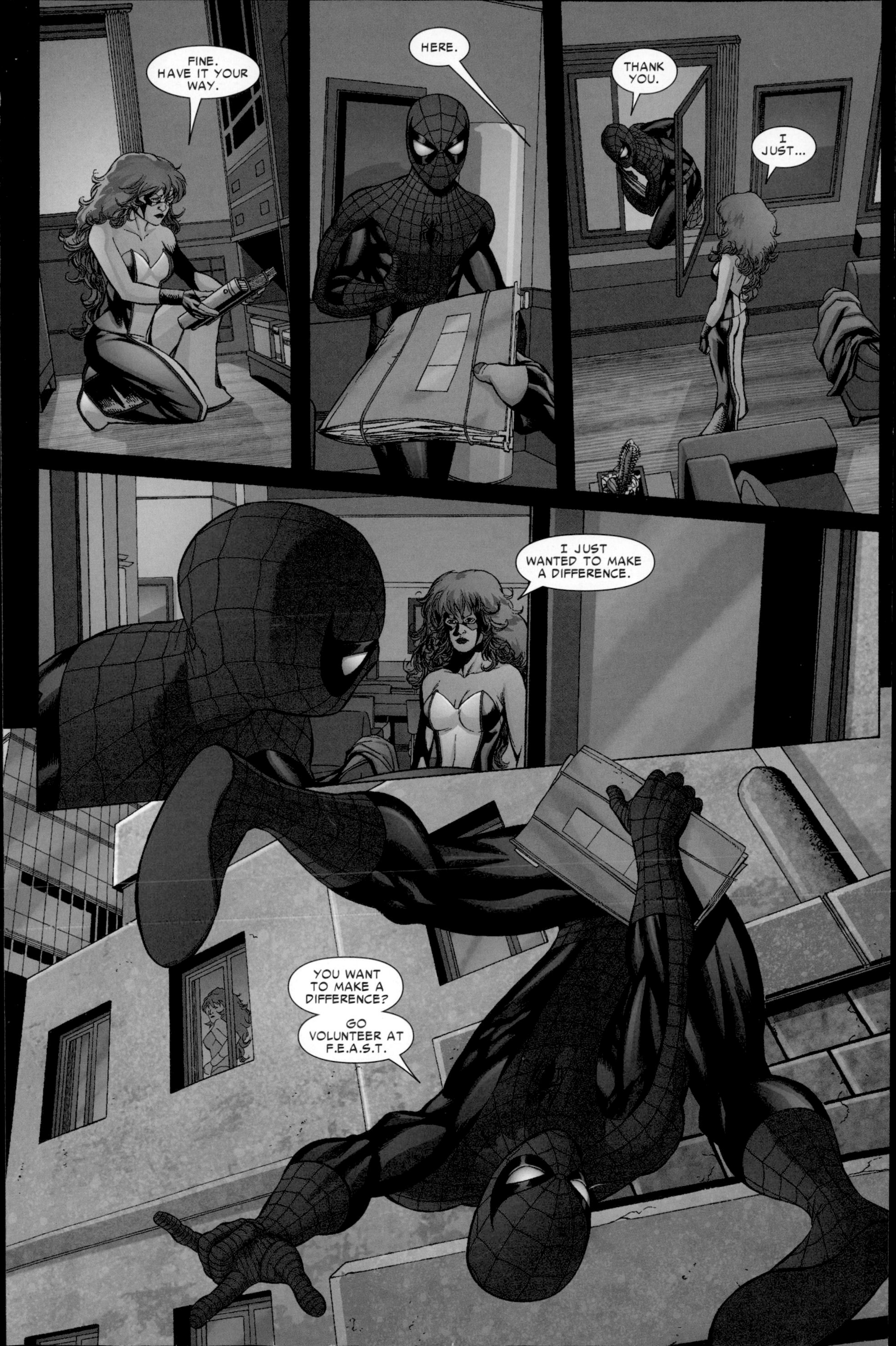
FINE. HAVE IT YOUR WAY.
HERE.
THANK YOU.
I JUST...
I JUST WANTED TO MAKE A DIFFERENCE.
YOU WANT TO MAKE A DIFFERENCE?
GO VOLUNTEER AT F.E.A.S.T.

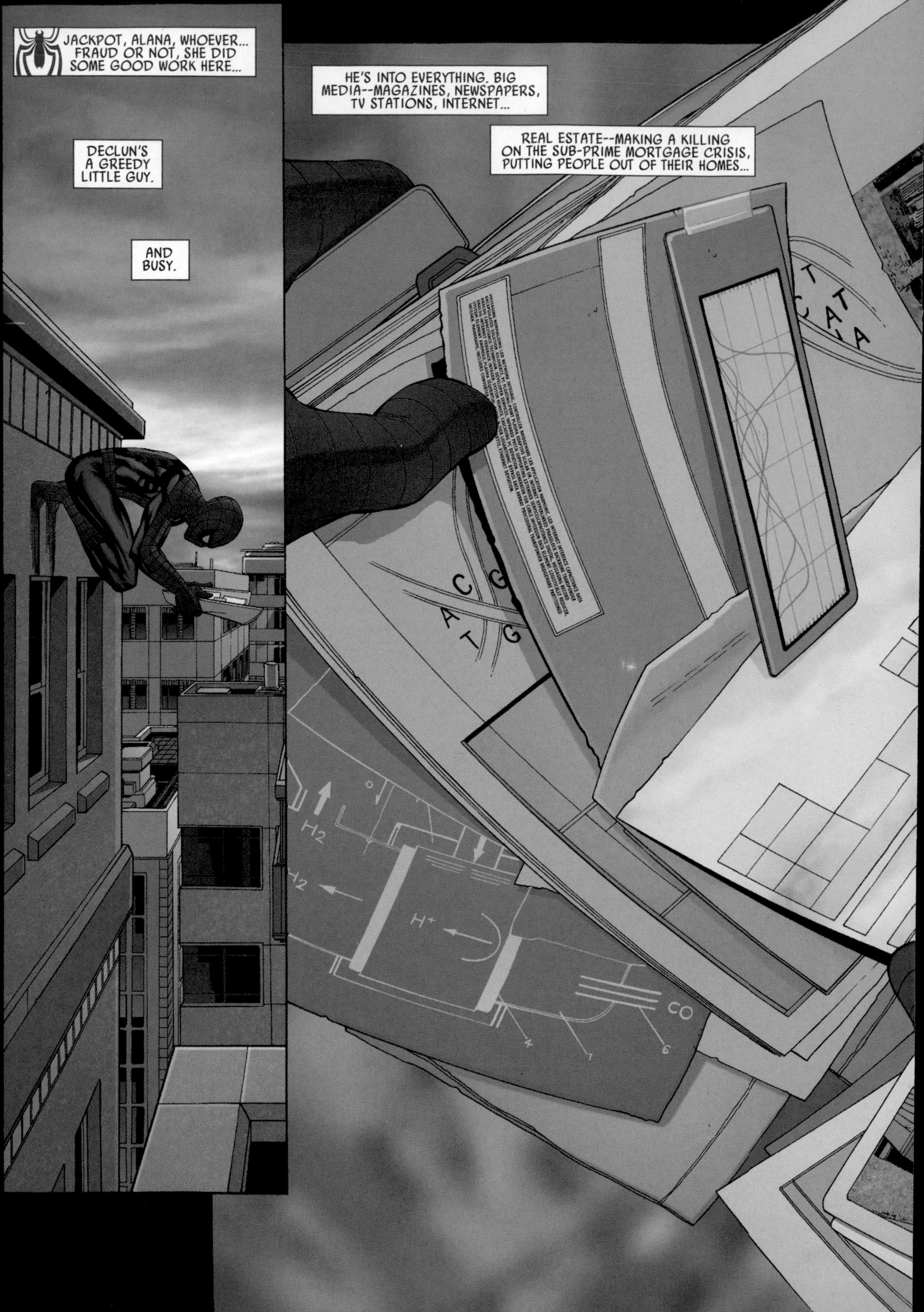
JACKPOT, ALANA, WHOEVER... FRAUD OR NOT, SHE DID SOME GOOD WORK HERE...
DECLUN'S A GREEDY LITTLE GUY.
AND BUSY.
HE'S INTO EVERYTHING. BIG MEDIA--MAGAZINES, NEWSPAPERS, TV STATIONS, INTERNET...
REAL ESTATE--MAKING A KILLING ON THE SUB-PRIME MORTGAGE CRISIS, PUTTING PEOPLE OUT OF THEIR HOMES...

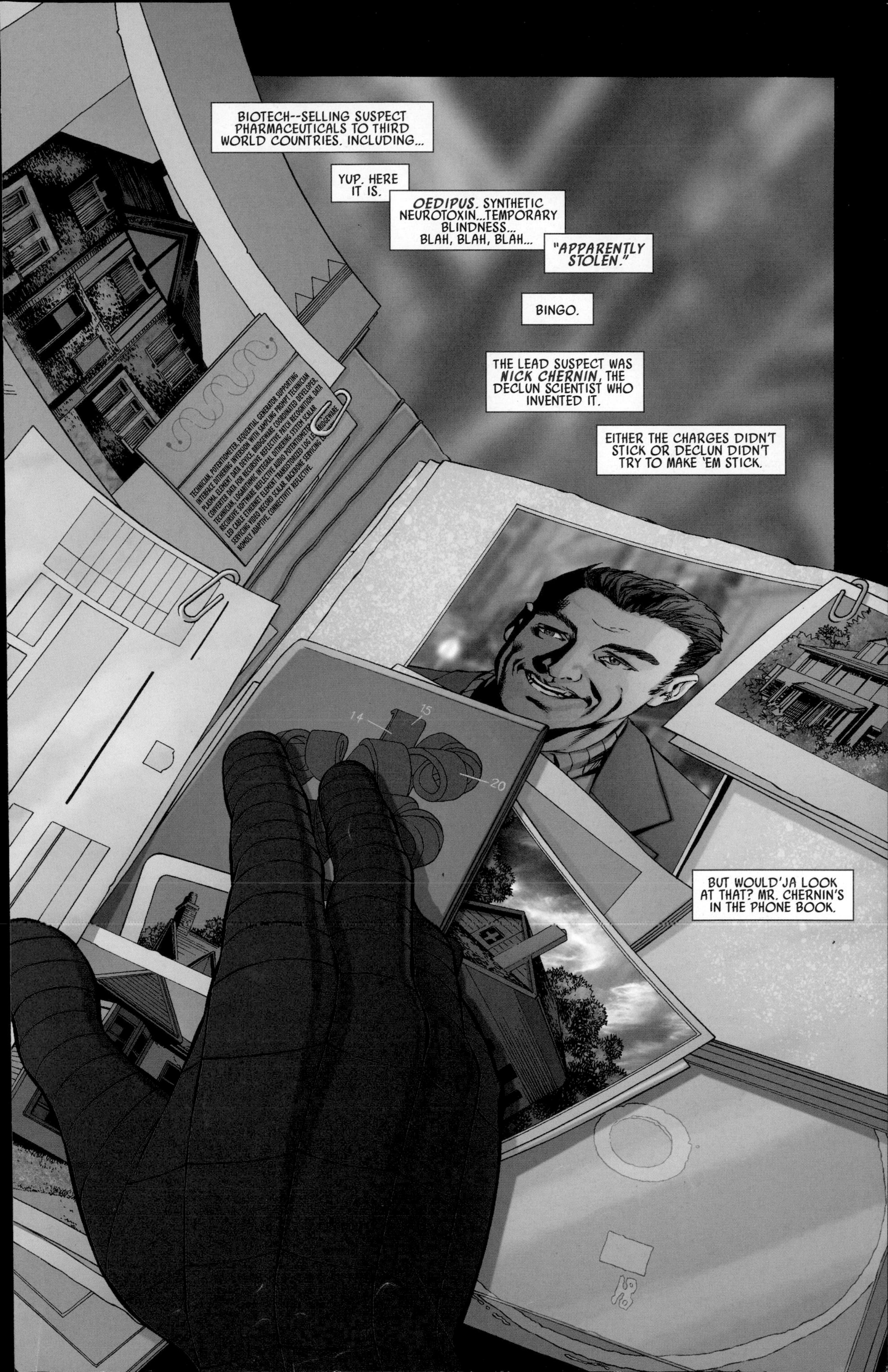
BIOTECH--SELLING SUSPECT PHARMACEUTICALS TO THIRD WORLD COUNTRIES. INCLUDING...
YUP. HERE IT IS.
OEDIPUS. SYNTHETIC NEUROTOXIN...TEMPORARY BLINDNESS... BLAH, BLAH, BLAH...
"APPARENTLY STOLEN."
BINGO.
THE LEAD SUSPECT WAS NICK CHERNIN, THE DECLUN SCIENTIST WHO INVENTED IT.
EITHER THE CHARGES DIDN'T STICK OR DECLUN DIDN'T TRY TO MAKE 'EM STICK.
14
15
20
BUT WOULD'JA LOOK AT THAT? MR. CHERNIN'S IN THE PHONE BOOK.

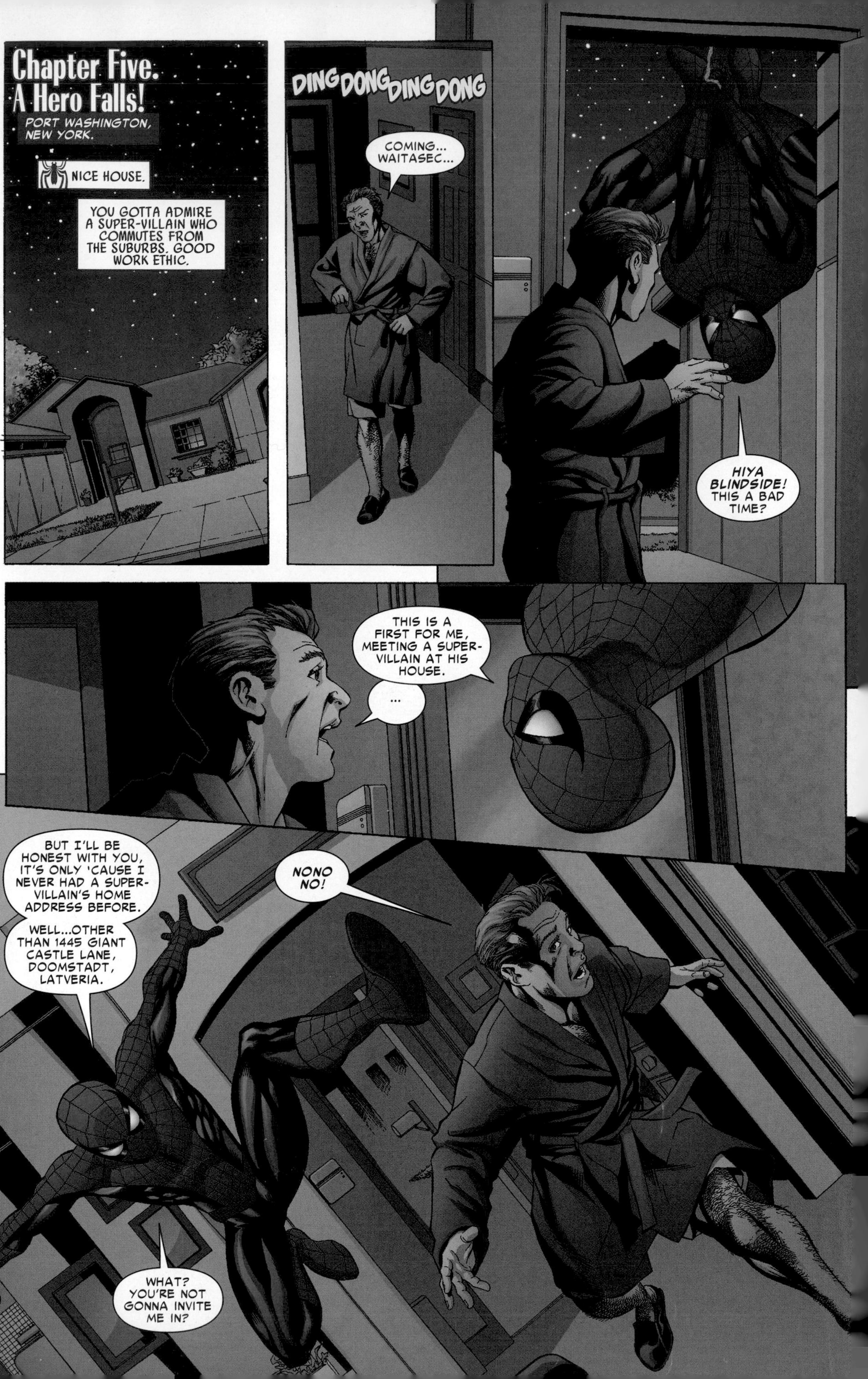
Chapter Five.
A Hero Falls!
PORT WASHINGTON, NEW YORK.
NICE HOUSE.
YOU GOTTA ADMIRE A SUPER-VILLAIN WHO COMMUTES FROM THE SUBURBS. GOOD WORK ETHIC.
DING DONG DING DONG
COMING... WAITASEC...
HIYA BLINDSIDE! THIS A BAD TIME?
THIS IS A FIRST FOR ME, MEETING A SUPER-VILLAIN AT HIS HOUSE.
...
BUT I'LL BE HONEST WITH YOU, IT'S ONLY 'CAUSE I NEVER HAD A SUPER-VILLAIN'S HOME ADDRESS BEFORE.
WELL...OTHER THAN 1445 GIANT CASTLE LANE, DOOMSTADT, LATVERIA.
NONO NO!
WHAT? YOU'RE NOT GONNA INVITE ME IN?

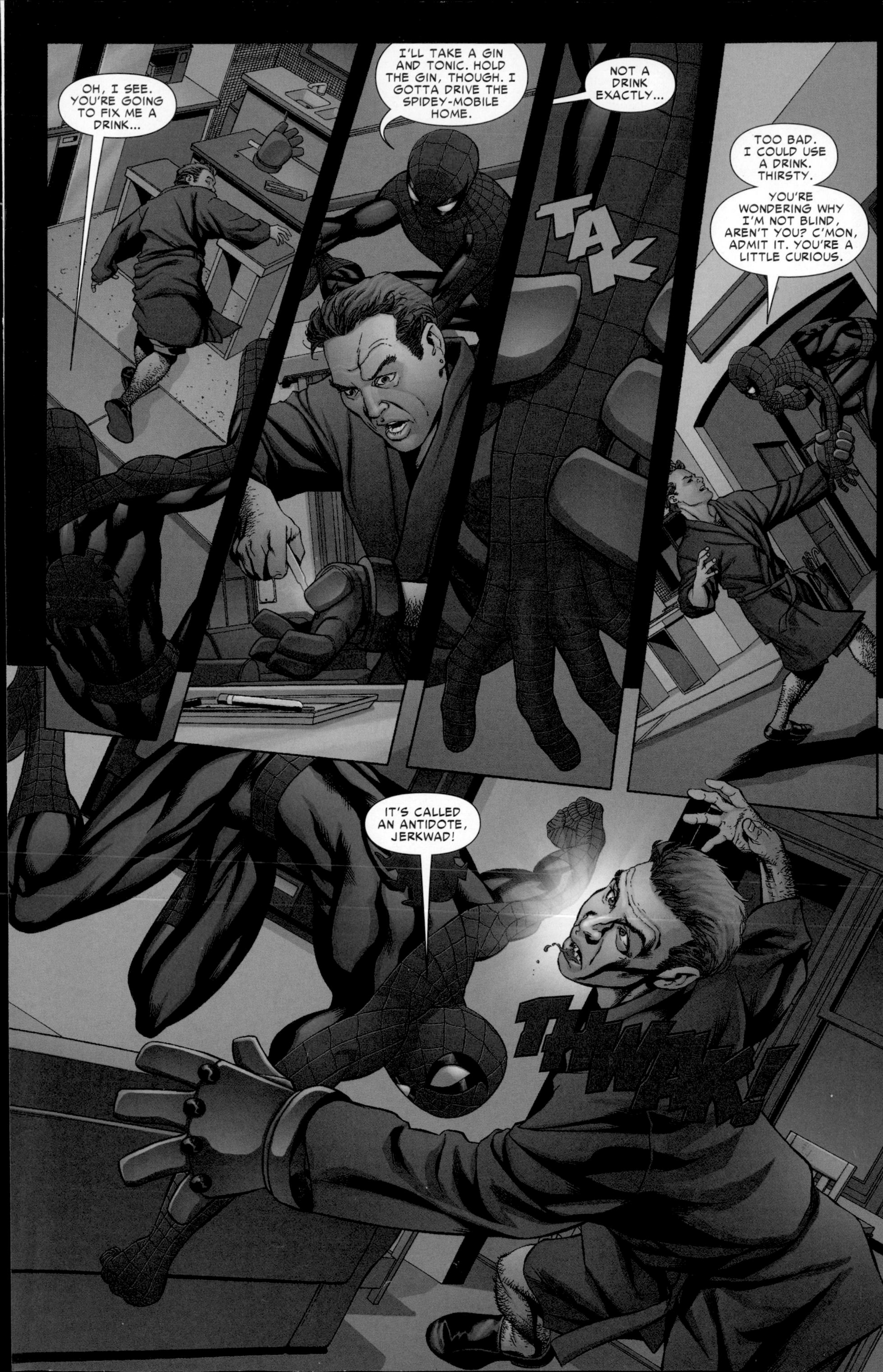
OH, I SEE. YOU'RE GOING TO FIX ME A DRINK...
I'LL TAKE A GIN AND TONIC. HOLD THE GIN, THOUGH. I GOTTA DRIVE THE SPIDEY-MOBILE HOME.
NOT A DRINK EXACTLY...
TAK
TOO BAD. I COULD USE A DRINK. THIRSTY.
YOU'RE WONDERING WHY I'M NOT BLIND, AREN'T YOU? C'MON, ADMIT IT. YOU'RE A LITTLE CURIOUS.
IT'S CALLED AN ANTIDOTE, JERKWAD!
THWAK!

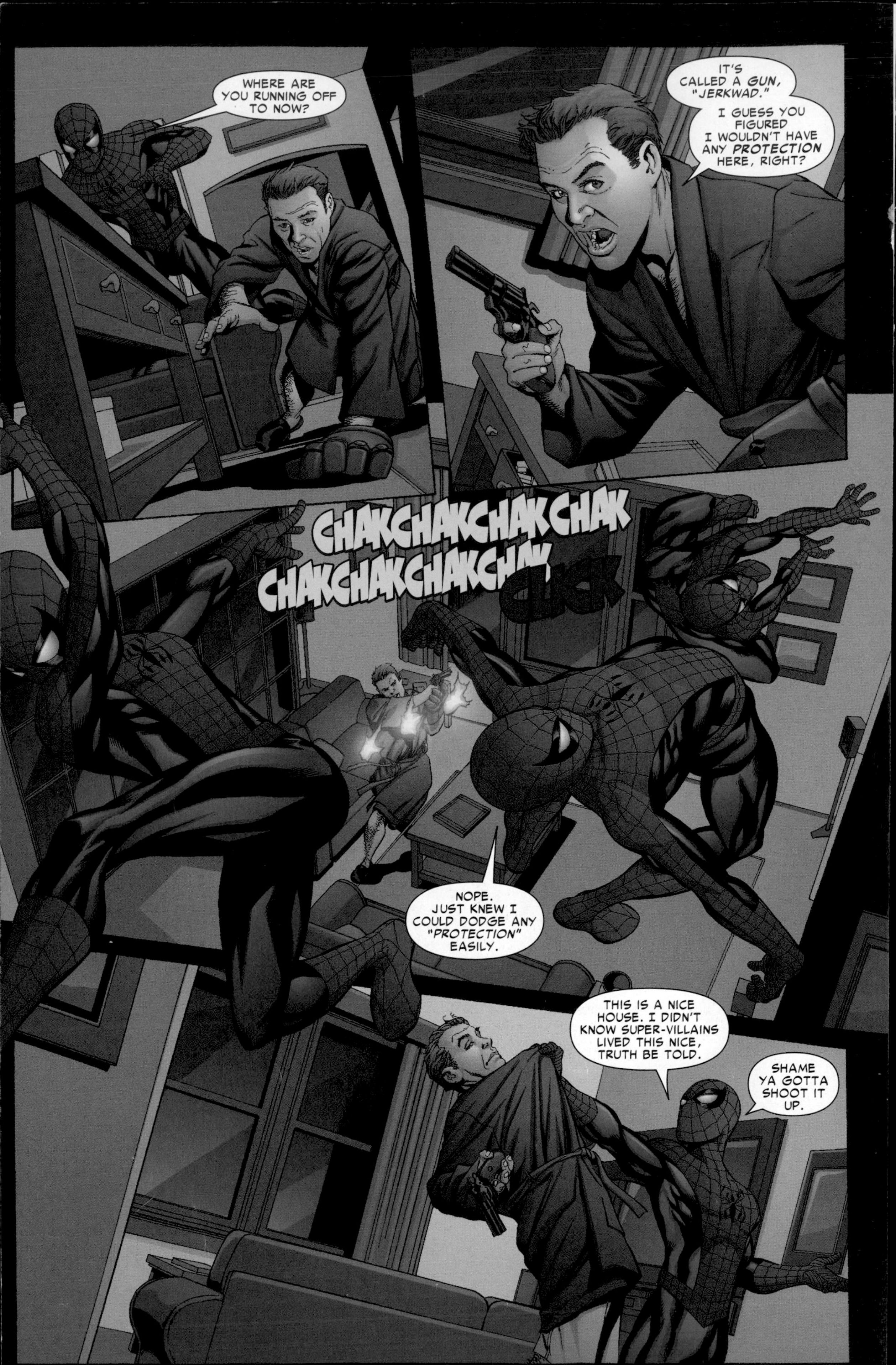
WHERE ARE YOU RUNNING OFF TO NOW?
IT'S CALLED A *GUN,* "JERKWAD."
I GUESS YOU FIGURED I WOULDN'T HAVE ANY ***PROTECTION*** HERE, RIGHT?
CHAKCHAKCHAKCHAK
CHAKCHAKCHAKCHAK
CLICK
NOPE. JUST KNEW I COULD DODGE ANY "*PROTECTION*" EASILY.
THIS IS A NICE HOUSE. I DIDN'T KNOW SUPER-VILLAINS LIVED THIS NICE, TRUTH BE TOLD.
SHAME YA GOTTA SHOOT IT UP.

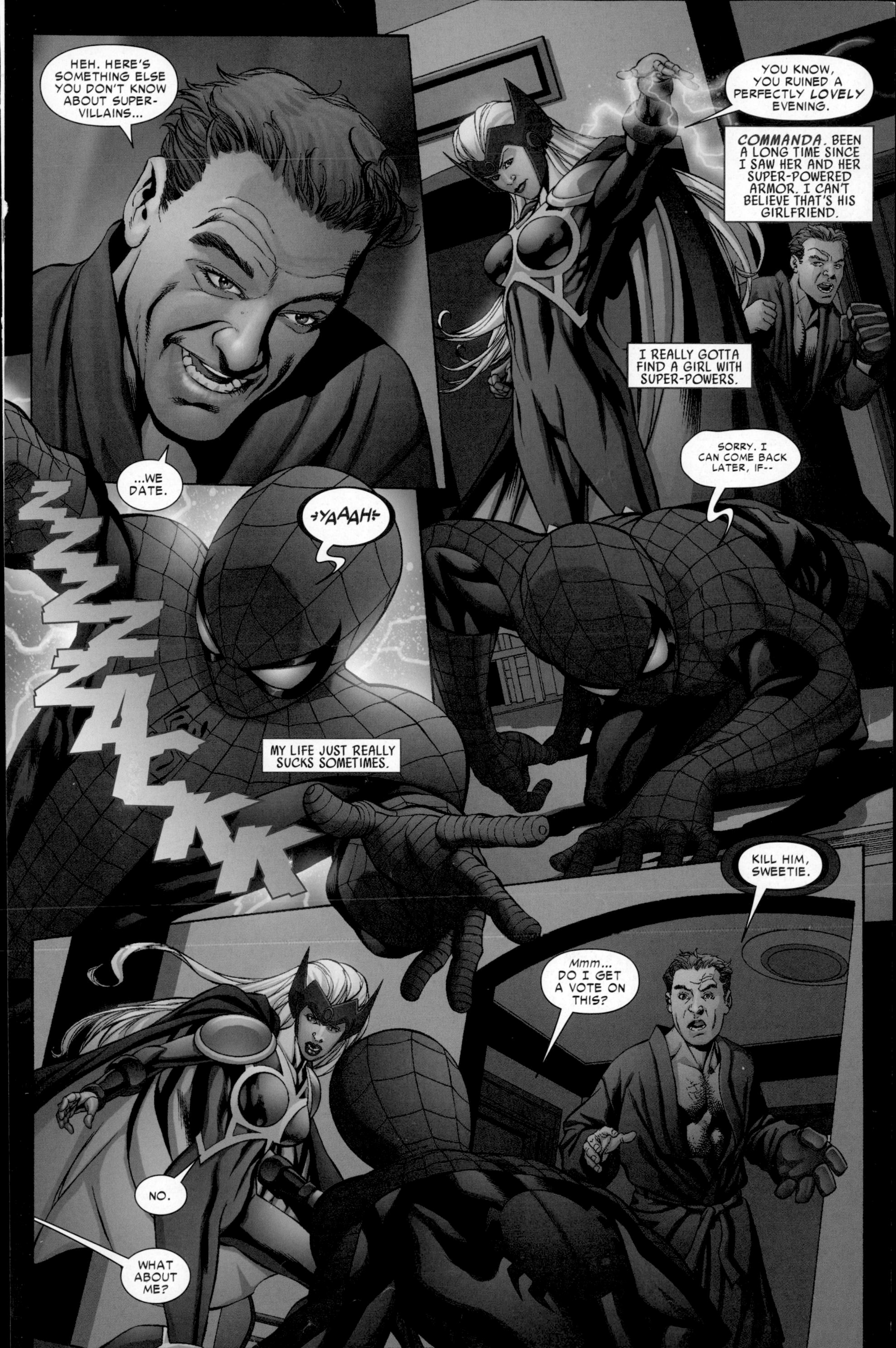

HEH. HERE'S SOMETHING ELSE YOU DON'T KNOW ABOUT SUPER-VILLAINS...
YOU KNOW, YOU RUINED A PERFECTLY LOVELY EVENING.
COMMANDA. BEEN A LONG TIME SINCE I SAW HER AND HER SUPER-POWERED ARMOR. I CAN'T BELIEVE THAT'S HIS GIRLFRIEND.
I REALLY GOTTA FIND A GIRL WITH SUPER-POWERS.
...WE DATE.
-YAAAH!-
ZZZZZACKK
SORRY. I CAN COME BACK LATER, IF--
MY LIFE JUST REALLY SUCKS SOMETIMES.
KILL HIM, SWEETIE.
Mmm... DO I GET A VOTE ON THIS?
NO.
WHAT ABOUT ME?

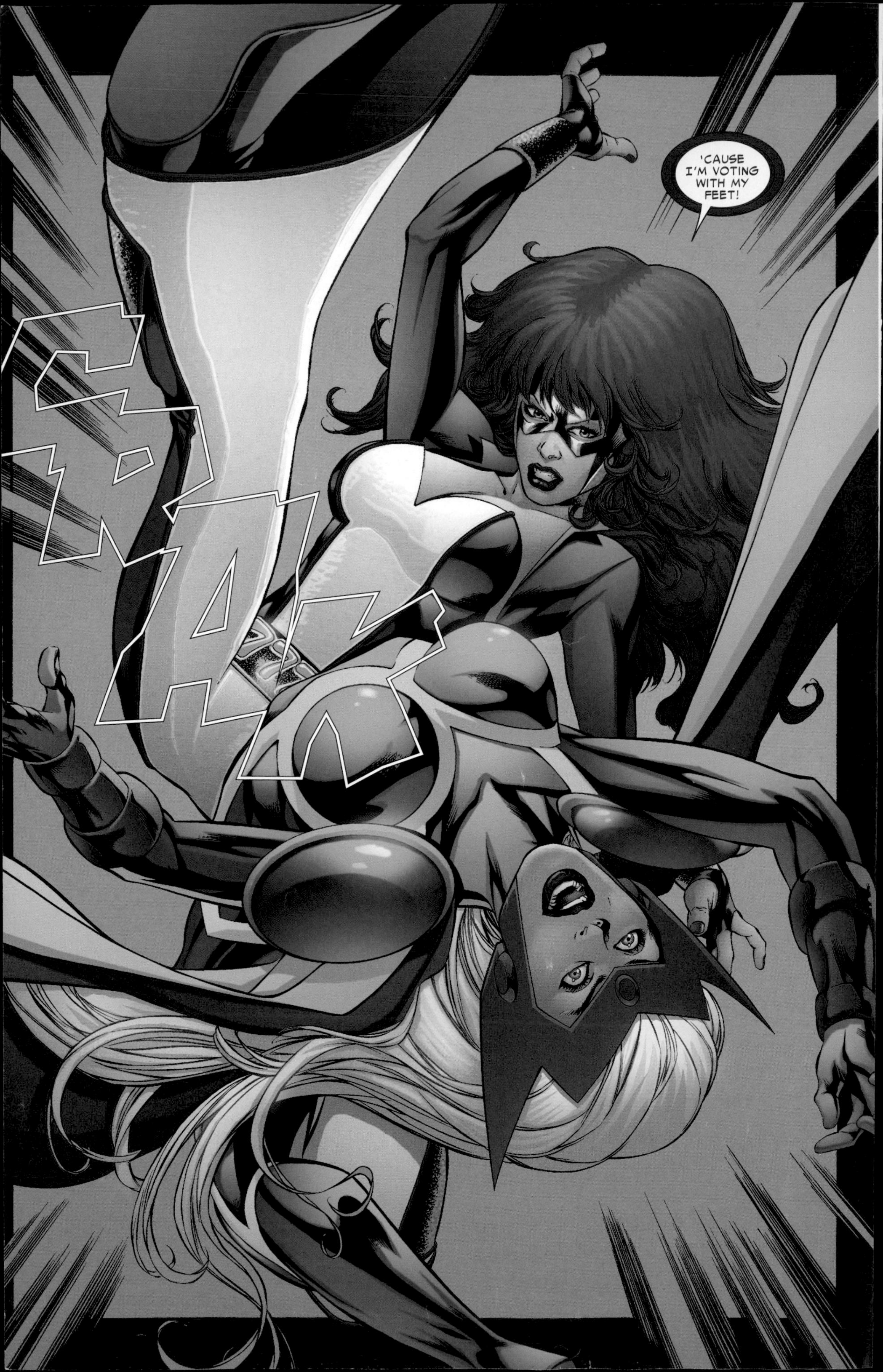
'CAUSE I'M VOTING WITH MY FEET!

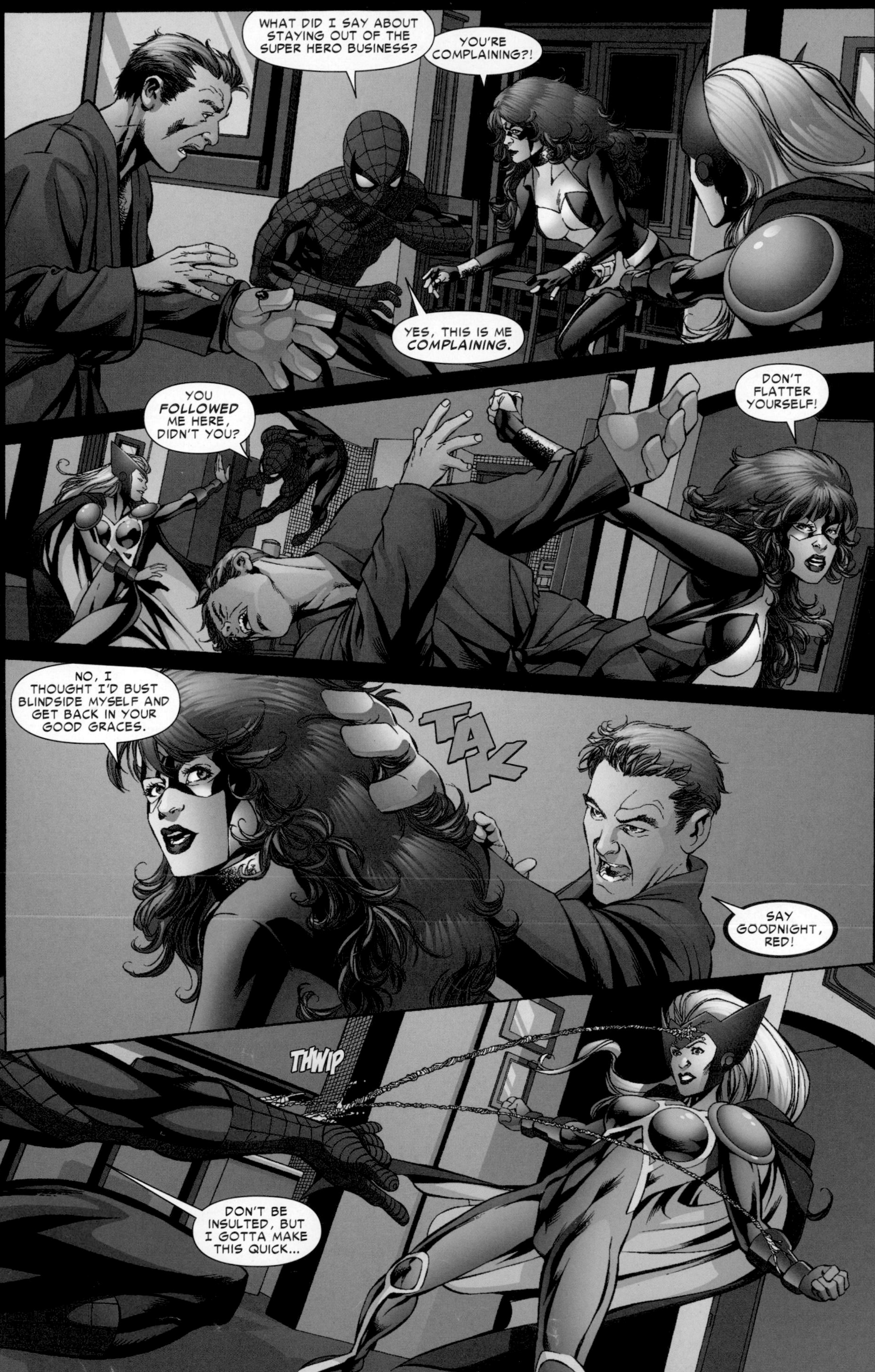
WHAT DID I SAY ABOUT STAYING OUT OF THE SUPER HERO BUSINESS?
YOU'RE COMPLAINING?!
YES, THIS IS ME COMPLAINING.
YOU FOLLOWED ME HERE, DIDN'T YOU?
DON'T FLATTER YOURSELF!
NO, I THOUGHT I'D BUST BLINDSIDE MYSELF AND GET BACK IN YOUR GOOD GRACES.
TAK
SAY GOODNIGHT, RED!
THWIP
DON'T BE INSULTED, BUT I GOTTA MAKE THIS QUICK...

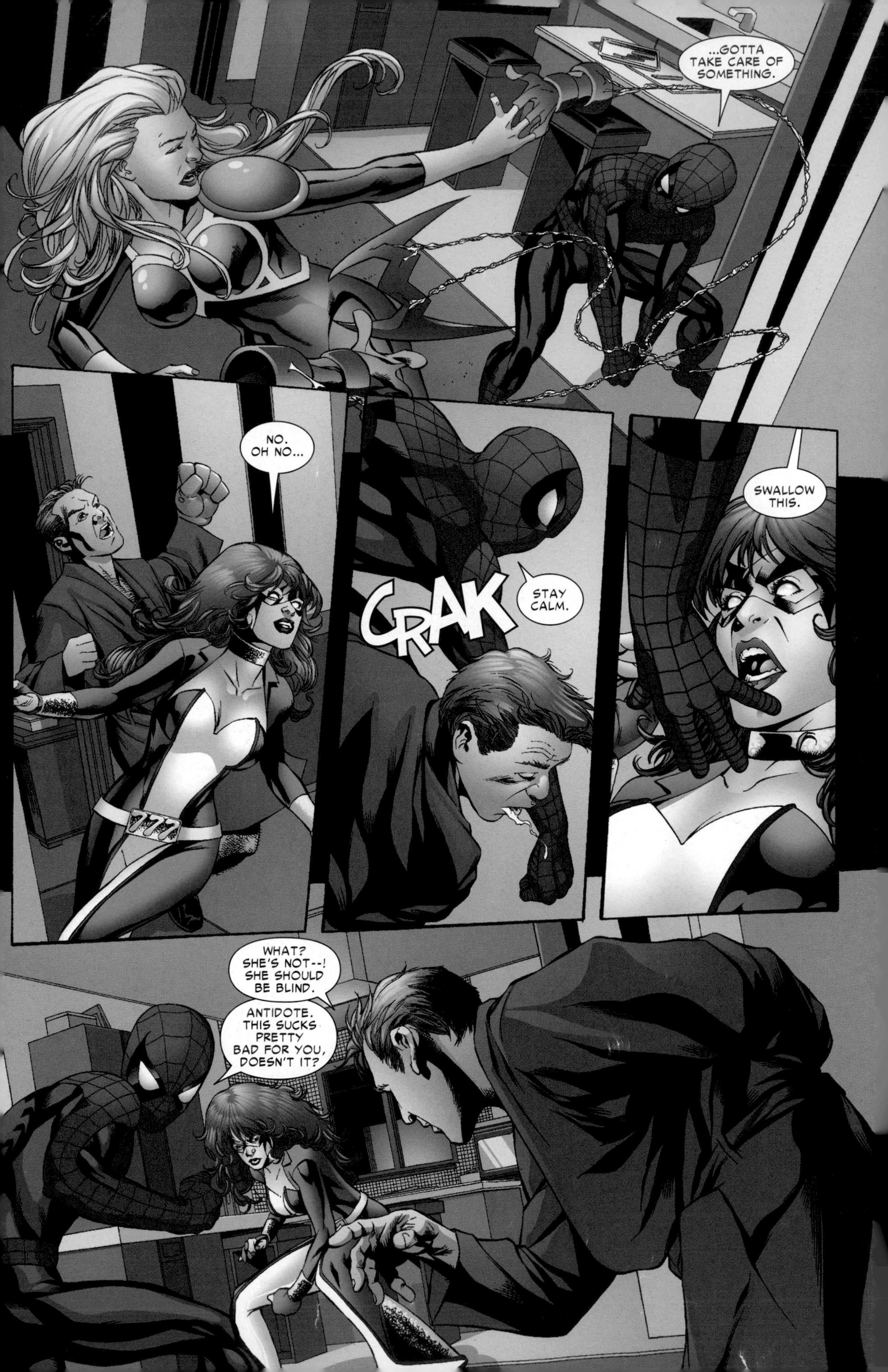
...GOTTA TAKE CARE OF SOMETHING.
NO. OH NO...
CRAK
STAY CALM.
SWALLOW THIS.
WHAT? SHE'S NOT--! SHE SHOULD BE BLIND.
ANTIDOTE. THIS SUCKS PRETTY BAD FOR YOU, DOESN'T IT?

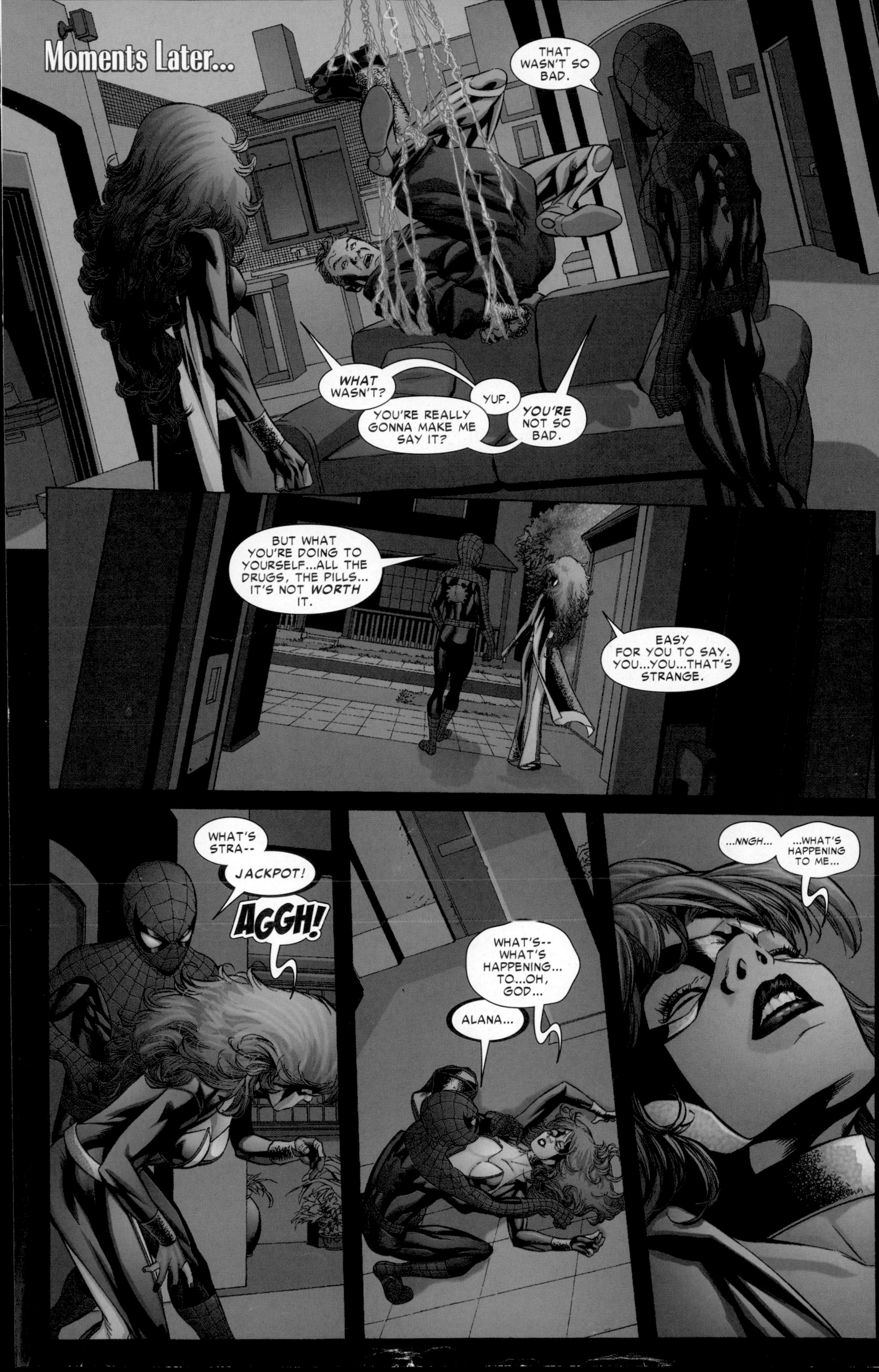
Moments Later...
THAT WASN'T SO BAD.
WHAT WASN'T?
YUP.
YOU'RE REALLY GONNA MAKE ME SAY IT?
YOU'RE NOT SO BAD.
BUT WHAT YOU'RE DOING TO YOURSELF...ALL THE DRUGS, THE PILLS... IT'S NOT WORTH IT.
EASY FOR YOU TO SAY. YOU...YOU...THAT'S STRANGE.
WHAT'S STRA--
JACKPOT!
AGGH!
WHAT'S-- WHAT'S HAPPENING... TO...OH, GOD...
ALANA...
...NNGH...
...WHAT'S HAPPENING TO ME...

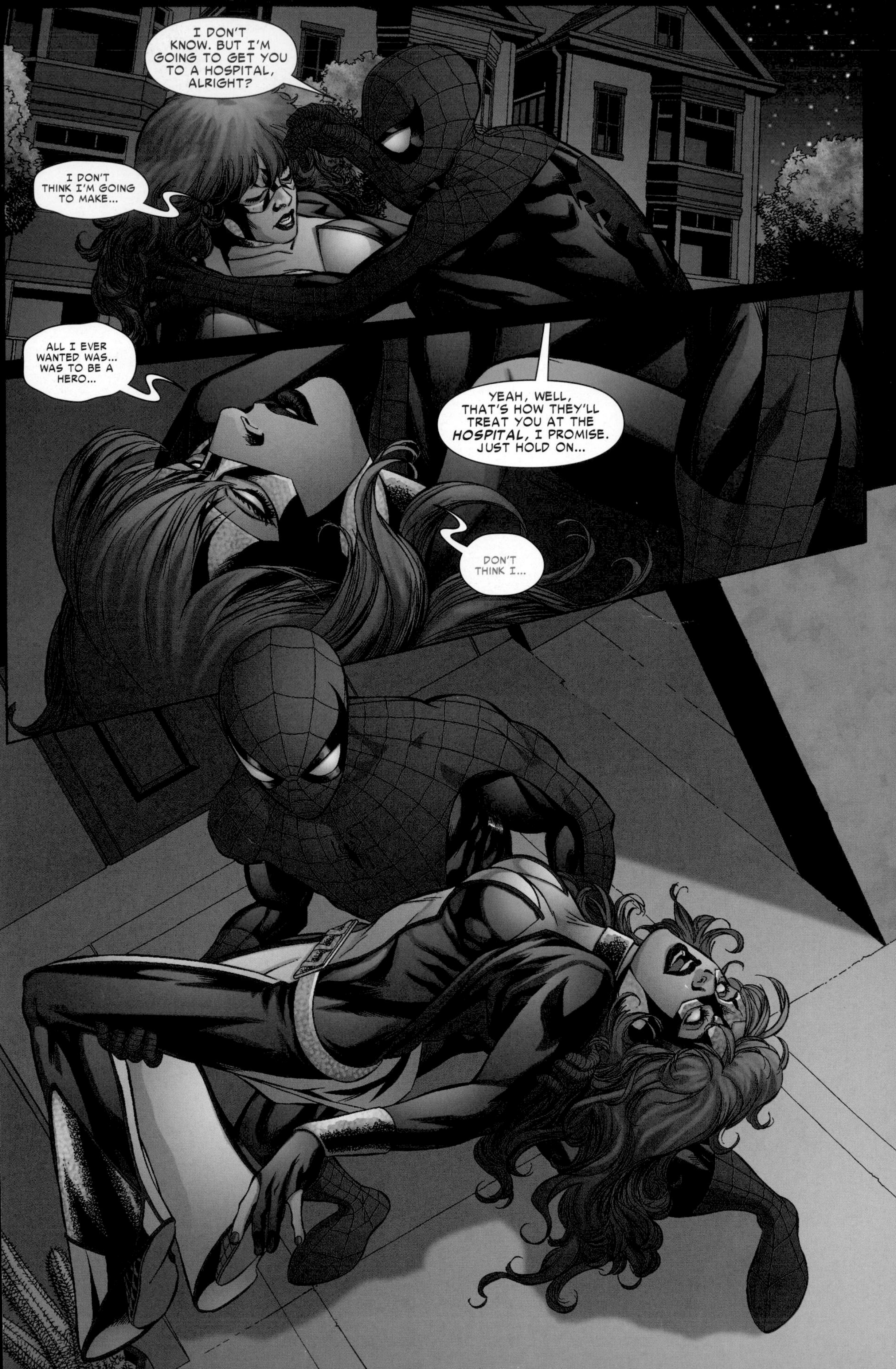
I DON'T KNOW. BUT I'M GOING TO GET YOU TO A HOSPITAL, ALRIGHT?
I DON'T THINK I'M GOING TO MAKE...
ALL I EVER WANTED WAS... WAS TO BE A HERO...
YEAH, WELL, THAT'S HOW THEY'LL TREAT YOU AT THE HOSPITAL, I PROMISE. JUST HOLD ON...
DON'T THINK I...

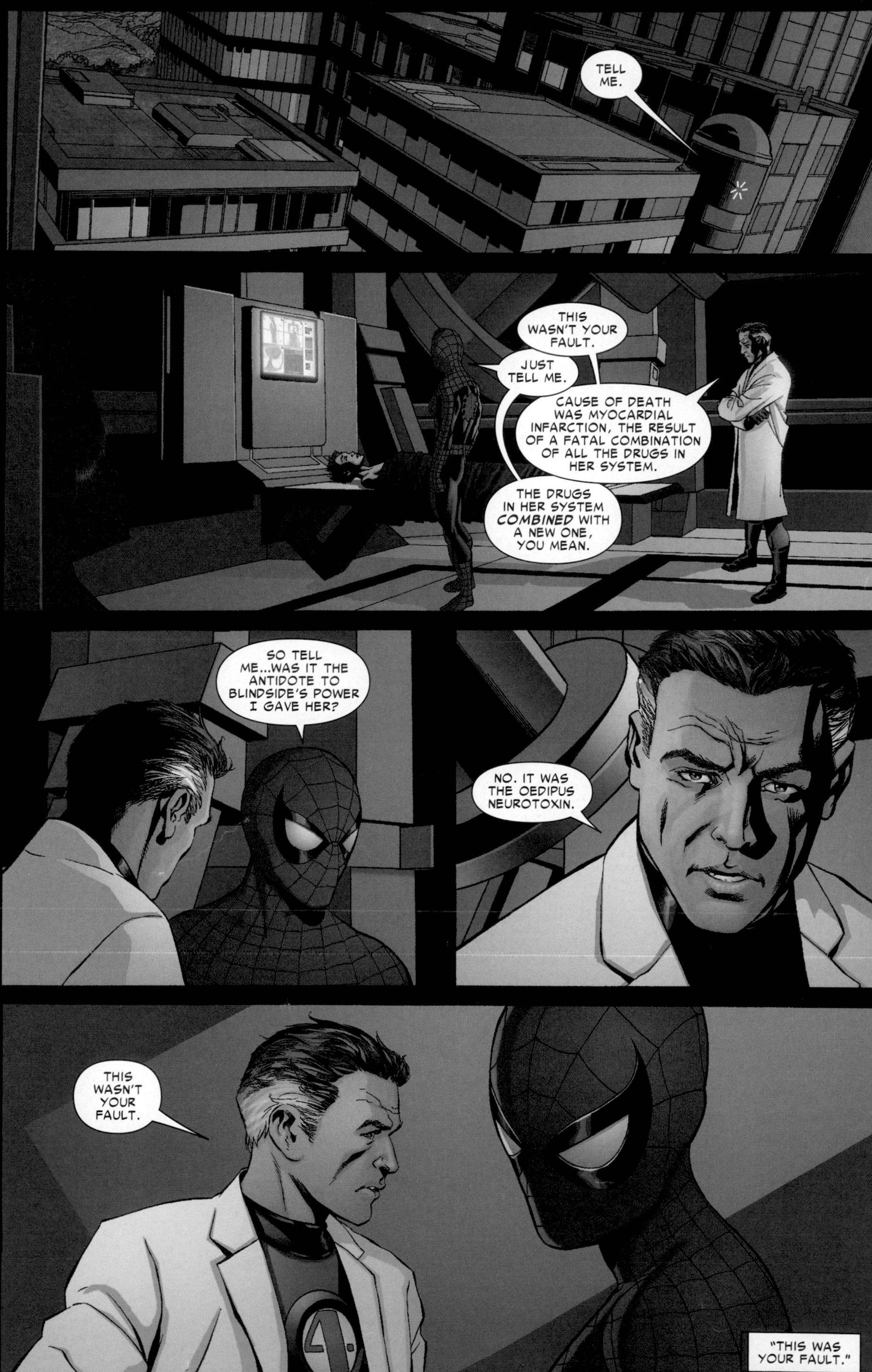
TELL ME.
THIS WASN'T YOUR FAULT.
JUST TELL ME.
CAUSE OF DEATH WAS MYOCARDIAL INFARCTION, THE RESULT OF A FATAL COMBINATION OF ALL THE DRUGS IN HER SYSTEM.
THE DRUGS IN HER SYSTEM *COMBINED* WITH A NEW ONE, YOU MEAN.
SO TELL ME...WAS IT THE ANTIDOTE TO BLINDSIDE'S POWER I GAVE HER?
NO. IT WAS THE OEDIPUS NEUROTOXIN.
THIS WASN'T YOUR FAULT.
"THIS WAS YOUR FAULT."

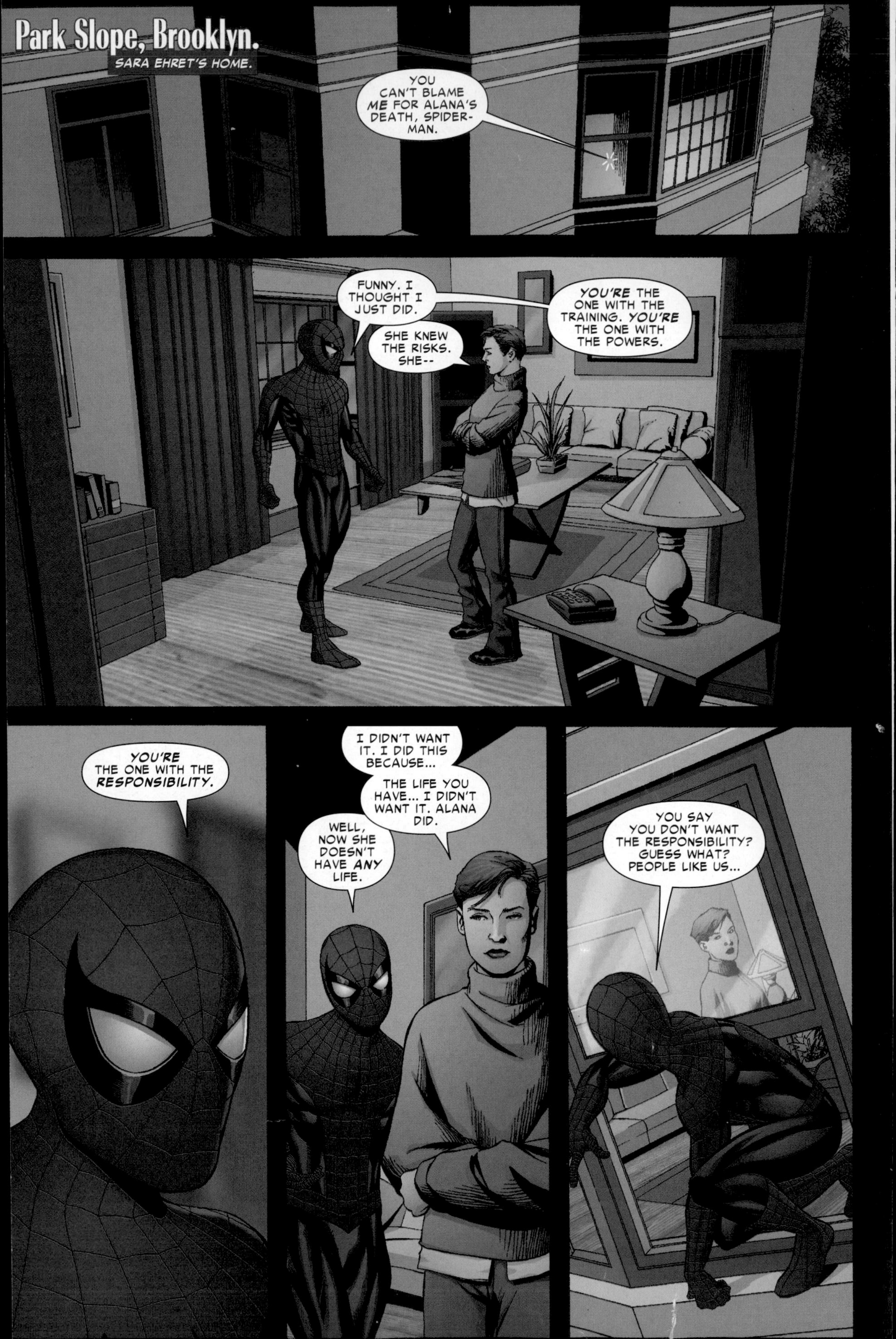
Park Slope, Brooklyn.
SARA EHRET'S HOME.
YOU CAN'T BLAME ME FOR ALANA'S DEATH, SPIDER-MAN.
FUNNY. I THOUGHT I JUST DID.
SHE KNEW THE RISKS. SHE--
YOU'RE THE ONE WITH THE TRAINING. YOU'RE THE ONE WITH THE POWERS.
YOU'RE THE ONE WITH THE RESPONSIBILITY.
I DIDN'T WANT IT. I DID THIS BECAUSE...
THE LIFE YOU HAVE... I DIDN'T WANT IT. ALANA DID.
WELL, NOW SHE DOESN'T HAVE ANY LIFE.
YOU SAY YOU DON'T WANT THE RESPONSIBILITY? GUESS WHAT? PEOPLE LIKE US...

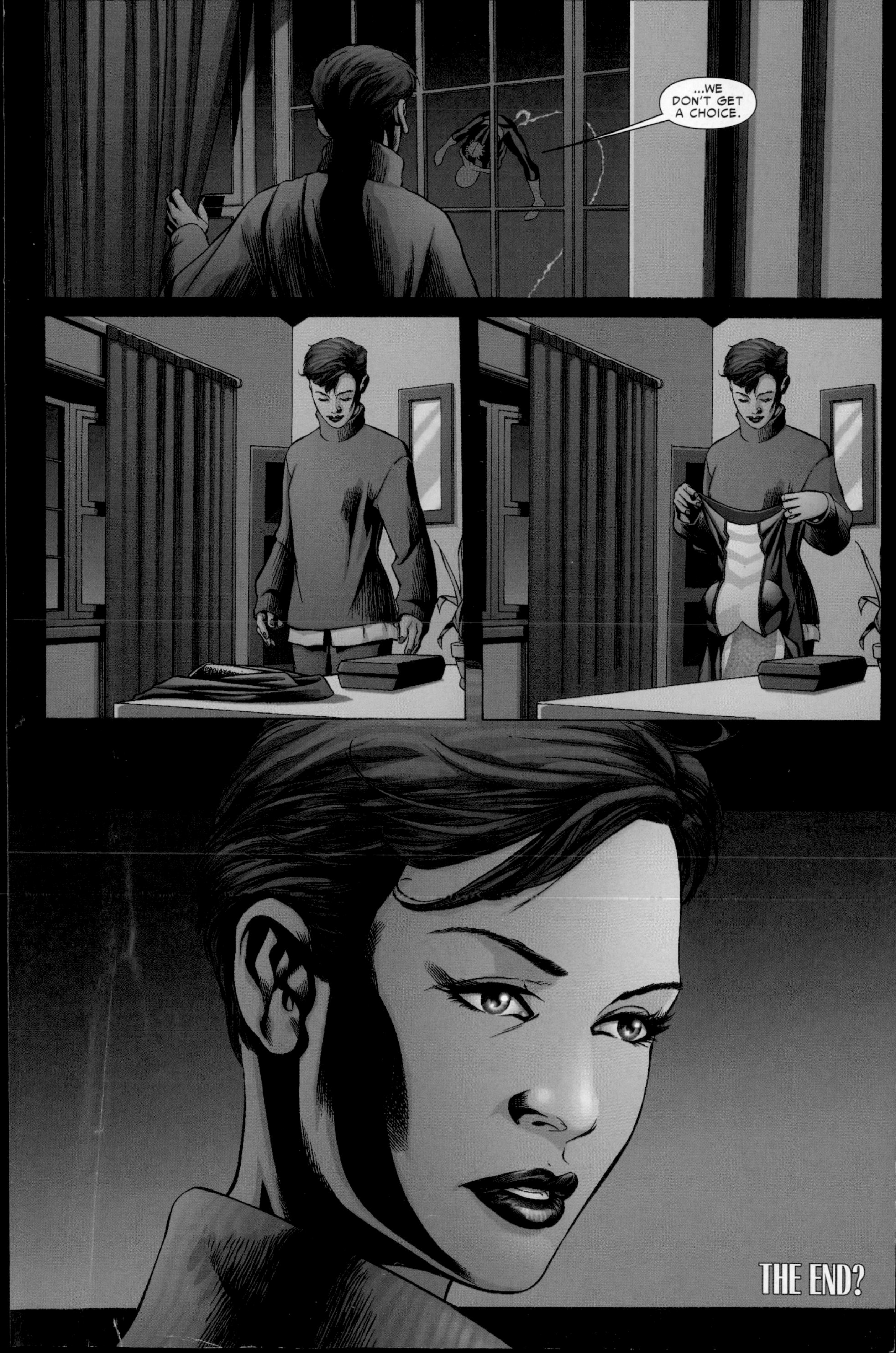
...WE DON'T GET A CHOICE.
THE END?

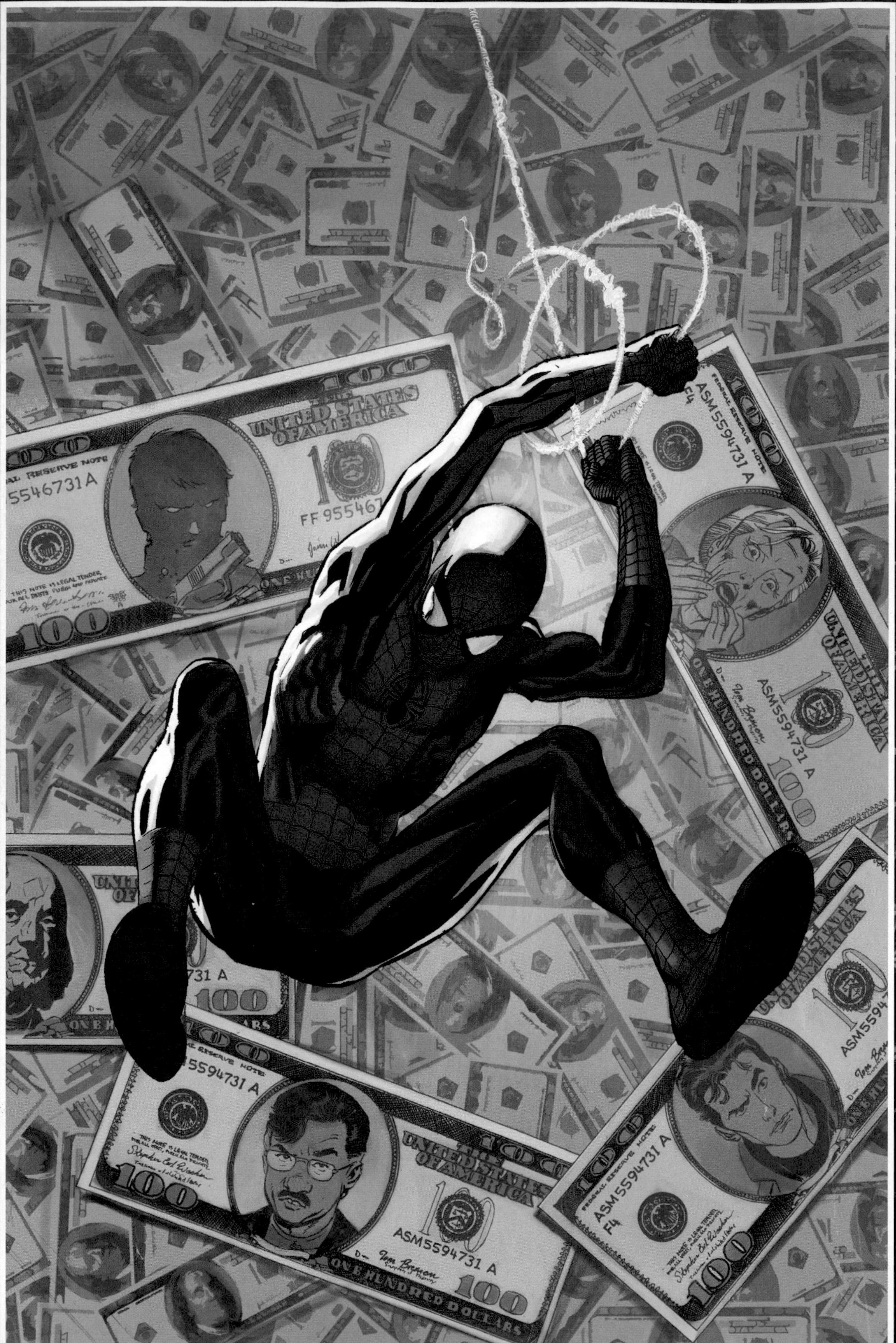

THE UNITED STATES OF AMERICA
FEDERAL RESERVE NOTE
5546731 A
FF 955467
THIS NOTE IS LEGAL TENDER FOR ALL DEBTS PUBLIC AND PRIVATE
100
ASM5594731 A
F4
ONE HUNDRED DOLLARS

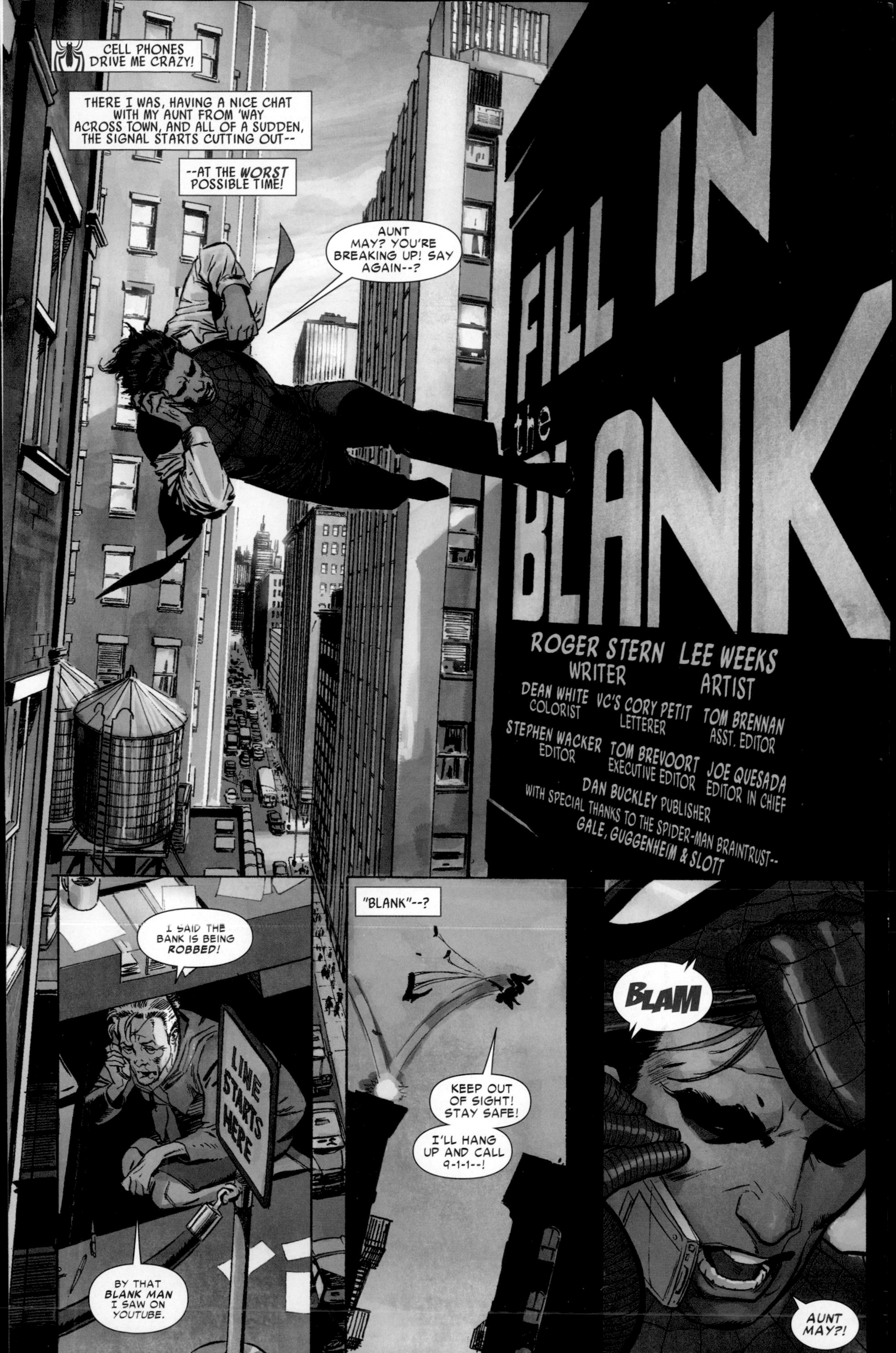

CELL PHONES DRIVE ME CRAZY!
THERE I WAS, HAVING A NICE CHAT WITH MY AUNT FROM 'WAY ACROSS TOWN, AND ALL OF A SUDDEN, THE SIGNAL STARTS CUTTING OUT--
--AT THE WORST POSSIBLE TIME!
AUNT MAY? YOU'RE BREAKING UP! SAY AGAIN--?
FILL IN the BLANK
ROGER STERN WRITER
LEE WEEKS ARTIST
DEAN WHITE COLORIST
VC'S CORY PETIT LETTERER
TOM BRENNAN ASST. EDITOR
STEPHEN WACKER EDITOR
TOM BREVOORT EXECUTIVE EDITOR
JOE QUESADA EDITOR IN CHIEF
DAN BUCKLEY PUBLISHER
WITH SPECIAL THANKS TO THE SPIDER-MAN BRAINTRUST-- GALE, GUGGENHEIM & SLOTT
I SAID THE BANK IS BEING ROBBED!
LINE STARTS HERE
BY THAT BLANK MAN I SAW ON YOUTUBE.
"BLANK"--?
KEEP OUT OF SIGHT! STAY SAFE!
I'LL HANG UP AND CALL 9-1-1--!
BLAM
AUNT MAY?!

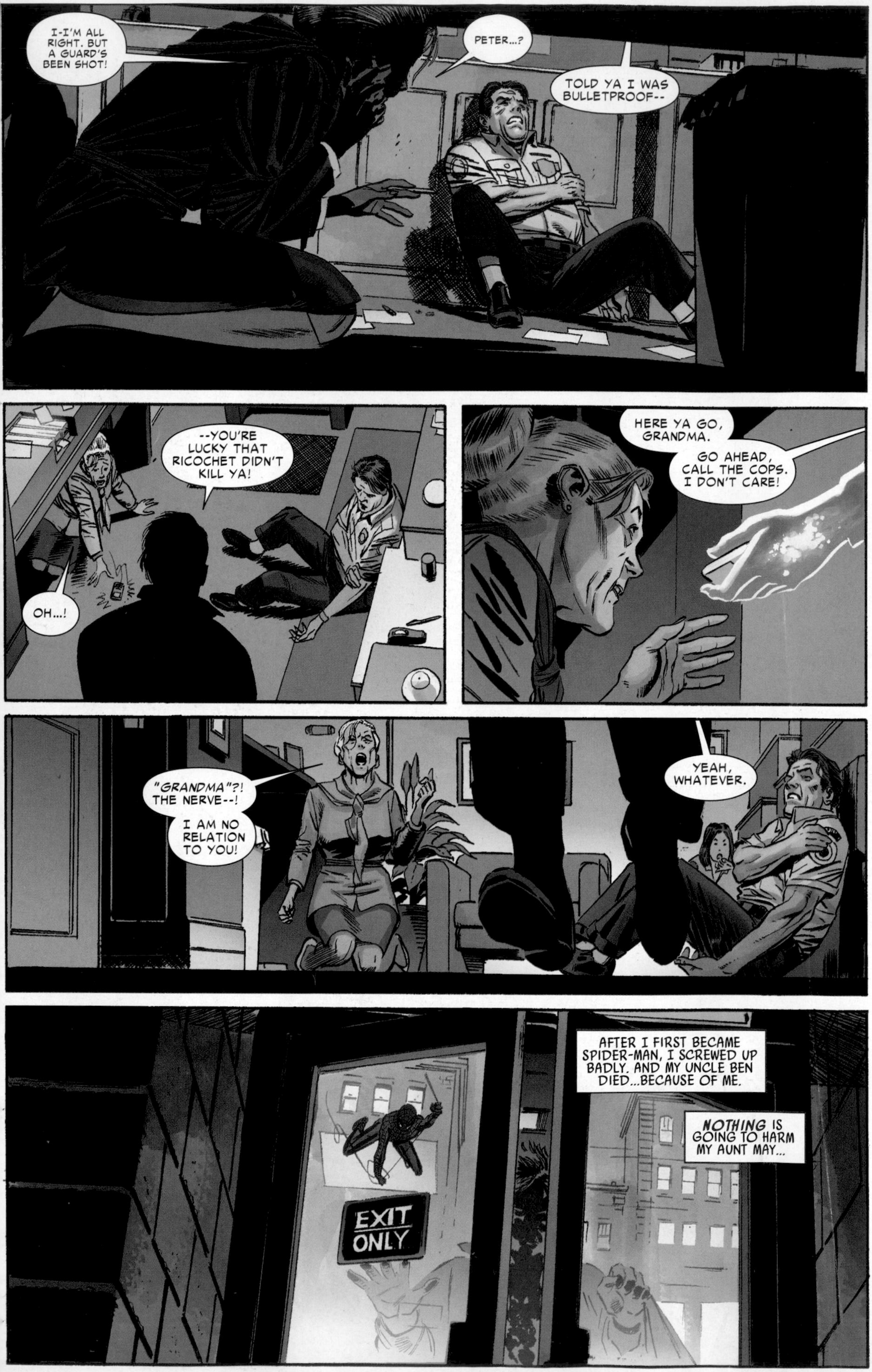
I-I'M ALL RIGHT. BUT A GUARD'S BEEN SHOT!
PETER...?
TOLD YA I WAS BULLETPROOF--
--YOU'RE LUCKY THAT RICOCHET DIDN'T KILL YA!
OH...!
HERE YA GO, GRANDMA.
GO AHEAD, CALL THE COPS. I DON'T CARE!
"GRANDMA"?! THE NERVE--!
I AM NO RELATION TO YOU!
YEAH, WHATEVER.
AFTER I FIRST BECAME SPIDER-MAN, I SCREWED UP BADLY. AND MY UNCLE BEN DIED...BECAUSE OF ME.
NOTHING IS GOING TO HARM MY AUNT MAY...
EXIT ONLY

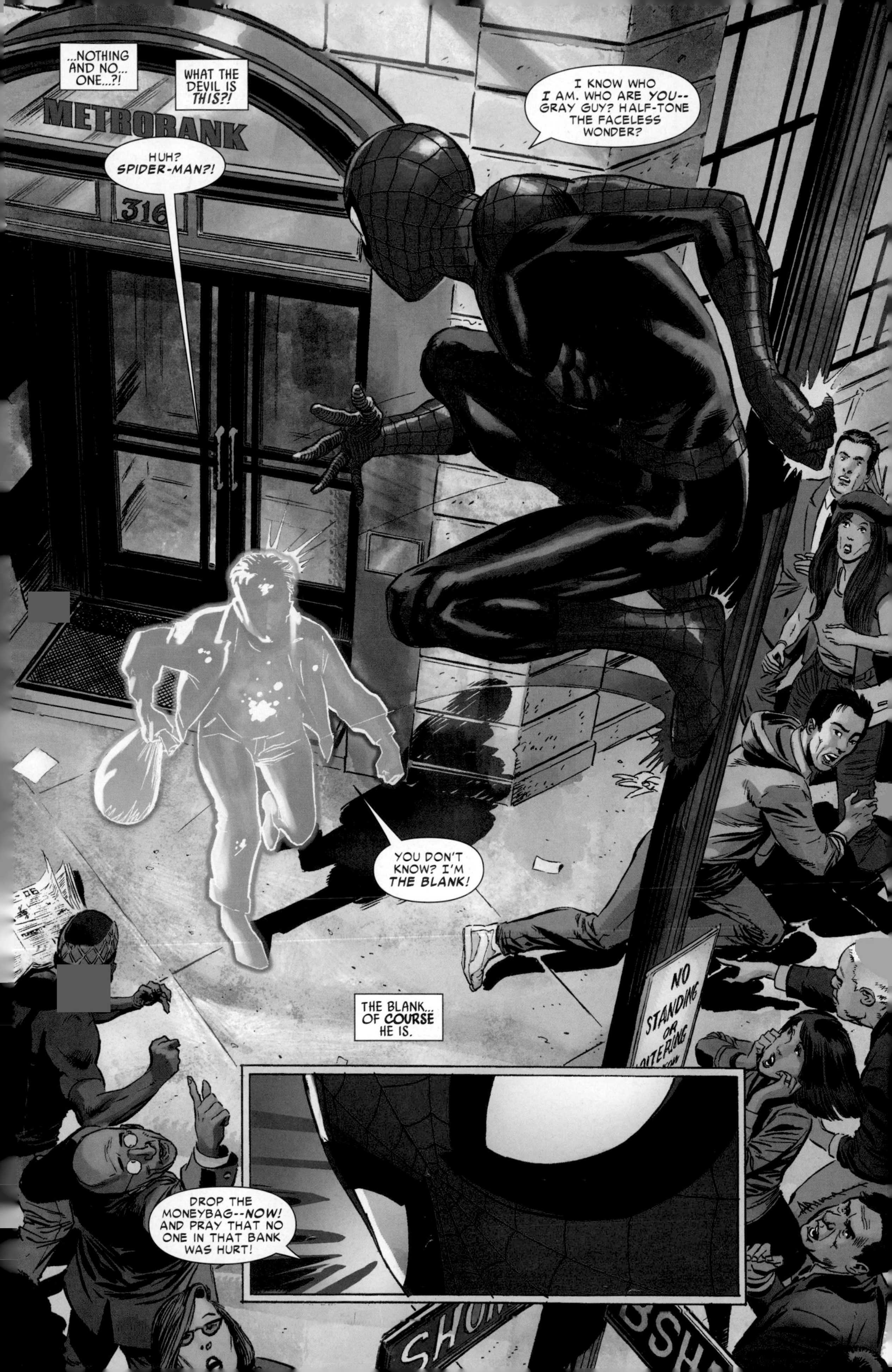
...NOTHING AND NO... ONE...?!
WHAT THE DEVIL IS THIS?!
METROBANK
316
HUH? SPIDER-MAN?!
I KNOW WHO I AM. WHO ARE YOU-- GRAY GUY? HALF-TONE THE FACELESS WONDER?
YOU DON'T KNOW? I'M THE BLANK!
THE BLANK... OF COURSE HE IS.
NO STANDING OR LOITERING
DROP THE MONEYBAG--NOW! AND PRAY THAT NO ONE IN THAT BANK WAS HURT!

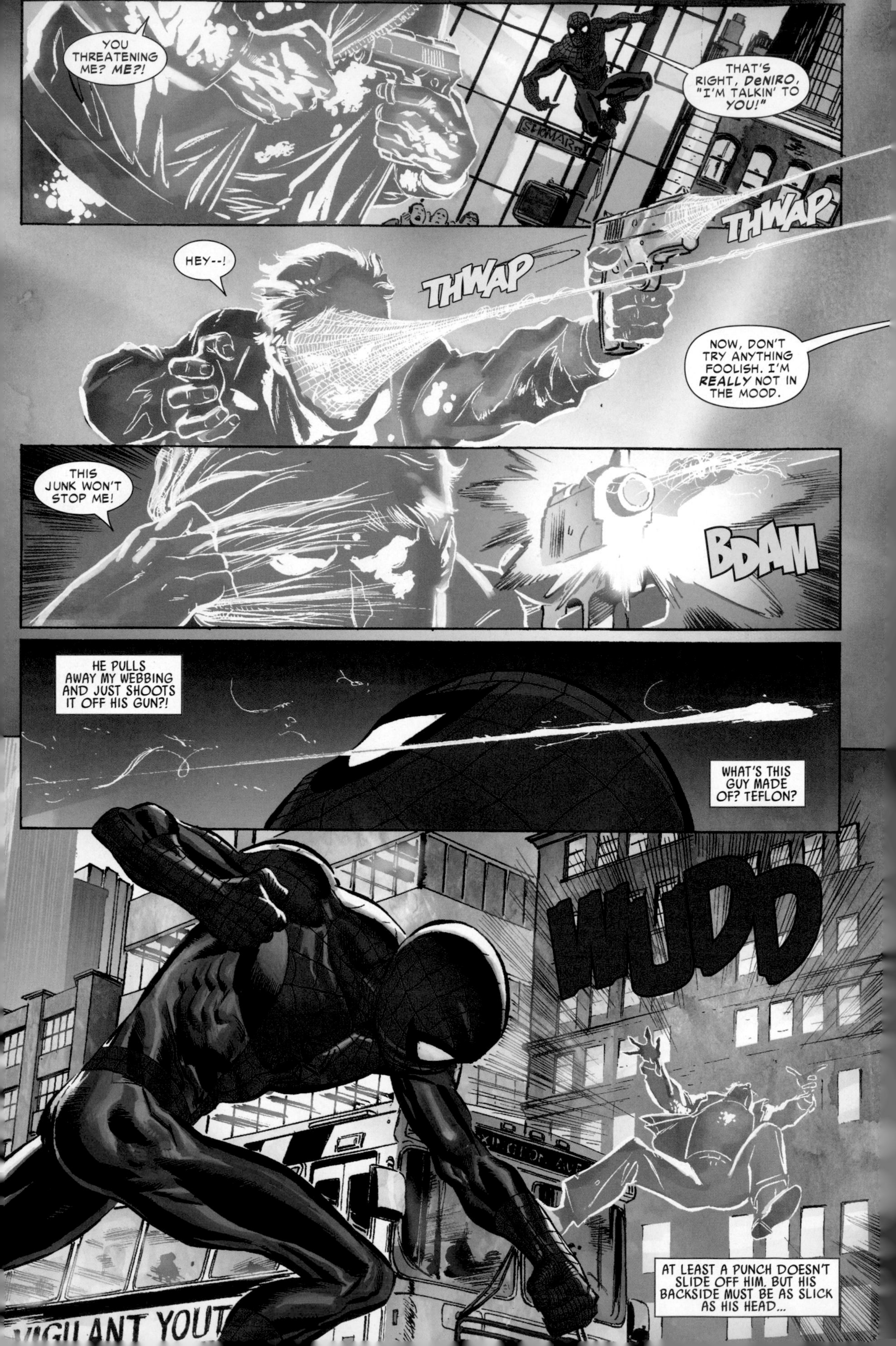
YOU THREATENING ME? *ME?!*
THAT'S RIGHT, *DeNIRO*, "I'M TALKIN' TO YOU!"
THWAP
THWAP
HEY--!
NOW, DON'T TRY ANYTHING FOOLISH. I'M *REALLY* NOT IN THE MOOD.
THIS JUNK WON'T STOP ME!
BDAM
HE PULLS AWAY MY WEBBING AND JUST SHOOTS IT OFF HIS GUN?!
WHAT'S THIS GUY MADE OF? TEFLON?
WUDD
AT LEAST A PUNCH DOESN'T SLIDE OFF HIM. BUT HIS BACKSIDE MUST BE AS SLICK AS HIS HEAD...
VIGILANT YOUT

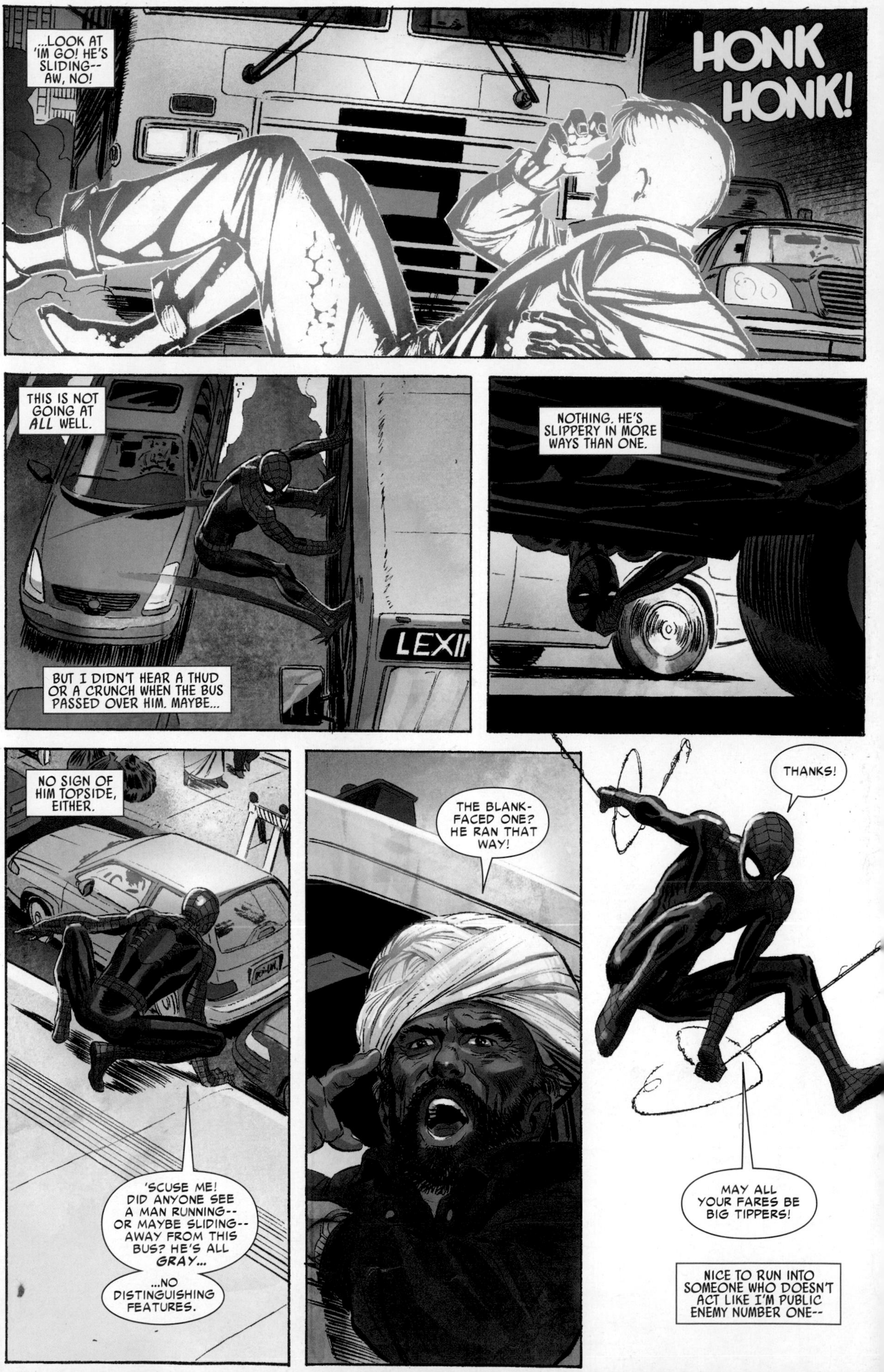
...LOOK AT 'IM GO! HE'S SLIDING-- AW, NO!
HONK HONK!
THIS IS NOT GOING AT ALL WELL.
LEXIN
BUT I DIDN'T HEAR A THUD OR A CRUNCH WHEN THE BUS PASSED OVER HIM. MAYBE...
NOTHING. HE'S SLIPPERY IN MORE WAYS THAN ONE.
NO SIGN OF HIM TOPSIDE, EITHER.
'SCUSE ME! DID ANYONE SEE A MAN RUNNING-- OR MAYBE SLIDING-- AWAY FROM THIS BUS? HE'S ALL GRAY...
...NO DISTINGUISHING FEATURES.
THE BLANK-FACED ONE? HE RAN THAT WAY!
THANKS!
MAY ALL YOUR FARES BE BIG TIPPERS!
NICE TO RUN INTO SOMEONE WHO DOESN'T ACT LIKE I'M PUBLIC ENEMY NUMBER ONE--

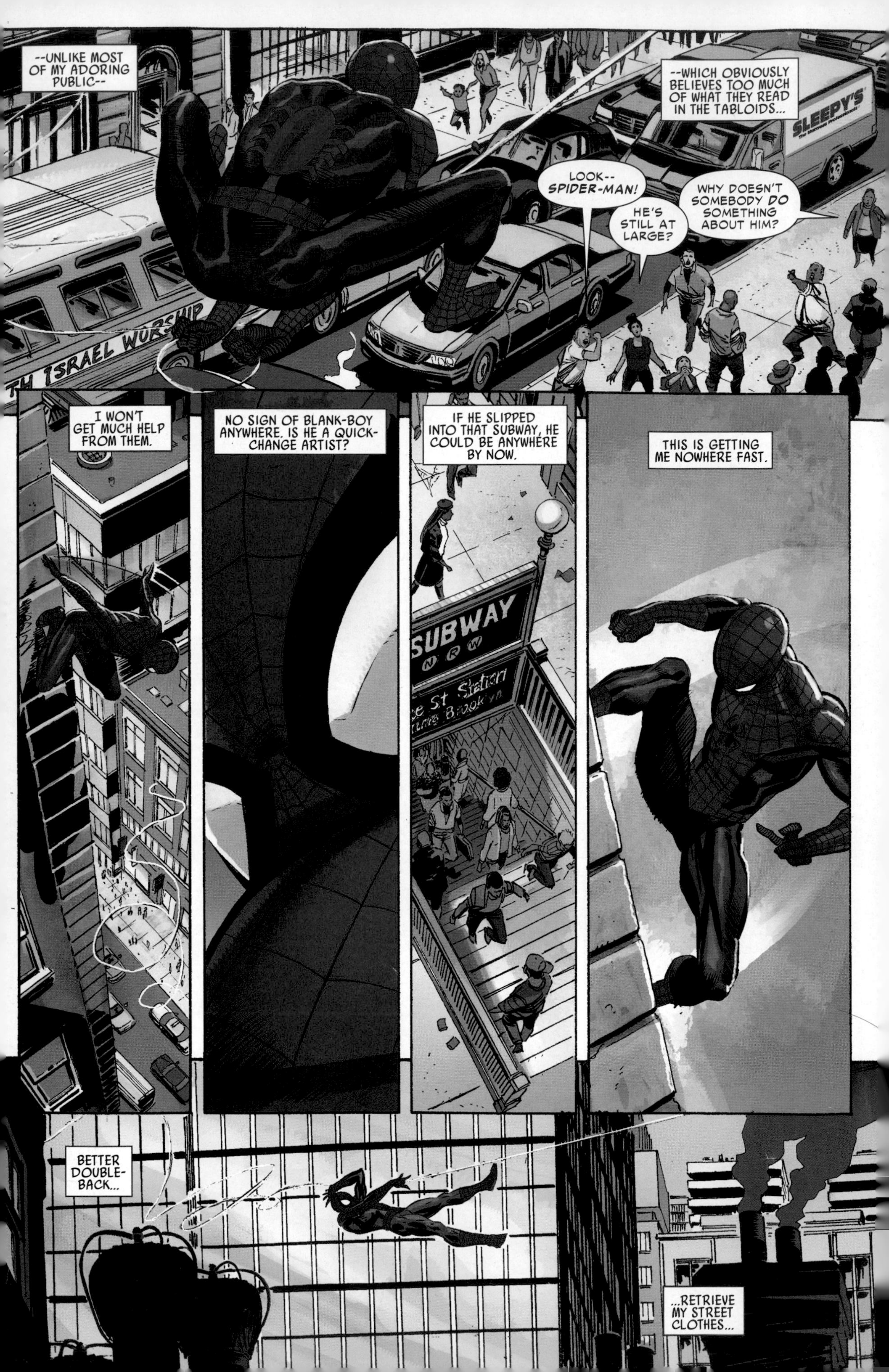
--UNLIKE MOST OF MY ADORING PUBLIC--
--WHICH OBVIOUSLY BELIEVES TOO MUCH OF WHAT THEY READ IN THE TABLOIDS...
SLEEPY'S
LOOK-- SPIDER-MAN!
HE'S STILL AT LARGE?
WHY DOESN'T SOMEBODY DO SOMETHING ABOUT HIM?
I WON'T GET MUCH HELP FROM THEM.
NO SIGN OF BLANK-BOY ANYWHERE. IS HE A QUICK-CHANGE ARTIST?
IF HE SLIPPED INTO THAT SUBWAY, HE COULD BE ANYWHERE BY NOW.
SUBWAY
N R W
THIS IS GETTING ME NOWHERE FAST.
BETTER DOUBLE-BACK...
...RETRIEVE MY STREET CLOTHES...

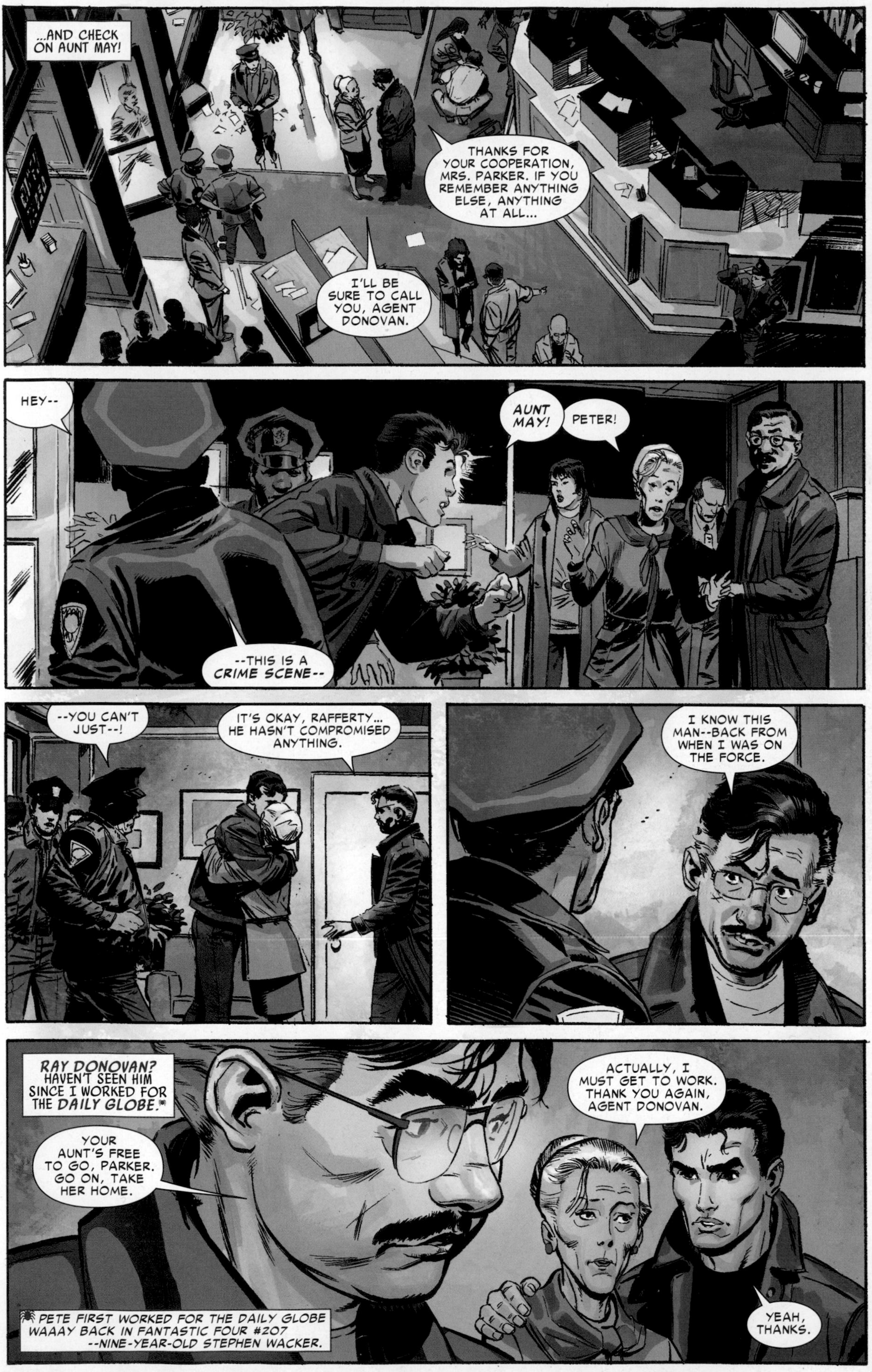

...AND CHECK ON AUNT MAY!
THANKS FOR YOUR COOPERATION, MRS. PARKER. IF YOU REMEMBER ANYTHING ELSE, ANYTHING AT ALL...
I'LL BE SURE TO CALL YOU, AGENT DONOVAN.
HEY--
AUNT MAY!
PETER!
--THIS IS A CRIME SCENE--
--YOU CAN'T JUST--!
IT'S OKAY, RAFFERTY... HE HASN'T COMPROMISED ANYTHING.
I KNOW THIS MAN--BACK FROM WHEN I WAS ON THE FORCE.
RAY DONOVAN? HAVEN'T SEEN HIM SINCE I WORKED FOR THE DAILY GLOBE.
YOUR AUNT'S FREE TO GO, PARKER. GO ON, TAKE HER HOME.
ACTUALLY, I MUST GET TO WORK. THANK YOU AGAIN, AGENT DONOVAN.
YEAH, THANKS.
PETE FIRST WORKED FOR THE DAILY GLOBE WAAAY BACK IN FANTASTIC FOUR #207 --NINE-YEAR-OLD STEPHEN WACKER.

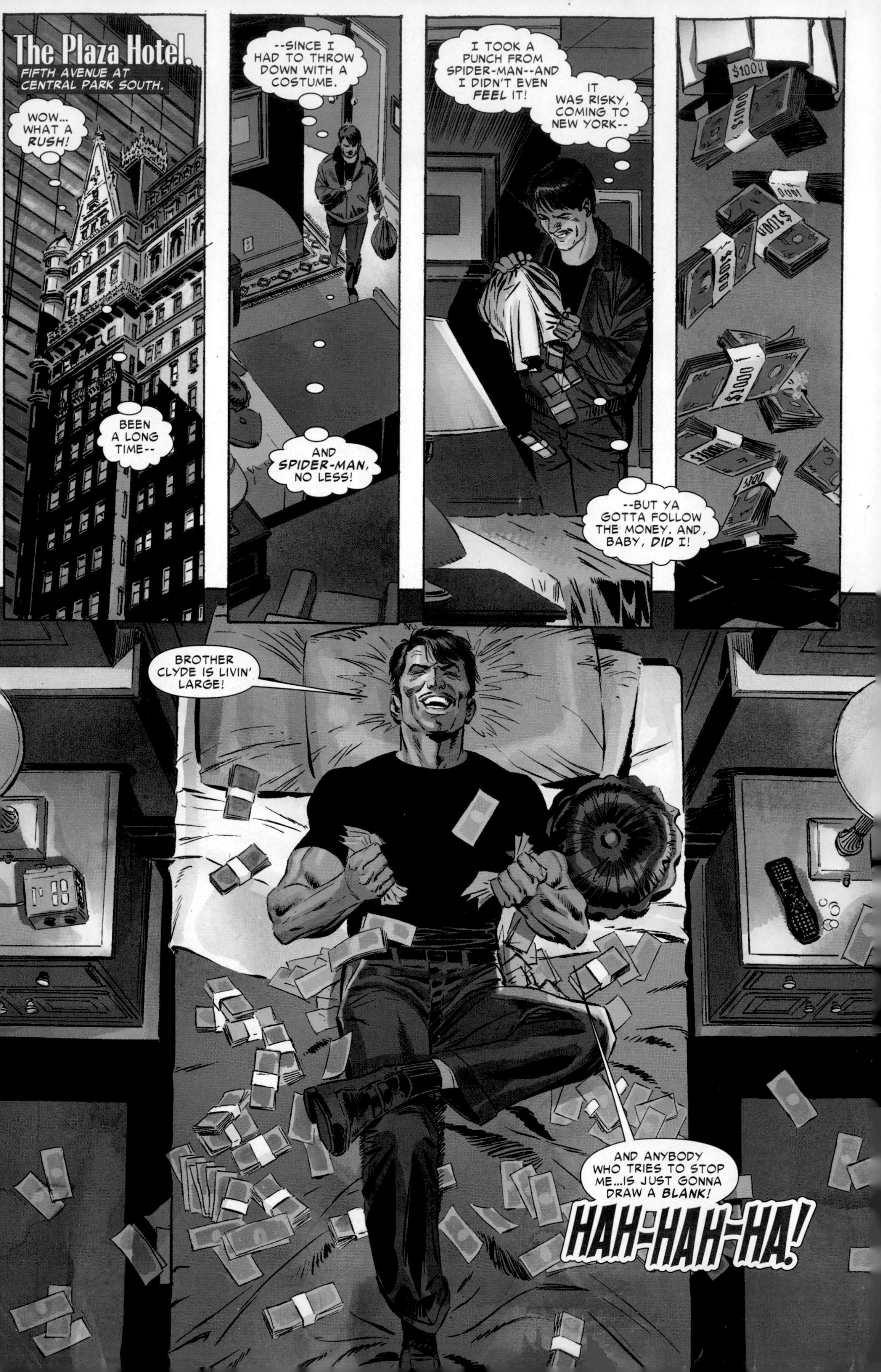
The Plaza Hotel.
FIFTH AVENUE AT CENTRAL PARK SOUTH.
WOW... WHAT A RUSH!
BEEN A LONG TIME--
--SINCE I HAD TO THROW DOWN WITH A COSTUME.
AND SPIDER-MAN, NO LESS!
I TOOK A PUNCH FROM SPIDER-MAN--AND I DIDN'T EVEN FEEL IT!
IT WAS RISKY, COMING TO NEW YORK--
--BUT YA GOTTA FOLLOW THE MONEY. AND, BABY, DID I!
BROTHER CLYDE IS LIVIN' LARGE!
AND ANYBODY WHO TRIES TO STOP ME...IS JUST GONNA DRAW A BLANK!
HAH-HAH-HA!

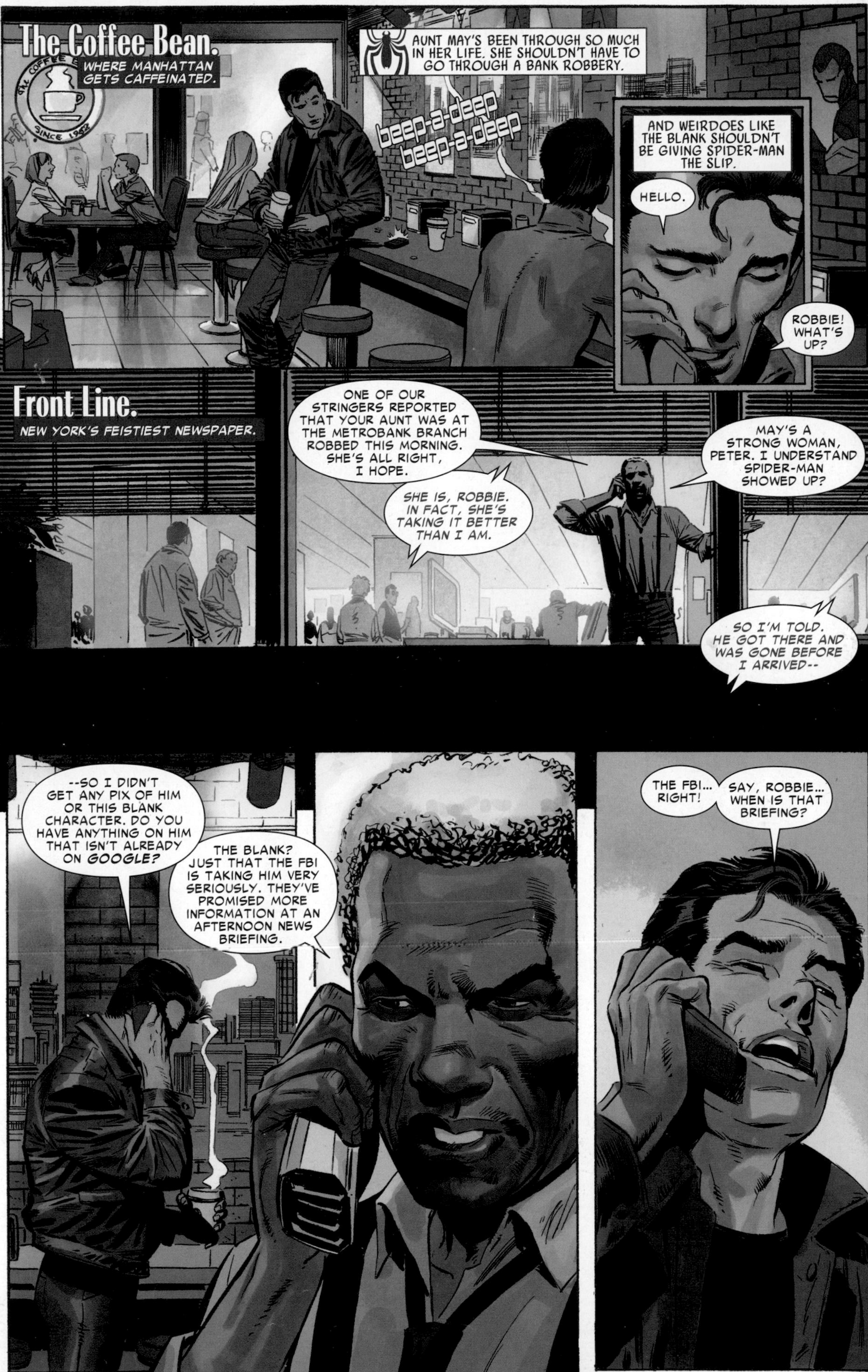
The Coffee Bean.
WHERE MANHATTAN GETS CAFFEINATED.
AUNT MAY'S BEEN THROUGH SO MUCH IN HER LIFE. SHE SHOULDN'T HAVE TO GO THROUGH A BANK ROBBERY.
beep-a-deep beep-a-deep
AND WEIRDOES LIKE THE BLANK SHOULDN'T BE GIVING SPIDER-MAN THE SLIP.
HELLO.
ROBBIE! WHAT'S UP?
Front Line.
NEW YORK'S FEISTIEST NEWSPAPER.
ONE OF OUR STRINGERS REPORTED THAT YOUR AUNT WAS AT THE METROBANK BRANCH ROBBED THIS MORNING. SHE'S ALL RIGHT, I HOPE.
SHE IS, ROBBIE. IN FACT, SHE'S TAKING IT BETTER THAN I AM.
MAY'S A STRONG WOMAN, PETER. I UNDERSTAND SPIDER-MAN SHOWED UP?
SO I'M TOLD. HE GOT THERE AND WAS GONE BEFORE I ARRIVED--
--SO I DIDN'T GET ANY PIX OF HIM OR THIS BLANK CHARACTER. DO YOU HAVE ANYTHING ON HIM THAT ISN'T ALREADY ON GOOGLE?
THE BLANK? JUST THAT THE FBI IS TAKING HIM VERY SERIOUSLY. THEY'VE PROMISED MORE INFORMATION AT AN AFTERNOON NEWS BRIEFING.
THE FBI... RIGHT!
SAY, ROBBIE... WHEN IS THAT BRIEFING?

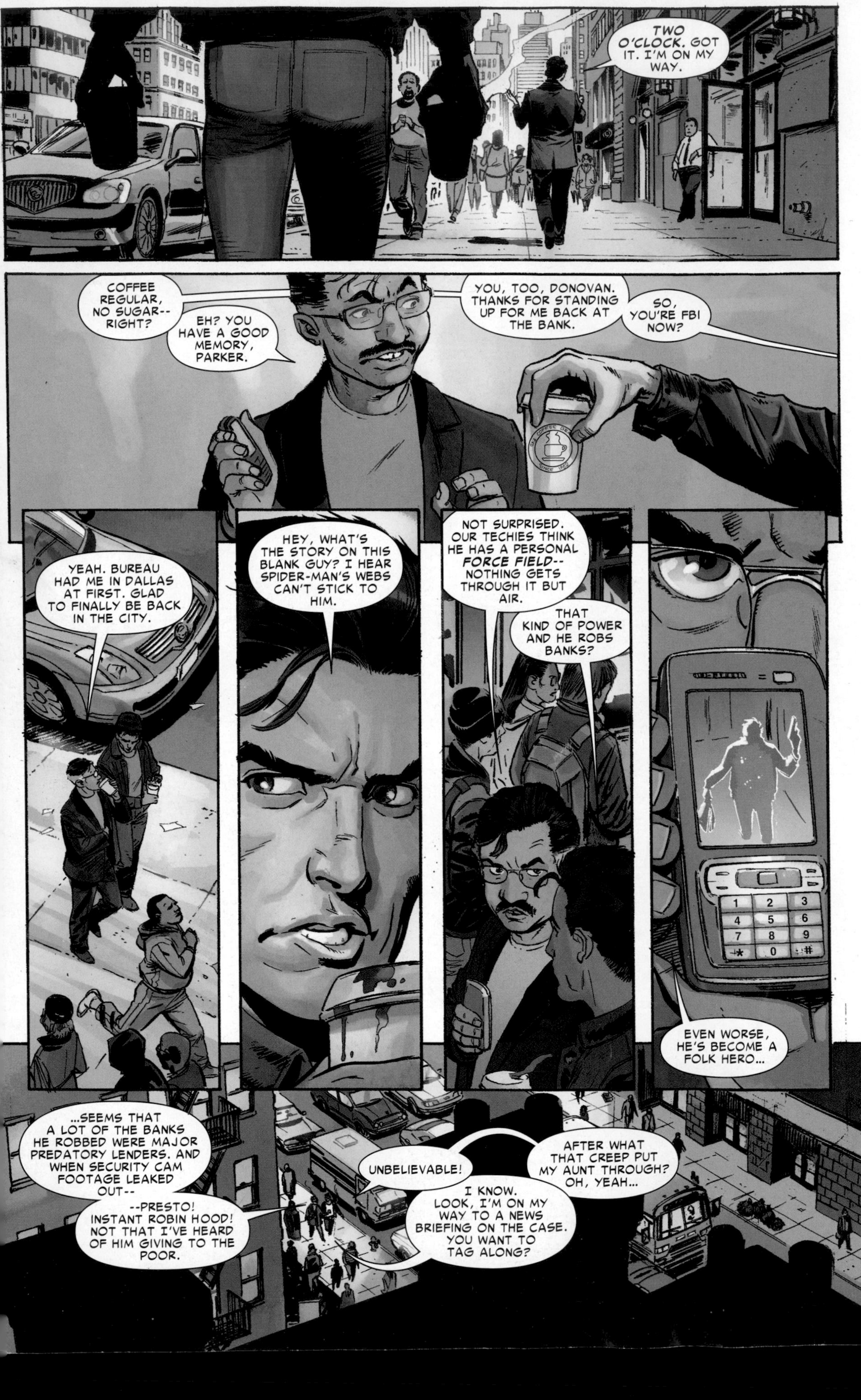
TWO O'CLOCK. GOT IT. I'M ON MY WAY.
COFFEE REGULAR, NO SUGAR-- RIGHT?
EH? YOU HAVE A GOOD MEMORY, PARKER.
YOU, TOO, DONOVAN. THANKS FOR STANDING UP FOR ME BACK AT THE BANK.
SO, YOU'RE FBI NOW?
YEAH. BUREAU HAD ME IN DALLAS AT FIRST. GLAD TO FINALLY BE BACK IN THE CITY.
HEY, WHAT'S THE STORY ON THIS BLANK GUY? I HEAR SPIDER-MAN'S WEBS CAN'T STICK TO HIM.
NOT SURPRISED. OUR TECHIES THINK HE HAS A PERSONAL FORCE FIELD-- NOTHING GETS THROUGH IT BUT AIR.
THAT KIND OF POWER AND HE ROBS BANKS?
EVEN WORSE, HE'S BECOME A FOLK HERO...
...SEEMS THAT A LOT OF THE BANKS HE ROBBED WERE MAJOR PREDATORY LENDERS. AND WHEN SECURITY CAM FOOTAGE LEAKED OUT--
--PRESTO! INSTANT ROBIN HOOD! NOT THAT I'VE HEARD OF HIM GIVING TO THE POOR.
UNBELIEVABLE!
AFTER WHAT THAT CREEP PUT MY AUNT THROUGH? OH, YEAH...
I KNOW. LOOK, I'M ON MY WAY TO A NEWS BRIEFING ON THE CASE. YOU WANT TO TAG ALONG?

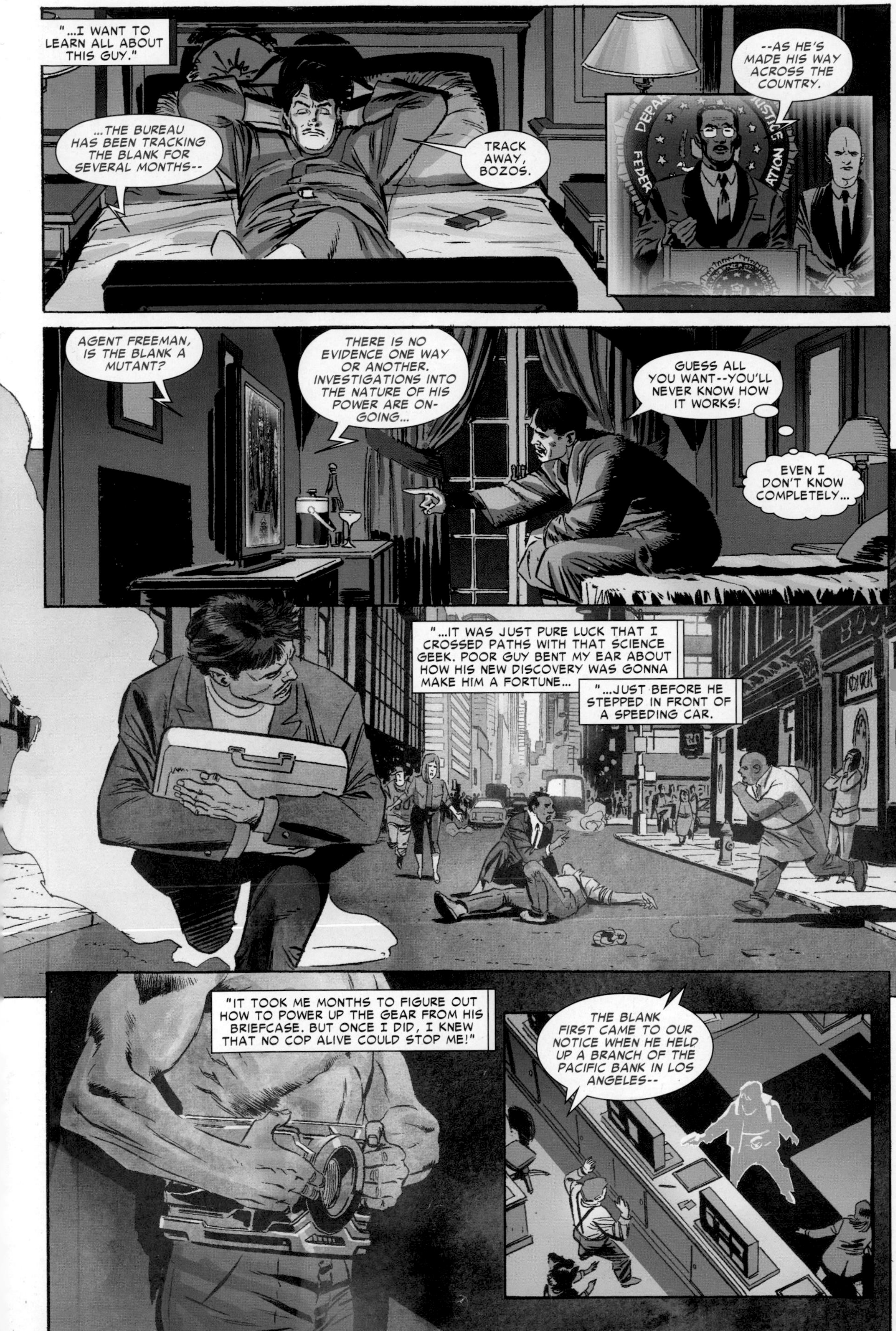

"...I WANT TO LEARN ALL ABOUT THIS GUY."
...THE BUREAU HAS BEEN TRACKING THE BLANK FOR SEVERAL MONTHS--
TRACK AWAY, BOZOS.
--AS HE'S MADE HIS WAY ACROSS THE COUNTRY.
AGENT FREEMAN, IS THE BLANK A MUTANT?
THERE IS NO EVIDENCE ONE WAY OR ANOTHER. INVESTIGATIONS INTO THE NATURE OF HIS POWER ARE ON-GOING...
GUESS ALL YOU WANT--YOU'LL NEVER KNOW HOW IT WORKS!
EVEN I DON'T KNOW COMPLETELY...
"...IT WAS JUST PURE LUCK THAT I CROSSED PATHS WITH THAT SCIENCE GEEK. POOR GUY BENT MY EAR ABOUT HOW HIS NEW DISCOVERY WAS GONNA MAKE HIM A FORTUNE...
"...JUST BEFORE HE STEPPED IN FRONT OF A SPEEDING CAR.
"IT TOOK ME MONTHS TO FIGURE OUT HOW TO POWER UP THE GEAR FROM HIS BRIEFCASE. BUT ONCE I DID, I KNEW THAT NO COP ALIVE COULD STOP ME!"
THE BLANK FIRST CAME TO OUR NOTICE WHEN HE HELD UP A BRANCH OF THE PACIFIC BANK IN LOS ANGELES--

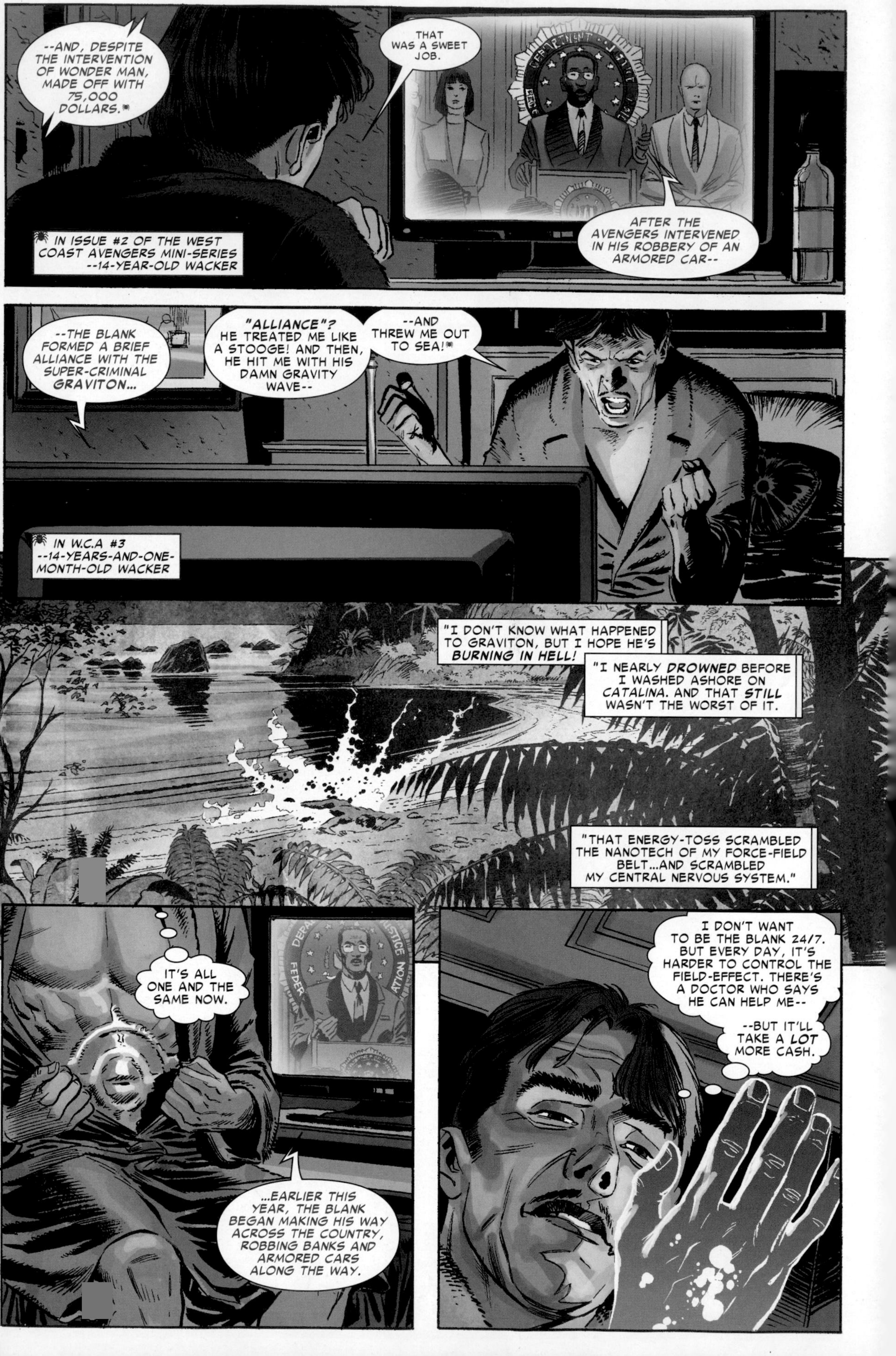
--AND, DESPITE THE INTERVENTION OF WONDER MAN, MADE OFF WITH 75,000 DOLLARS.*
THAT WAS A SWEET JOB.
AFTER THE AVENGERS INTERVENED IN HIS ROBBERY OF AN ARMORED CAR--
*IN ISSUE #2 OF THE WEST COAST AVENGERS MINI-SERIES --14-YEAR-OLD WACKER
--THE BLANK FORMED A BRIEF ALLIANCE WITH THE SUPER-CRIMINAL GRAVITON...
"ALLIANCE"? HE TREATED ME LIKE A STOOGE! AND THEN, HE HIT ME WITH HIS DAMN GRAVITY WAVE--
--AND THREW ME OUT TO SEA!*
*IN W.C.A #3 --14-YEARS-AND-ONE-MONTH-OLD WACKER
"I DON'T KNOW WHAT HAPPENED TO GRAVITON, BUT I HOPE HE'S BURNING IN HELL!
"I NEARLY DROWNED BEFORE I WASHED ASHORE ON CATALINA. AND THAT STILL WASN'T THE WORST OF IT.
"THAT ENERGY-TOSS SCRAMBLED THE NANOTECH OF MY FORCE-FIELD BELT...AND SCRAMBLED MY CENTRAL NERVOUS SYSTEM."
IT'S ALL ONE AND THE SAME NOW.
...EARLIER THIS YEAR, THE BLANK BEGAN MAKING HIS WAY ACROSS THE COUNTRY, ROBBING BANKS AND ARMORED CARS ALONG THE WAY.
I DON'T WANT TO BE THE BLANK 24/7. BUT EVERY DAY, IT'S HARDER TO CONTROL THE FIELD-EFFECT. THERE'S A DOCTOR WHO SAYS HE CAN HELP ME--
--BUT IT'LL TAKE A LOT MORE CASH.

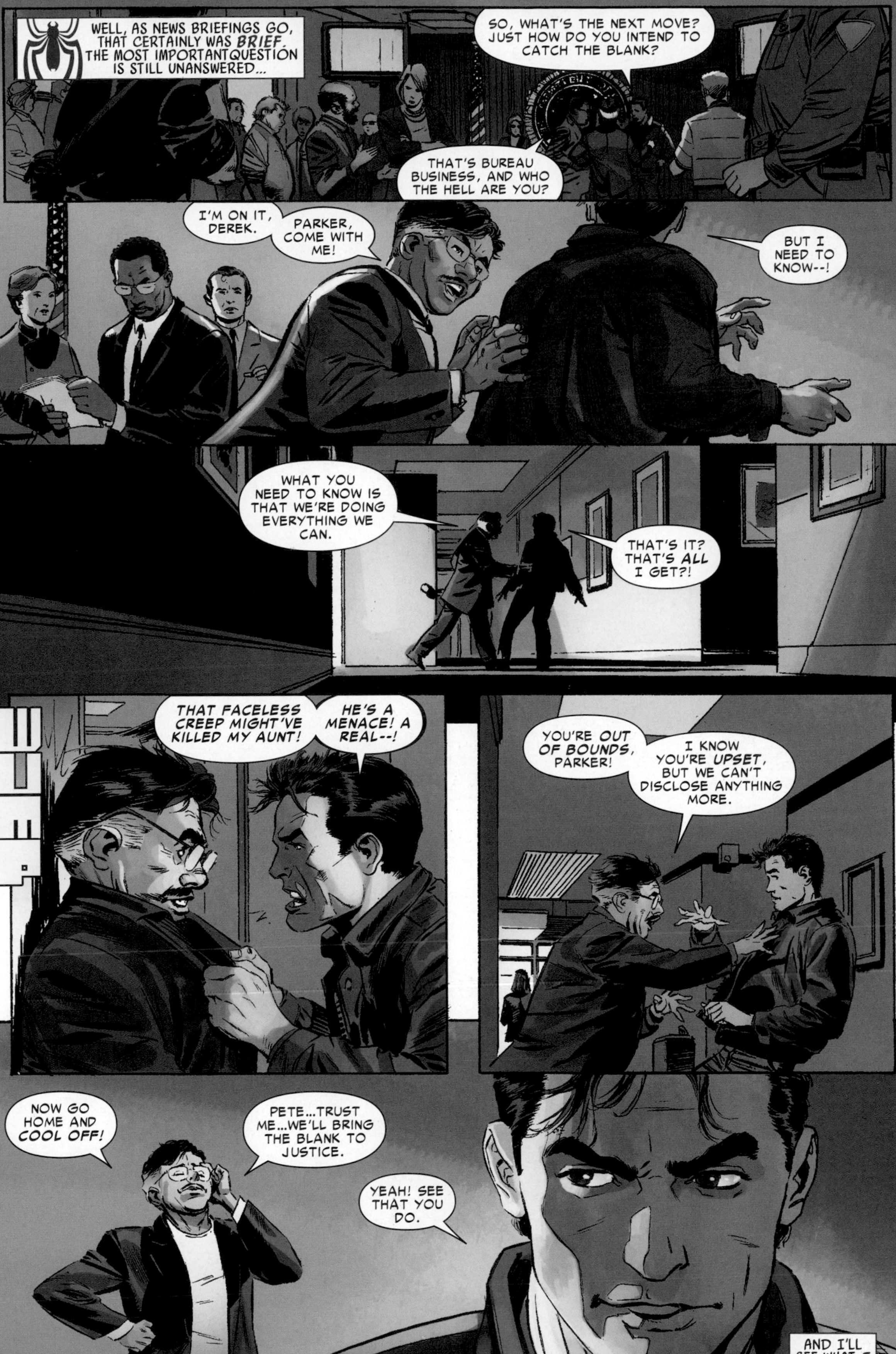

WELL, AS NEWS BRIEFINGS GO, THAT CERTAINLY WAS BRIEF. THE MOST IMPORTANTQUESTION IS STILL UNANSWERED...
SO, WHAT'S THE NEXT MOVE? JUST HOW DO YOU INTEND TO CATCH THE BLANK?
THAT'S BUREAU BUSINESS, AND WHO THE HELL ARE YOU?
I'M ON IT, DEREK.
PARKER, COME WITH ME!
BUT I NEED TO KNOW--!
WHAT YOU NEED TO KNOW IS THAT WE'RE DOING EVERYTHING WE CAN.
THAT'S IT? THAT'S ALL I GET?!
THAT FACELESS CREEP MIGHT'VE KILLED MY AUNT!
HE'S A MENACE! A REAL--!
YOU'RE OUT OF BOUNDS, PARKER!
I KNOW YOU'RE UPSET, BUT WE CAN'T DISCLOSE ANYTHING MORE.
NOW GO HOME AND COOL OFF!
PETE...TRUST ME...WE'LL BRING THE BLANK TO JUSTICE.
YEAH! SEE THAT YOU DO.
AND I'LL SEE WHAT I CAN DO.

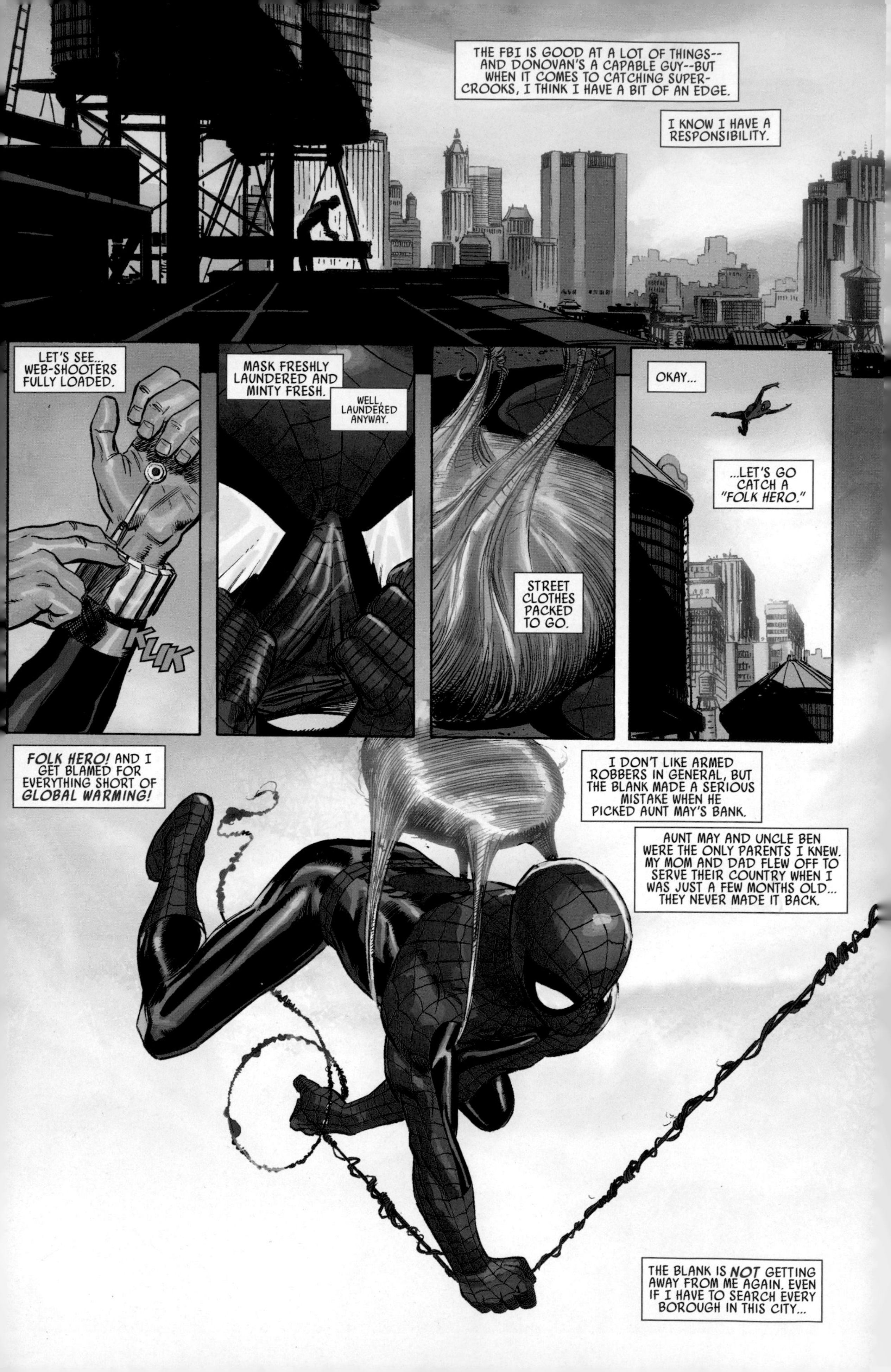
THE FBI IS GOOD AT A LOT OF THINGS-- AND DONOVAN'S A CAPABLE GUY--BUT WHEN IT COMES TO CATCHING SUPER-CROOKS, I THINK I HAVE A BIT OF AN EDGE.
I KNOW I HAVE A RESPONSIBILITY.
LET'S SEE... WEB-SHOOTERS FULLY LOADED.
KLIK
MASK FRESHLY LAUNDERED AND MINTY FRESH.
WELL, LAUNDERED ANYWAY.
STREET CLOTHES PACKED TO GO.
OKAY...
...LET'S GO CATCH A "FOLK HERO."
FOLK HERO! AND I GET BLAMED FOR EVERYTHING SHORT OF GLOBAL WARMING!
I DON'T LIKE ARMED ROBBERS IN GENERAL, BUT THE BLANK MADE A SERIOUS MISTAKE WHEN HE PICKED AUNT MAY'S BANK.
AUNT MAY AND UNCLE BEN WERE THE ONLY PARENTS I KNEW. MY MOM AND DAD FLEW OFF TO SERVE THEIR COUNTRY WHEN I WAS JUST A FEW MONTHS OLD... THEY NEVER MADE IT BACK.
THE BLANK IS NOT GETTING AWAY FROM ME AGAIN. EVEN IF I HAVE TO SEARCH EVERY BOROUGH IN THIS CITY...

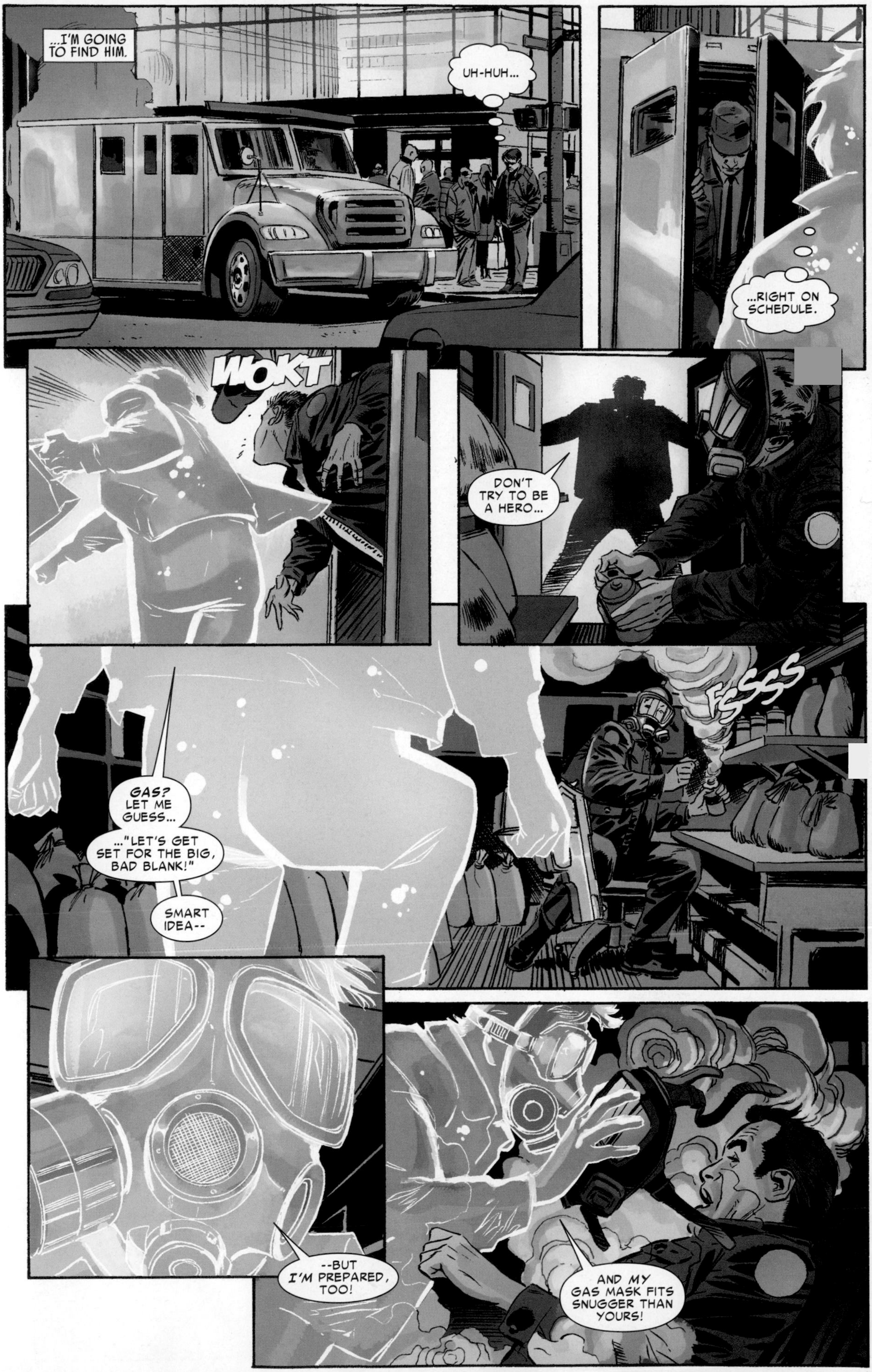

...I'M GOING TO FIND HIM.
UH-HUH...
...RIGHT ON SCHEDULE.
WOKT
DON'T TRY TO BE A HERO...
FSSSS
GAS? LET ME GUESS...
..."LET'S GET SET FOR THE BIG, BAD BLANK!"
SMART IDEA--
--BUT I'M PREPARED, TOO!
AND MY GAS MASK FITS SNUGGER THAN YOURS!

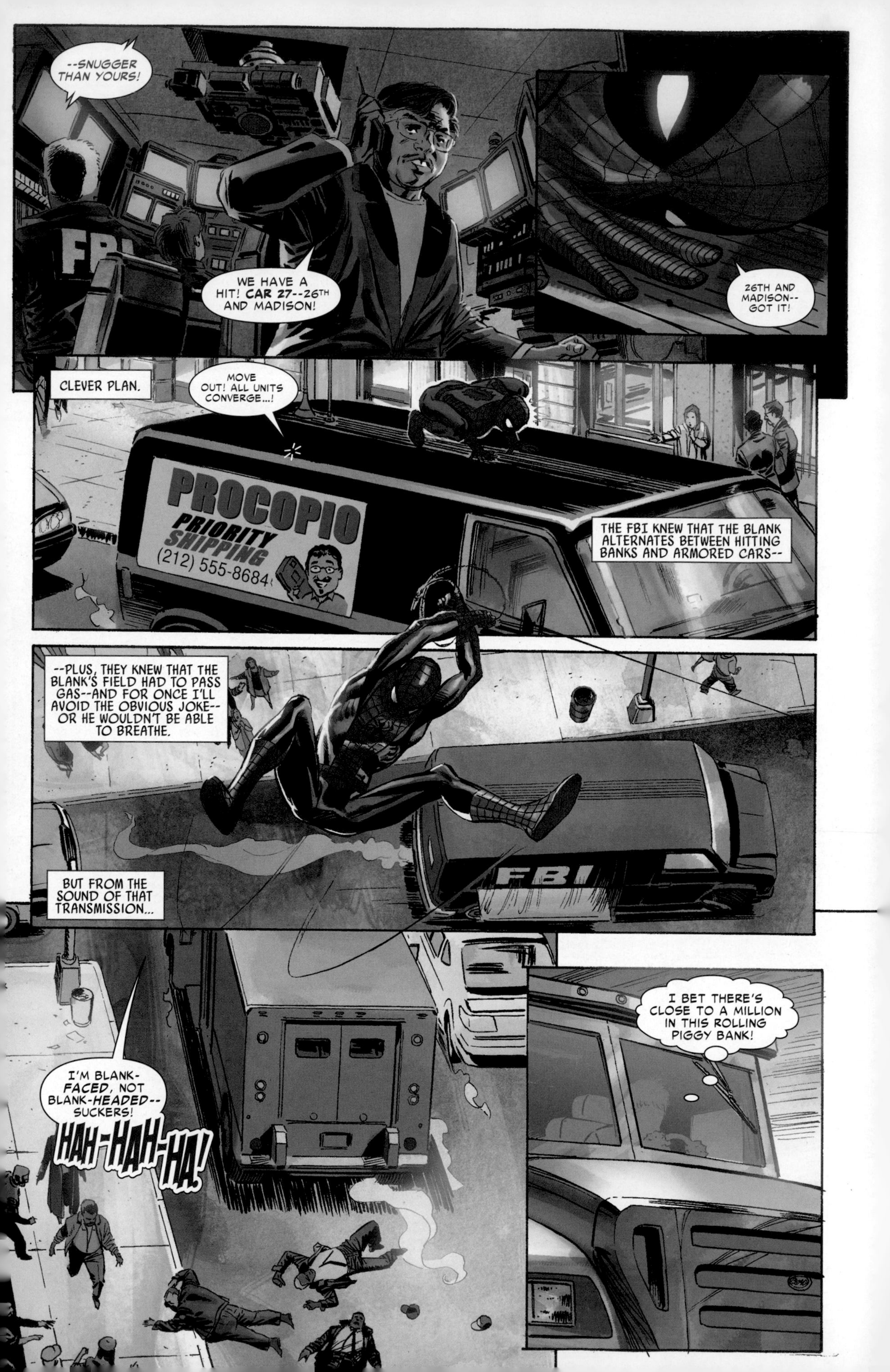
--SNUGGER THAN YOURS!
WE HAVE A HIT! CAR 27--26TH AND MADISON!
26TH AND MADISON--GOT IT!
CLEVER PLAN.
MOVE OUT! ALL UNITS CONVERGE...!
PROCOPIO PRIORITY SHIPPING (212) 555-8684
THE FBI KNEW THAT THE BLANK ALTERNATES BETWEEN HITTING BANKS AND ARMORED CARS--
--PLUS, THEY KNEW THAT THE BLANK'S FIELD HAD TO PASS GAS--AND FOR ONCE I'LL AVOID THE OBVIOUS JOKE--OR HE WOULDN'T BE ABLE TO BREATHE.
FBI
BUT FROM THE SOUND OF THAT TRANSMISSION...
I'M BLANK-FACED, NOT BLANK-HEADED--SUCKERS!
HAH-HAH-HA!
I BET THERE'S CLOSE TO A MILLION IN THIS ROLLING PIGGY BANK!

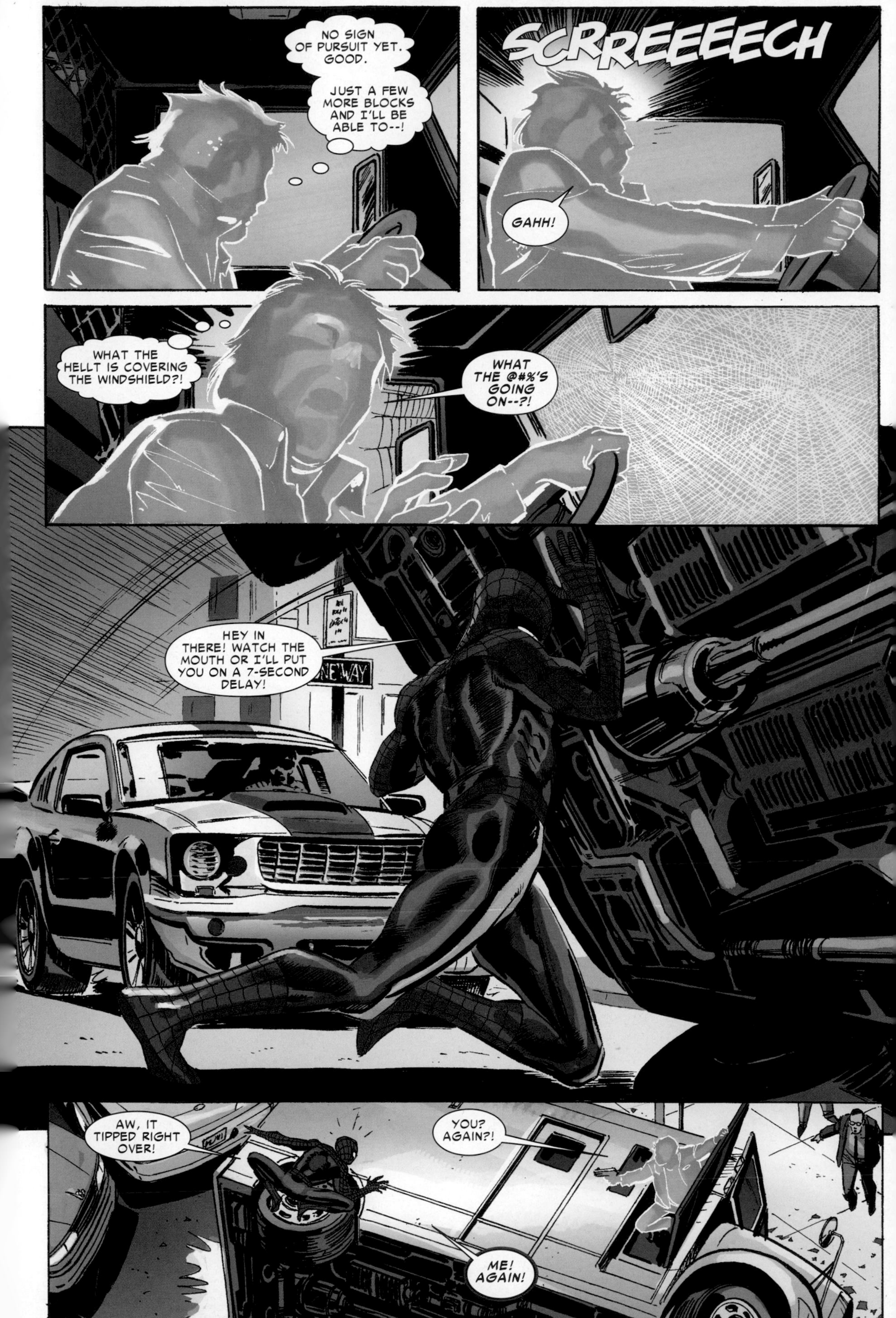
NO SIGN OF PURSUIT YET. GOOD.
JUST A FEW MORE BLOCKS AND I'LL BE ABLE TO--!
SCRREEEEECH
GAHH!
WHAT THE HELLT IS COVERING THE WINDSHIELD?!
WHAT THE @#%'S GOING ON--?!
HEY IN THERE! WATCH THE MOUTH OR I'LL PUT YOU ON A 7-SECOND DELAY!
ONE WAY
AW, IT TIPPED RIGHT OVER!
YOU? AGAIN?!
ME! AGAIN!

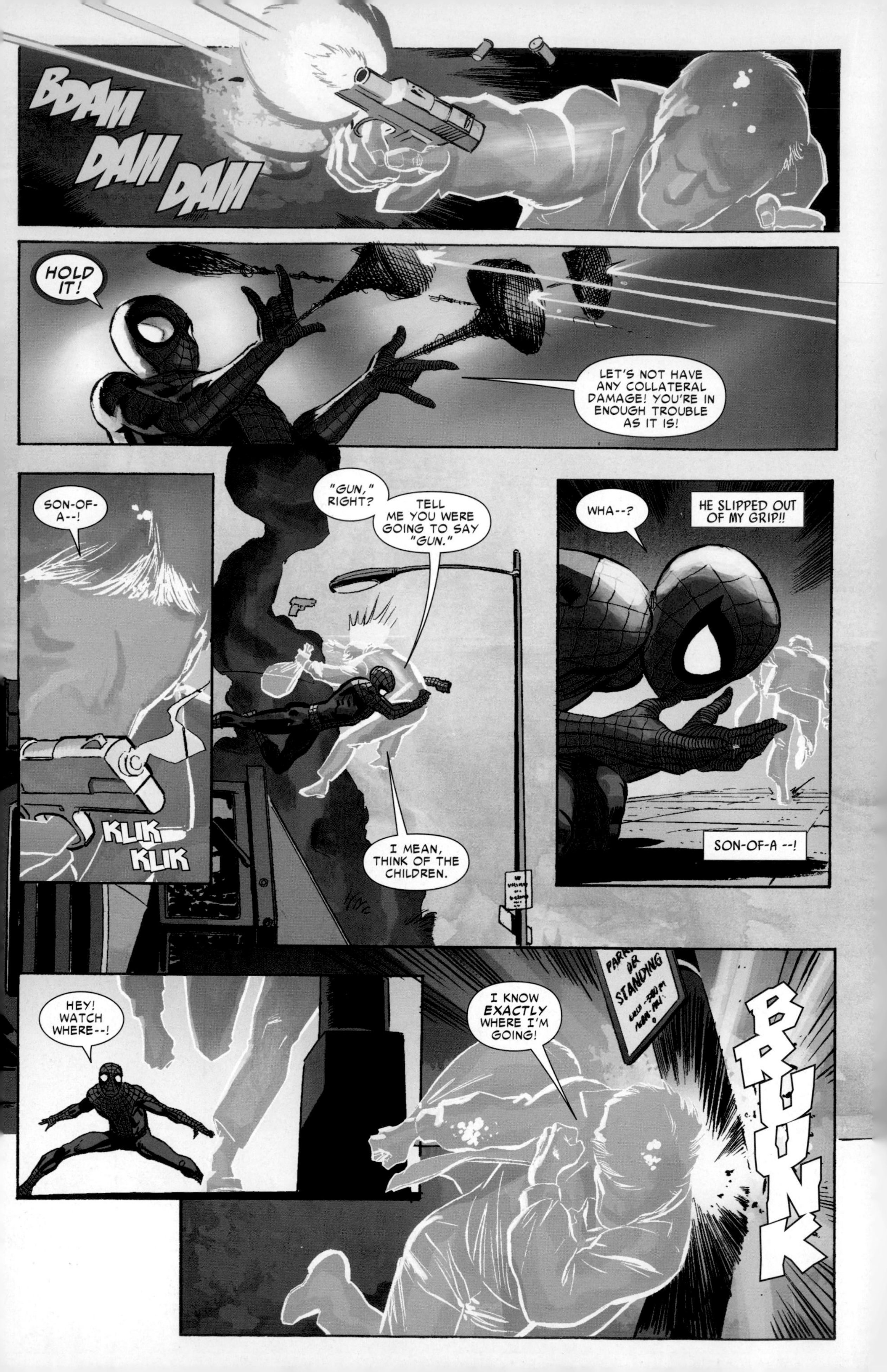
BDAM DAM DAM
HOLD IT!
LET'S NOT HAVE ANY COLLATERAL DAMAGE! YOU'RE IN ENOUGH TROUBLE AS IT IS!
SON-OF-A--!
KLIK KLIK
"GUN," RIGHT?
TELL ME YOU WERE GOING TO SAY "GUN."
I MEAN, THINK OF THE CHILDREN.
WHA--?
HE SLIPPED OUT OF MY GRIP!!
SON-OF-A --!
HEY! WATCH WHERE--!
I KNOW EXACTLY WHERE I'M GOING!
BRUNK

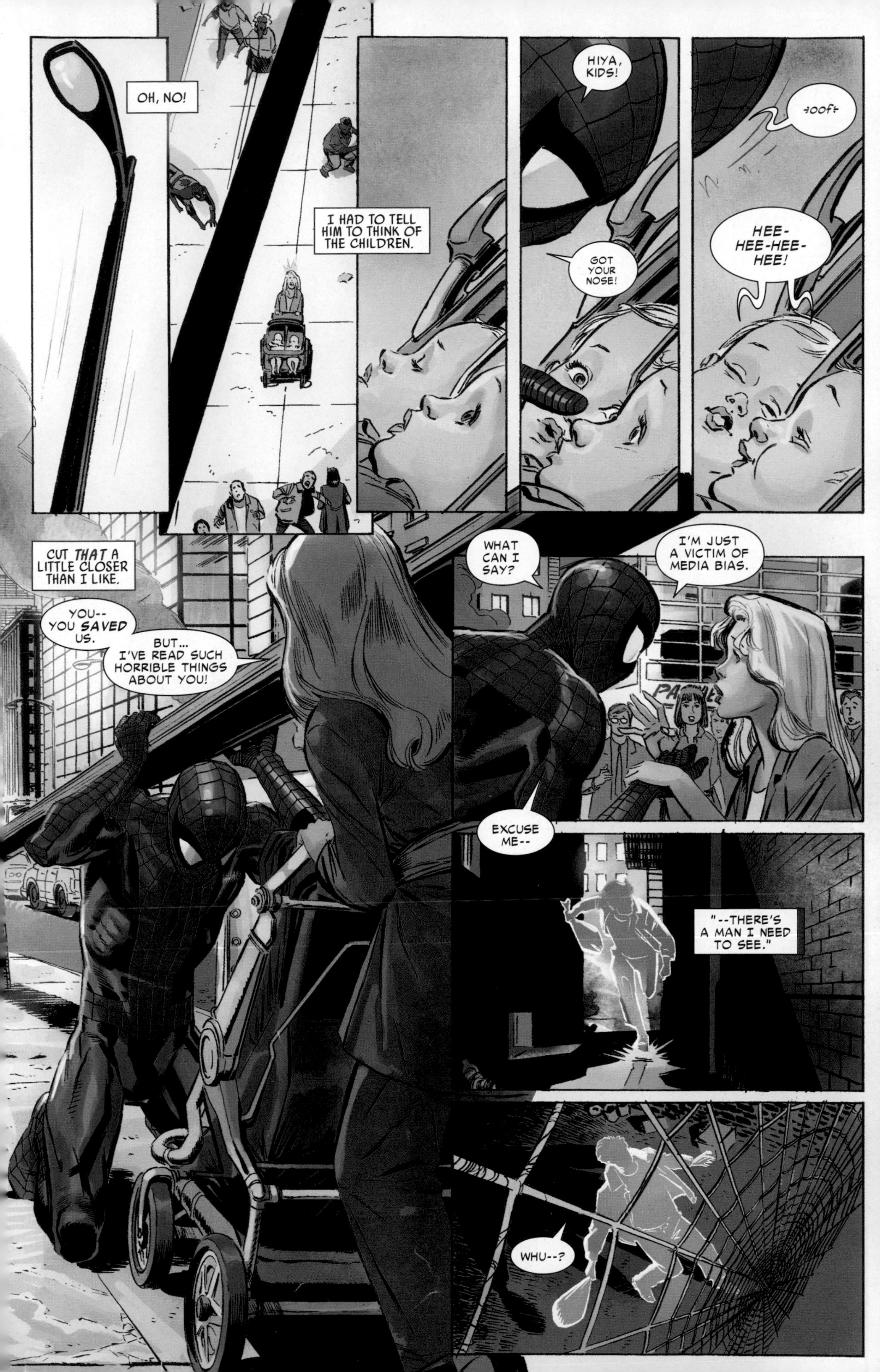
OH, NO!
I HAD TO TELL HIM TO THINK OF THE CHILDREN.
HIYA, KIDS!
GOT YOUR NOSE!
OOF
HEE-HEE-HEE-HEE!
CUT THAT A LITTLE CLOSER THAN I LIKE.
YOU-- YOU SAVED US.
BUT... I'VE READ SUCH HORRIBLE THINGS ABOUT YOU!
WHAT CAN I SAY?
I'M JUST A VICTIM OF MEDIA BIAS.
EXCUSE ME--
"--THERE'S A MAN I NEED TO SEE."
WHU--?

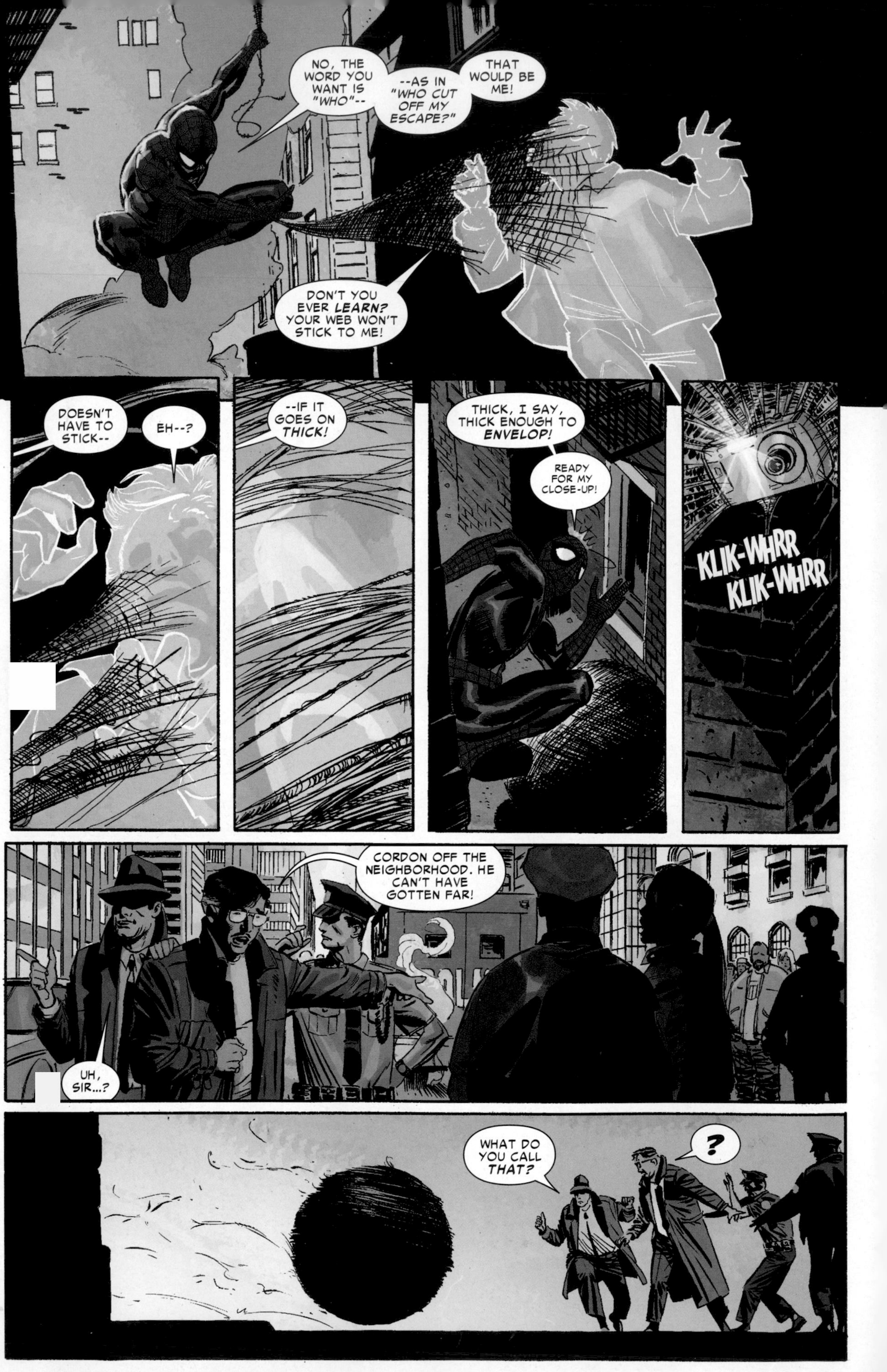
NO, THE WORD YOU WANT IS "WHO"--
--AS IN "WHO CUT OFF MY ESCAPE?"
THAT WOULD BE ME!
DON'T YOU EVER LEARN? YOUR WEB WON'T STICK TO ME!
DOESN'T HAVE TO STICK--
EH--?
--IF IT GOES ON THICK!
THICK, I SAY, THICK ENOUGH TO ENVELOP!
READY FOR MY CLOSE-UP!
KLIK-WHRR
KLIK-WHRR
CORDON OFF THE NEIGHBORHOOD. HE CAN'T HAVE GOTTEN FAR!
UH, SIR...?
WHAT DO YOU CALL THAT?
?

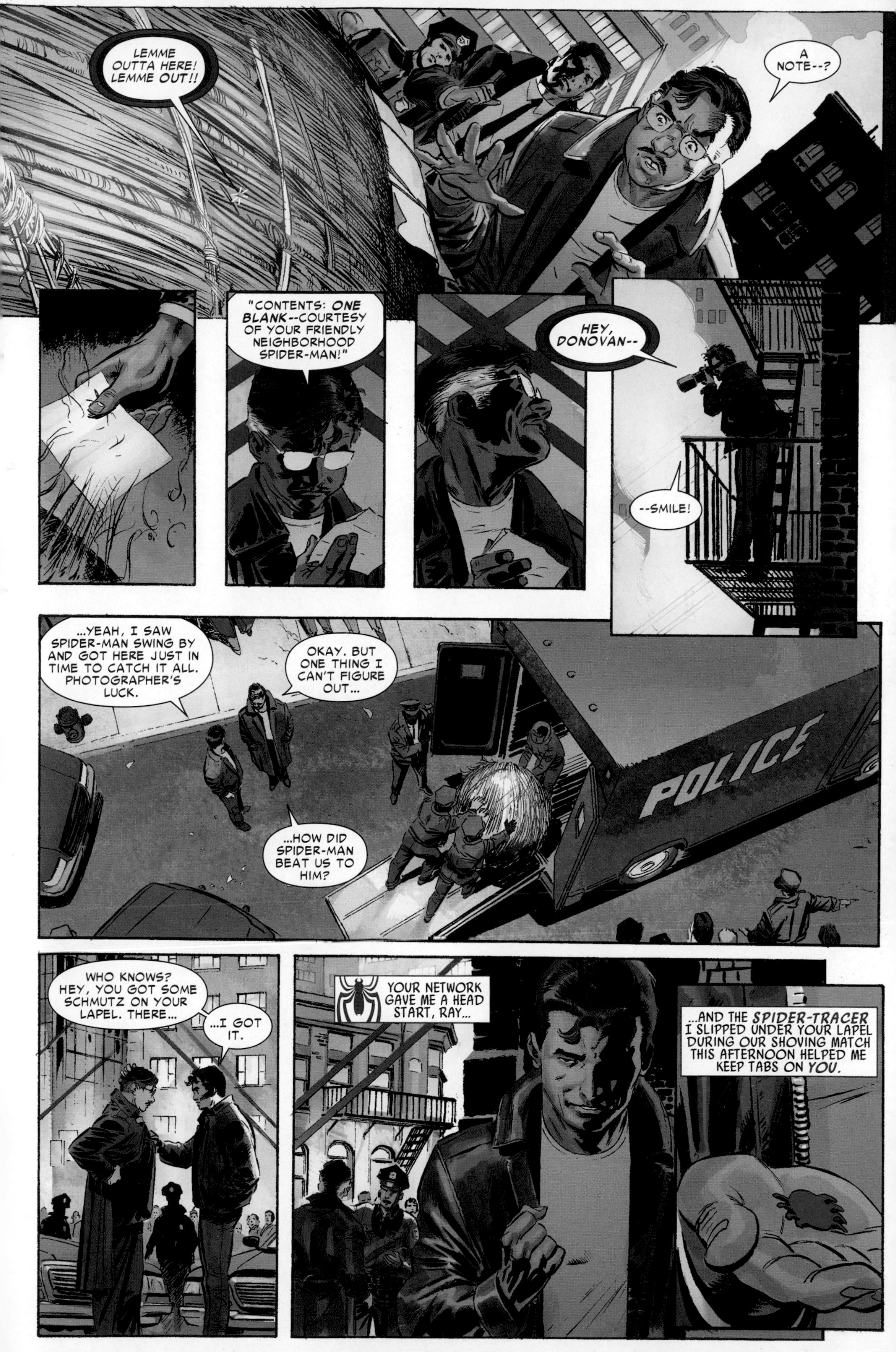
LEMME OUTTA HERE! LEMME OUT!!
A NOTE--?
"CONTENTS: ONE BLANK--COURTESY OF YOUR FRIENDLY NEIGHBORHOOD SPIDER-MAN!"
HEY, DONOVAN--
--SMILE!
...YEAH, I SAW SPIDER-MAN SWING BY AND GOT HERE JUST IN TIME TO CATCH IT ALL. PHOTOGRAPHER'S LUCK.
OKAY. BUT ONE THING I CAN'T FIGURE OUT...
...HOW DID SPIDER-MAN BEAT US TO HIM?
POLICE
WHO KNOWS? HEY, YOU GOT SOME SCHMUTZ ON YOUR LAPEL. THERE...
...I GOT IT.
YOUR NETWORK GAVE ME A HEAD START, RAY...
...AND THE SPIDER-TRACER I SLIPPED UNDER YOUR LAPEL DURING OUR SHOVING MATCH THIS AFTERNOON HELPED ME KEEP TABS ON YOU.

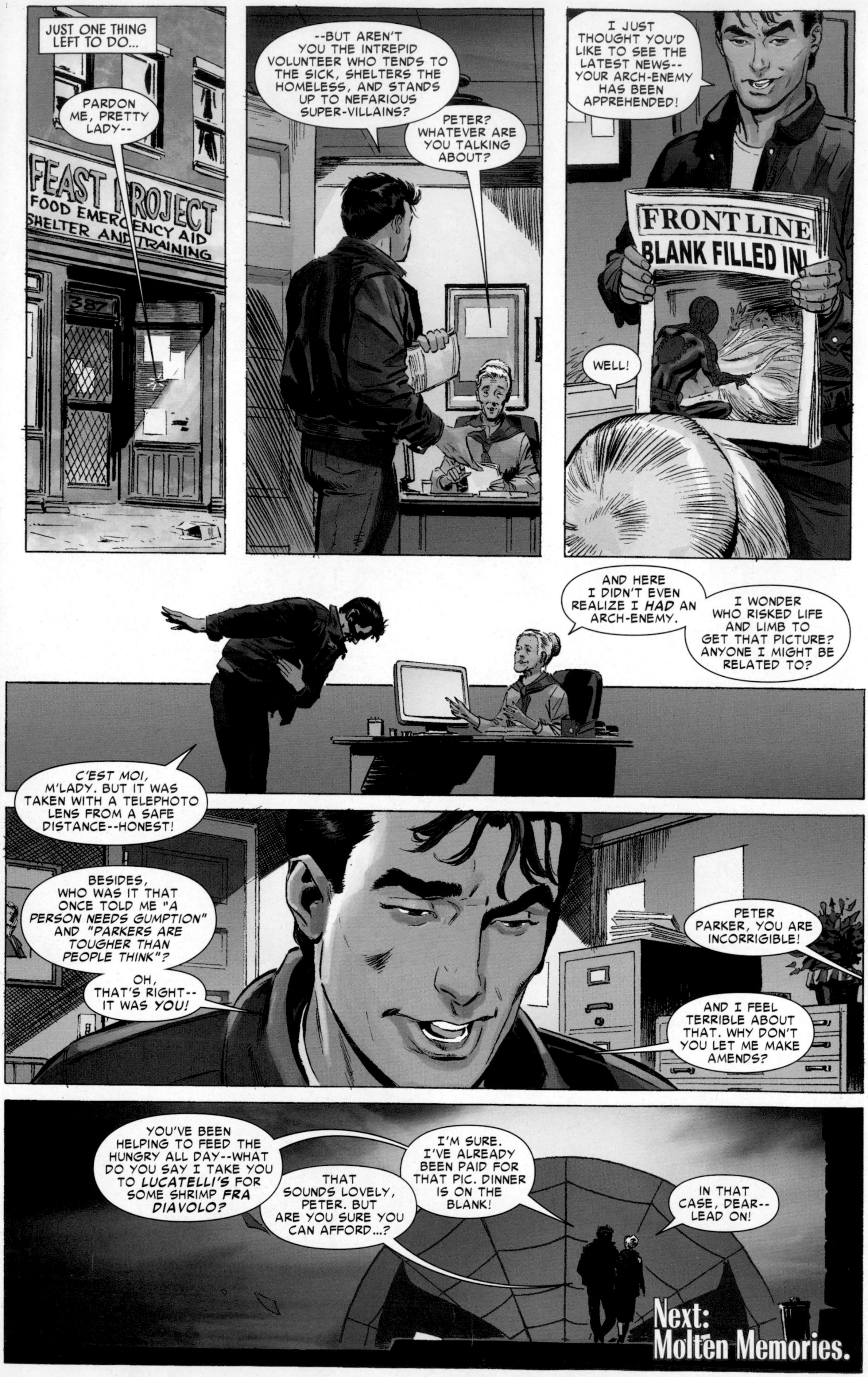
JUST ONE THING LEFT TO DO...
PARDON ME, PRETTY LADY--
FEAST PROJECT
FOOD EMERGENCY AID SHELTER AND TRAINING
387
--BUT AREN'T YOU THE INTREPID VOLUNTEER WHO TENDS TO THE SICK, SHELTERS THE HOMELESS, AND STANDS UP TO NEFARIOUS SUPER-VILLAINS?
PETER? WHATEVER ARE YOU TALKING ABOUT?
I JUST THOUGHT YOU'D LIKE TO SEE THE LATEST NEWS-- YOUR ARCH-ENEMY HAS BEEN APPREHENDED!
FRONT LINE
BLANK FILLED IN!
WELL!
AND HERE I DIDN'T EVEN REALIZE I *HAD* AN ARCH-ENEMY.
I WONDER WHO RISKED LIFE AND LIMB TO GET THAT PICTURE? ANYONE I MIGHT BE RELATED TO?
C'EST MOI, M'LADY. BUT IT WAS TAKEN WITH A TELEPHOTO LENS FROM A SAFE DISTANCE--HONEST!
BESIDES, WHO WAS IT THAT ONCE TOLD ME "*A PERSON NEEDS GUMPTION*" AND "*PARKERS ARE TOUGHER THAN PEOPLE THINK*"?
OH, THAT'S RIGHT-- IT WAS *YOU!*
PETER PARKER, YOU ARE INCORRIGIBLE!
AND I FEEL TERRIBLE ABOUT THAT. WHY DON'T YOU LET ME MAKE AMENDS?
YOU'VE BEEN HELPING TO FEED THE HUNGRY ALL DAY--WHAT DO YOU SAY I TAKE YOU TO *LUCATELLI'S* FOR SOME SHRIMP *FRA DIAVOLO?*
THAT SOUNDS LOVELY, PETER. BUT ARE YOU SURE YOU CAN AFFORD...?
I'M SURE. I'VE ALREADY BEEN PAID FOR THAT PIC. DINNER IS ON THE BLANK!
IN THAT CASE, DEAR-- LEAD ON!
Next: Molten Memories.

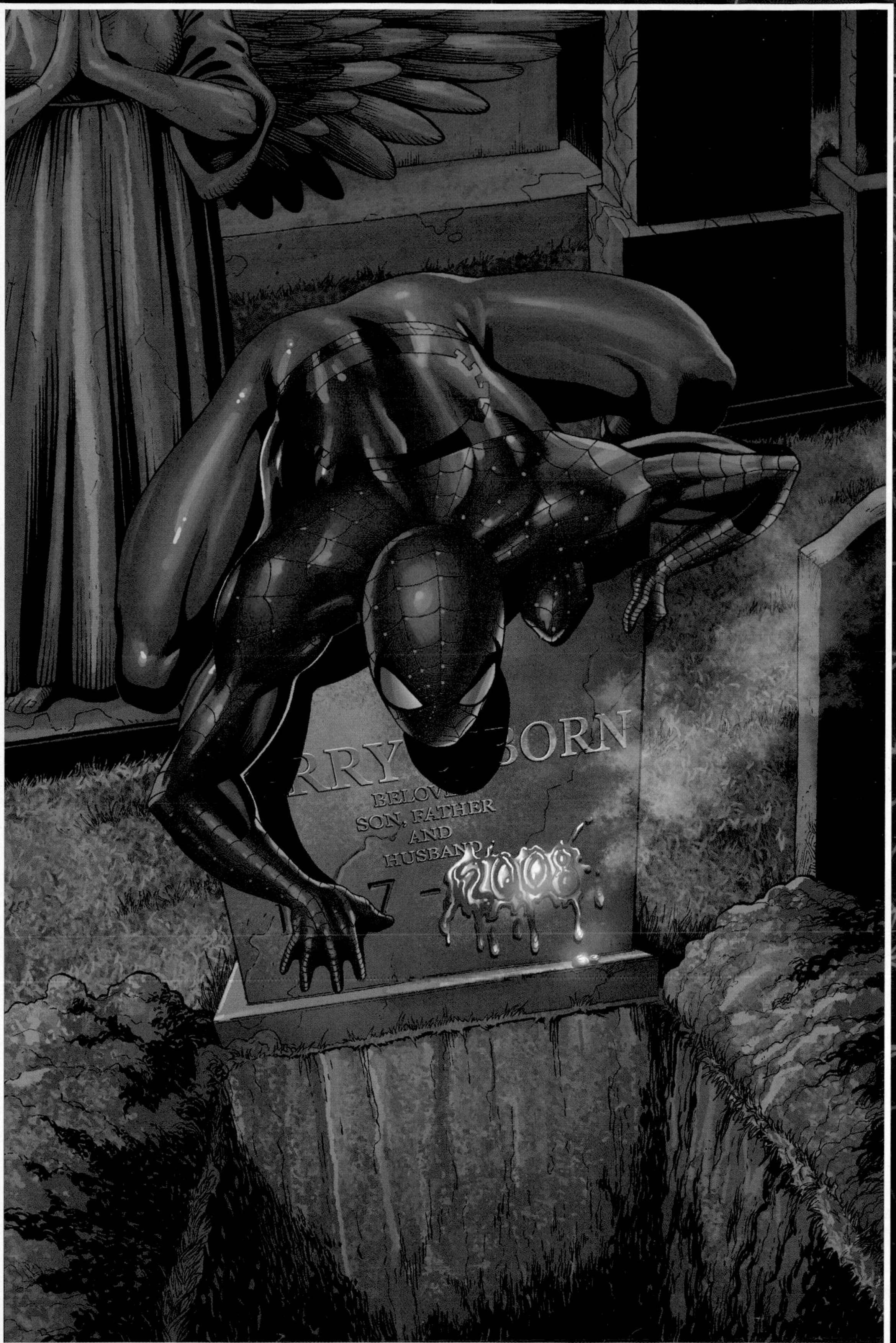
RRY
BORN
BELOV
SON, FATHER
AND
HUSBAND
2008

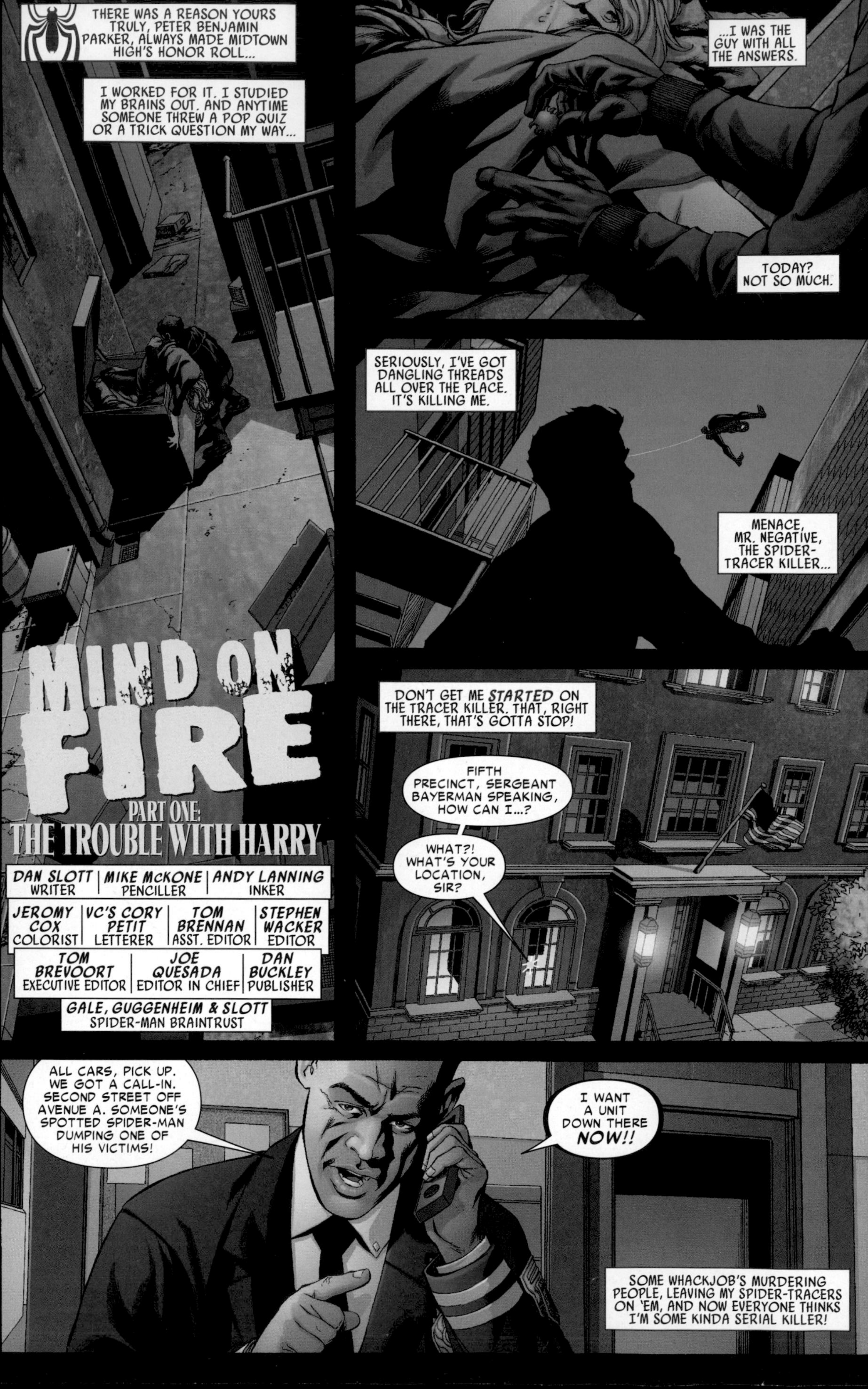
THERE WAS A REASON YOURS TRULY, PETER BENJAMIN PARKER, ALWAYS MADE MIDTOWN HIGH'S HONOR ROLL...
I WORKED FOR IT. I STUDIED MY BRAINS OUT. AND ANYTIME SOMEONE THREW A POP QUIZ OR A TRICK QUESTION MY WAY...
...I WAS THE GUY WITH ALL THE ANSWERS.
TODAY? NOT SO MUCH.
SERIOUSLY, I'VE GOT DANGLING THREADS ALL OVER THE PLACE. IT'S KILLING ME.
MENACE, MR. NEGATIVE, THE SPIDER-TRACER KILLER...
MIND ON FIRE
PART ONE: THE TROUBLE WITH HARRY
DAN SLOTT WRITER | MIKE McKONE PENCILLER | ANDY LANNING INKER
JEROMY COX COLORIST | VC'S CORY PETIT LETTERER | TOM BRENNAN ASST. EDITOR | STEPHEN WACKER EDITOR
TOM BREVOORT EXECUTIVE EDITOR | JOE QUESADA EDITOR IN CHIEF | DAN BUCKLEY PUBLISHER
GALE, GUGGENHEIM & SLOTT SPIDER-MAN BRAINTRUST
DON'T GET ME STARTED ON THE TRACER KILLER. THAT, RIGHT THERE, THAT'S GOTTA STOP!
FIFTH PRECINCT, SERGEANT BAYERMAN SPEAKING, HOW CAN I...?
WHAT?! WHAT'S YOUR LOCATION, SIR?
ALL CARS, PICK UP. WE GOT A CALL-IN. SECOND STREET OFF AVENUE A. SOMEONE'S SPOTTED SPIDER-MAN DUMPING ONE OF HIS VICTIMS!
I WANT A UNIT DOWN THERE NOW!!
SOME WHACKJOB'S MURDERING PEOPLE, LEAVING MY SPIDER-TRACERS ON 'EM, AND NOW EVERYONE THINKS I'M SOME KINDA SERIAL KILLER!

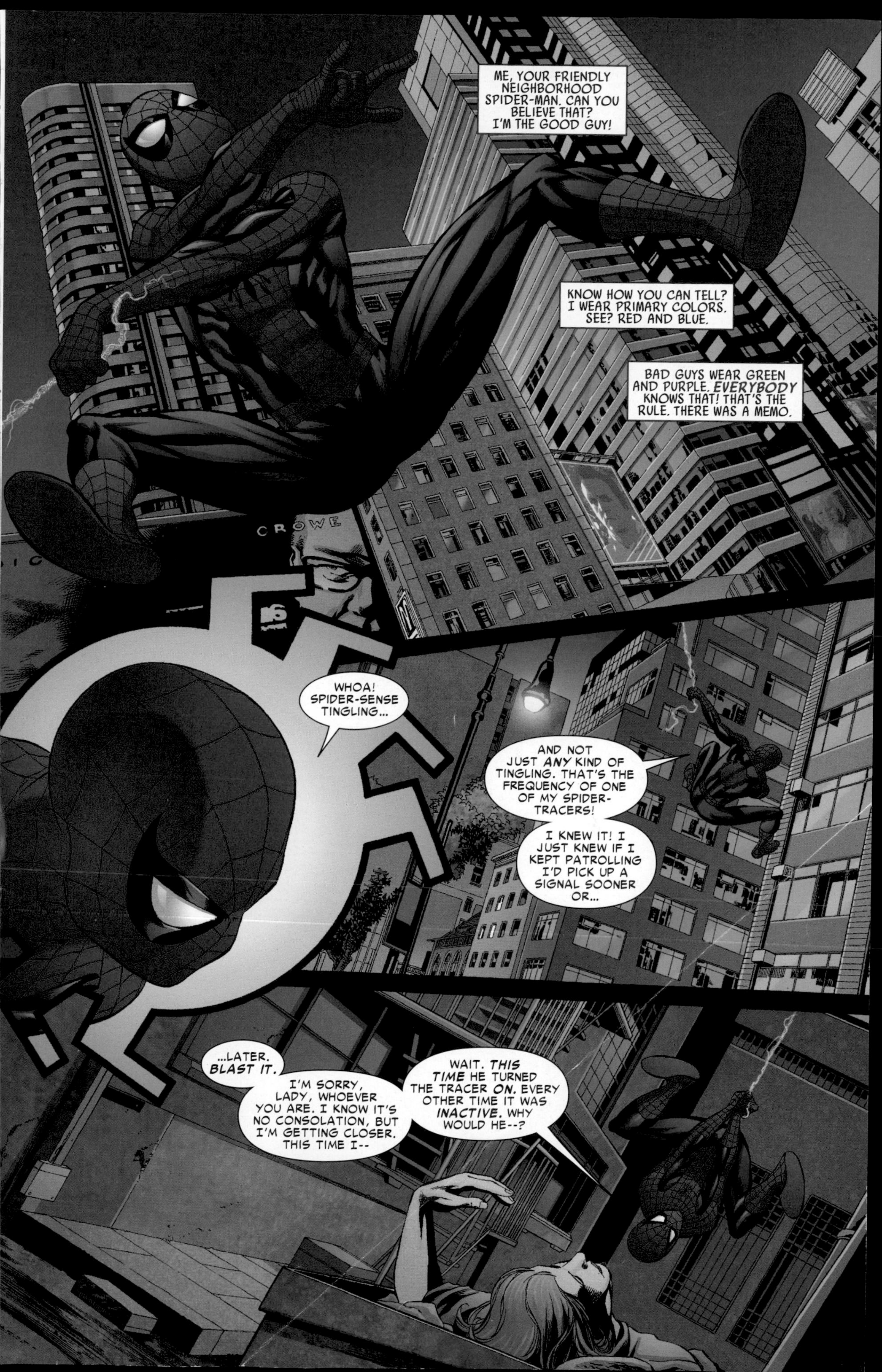
ME, YOUR FRIENDLY NEIGHBORHOOD SPIDER-MAN. CAN YOU BELIEVE THAT? I'M THE GOOD GUY!
KNOW HOW YOU CAN TELL? I WEAR PRIMARY COLORS. SEE? RED AND BLUE.
BAD GUYS WEAR GREEN AND PURPLE. EVERYBODY KNOWS THAT! THAT'S THE RULE. THERE WAS A MEMO.
CROWE
WHOA! SPIDER-SENSE TINGLING...
AND NOT JUST ANY KIND OF TINGLING. THAT'S THE FREQUENCY OF ONE OF MY SPIDER-TRACERS!
I KNEW IT! I JUST KNEW IF I KEPT PATROLLING I'D PICK UP A SIGNAL SOONER OR...
...LATER. BLAST IT.
I'M SORRY, LADY, WHOEVER YOU ARE. I KNOW IT'S NO CONSOLATION, BUT I'M GETTING CLOSER. THIS TIME I--
WAIT. THIS TIME HE TURNED THE TRACER ON. EVERY OTHER TIME IT WAS INACTIVE. WHY WOULD HE--?

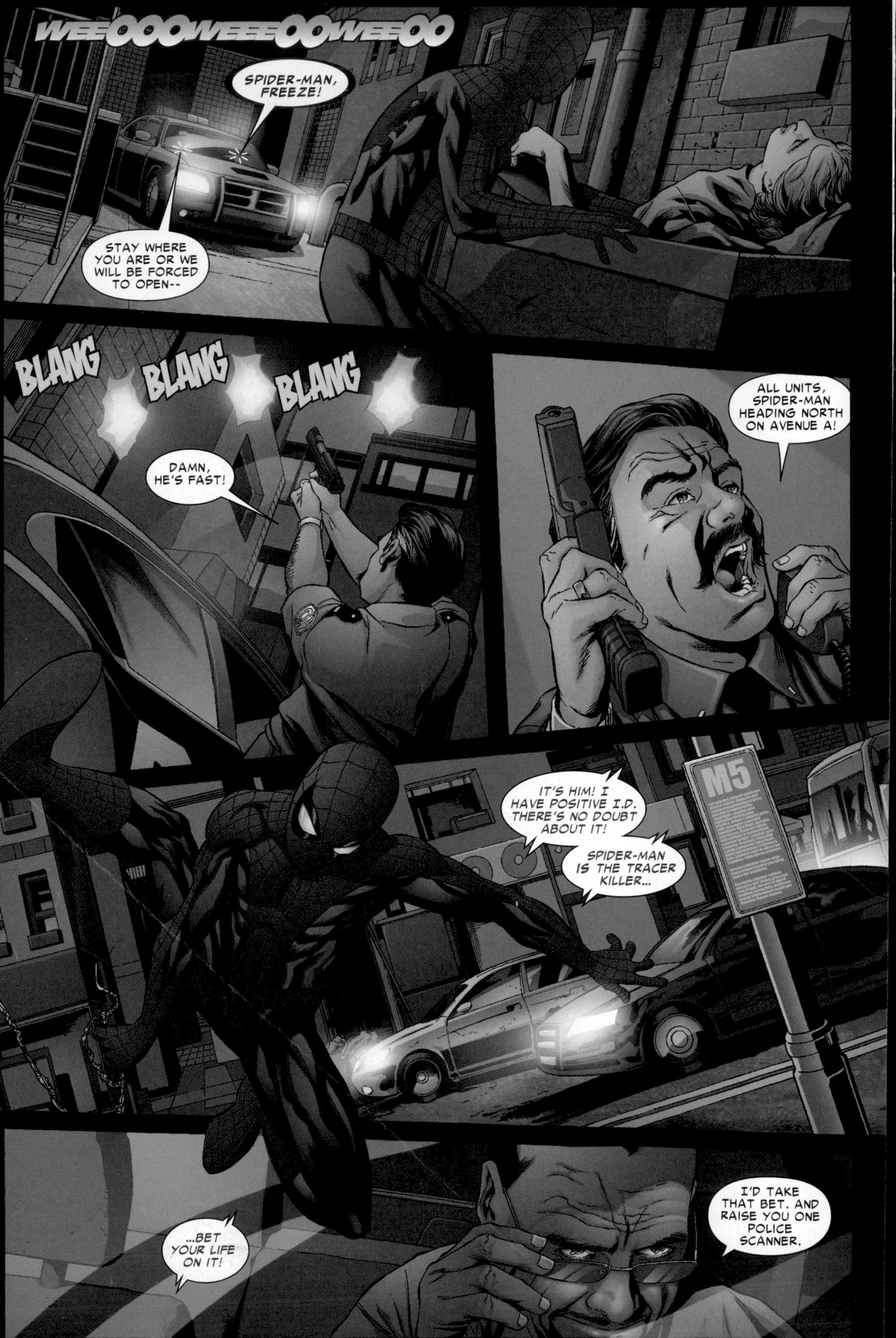
WEEOOOWEEEOOWEEOO
SPIDER-MAN, FREEZE!
STAY WHERE YOU ARE OR WE WILL BE FORCED TO OPEN--
BLANG
BLANG
BLANG
DAMN, HE'S FAST!
ALL UNITS, SPIDER-MAN HEADING NORTH ON AVENUE A!
IT'S HIM! I HAVE POSITIVE I.D. THERE'S NO DOUBT ABOUT IT!
SPIDER-MAN IS THE TRACER KILLER...
M5
...BET YOUR LIFE ON IT!
I'D TAKE THAT BET. AND RAISE YOU ONE POLICE SCANNER.

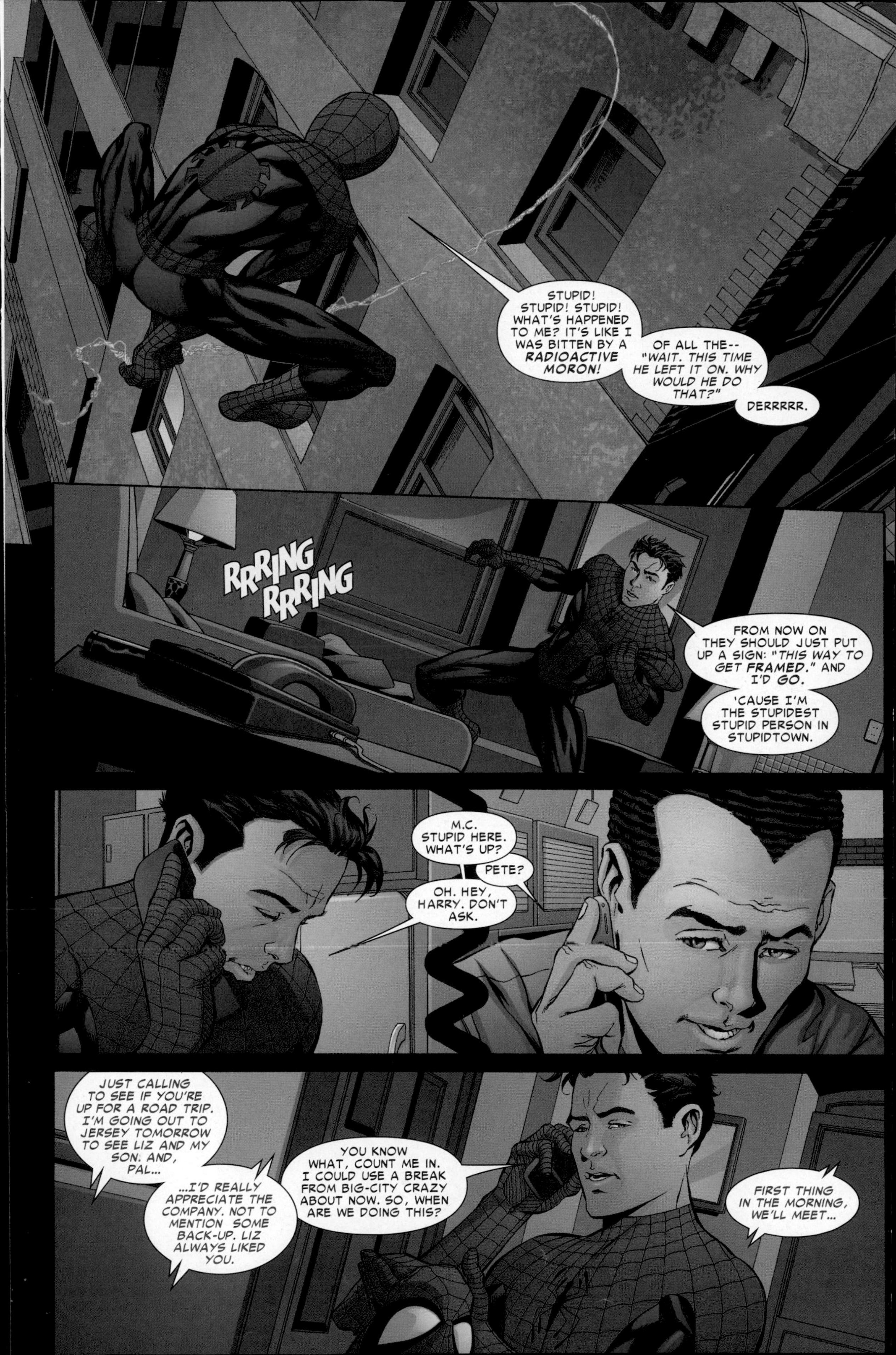
STUPID! STUPID! STUPID! WHAT'S HAPPENED TO ME? IT'S LIKE I WAS BITTEN BY A RADIOACTIVE MORON!
OF ALL THE-- "WAIT. THIS TIME HE LEFT IT ON. WHY WOULD HE DO THAT?"
DERRRRR.
RRRING RRRING
FROM NOW ON THEY SHOULD JUST PUT UP A SIGN: "THIS WAY TO GET FRAMED." AND I'D GO.
'CAUSE I'M THE STUPIDEST STUPID PERSON IN STUPIDTOWN.
M.C. STUPID HERE. WHAT'S UP?
PETE?
OH. HEY, HARRY. DON'T ASK.
JUST CALLING TO SEE IF YOU'RE UP FOR A ROAD TRIP. I'M GOING OUT TO JERSEY TOMORROW TO SEE LIZ AND MY SON. AND, PAL...
...I'D REALLY APPRECIATE THE COMPANY. NOT TO MENTION SOME BACK-UP. LIZ ALWAYS LIKED YOU.
YOU KNOW WHAT, COUNT ME IN. I COULD USE A BREAK FROM BIG-CITY CRAZY ABOUT NOW. SO, WHEN ARE WE DOING THIS?
FIRST THING IN THE MORNING, WE'LL MEET...

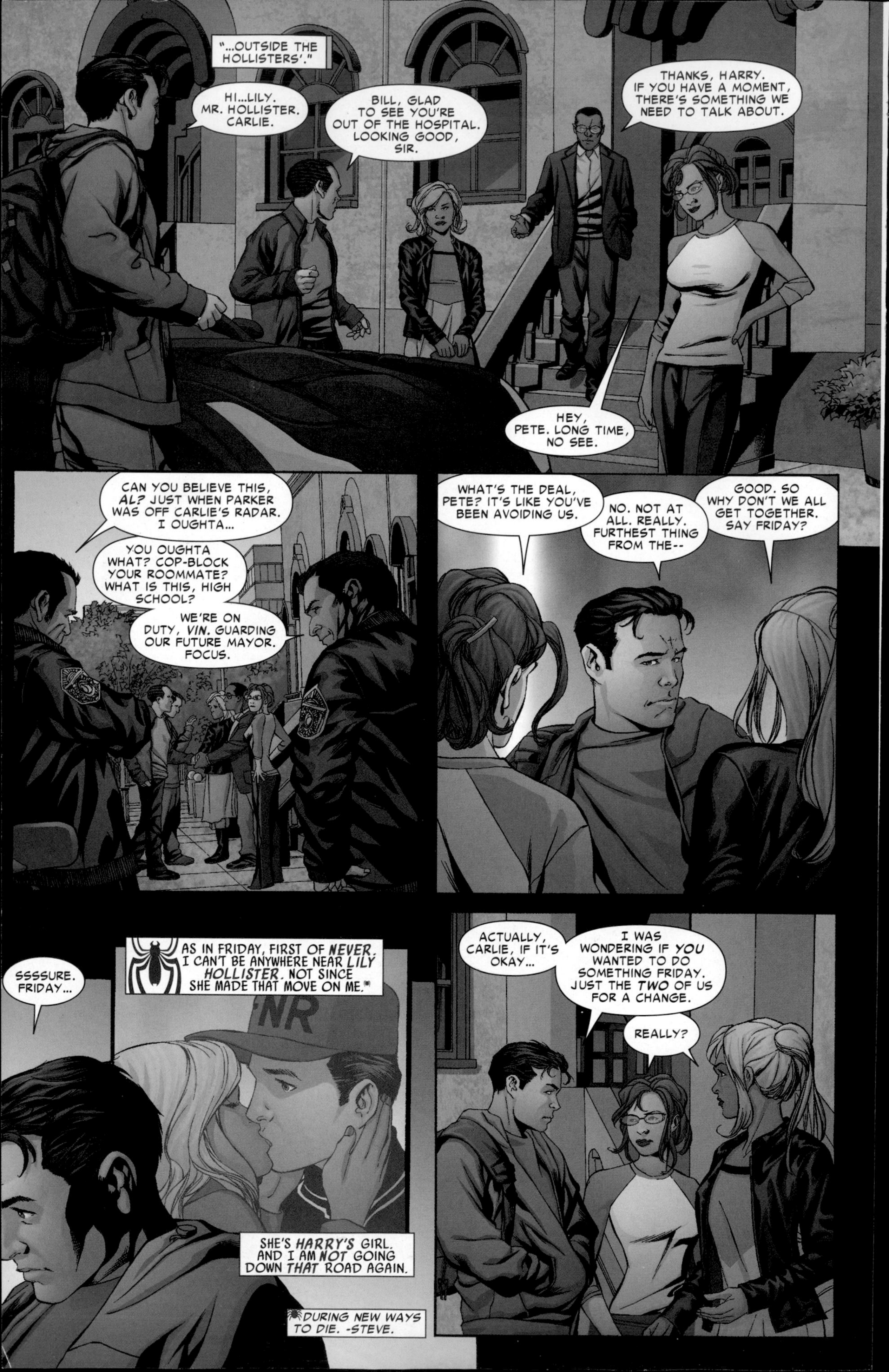
"...OUTSIDE THE HOLLISTERS'."
HI...LILY. MR. HOLLISTER. CARLIE.
BILL, GLAD TO SEE YOU'RE OUT OF THE HOSPITAL. LOOKING GOOD, SIR.
THANKS, HARRY. IF YOU HAVE A MOMENT, THERE'S SOMETHING WE NEED TO TALK ABOUT.
HEY, PETE. LONG TIME, NO SEE.
CAN YOU BELIEVE THIS, AL? JUST WHEN PARKER WAS OFF CARLIE'S RADAR. I OUGHTA...
YOU OUGHTA WHAT? COP-BLOCK YOUR ROOMMATE? WHAT IS THIS, HIGH SCHOOL?
WE'RE ON DUTY, VIN. GUARDING OUR FUTURE MAYOR. FOCUS.
WHAT'S THE DEAL, PETE? IT'S LIKE YOU'VE BEEN AVOIDING US.
NO. NOT AT ALL. REALLY. FURTHEST THING FROM THE--
GOOD. SO WHY DON'T WE ALL GET TOGETHER. SAY FRIDAY?
SSSSURE. FRIDAY...
AS IN FRIDAY, FIRST OF NEVER. I CAN'T BE ANYWHERE NEAR LILY HOLLISTER. NOT SINCE SHE MADE THAT MOVE ON ME.*
FNR
SHE'S HARRY'S GIRL. AND I AM NOT GOING DOWN THAT ROAD AGAIN.
*DURING NEW WAYS TO DIE. -STEVE.
ACTUALLY, CARLIE, IF IT'S OKAY...
I WAS WONDERING IF YOU WANTED TO DO SOMETHING FRIDAY. JUST THE TWO OF US FOR A CHANGE.
REALLY?

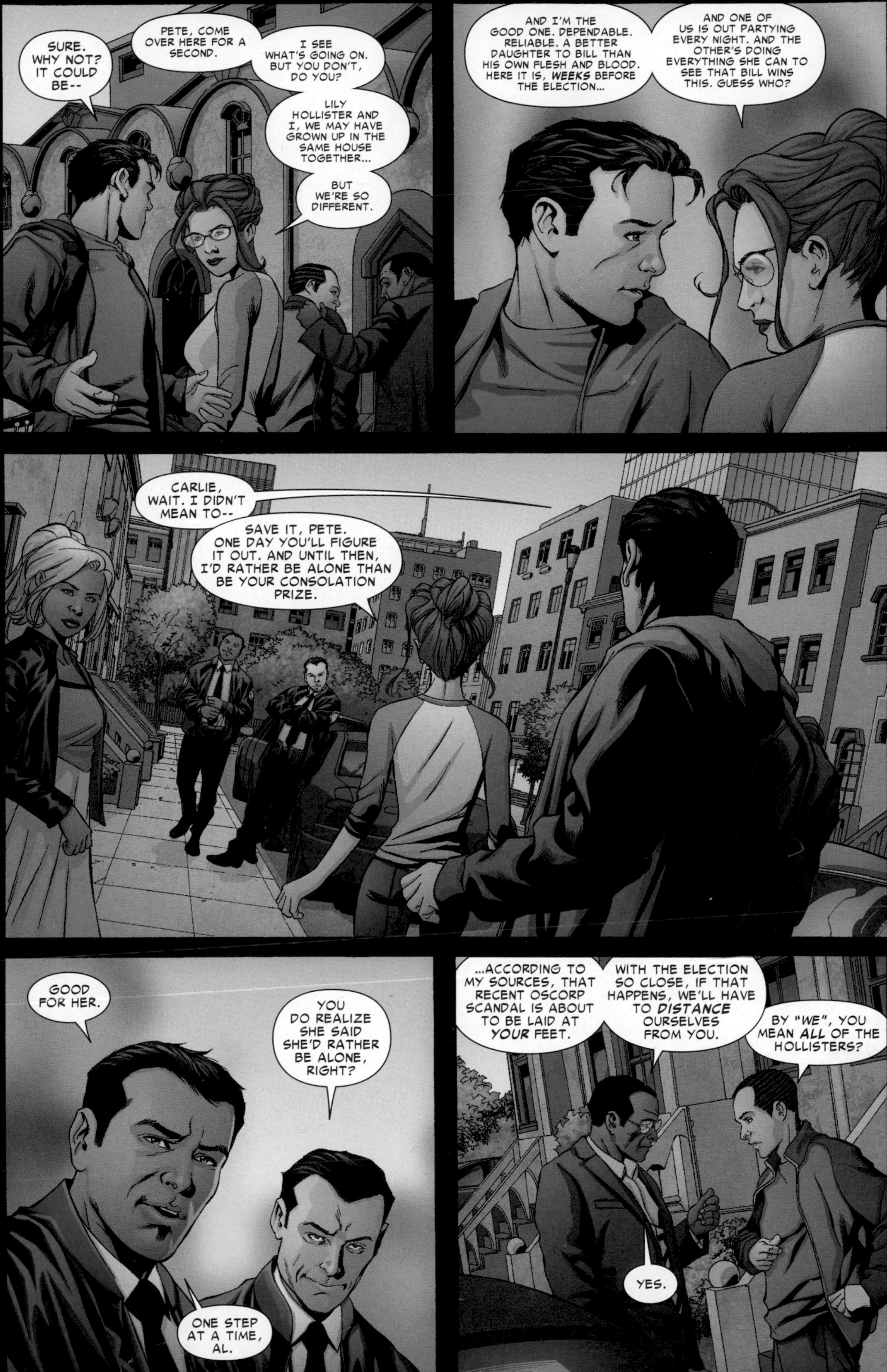
SURE. WHY NOT? IT COULD BE--
PETE, COME OVER HERE FOR A SECOND.
I SEE WHAT'S GOING ON. BUT YOU DON'T, DO YOU?
LILY HOLLISTER AND I, WE MAY HAVE GROWN UP IN THE SAME HOUSE TOGETHER...
BUT WE'RE SO DIFFERENT.
AND I'M THE GOOD ONE. DEPENDABLE. RELIABLE. A BETTER DAUGHTER TO BILL THAN HIS OWN FLESH AND BLOOD. HERE IT IS, WEEKS BEFORE THE ELECTION...
AND ONE OF US IS OUT PARTYING EVERY NIGHT. AND THE OTHER'S DOING EVERYTHING SHE CAN TO SEE THAT BILL WINS THIS. GUESS WHO?
CARLIE, WAIT. I DIDN'T MEAN TO--
SAVE IT, PETE. ONE DAY YOU'LL FIGURE IT OUT. AND UNTIL THEN, I'D RATHER BE ALONE THAN BE YOUR CONSOLATION PRIZE.
GOOD FOR HER.
YOU DO REALIZE SHE SAID SHE'D RATHER BE ALONE, RIGHT?
ONE STEP AT A TIME, AL.
...ACCORDING TO MY SOURCES, THAT RECENT OSCORP SCANDAL IS ABOUT TO BE LAID AT YOUR FEET.
WITH THE ELECTION SO CLOSE, IF THAT HAPPENS, WE'LL HAVE TO DISTANCE OURSELVES FROM YOU.
BY "WE", YOU MEAN ALL OF THE HOLLISTERS?
YES.

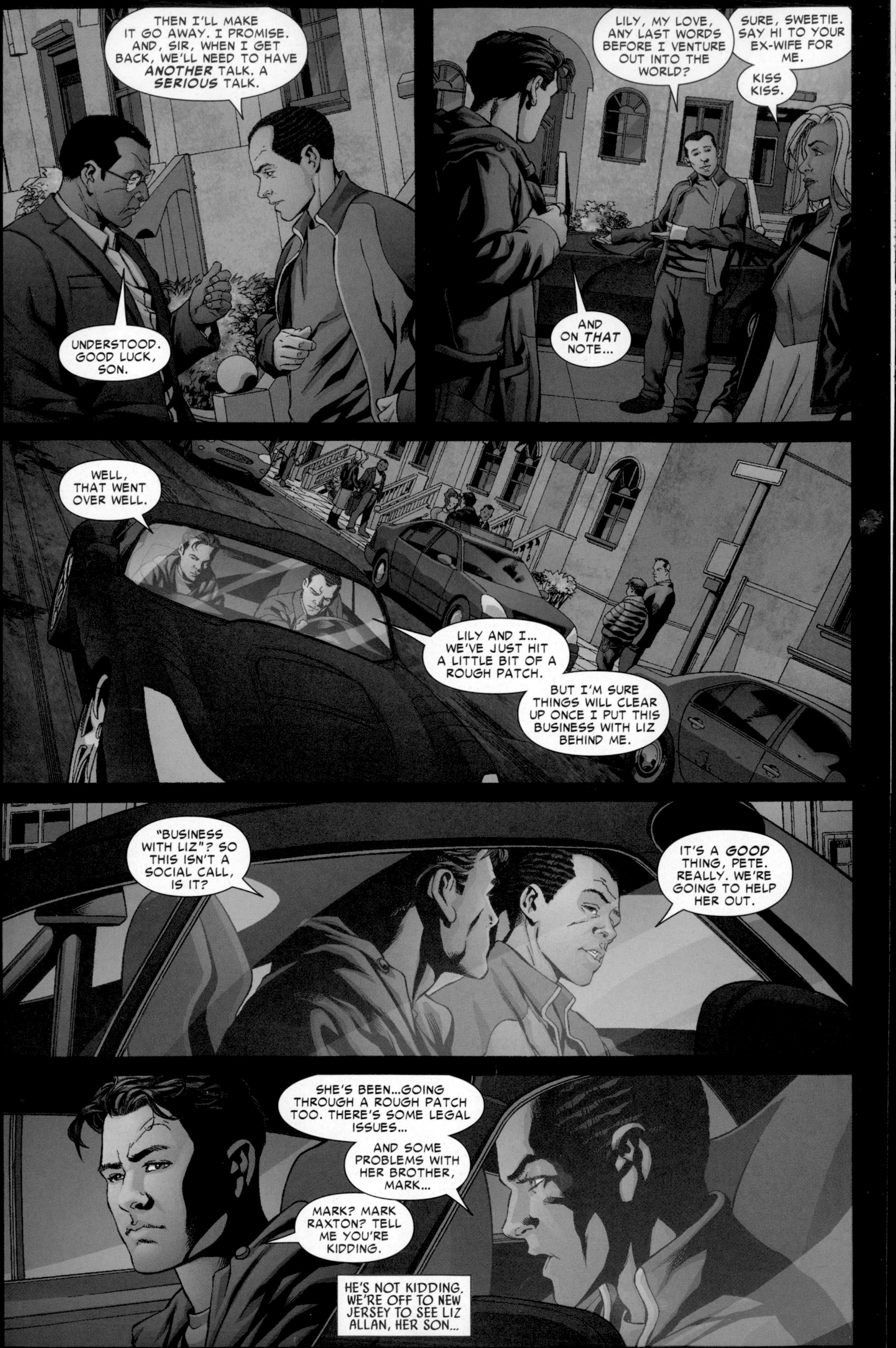
THEN I'LL MAKE IT GO AWAY. I PROMISE. AND, SIR, WHEN I GET BACK, WE'LL NEED TO HAVE ANOTHER TALK. A SERIOUS TALK.
UNDERSTOOD. GOOD LUCK, SON.
LILY, MY LOVE, ANY LAST WORDS BEFORE I VENTURE OUT INTO THE WORLD?
SURE, SWEETIE. SAY HI TO YOUR EX-WIFE FOR ME.
KISS KISS.
AND ON THAT NOTE...
WELL, THAT WENT OVER WELL.
LILY AND I... WE'VE JUST HIT A LITTLE BIT OF A ROUGH PATCH.
BUT I'M SURE THINGS WILL CLEAR UP ONCE I PUT THIS BUSINESS WITH LIZ BEHIND ME.
"BUSINESS WITH LIZ"? SO THIS ISN'T A SOCIAL CALL, IS IT?
IT'S A GOOD THING, PETE. REALLY. WE'RE GOING TO HELP HER OUT.
SHE'S BEEN...GOING THROUGH A ROUGH PATCH TOO. THERE'S SOME LEGAL ISSUES...
AND SOME PROBLEMS WITH HER BROTHER, MARK...
MARK? MARK RAXTON? TELL ME YOU'RE KIDDING.
HE'S NOT KIDDING. WE'RE OFF TO NEW JERSEY TO SEE LIZ ALLAN, HER SON...

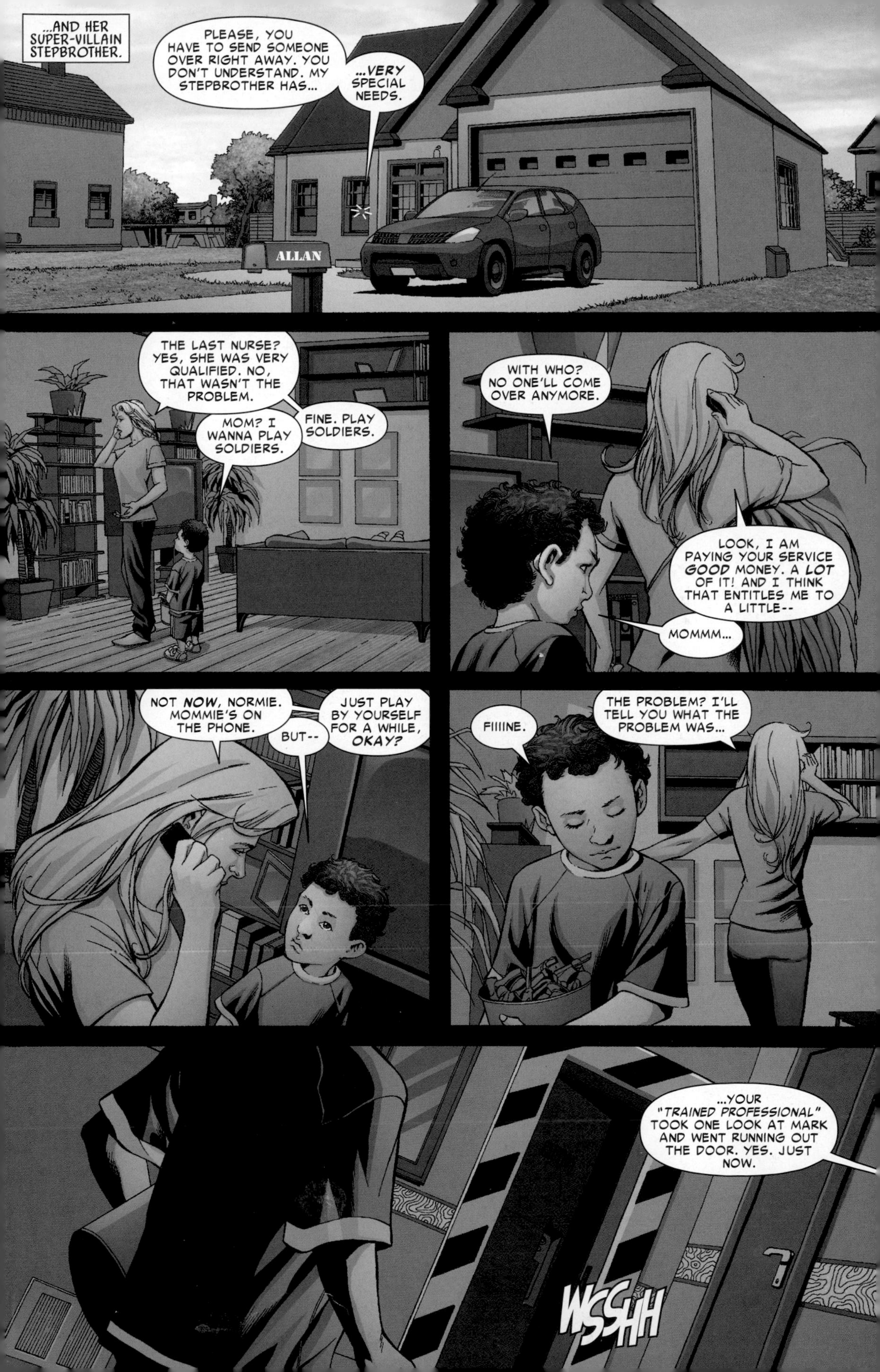
...AND HER SUPER-VILLAIN STEPBROTHER.
PLEASE, YOU HAVE TO SEND SOMEONE OVER RIGHT AWAY. YOU DON'T UNDERSTAND. MY STEPBROTHER HAS...
...VERY SPECIAL NEEDS.
ALLAN
THE LAST NURSE? YES, SHE WAS VERY QUALIFIED. NO, THAT WASN'T THE PROBLEM.
MOM? I WANNA PLAY SOLDIERS.
FINE. PLAY SOLDIERS.
WITH WHO? NO ONE'LL COME OVER ANYMORE.
LOOK, I AM PAYING YOUR SERVICE GOOD MONEY. A LOT OF IT! AND I THINK THAT ENTITLES ME TO A LITTLE--
MOMMM...
NOT NOW, NORMIE. MOMMIE'S ON THE PHONE.
BUT--
JUST PLAY BY YOURSELF FOR A WHILE, OKAY?
FIIIINE.
THE PROBLEM? I'LL TELL YOU WHAT THE PROBLEM WAS...
...YOUR "TRAINED PROFESSIONAL" TOOK ONE LOOK AT MARK AND WENT RUNNING OUT THE DOOR. YES. JUST NOW.
WSSHH

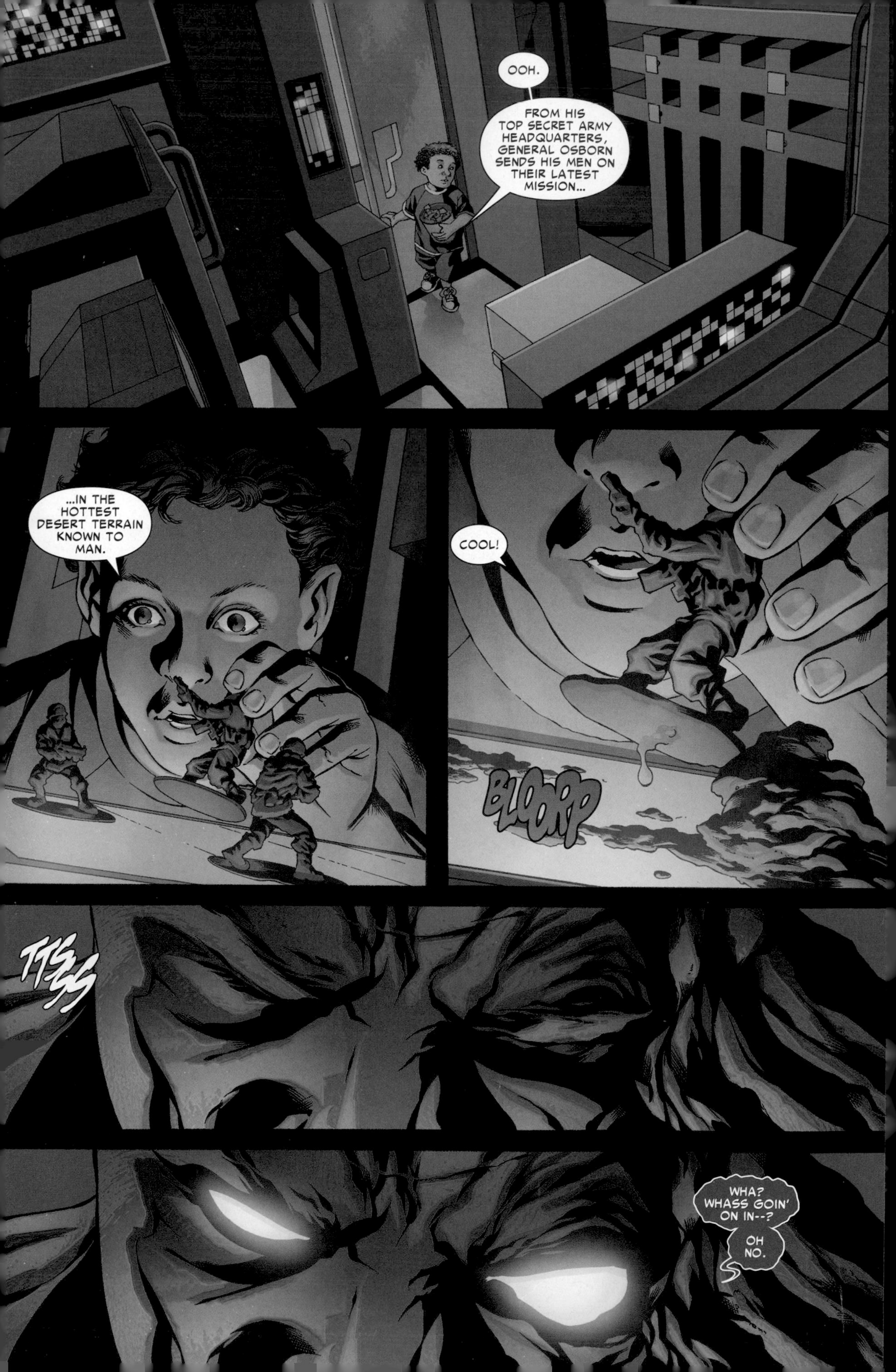
OOH.
FROM HIS TOP SECRET ARMY HEADQUARTERS, GENERAL OSBORN SENDS HIS MEN ON THEIR LATEST MISSION...
...IN THE HOTTEST DESERT TERRAIN KNOWN TO MAN.
COOL!
BLOORP
TTSSS
WHA? WHASS GOIN' ON IN--?
OH NO.

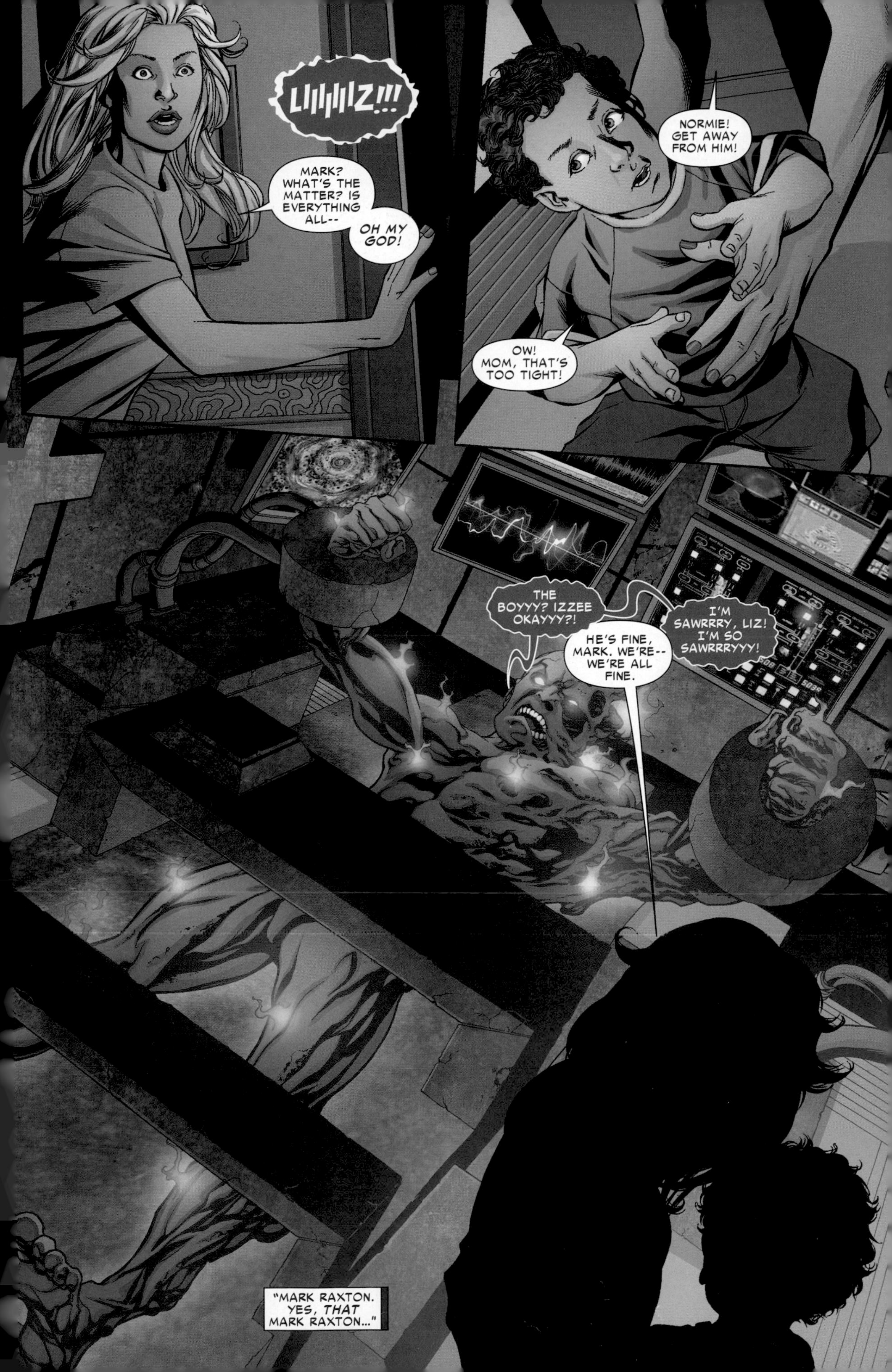
LIIIIIIZ!!!
MARK? WHAT'S THE MATTER? IS EVERYTHING ALL--
OH MY GOD!
NORMIE! GET AWAY FROM HIM!
OW! MOM, THAT'S TOO TIGHT!
THE BOYYY? IZZEE OKAYYY?!
HE'S FINE, MARK. WE'RE-- WE'RE ALL FINE.
I'M SAWRRRY, LIZ! I'M SO SAWRRRYYY!
"MARK RAXTON. YES, *THAT* MARK RAXTON..."

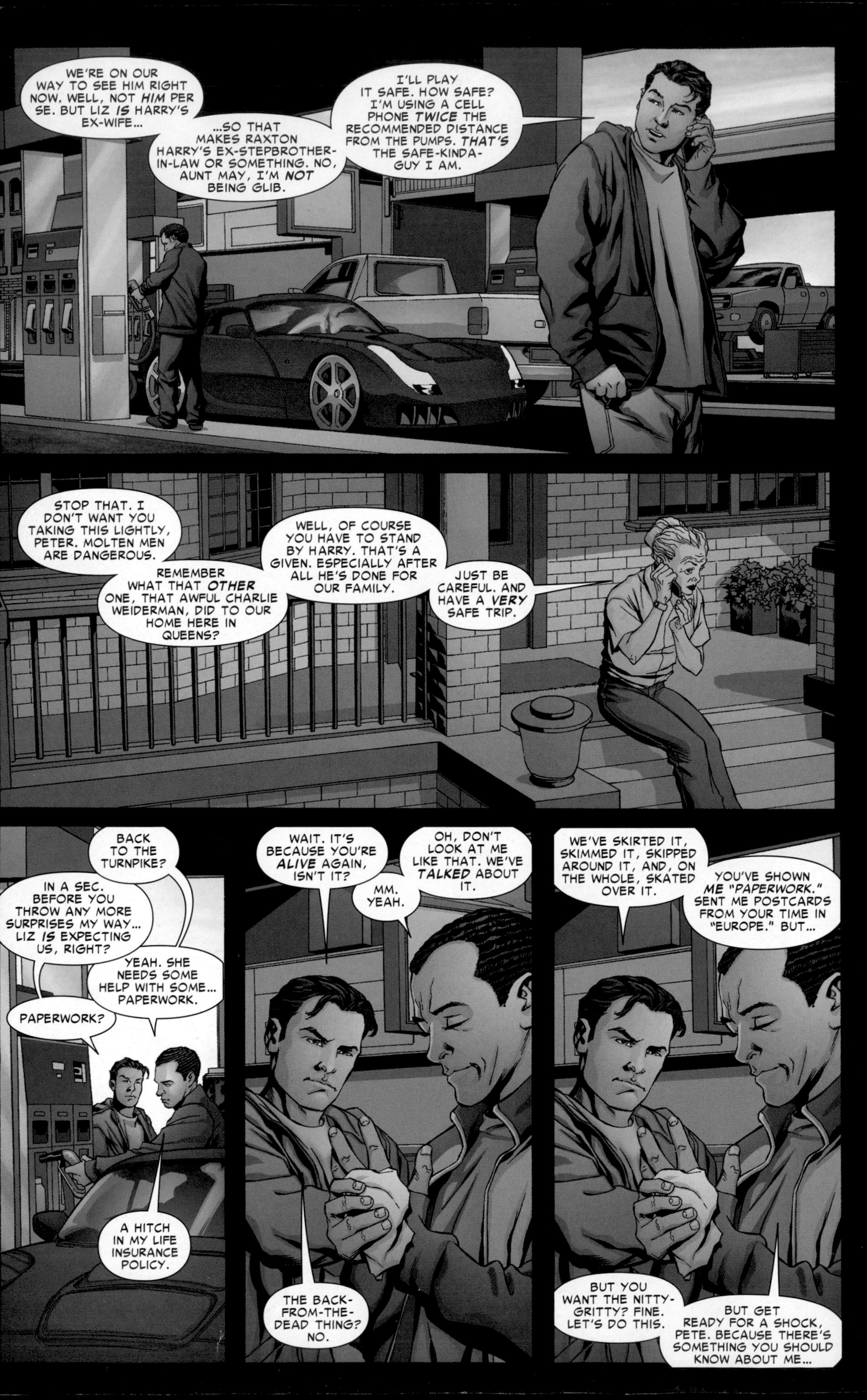
WE'RE ON OUR WAY TO SEE HIM RIGHT NOW. WELL, NOT *HIM* PER SE. BUT LIZ *IS* HARRY'S EX-WIFE...
...SO THAT MAKES RAXTON HARRY'S EX-STEPBROTHER-IN-LAW OR SOMETHING. NO, AUNT MAY, I'M *NOT* BEING GLIB.
I'LL PLAY IT SAFE. HOW SAFE? I'M USING A CELL PHONE *TWICE* THE RECOMMENDED DISTANCE FROM THE PUMPS. *THAT'S* THE SAFE-KINDA-GUY I AM.
STOP THAT. I DON'T WANT YOU TAKING THIS LIGHTLY, PETER. MOLTEN MEN ARE DANGEROUS.
REMEMBER WHAT THAT *OTHER* ONE, THAT AWFUL CHARLIE WEIDERMAN, DID TO OUR HOME HERE IN QUEENS?
WELL, OF COURSE YOU HAVE TO STAND BY HARRY. THAT'S A GIVEN. ESPECIALLY AFTER ALL HE'S DONE FOR OUR FAMILY.
JUST BE CAREFUL. AND HAVE A *VERY* SAFE TRIP.
BACK TO THE TURNPIKE?
IN A SEC. BEFORE YOU THROW ANY MORE SURPRISES MY WAY... LIZ *IS* EXPECTING US, RIGHT?
YEAH. SHE NEEDS SOME HELP WITH SOME... PAPERWORK.
PAPERWORK?
A HITCH IN MY LIFE INSURANCE POLICY.
WAIT. IT'S BECAUSE YOU'RE *ALIVE* AGAIN, ISN'T IT?
OH, DON'T LOOK AT ME LIKE THAT. WE'VE *TALKED* ABOUT IT.
MM. YEAH.
THE BACK-FROM-THE-DEAD THING? NO.
WE'VE SKIRTED IT, SKIMMED IT, SKIPPED AROUND IT, AND, ON THE WHOLE, SKATED OVER IT.
YOU'VE SHOWN *ME* "*PAPERWORK*." SENT ME POSTCARDS FROM YOUR TIME IN "EUROPE." BUT...
BUT YOU WANT THE NITTY-GRITTY? FINE. LET'S DO THIS.
BUT GET READY FOR A SHOCK, PETE. BECAUSE THERE'S SOMETHING YOU SHOULD KNOW ABOUT ME...

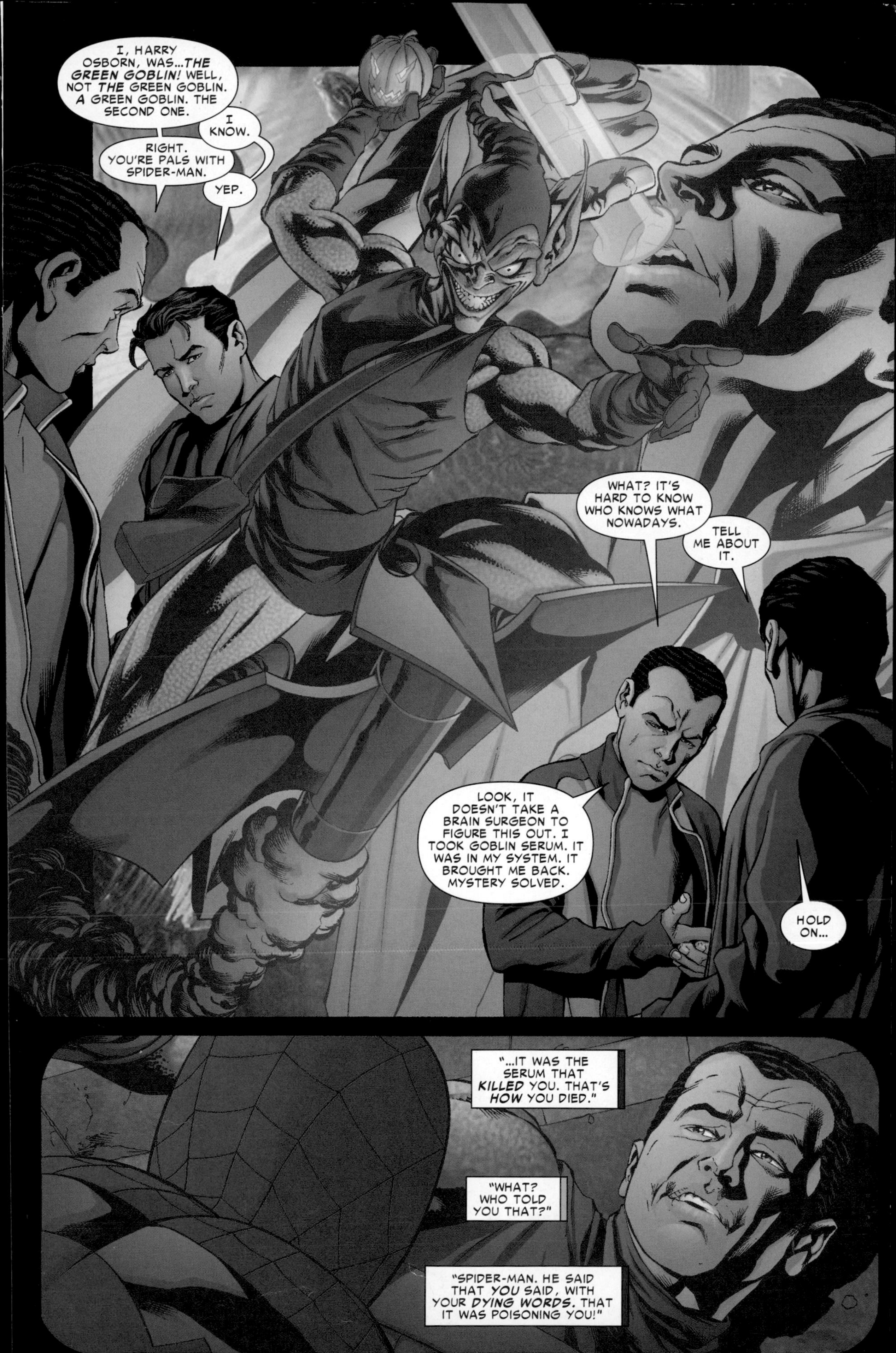
I, HARRY OSBORN, WAS...*THE GREEN GOBLIN!* WELL, NOT *THE* GREEN GOBLIN. A GREEN GOBLIN. THE SECOND ONE.
I KNOW.
RIGHT. YOU'RE PALS WITH SPIDER-MAN.
YEP.
WHAT? IT'S HARD TO KNOW WHO KNOWS WHAT NOWADAYS.
TELL ME ABOUT IT.
LOOK, IT DOESN'T TAKE A BRAIN SURGEON TO FIGURE THIS OUT. I TOOK GOBLIN SERUM. IT WAS IN MY SYSTEM. IT BROUGHT ME BACK. MYSTERY SOLVED.
HOLD ON...
"...IT WAS THE SERUM THAT *KILLED* YOU. THAT'S *HOW* YOU DIED."
"WHAT? WHO TOLD YOU THAT?"
"SPIDER-MAN. HE SAID THAT *YOU* SAID, WITH YOUR *DYING WORDS*, THAT IT WAS POISONING YOU!"

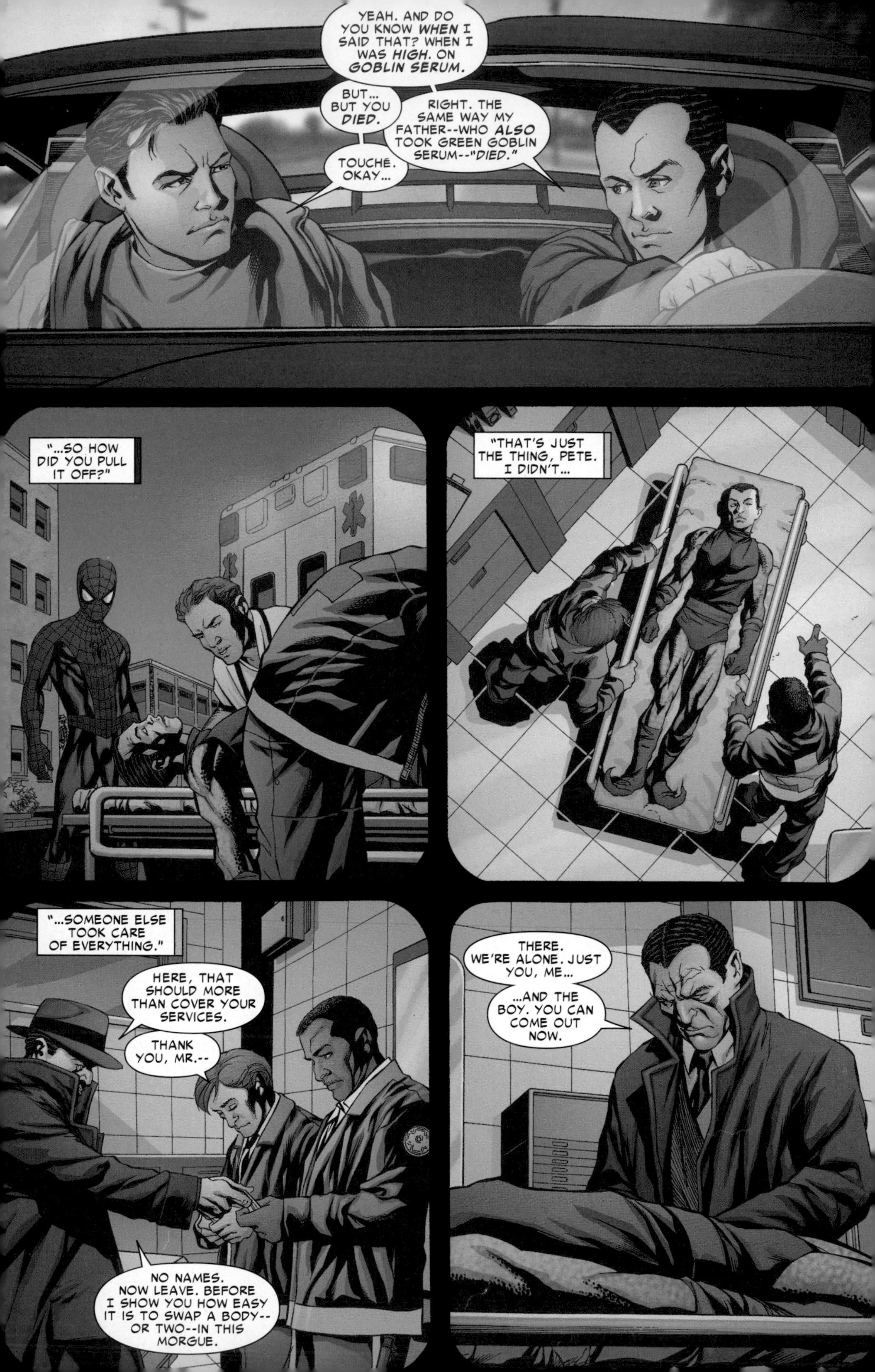
YEAH. AND DO YOU KNOW WHEN I SAID THAT? WHEN I WAS HIGH. ON GOBLIN SERUM.
BUT... BUT YOU DIED.
RIGHT. THE SAME WAY MY FATHER--WHO ALSO TOOK GREEN GOBLIN SERUM--"DIED."
TOUCHÉ. OKAY...
"...SO HOW DID YOU PULL IT OFF?"
"THAT'S JUST THE THING, PETE. I DIDN'T...
"...SOMEONE ELSE TOOK CARE OF EVERYTHING."
HERE, THAT SHOULD MORE THAN COVER YOUR SERVICES.
THANK YOU, MR.--
NO NAMES. NOW LEAVE. BEFORE I SHOW YOU HOW EASY IT IS TO SWAP A BODY--OR TWO--IN THIS MORGUE.
THERE. WE'RE ALONE. JUST YOU, ME...
...AND THE BOY. YOU CAN COME OUT NOW.

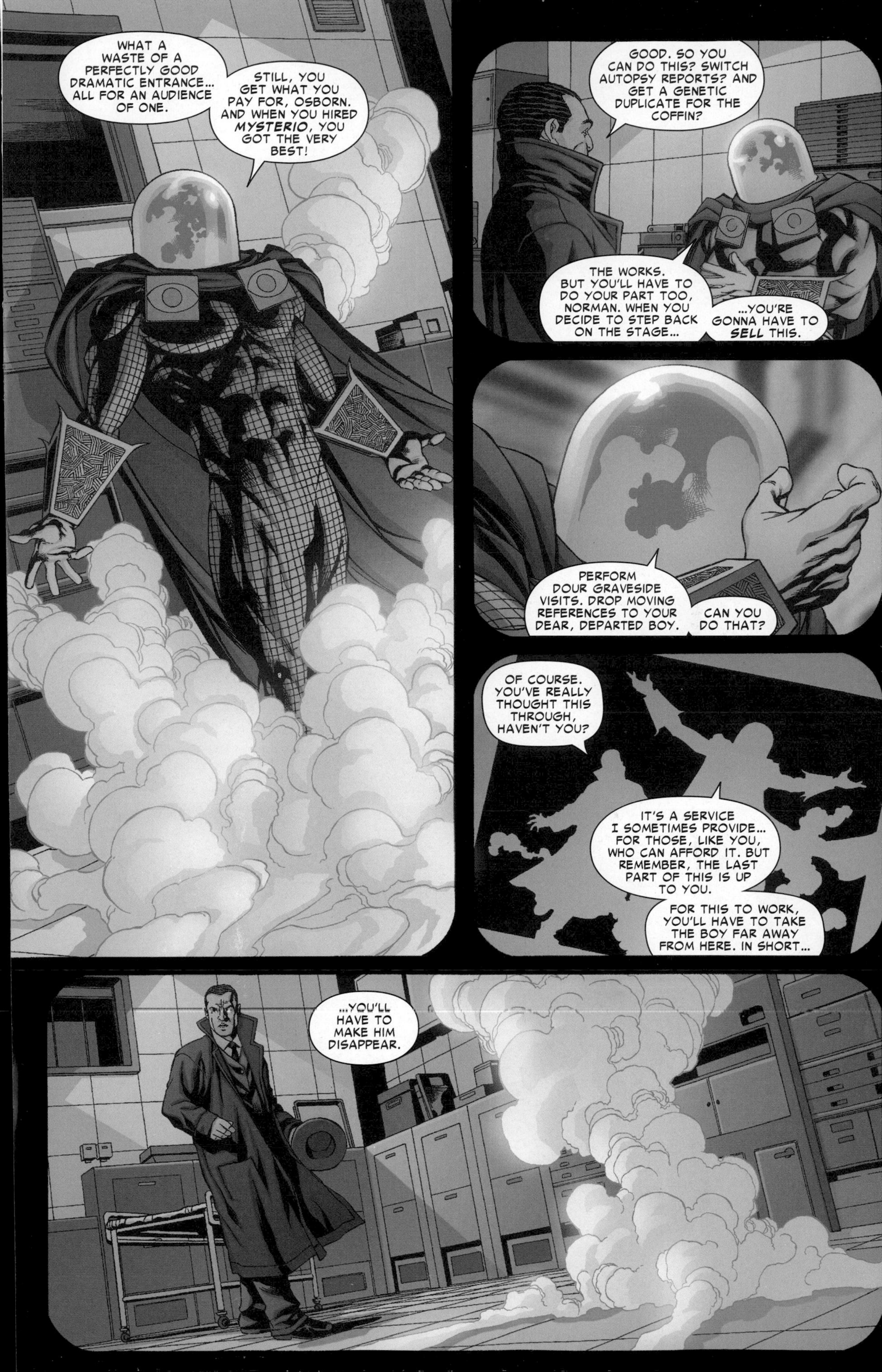
WHAT A WASTE OF A PERFECTLY GOOD DRAMATIC ENTRANCE... ALL FOR AN AUDIENCE OF ONE.
STILL, YOU GET WHAT YOU PAY FOR, OSBORN. AND WHEN YOU HIRED MYSTERIO, YOU GOT THE VERY BEST!
GOOD. SO YOU CAN DO THIS? SWITCH AUTOPSY REPORTS? AND GET A GENETIC DUPLICATE FOR THE COFFIN?
THE WORKS. BUT YOU'LL HAVE TO DO YOUR PART TOO, NORMAN. WHEN YOU DECIDE TO STEP BACK ON THE STAGE...
...YOU'RE GONNA HAVE TO SELL THIS.
PERFORM DOUR GRAVESIDE VISITS. DROP MOVING REFERENCES TO YOUR DEAR, DEPARTED BOY.
CAN YOU DO THAT?
OF COURSE. YOU'VE REALLY THOUGHT THIS THROUGH, HAVEN'T YOU?
IT'S A SERVICE I SOMETIMES PROVIDE... FOR THOSE, LIKE YOU, WHO CAN AFFORD IT. BUT REMEMBER, THE LAST PART OF THIS IS UP TO YOU.
FOR THIS TO WORK, YOU'LL HAVE TO TAKE THE BOY FAR AWAY FROM HERE. IN SHORT...
...YOU'LL HAVE TO MAKE HIM DISAPPEAR.

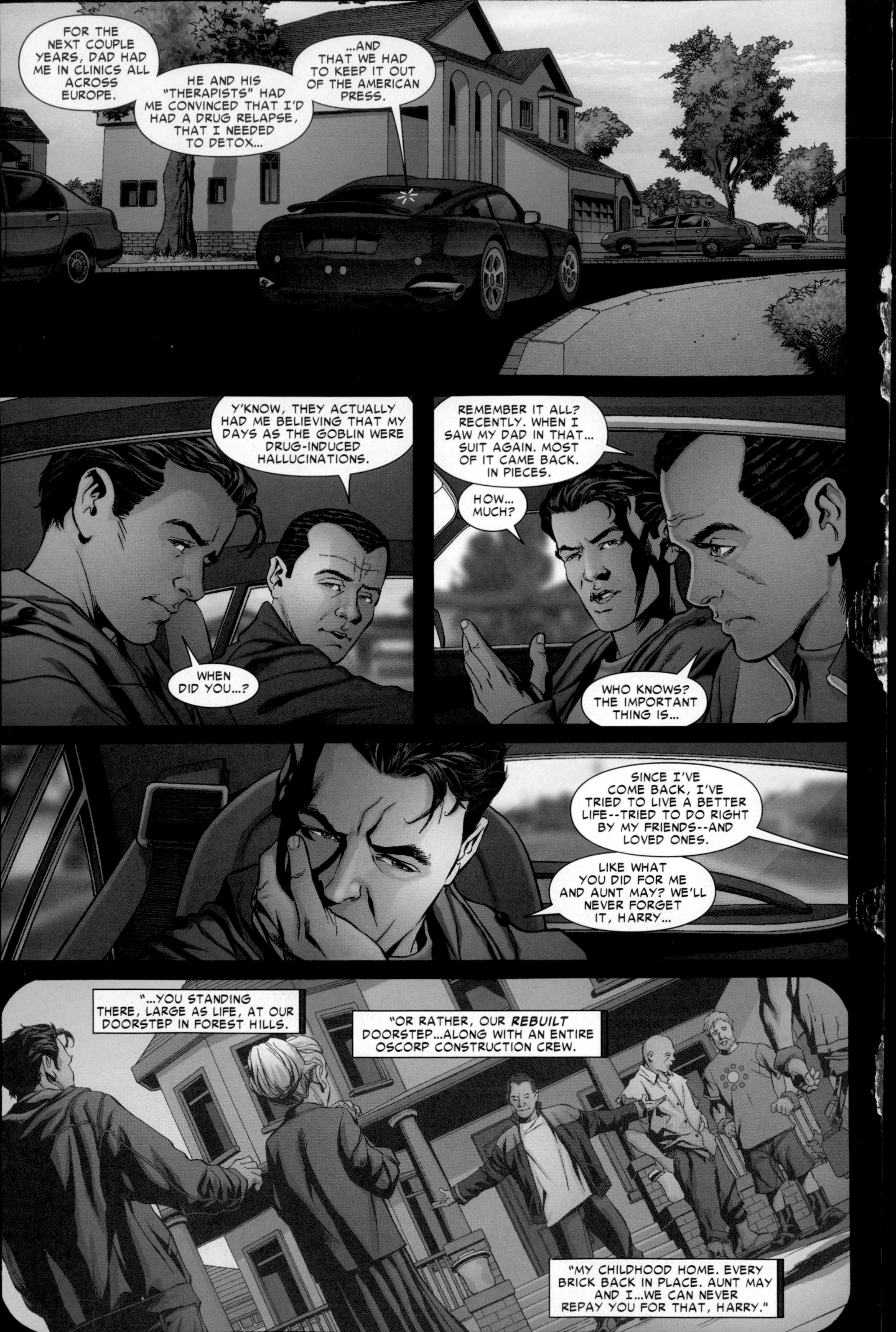
FOR THE NEXT COUPLE YEARS, DAD HAD ME IN CLINICS ALL ACROSS EUROPE.
HE AND HIS "THERAPISTS" HAD ME CONVINCED THAT I'D HAD A DRUG RELAPSE, THAT I NEEDED TO DETOX...
...AND THAT WE HAD TO KEEP IT OUT OF THE AMERICAN PRESS.
Y'KNOW, THEY ACTUALLY HAD ME BELIEVING THAT MY DAYS AS THE GOBLIN WERE DRUG-INDUCED HALLUCINATIONS.
WHEN DID YOU...?
REMEMBER IT ALL? RECENTLY. WHEN I SAW MY DAD IN THAT... SUIT AGAIN. MOST OF IT CAME BACK. IN PIECES.
HOW... MUCH?
WHO KNOWS? THE IMPORTANT THING IS...
SINCE I'VE COME BACK, I'VE TRIED TO LIVE A BETTER LIFE--TRIED TO DO RIGHT BY MY FRIENDS--AND LOVED ONES.
LIKE WHAT YOU DID FOR ME AND AUNT MAY? WE'LL NEVER FORGET IT, HARRY...
"...YOU STANDING THERE, LARGE AS LIFE, AT OUR DOORSTEP IN FOREST HILLS.
"OR RATHER, OUR *REBUILT* DOORSTEP...ALONG WITH AN ENTIRE OSCORP CONSTRUCTION CREW.
"MY CHILDHOOD HOME. EVERY BRICK BACK IN PLACE. AUNT MAY AND I...WE CAN NEVER REPAY YOU FOR THAT, HARRY."

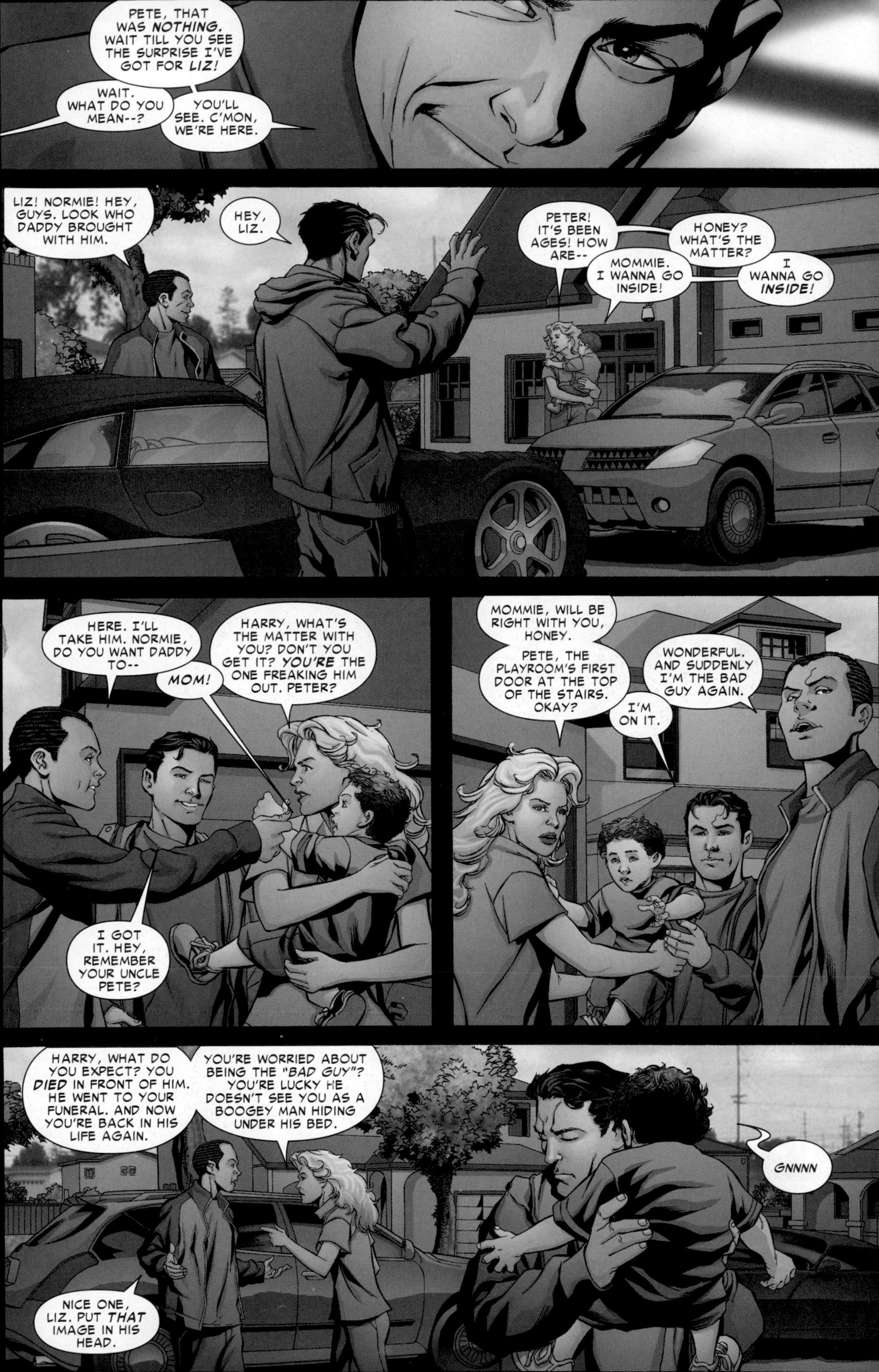
PETE, THAT WAS NOTHING. WAIT TILL YOU SEE THE SURPRISE I'VE GOT FOR LIZ!
WAIT. WHAT DO YOU MEAN--?
YOU'LL SEE. C'MON, WE'RE HERE.
LIZ! NORMIE! HEY, GUYS. LOOK WHO DADDY BROUGHT WITH HIM.
HEY, LIZ.
PETER! IT'S BEEN AGES! HOW ARE--
HONEY? WHAT'S THE MATTER?
MOMMIE. I WANNA GO INSIDE!
I WANNA GO INSIDE!
HERE. I'LL TAKE HIM. NORMIE, DO YOU WANT DADDY TO--
MOM!
HARRY, WHAT'S THE MATTER WITH YOU? DON'T YOU GET IT? YOU'RE THE ONE FREAKING HIM OUT. PETER?
I GOT IT. HEY, REMEMBER YOUR UNCLE PETE?
MOMMIE, WILL BE RIGHT WITH YOU, HONEY.
PETE, THE PLAYROOM'S FIRST DOOR AT THE TOP OF THE STAIRS. OKAY?
I'M ON IT.
WONDERFUL. AND SUDDENLY I'M THE BAD GUY AGAIN.
HARRY, WHAT DO YOU EXPECT? YOU DIED IN FRONT OF HIM. HE WENT TO YOUR FUNERAL. AND NOW YOU'RE BACK IN HIS LIFE AGAIN.
YOU'RE WORRIED ABOUT BEING THE "BAD GUY"? YOU'RE LUCKY HE DOESN'T SEE YOU AS A BOOGEY MAN HIDING UNDER HIS BED.
GNNNN
NICE ONE, LIZ. PUT THAT IMAGE IN HIS HEAD.

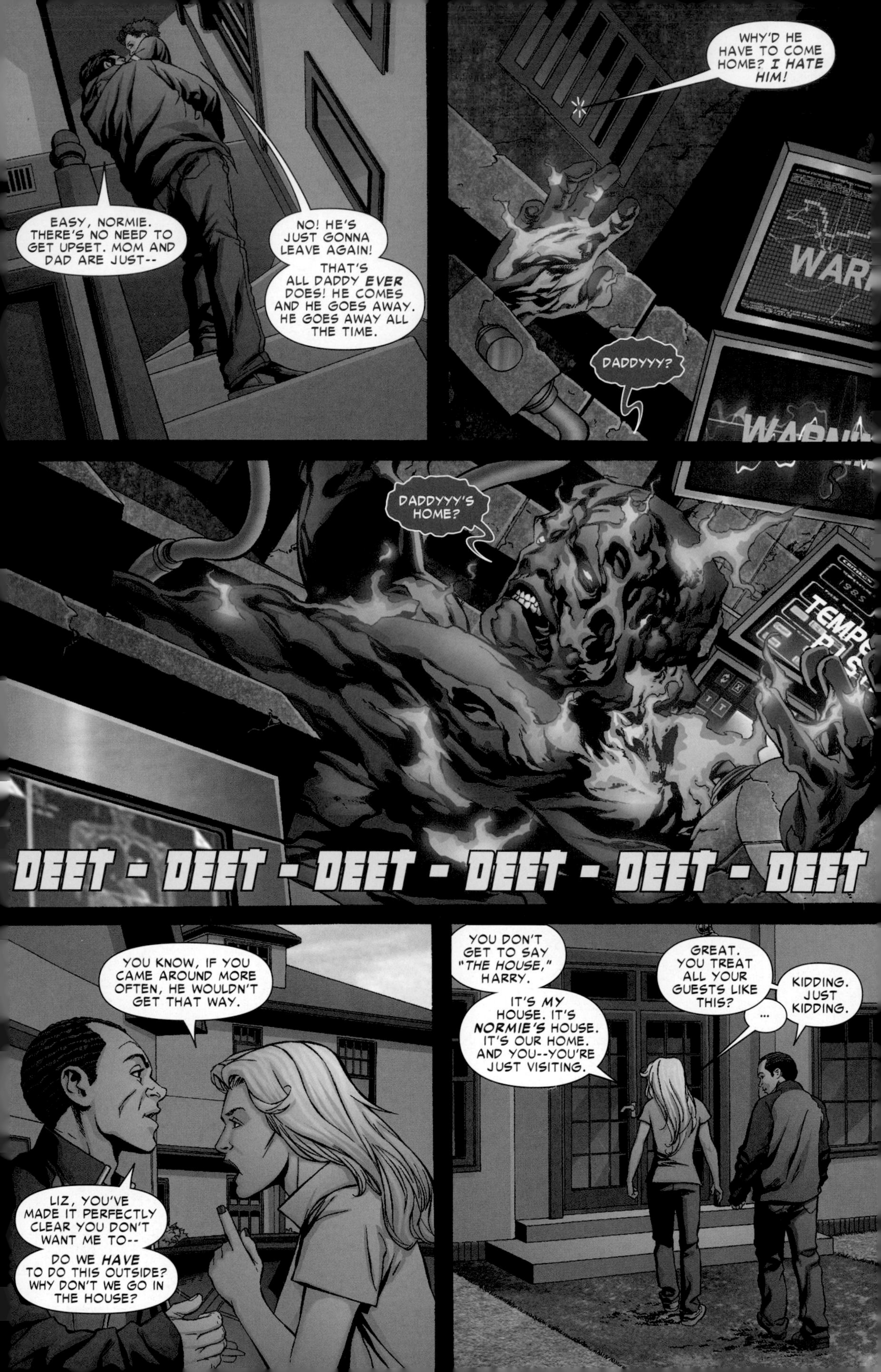
EASY, NORMIE. THERE'S NO NEED TO GET UPSET. MOM AND DAD ARE JUST--
NO! HE'S JUST GONNA LEAVE AGAIN!
THAT'S ALL DADDY EVER DOES! HE COMES AND HE GOES AWAY. HE GOES AWAY ALL THE TIME.
WHY'D HE HAVE TO COME HOME? I HATE HIM!
DADDYYY?
DADDYYY'S HOME?
DEET - DEET - DEET - DEET - DEET - DEET
YOU KNOW, IF YOU CAME AROUND MORE OFTEN, HE WOULDN'T GET THAT WAY.
LIZ, YOU'VE MADE IT PERFECTLY CLEAR YOU DON'T WANT ME TO--
DO WE HAVE TO DO THIS OUTSIDE? WHY DON'T WE GO IN THE HOUSE?
YOU DON'T GET TO SAY "THE HOUSE," HARRY.
IT'S MY HOUSE. IT'S NORMIE'S HOUSE. IT'S OUR HOME. AND YOU--YOU'RE JUST VISITING.
GREAT. YOU TREAT ALL YOUR GUESTS LIKE THIS?
...
KIDDING. JUST KIDDING.

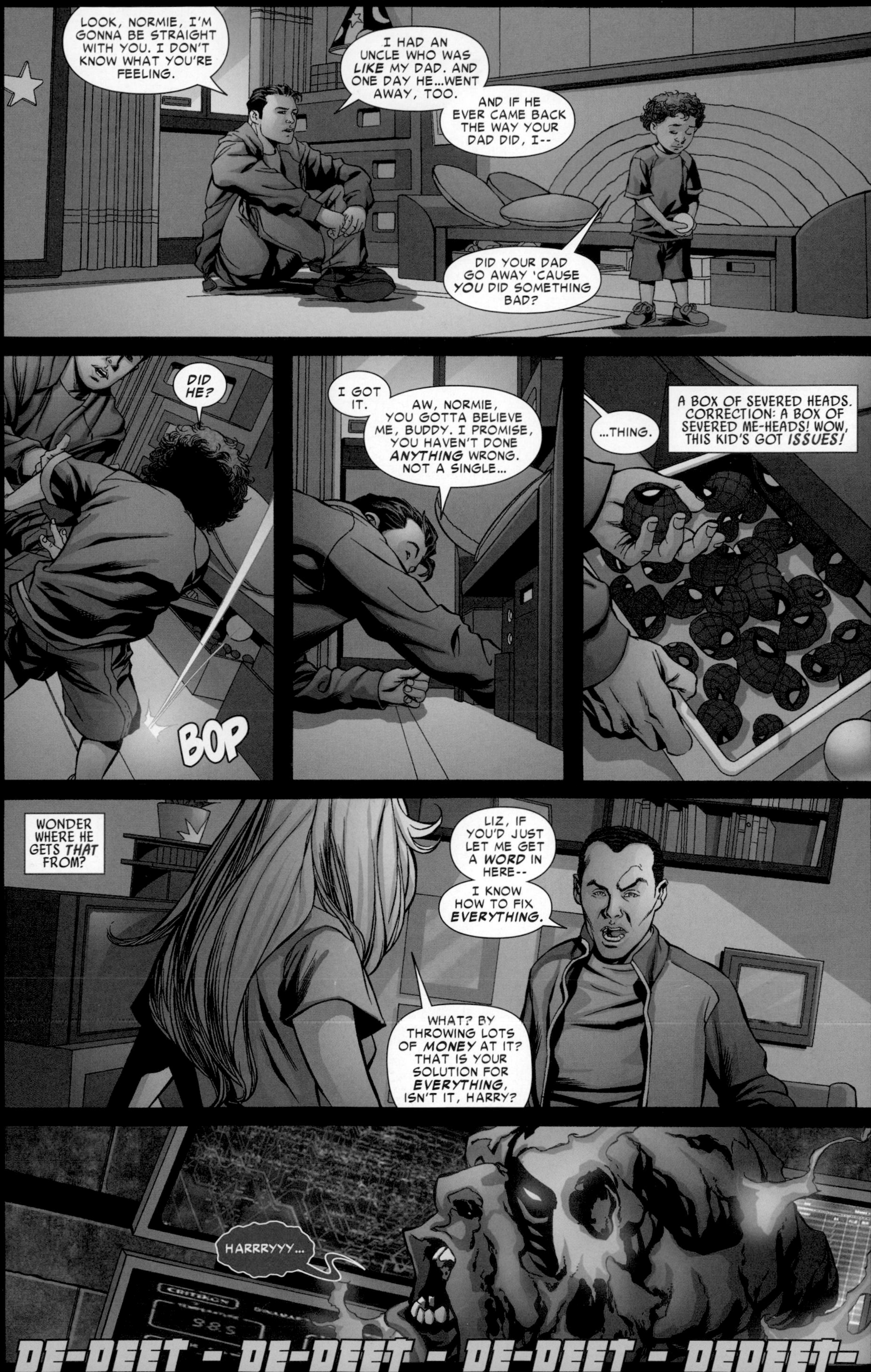
LOOK, NORMIE, I'M GONNA BE STRAIGHT WITH YOU. I DON'T KNOW WHAT YOU'RE FEELING.
I HAD AN UNCLE WHO WAS LIKE MY DAD. AND ONE DAY HE...WENT AWAY, TOO.
AND IF HE EVER CAME BACK THE WAY YOUR DAD DID, I--
DID YOUR DAD GO AWAY 'CAUSE YOU DID SOMETHING BAD?
DID HE?
BOP
I GOT IT.
AW, NORMIE, YOU GOTTA BELIEVE ME, BUDDY. I PROMISE, YOU HAVEN'T DONE ANYTHING WRONG. NOT A SINGLE...
...THING.
A BOX OF SEVERED HEADS. CORRECTION: A BOX OF SEVERED ME-HEADS! WOW, THIS KID'S GOT ISSUES!
WONDER WHERE HE GETS THAT FROM?
LIZ, IF YOU'D JUST LET ME GET A WORD IN HERE--
I KNOW HOW TO FIX EVERYTHING.
WHAT? BY THROWING LOTS OF MONEY AT IT? THAT IS YOUR SOLUTION FOR EVERYTHING, ISN'T IT, HARRY?
HARRRYYY...
DE-DEET - DE-DEET - DE-DEET - DEDEET-

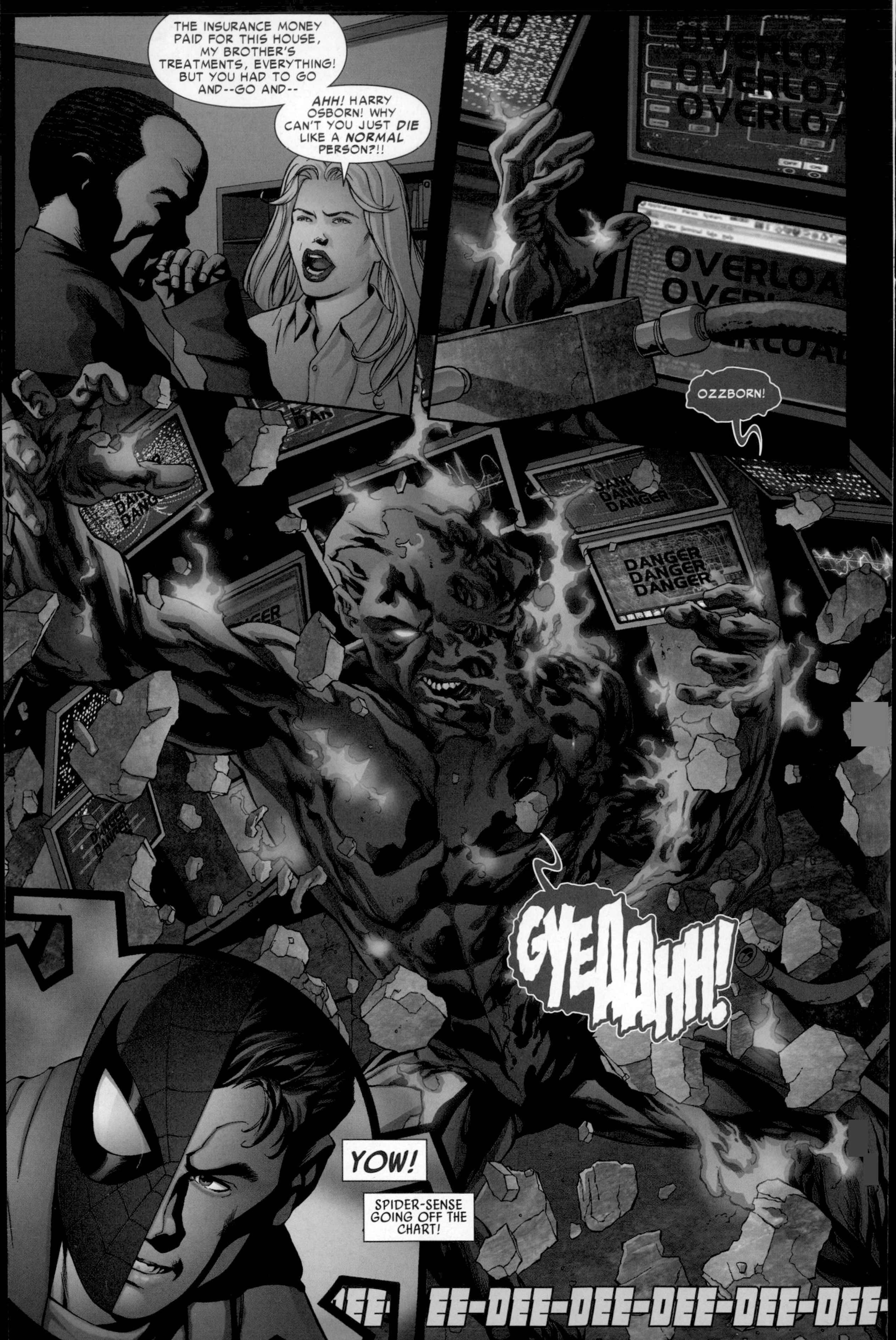
THE INSURANCE MONEY PAID FOR THIS HOUSE, MY BROTHER'S TREATMENTS, EVERYTHING! BUT YOU HAD TO GO AND--GO AND--
AHH! HARRY OSBORN! WHY CAN'T YOU JUST DIE LIKE A NORMAL PERSON?!!
OVERLOAD
OVERLOAD
OVERLOAD
OZZBORN!
DANGER
DANGER
DANGER
GYEAAHH!
YOW!
SPIDER-SENSE GOING OFF THE CHART!
EE-DEE-DEE-DEE-DEE-DEE-

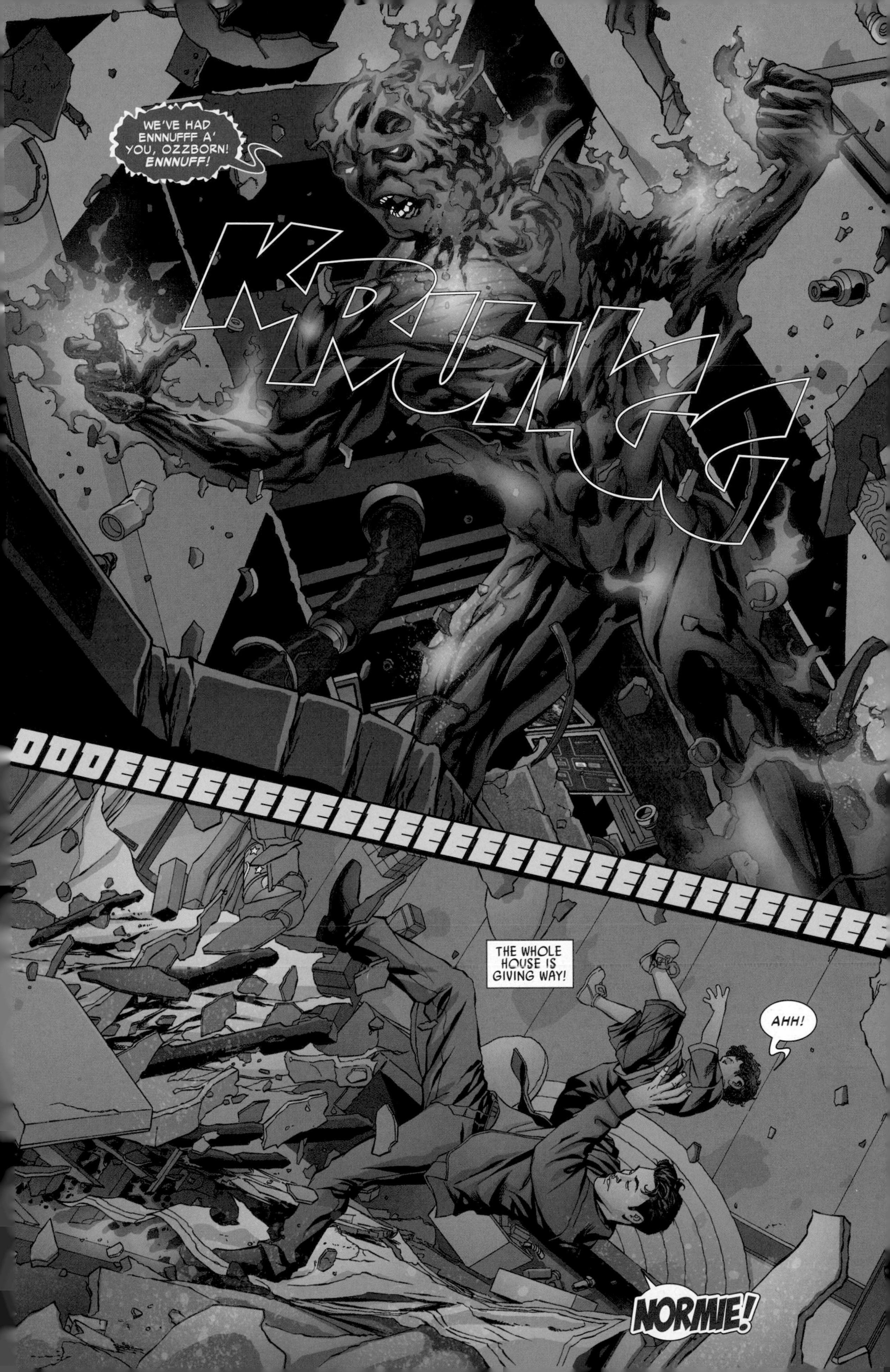

WE'VE HAD ENNNUFFF A' YOU, OZZBORN! *ENNNUFF!*
KRUNG
DDDEEEEEEEEEEEEEEEEEEEEEEEEEE
THE WHOLE HOUSE IS GIVING WAY!
AHH!
NORMIE!

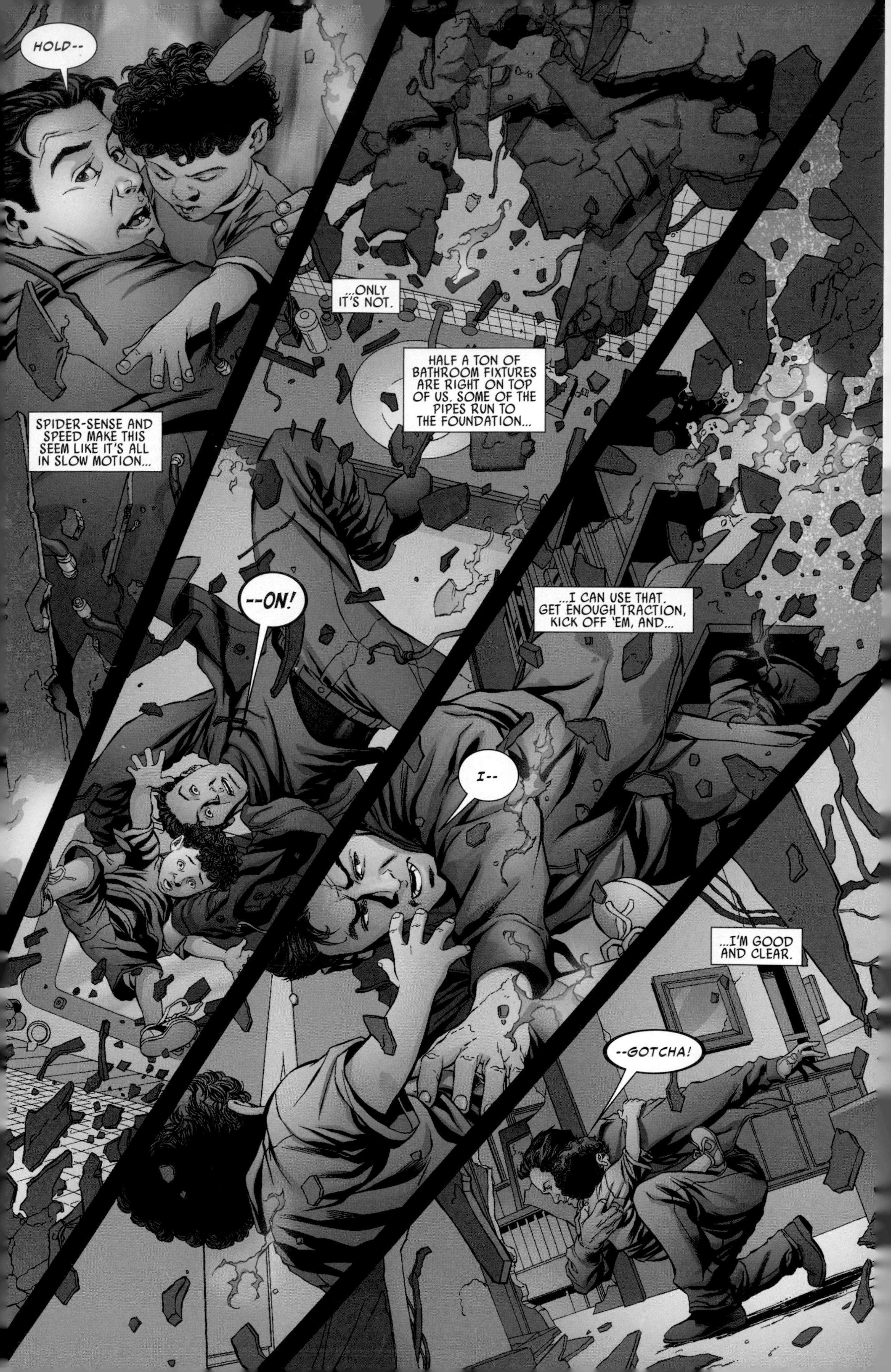
HOLD--
SPIDER-SENSE AND SPEED MAKE THIS SEEM LIKE IT'S ALL IN SLOW MOTION...
...ONLY IT'S NOT.
HALF A TON OF BATHROOM FIXTURES ARE RIGHT ON TOP OF US. SOME OF THE PIPES RUN TO THE FOUNDATION...
--ON!
...I CAN USE THAT. GET ENOUGH TRACTION, KICK OFF 'EM, AND...
I--
...I'M GOOD AND CLEAR.
--GOTCHA!

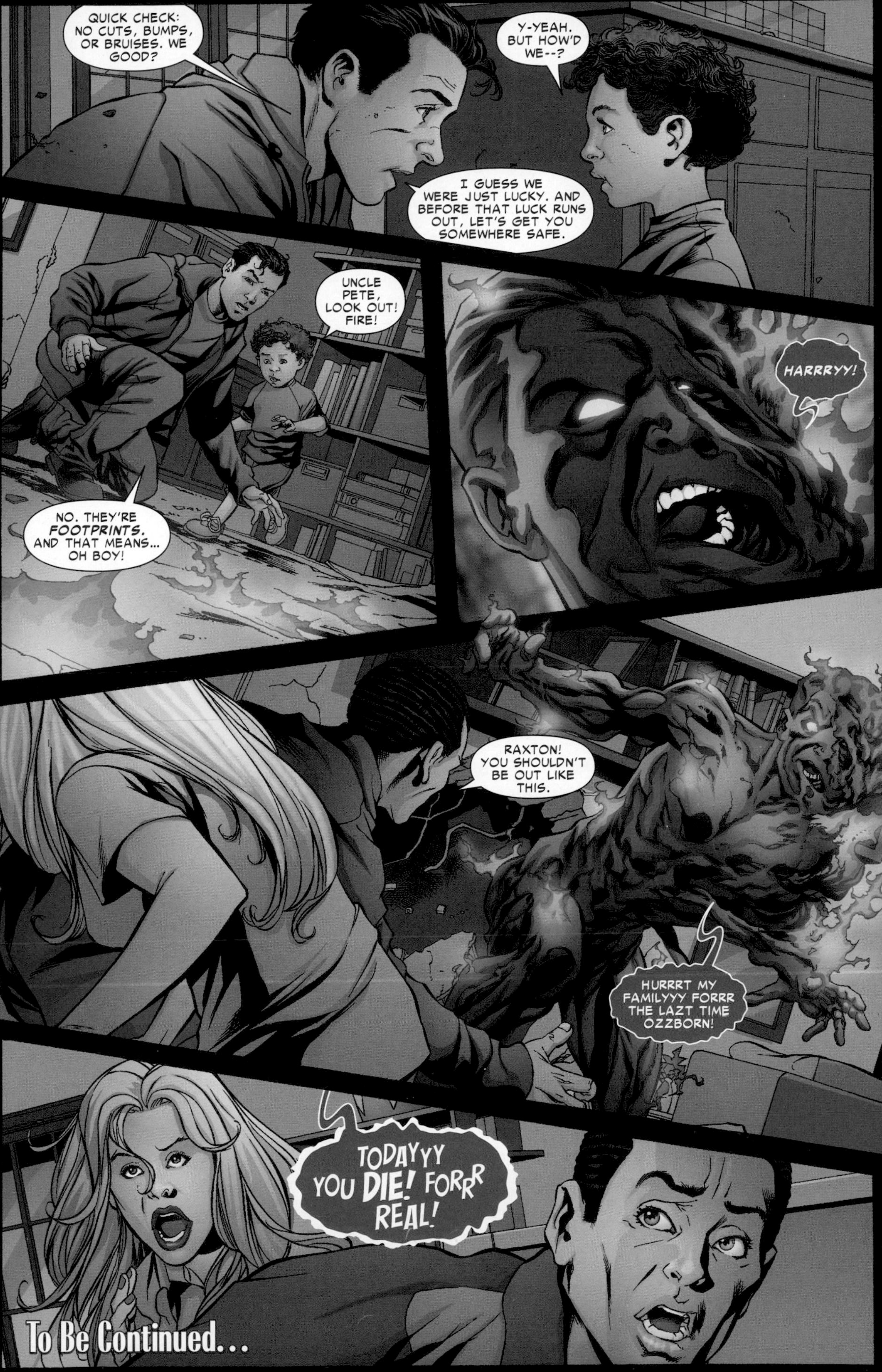
QUICK CHECK: NO CUTS, BUMPS, OR BRUISES. WE GOOD?
Y-YEAH. BUT HOW'D WE--?
I GUESS WE WERE JUST LUCKY. AND BEFORE THAT LUCK RUNS OUT, LET'S GET YOU SOMEWHERE SAFE.
UNCLE PETE, LOOK OUT! FIRE!
NO. THEY'RE FOOTPRINTS. AND THAT MEANS... OH BOY!
HARRRYY!
RAXTON! YOU SHOULDN'T BE OUT LIKE THIS.
HURRRT MY FAMILYYY FORRR THE LAZT TIME OZZBORN!
TODAYYY YOU DIE! FORRR REAL!
To Be Continued...

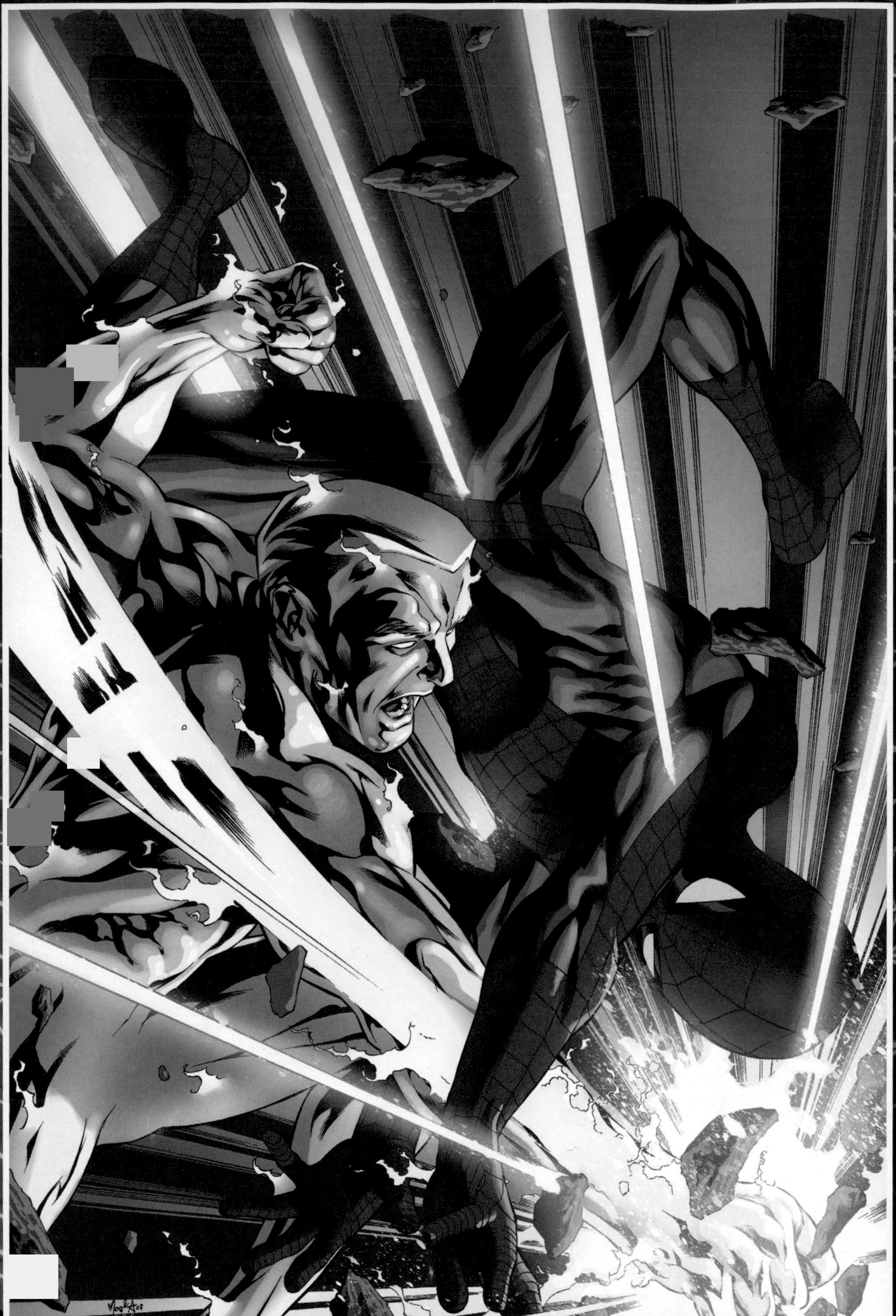

AMAZING SPIDER-MAN #582

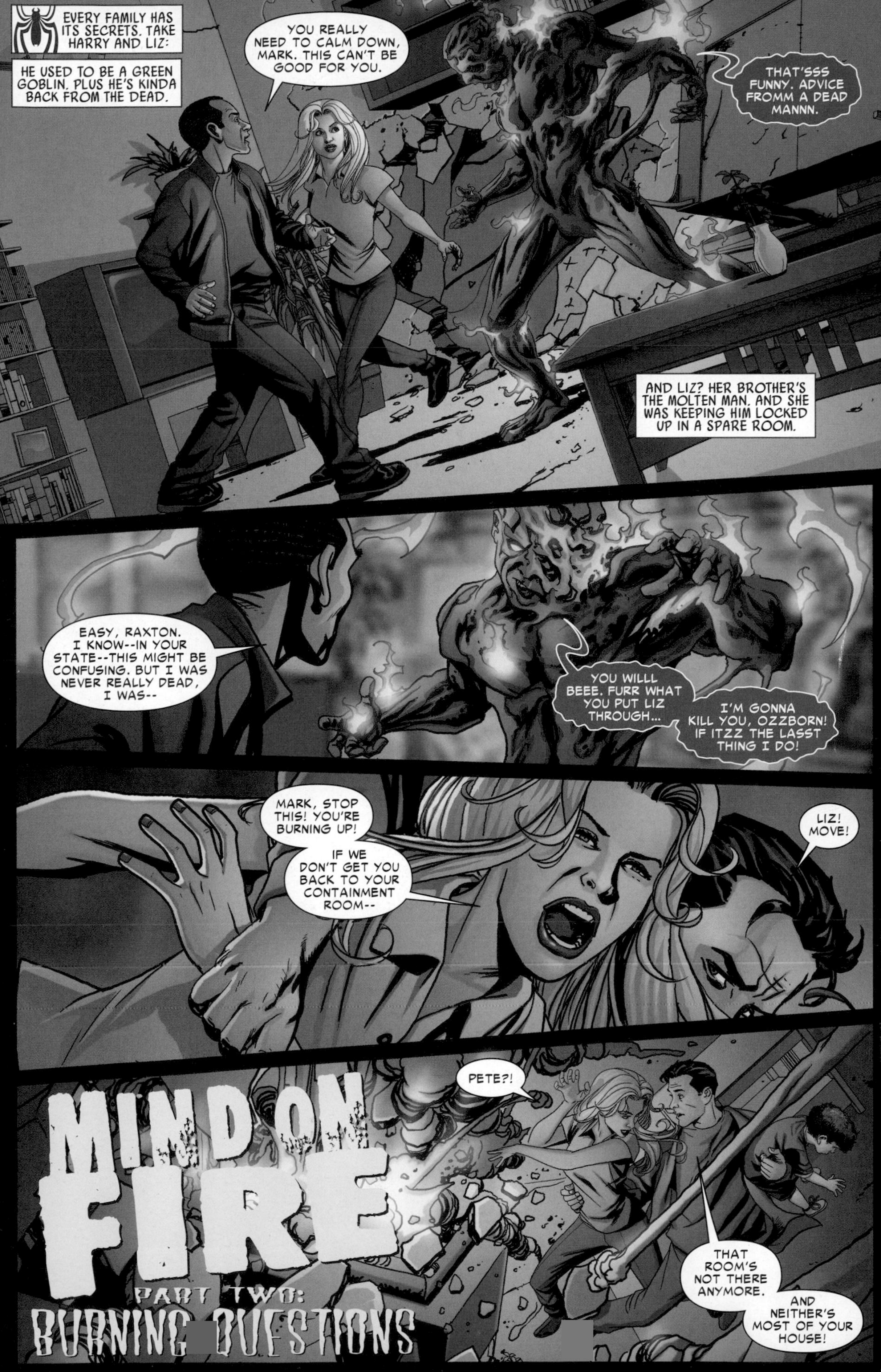
EVERY FAMILY HAS ITS SECRETS. TAKE HARRY AND LIZ:
HE USED TO BE A GREEN GOBLIN. PLUS HE'S KINDA BACK FROM THE DEAD.
YOU REALLY NEED TO CALM DOWN, MARK. THIS CAN'T BE GOOD FOR YOU.
THAT'SSS FUNNY. ADVICE FROMM A DEAD MANNN.
AND LIZ? HER BROTHER'S THE MOLTEN MAN. AND SHE WAS KEEPING HIM LOCKED UP IN A SPARE ROOM.
EASY, RAXTON. I KNOW--IN YOUR STATE--THIS MIGHT BE CONFUSING. BUT I WAS NEVER REALLY DEAD, I WAS--
YOU WILLL BEEE. FURR WHAT YOU PUT LIZ THROUGH...
I'M GONNA KILL YOU, OZZBORN! IF ITZZ THE LASST THING I DO!
MARK, STOP THIS! YOU'RE BURNING UP!
IF WE DON'T GET YOU BACK TO YOUR CONTAINMENT ROOM--
LIZ! MOVE!
PETE?!
MIND ON FIRE
PART TWO:
BURNING QUESTIONS
THAT ROOM'S NOT THERE ANYMORE.
AND NEITHER'S MOST OF YOUR HOUSE!

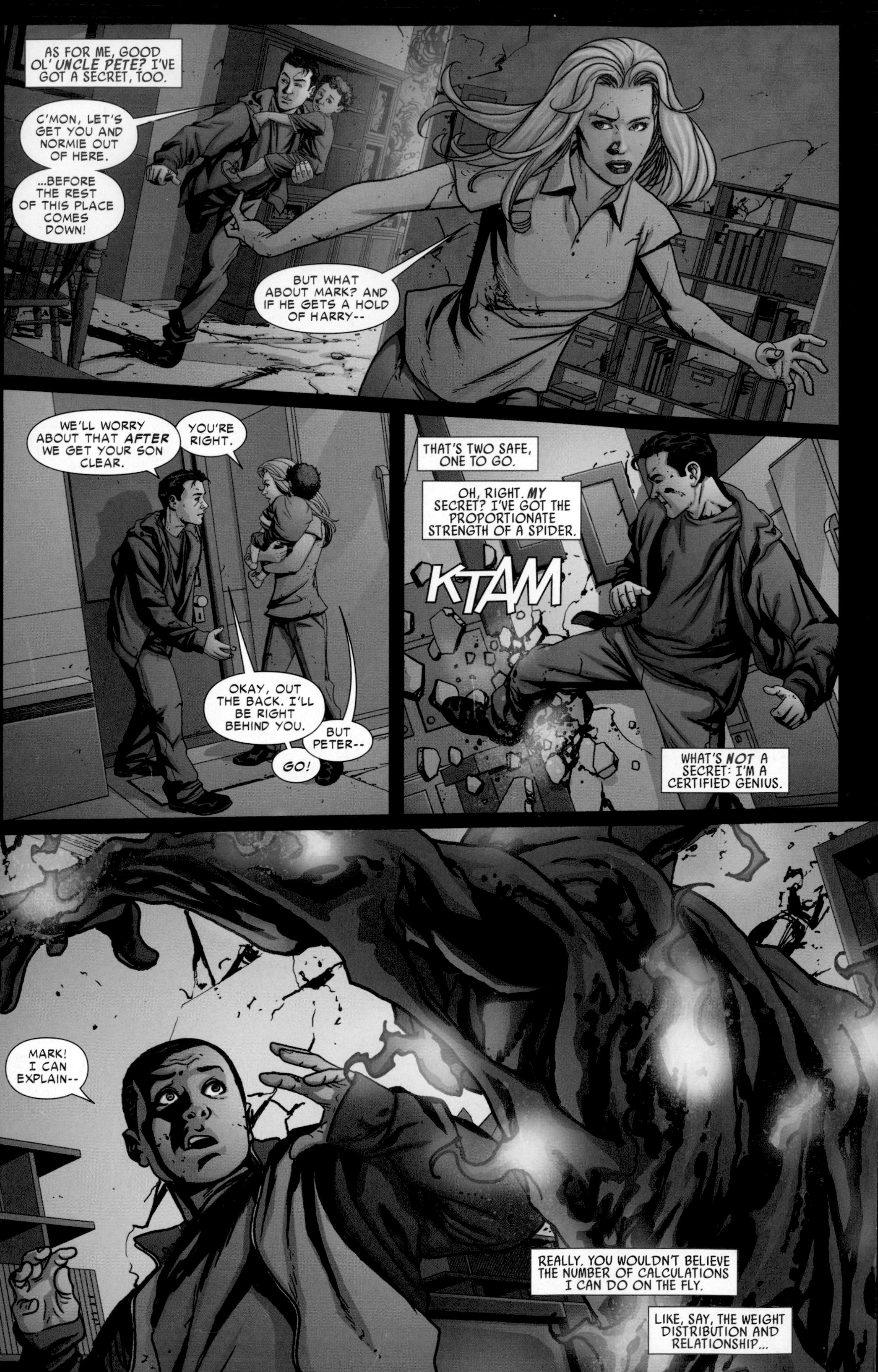

AS FOR ME, GOOD OL' UNCLE PETE? I'VE GOT A SECRET, TOO.
C'MON, LET'S GET YOU AND NORMIE OUT OF HERE.
...BEFORE THE REST OF THIS PLACE COMES DOWN!
BUT WHAT ABOUT MARK? AND IF HE GETS A HOLD OF HARRY--
WE'LL WORRY ABOUT THAT AFTER WE GET YOUR SON CLEAR.
YOU'RE RIGHT.
OKAY, OUT THE BACK. I'LL BE RIGHT BEHIND YOU.
BUT PETER--
GO!
THAT'S TWO SAFE, ONE TO GO.
OH, RIGHT. MY SECRET? I'VE GOT THE PROPORTIONATE STRENGTH OF A SPIDER.
KTAM
WHAT'S NOT A SECRET: I'M A CERTIFIED GENIUS.
MARK! I CAN EXPLAIN--
REALLY. YOU WOULDN'T BELIEVE THE NUMBER OF CALCULATIONS I CAN DO ON THE FLY.
LIKE, SAY, THE WEIGHT DISTRIBUTION AND RELATIONSHIP...

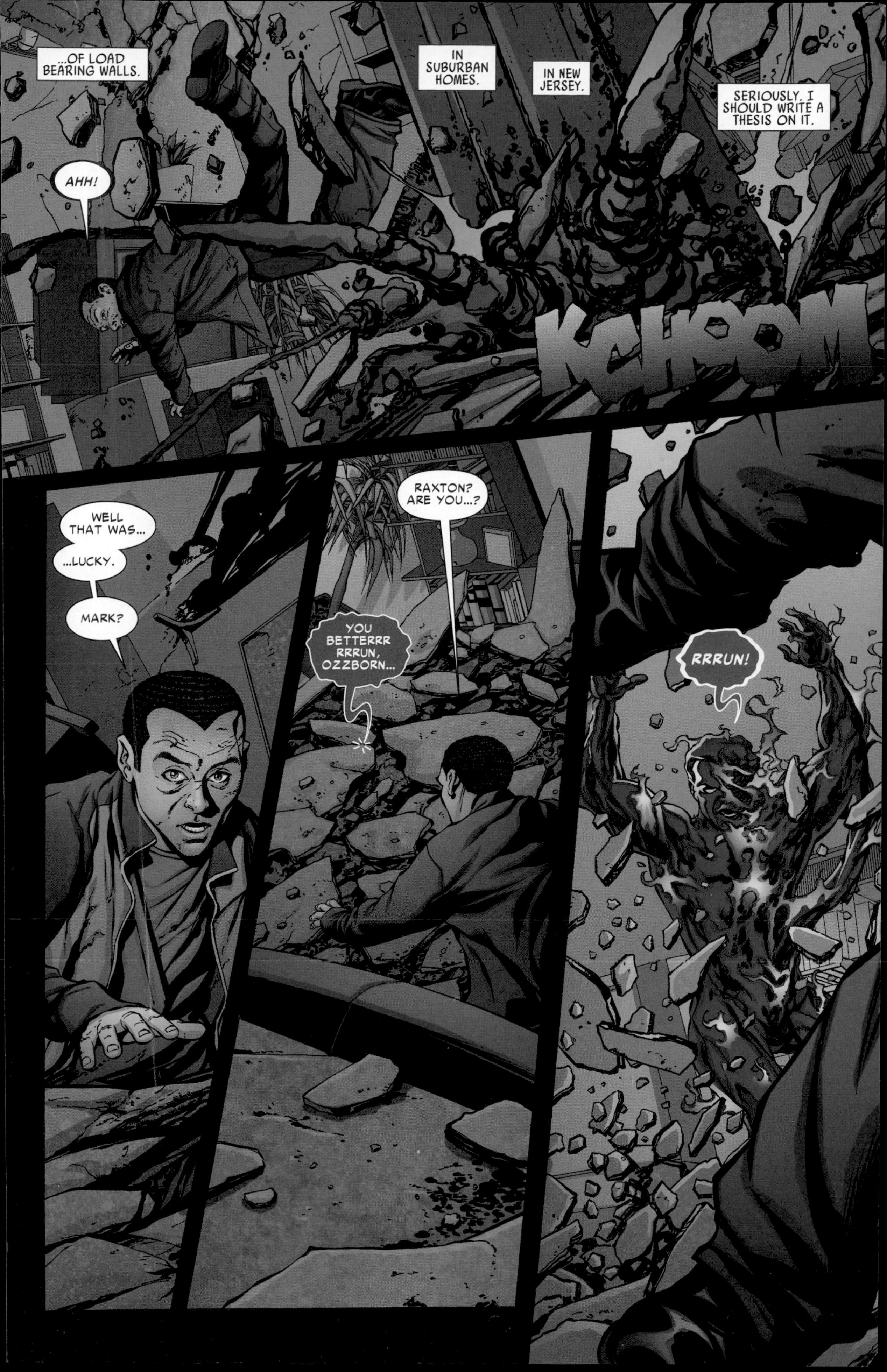
...OF LOAD BEARING WALLS.
IN SUBURBAN HOMES.
IN NEW JERSEY.
SERIOUSLY. I SHOULD WRITE A THESIS ON IT.
AHH!
KCHOOM
WELL THAT WAS...
...LUCKY.
MARK?
RAXTON? ARE YOU...?
YOU BETTERRR RRRUN, OZZBORN...
RRRUN!

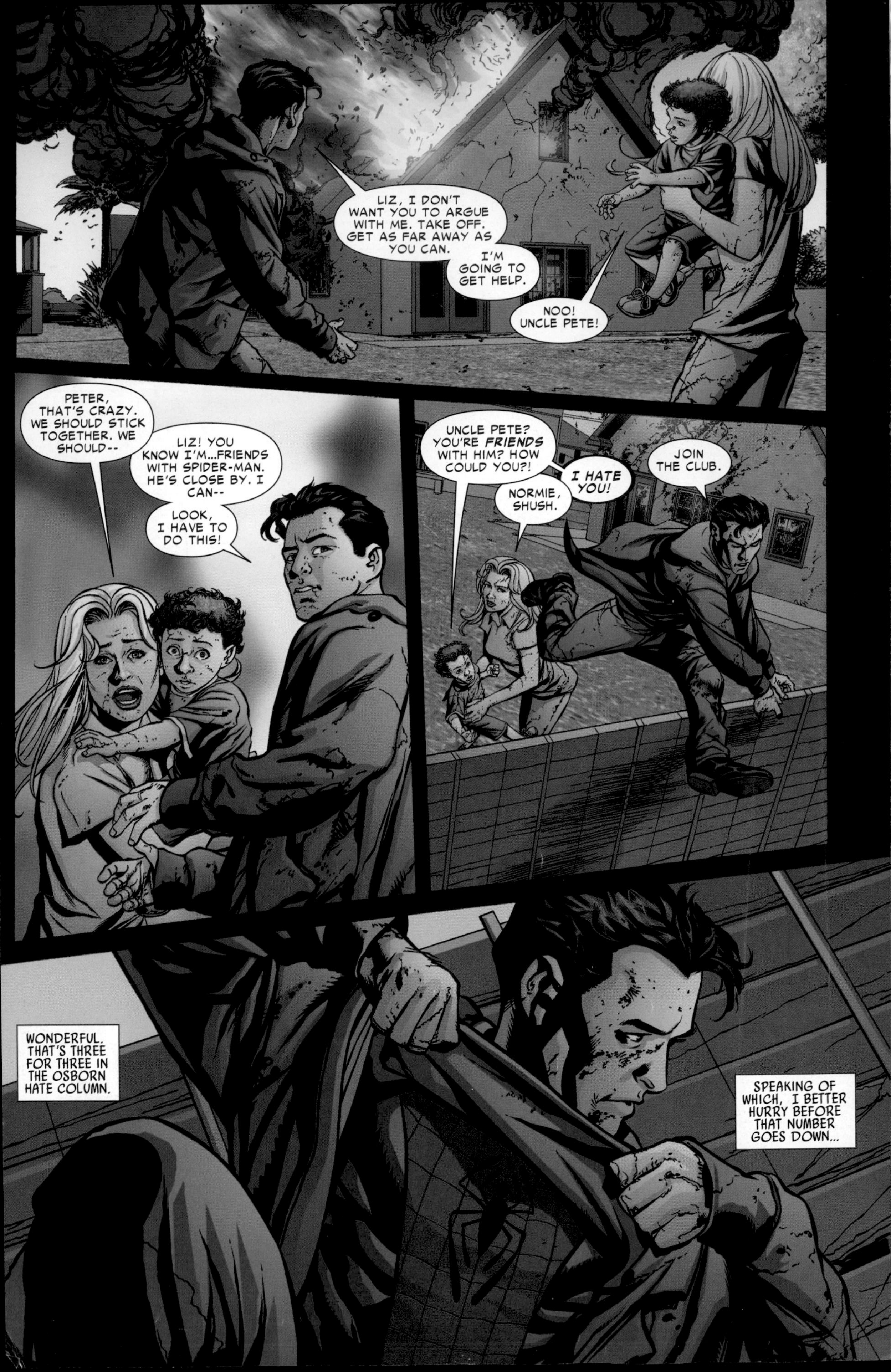
LIZ, I DON'T WANT YOU TO ARGUE WITH ME. TAKE OFF. GET AS FAR AWAY AS YOU CAN.
I'M GOING TO GET HELP.
NOO! UNCLE PETE!
PETER, THAT'S CRAZY. WE SHOULD STICK TOGETHER. WE SHOULD--
LIZ! YOU KNOW I'M...FRIENDS WITH SPIDER-MAN. HE'S CLOSE BY. I CAN--
LOOK, I HAVE TO DO THIS!
UNCLE PETE? YOU'RE FRIENDS WITH HIM? HOW COULD YOU?!
I HATE YOU!
NORMIE, SHUSH.
JOIN THE CLUB.
WONDERFUL. THAT'S THREE FOR THREE IN THE OSBORN HATE COLUMN.
SPEAKING OF WHICH, I BETTER HURRY BEFORE THAT NUMBER GOES DOWN...

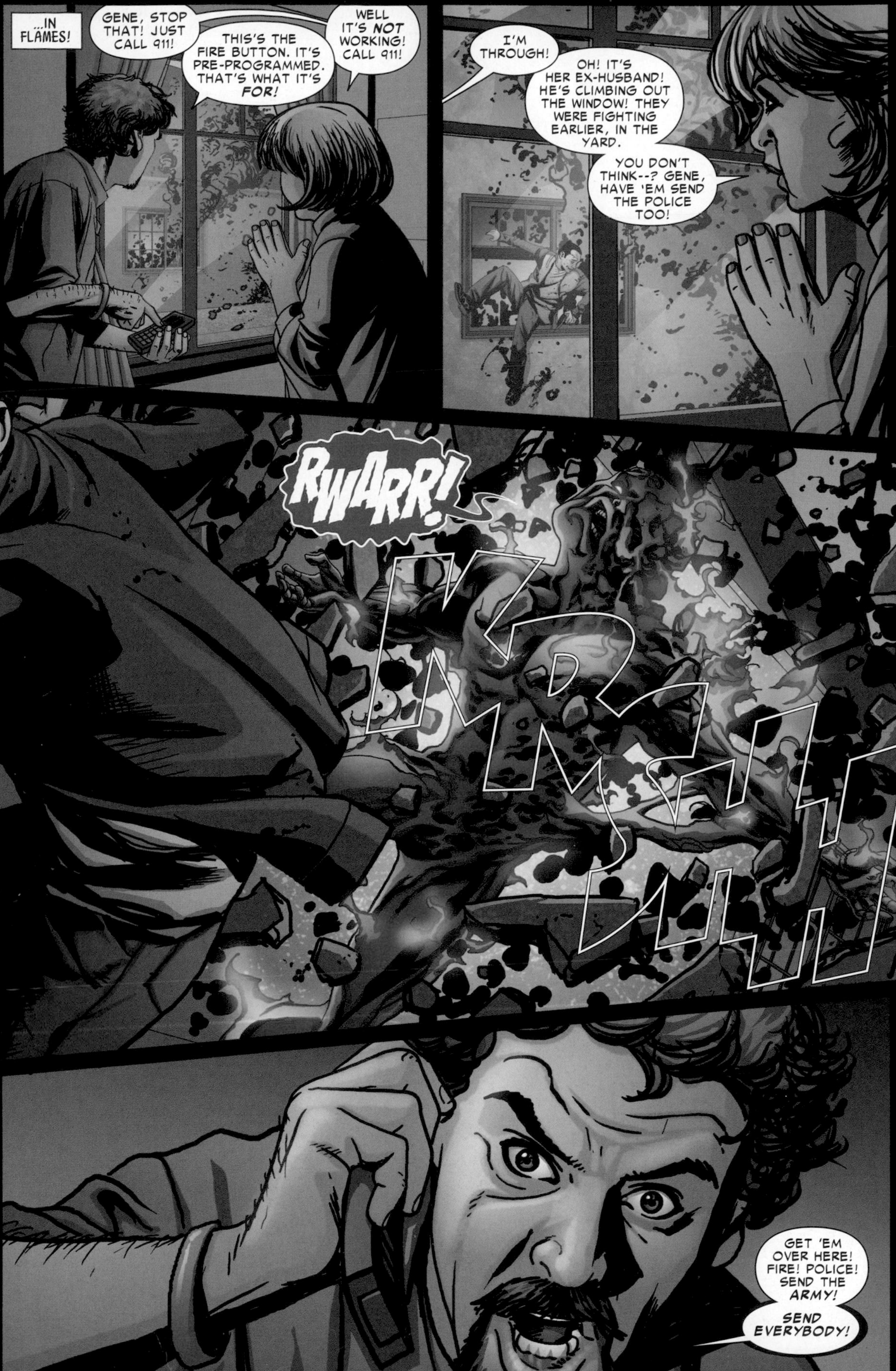
...IN FLAMES!
GENE, STOP THAT! JUST CALL 911!
THIS'S THE FIRE BUTTON. IT'S PRE-PROGRAMMED. THAT'S WHAT IT'S *FOR!*
WELL IT'S *NOT* WORKING! CALL 911!
I'M THROUGH!
OH! IT'S HER EX-HUSBAND! HE'S CLIMBING OUT THE WINDOW! THEY WERE FIGHTING EARLIER, IN THE YARD.
YOU DON'T THINK--? GENE, HAVE 'EM SEND THE POLICE TOO!
RWARR!
GET 'EM OVER HERE! FIRE! POLICE! SEND THE *ARMY!*
SEND EVERYBODY!

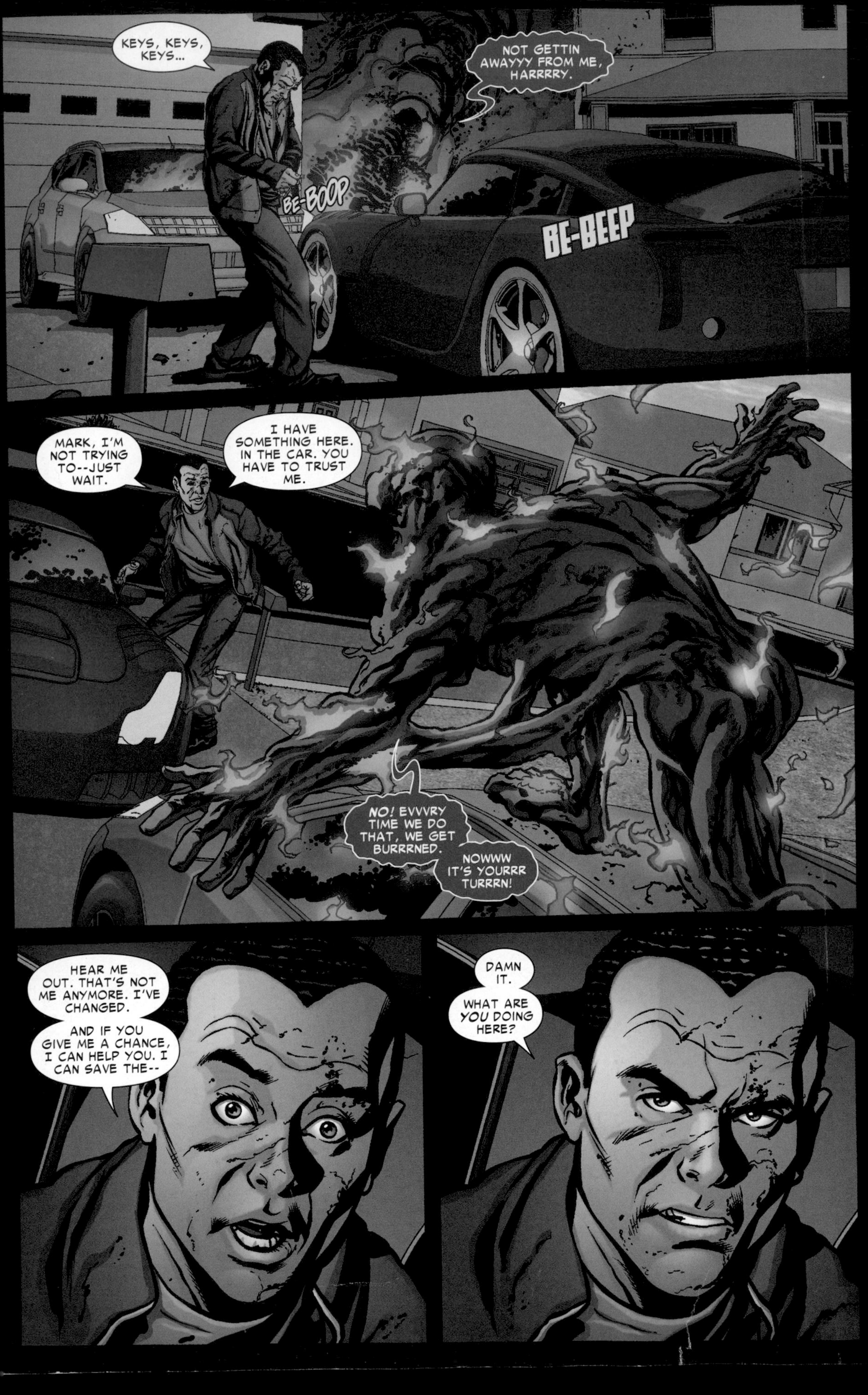
KEYS, KEYS, KEYS...
NOT GETTIN AWAYYY FROM ME, HARRRRY.
BE-BOOP
BE-BEEP
MARK, I'M NOT TRYING TO--JUST WAIT.
I HAVE SOMETHING HERE. IN THE CAR. YOU HAVE TO TRUST ME.
NO! EVVVRY TIME WE DO THAT, WE GET BURRRNED.
NOWWW IT'S YOURRR TURRRN!
HEAR ME OUT. THAT'S NOT ME ANYMORE. I'VE CHANGED.
AND IF YOU GIVE ME A CHANCE, I CAN HELP YOU. I CAN SAVE THE--
DAMN IT.
WHAT ARE YOU DOING HERE?

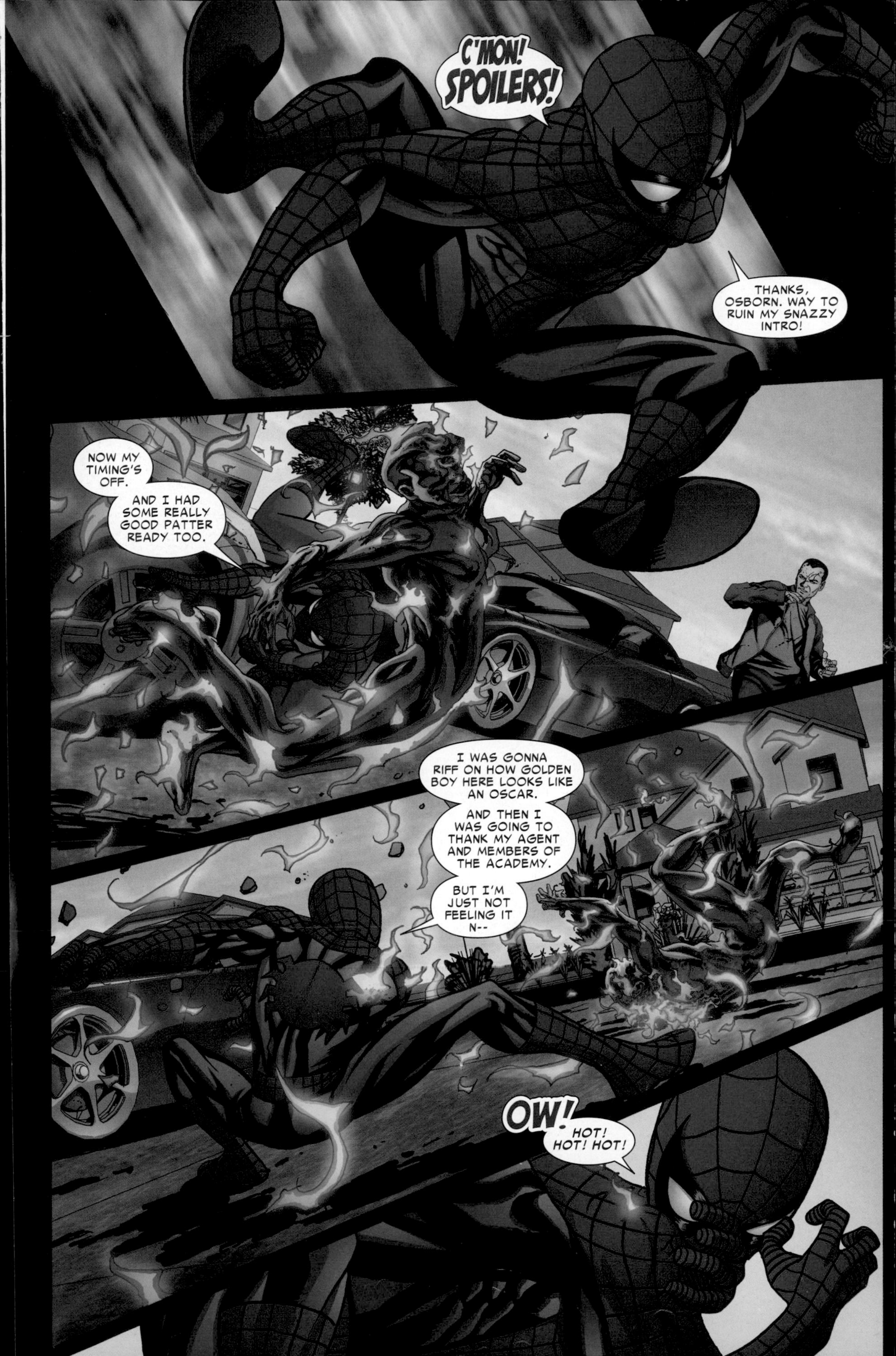
C'MON! SPOILERS!
THANKS, OSBORN. WAY TO RUIN MY SNAZZY INTRO!
NOW MY TIMING'S OFF.
AND I HAD SOME REALLY GOOD PATTER READY TOO.
I WAS GONNA RIFF ON HOW GOLDEN BOY HERE LOOKS LIKE AN OSCAR.
AND THEN I WAS GOING TO THANK MY AGENT AND MEMBERS OF THE ACADEMY.
BUT I'M JUST NOT FEELING IT N--
OW!
HOT! HOT! HOT!

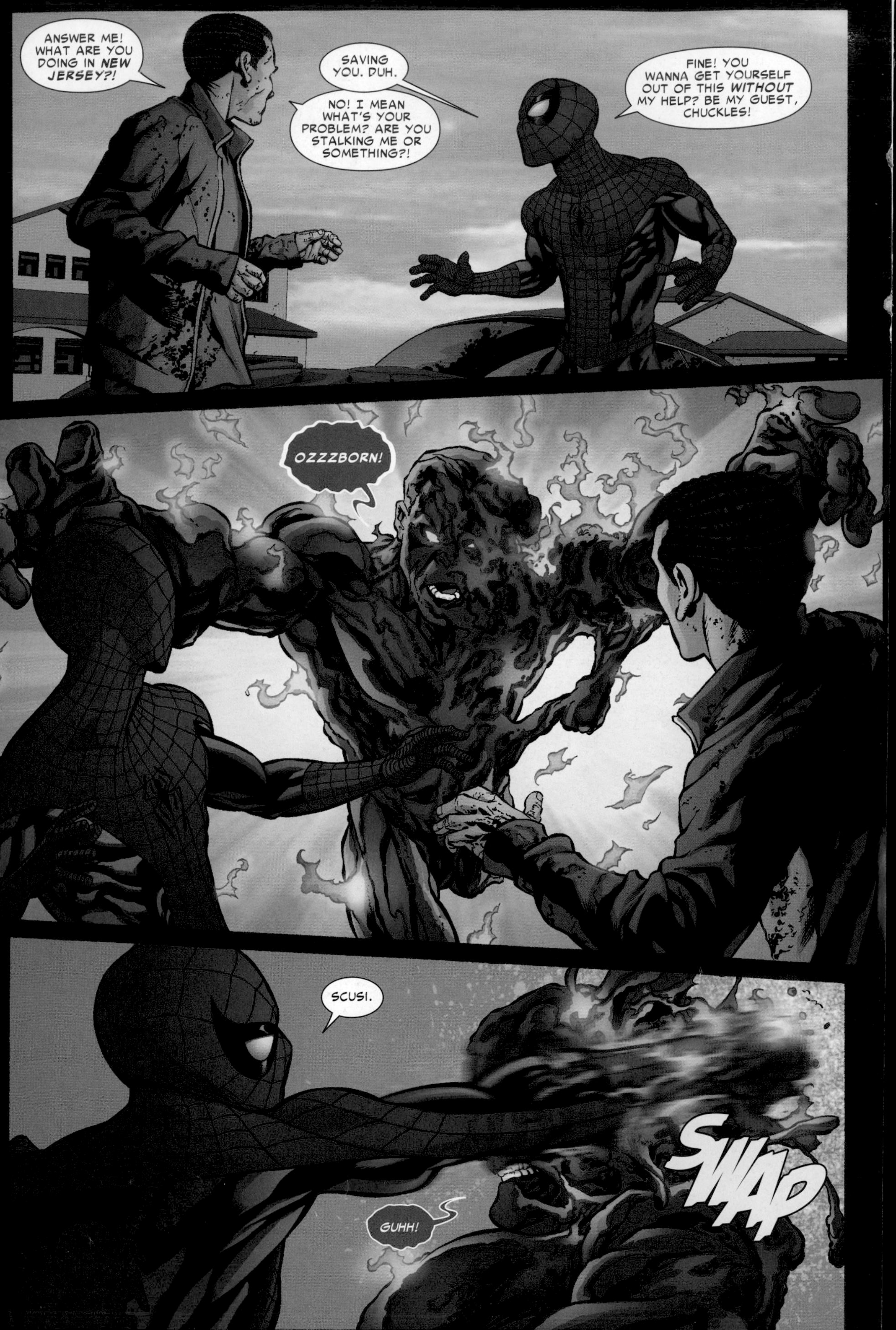

ANSWER ME! WHAT ARE YOU DOING IN NEW JERSEY?!
SAVING YOU. DUH.
NO! I MEAN WHAT'S YOUR PROBLEM? ARE YOU STALKING ME OR SOMETHING?!
FINE! YOU WANNA GET YOURSELF OUT OF THIS WITHOUT MY HELP? BE MY GUEST, CHUCKLES!
OZZZBORN!
SCUSI.
SWAP
GUHH!

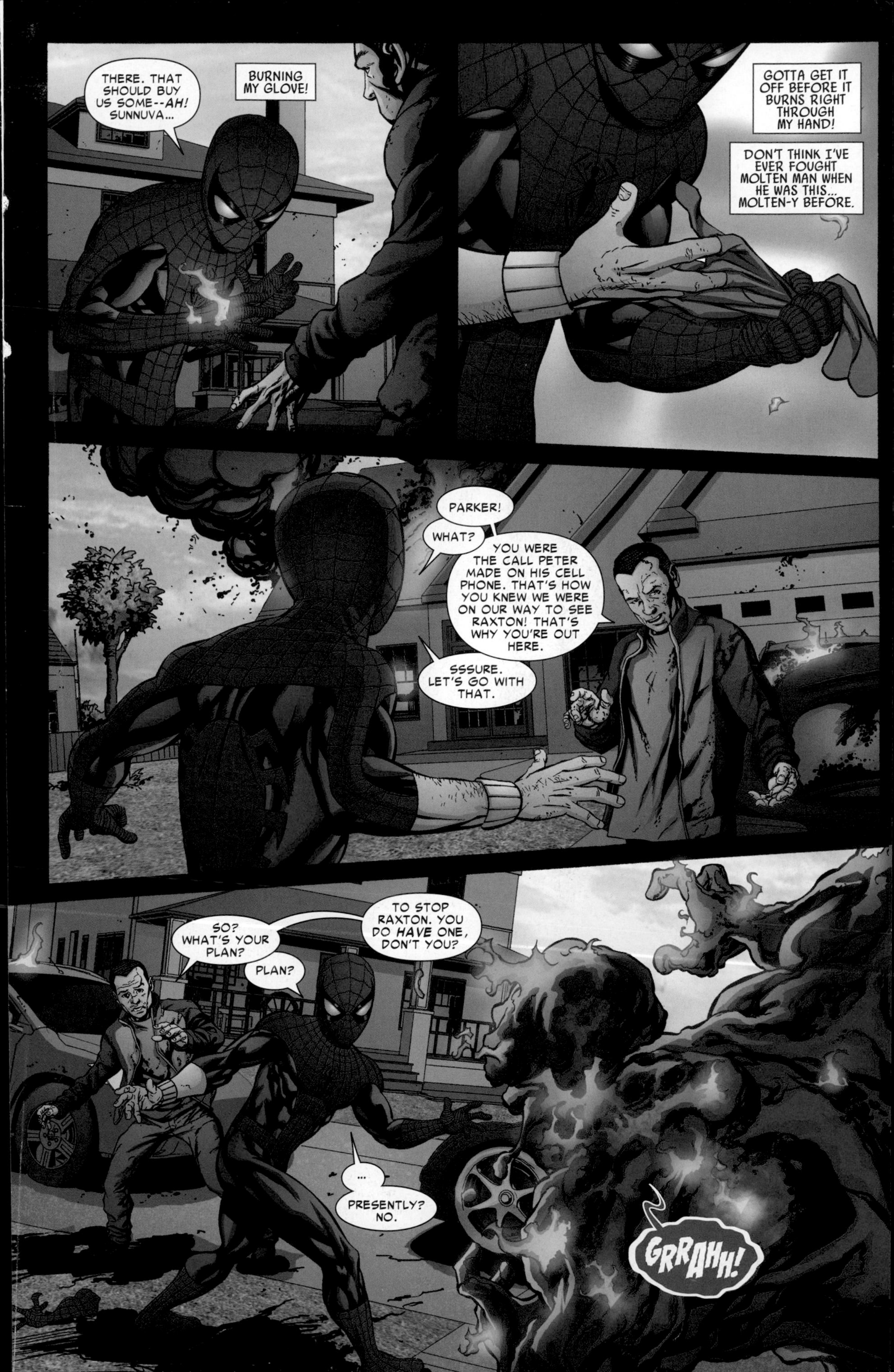
THERE. THAT SHOULD BUY US SOME--*AH!* SUNNUVA...
BURNING MY GLOVE!
GOTTA GET IT OFF BEFORE IT BURNS RIGHT THROUGH MY HAND!
DON'T THINK I'VE EVER FOUGHT MOLTEN MAN WHEN HE WAS THIS... MOLTEN-Y BEFORE.
PARKER!
WHAT?
YOU WERE THE CALL PETER MADE ON HIS CELL PHONE. THAT'S HOW YOU KNEW WE WERE ON OUR WAY TO SEE RAXTON! THAT'S WHY YOU'RE OUT HERE.
SSSURE. LET'S GO WITH THAT.
SO? WHAT'S YOUR PLAN?
PLAN?
TO STOP RAXTON. YOU DO *HAVE* ONE, DON'T YOU?
...
PRESENTLY? NO.
GRRAHH!

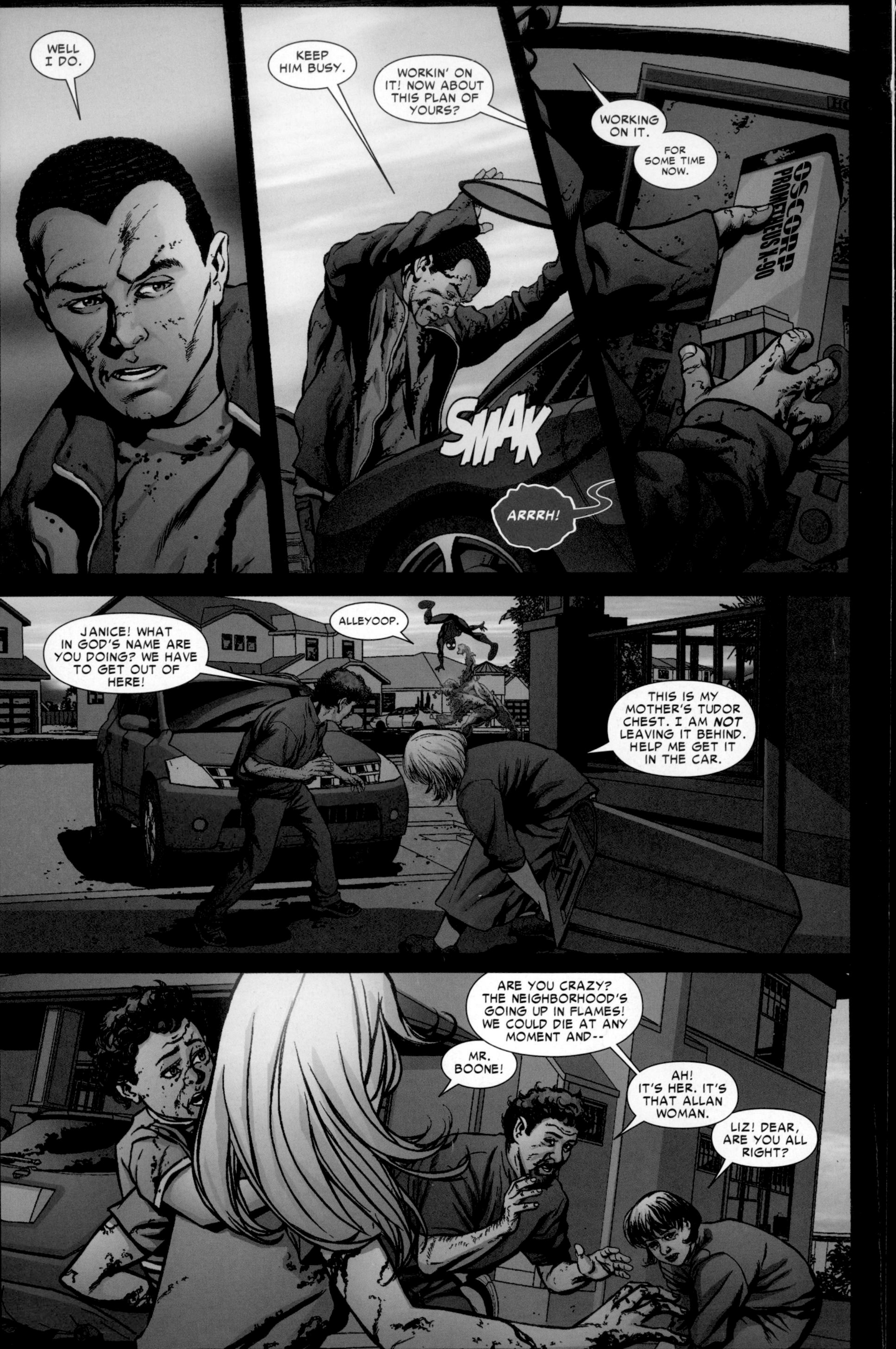
WELL I DO.
KEEP HIM BUSY.
WORKIN' ON IT! NOW ABOUT THIS PLAN OF YOURS?
WORKING ON IT.
FOR SOME TIME NOW.
OSCORP PROMETHEUS X-90
SMAK
ARRRH!
JANICE! WHAT IN GOD'S NAME ARE YOU DOING? WE HAVE TO GET OUT OF HERE!
ALLEYOOP.
THIS IS MY MOTHER'S TUDOR CHEST. I AM NOT LEAVING IT BEHIND. HELP ME GET IT IN THE CAR.
ARE YOU CRAZY? THE NEIGHBORHOOD'S GOING UP IN FLAMES! WE COULD DIE AT ANY MOMENT AND--
MR. BOONE!
AH! IT'S HER. IT'S THAT ALLAN WOMAN.
LIZ! DEAR, ARE YOU ALL RIGHT?

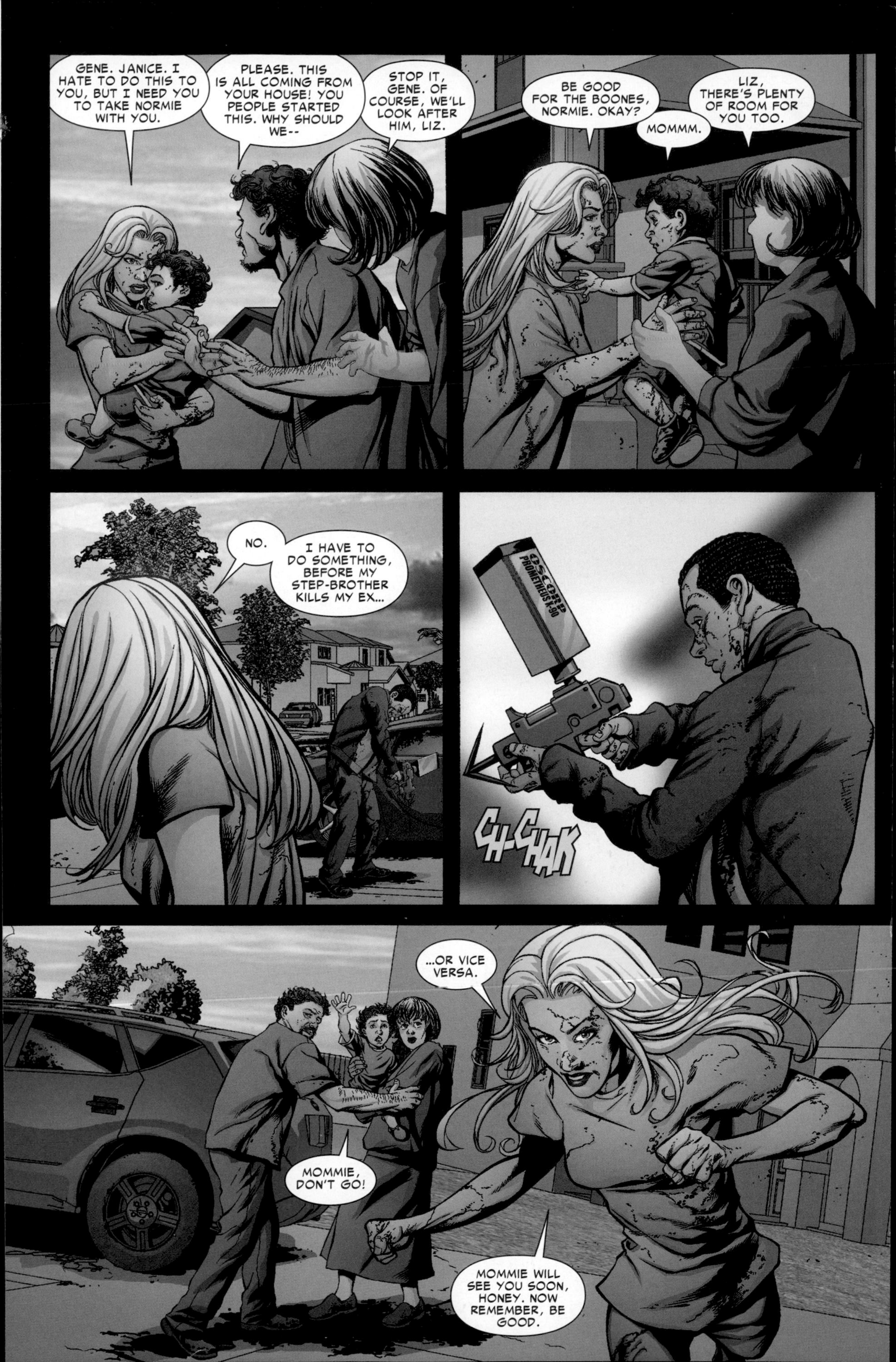
GENE. JANICE. I HATE TO DO THIS TO YOU, BUT I NEED YOU TO TAKE NORMIE WITH YOU.
PLEASE. THIS IS ALL COMING FROM YOUR HOUSE! YOU PEOPLE STARTED THIS. WHY SHOULD WE--
STOP IT, GENE. OF COURSE, WE'LL LOOK AFTER HIM, LIZ.
BE GOOD FOR THE BOONES, NORMIE. OKAY?
MOMMM.
LIZ, THERE'S PLENTY OF ROOM FOR YOU TOO.
NO.
I HAVE TO DO SOMETHING, BEFORE MY STEP-BROTHER KILLS MY EX...
OSCORP PROMETHEUS X-90
CH-CHAK
...OR VICE VERSA.
MOMMIE, DON'T GO!
MOMMIE WILL SEE YOU SOON, HONEY. NOW REMEMBER, BE GOOD.

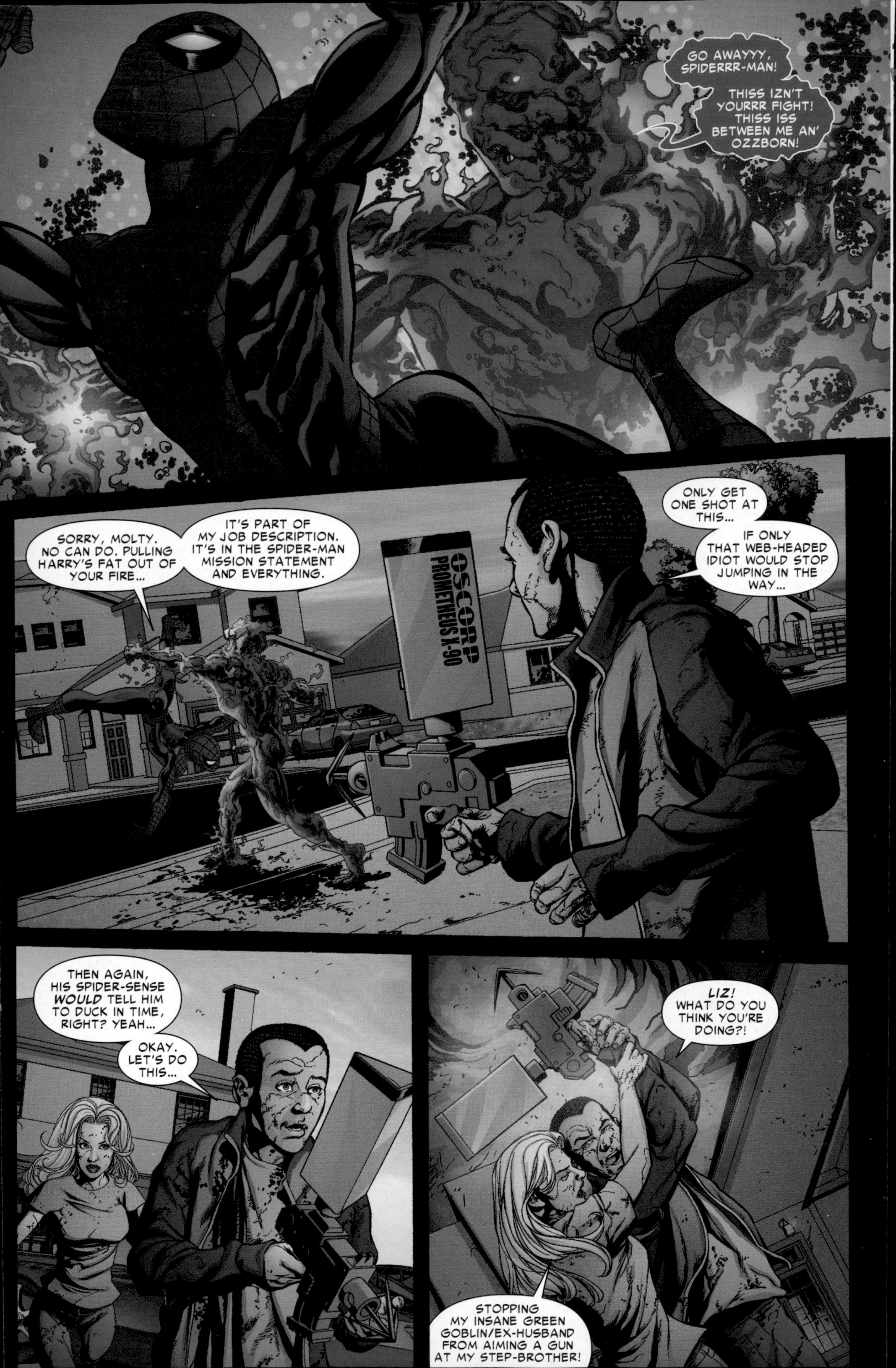
GO AWAYYY, SPIDERRR-MAN!
THISS IZN'T YOURRR FIGHT! THISS ISS BETWEEN ME AN' OZZBORN!
SORRY, MOLTY. NO CAN DO. PULLING HARRY'S FAT OUT OF YOUR FIRE...
IT'S PART OF MY JOB DESCRIPTION. IT'S IN THE SPIDER-MAN MISSION STATEMENT AND EVERYTHING.
OSCORP PROMETHEUS X-90
ONLY GET ONE SHOT AT THIS...
IF ONLY THAT WEB-HEADED IDIOT WOULD STOP JUMPING IN THE WAY...
THEN AGAIN, HIS SPIDER-SENSE WOULD TELL HIM TO DUCK IN TIME, RIGHT? YEAH...
OKAY. LET'S DO THIS...
LIZ! WHAT DO YOU THINK YOU'RE DOING?!
STOPPING MY INSANE GREEN GOBLIN/EX-HUSBAND FROM AIMING A GUN AT MY STEP-BROTHER!

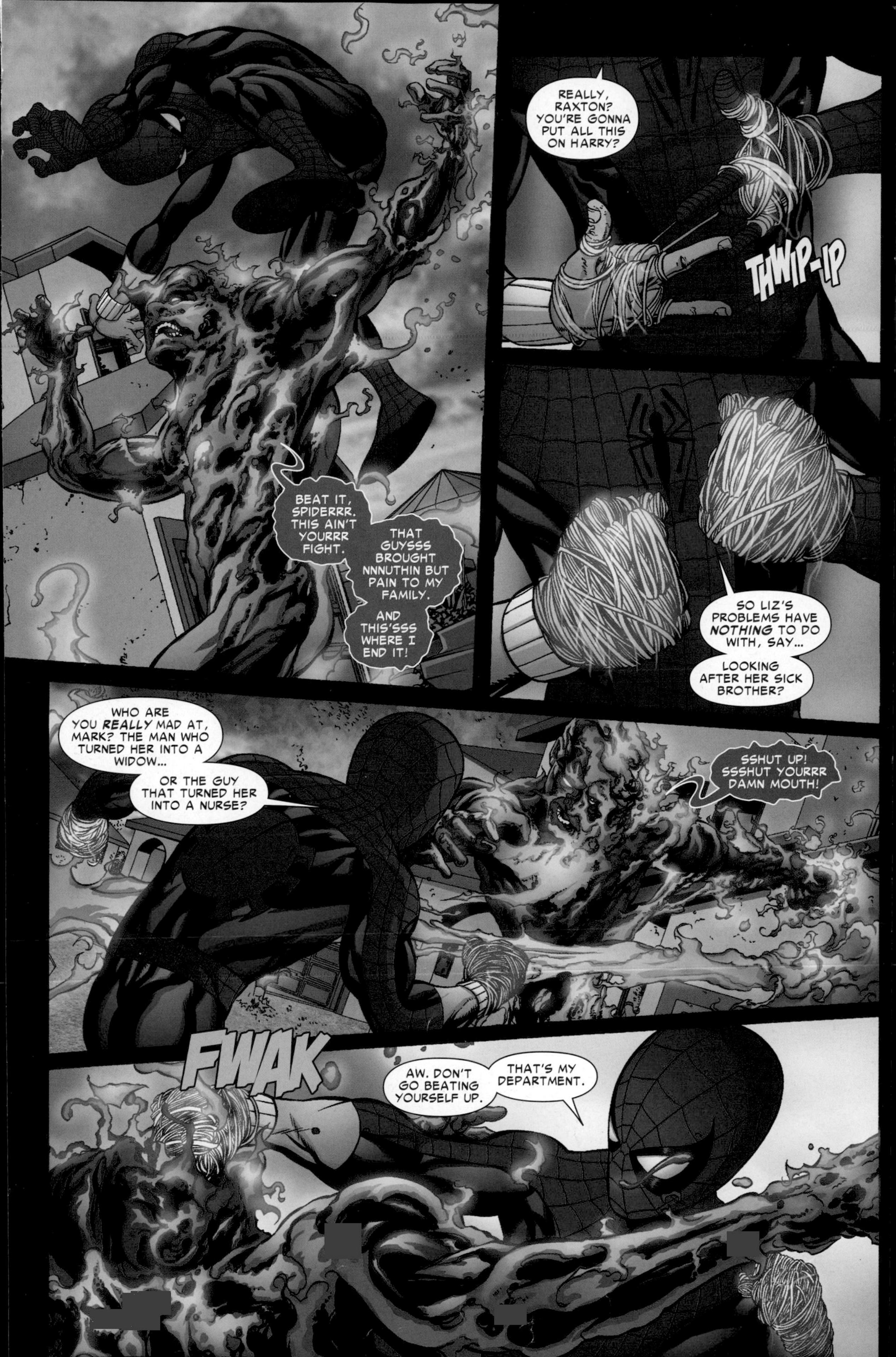
BEAT IT, SPIDERRR. THIS AIN'T YOURRR FIGHT.
THAT GUYSSS BROUGHT NNNUTHIN BUT PAIN TO MY FAMILY.
AND THIS'SSS WHERE I END IT!
REALLY, RAXTON? YOU'RE GONNA PUT ALL THIS ON HARRY?
THWIP-UP
SO LIZ'S PROBLEMS HAVE *NOTHING* TO DO WITH, SAY...
LOOKING AFTER HER SICK BROTHER?
WHO ARE YOU *REALLY* MAD AT, MARK? THE MAN WHO TURNED HER INTO A WIDOW...
OR THE GUY THAT TURNED HER INTO A NURSE?
SSHUT UP! SSSHUT YOURRR DAMN MOUTH!
FWAK
AW. DON'T GO BEATING YOURSELF UP.
THAT'S MY DEPARTMENT.

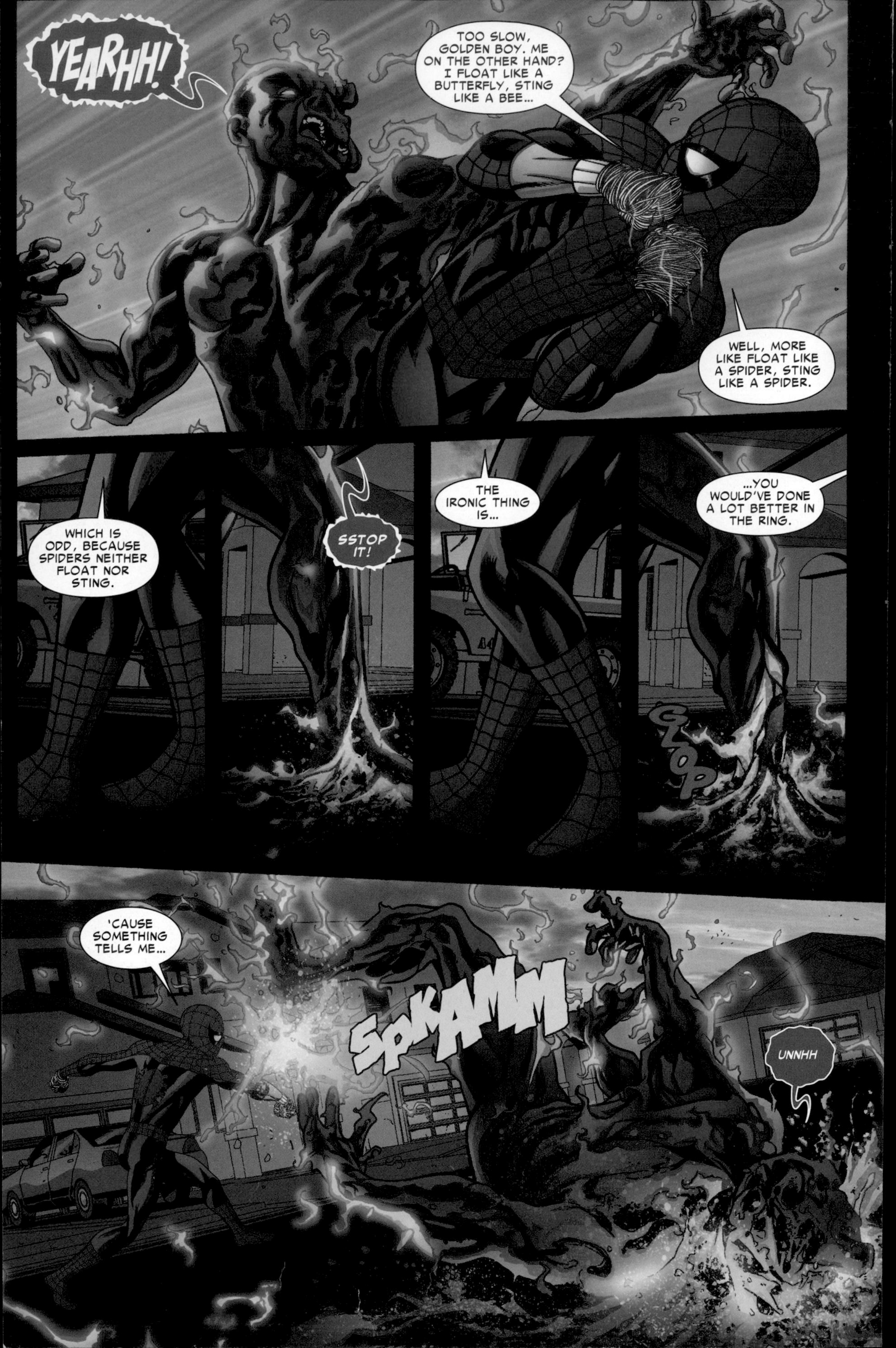
YEARHH!
TOO SLOW, GOLDEN BOY. ME ON THE OTHER HAND? I FLOAT LIKE A BUTTERFLY, STING LIKE A BEE...
WELL, MORE LIKE FLOAT LIKE A SPIDER, STING LIKE A SPIDER.
WHICH IS ODD, BECAUSE SPIDERS NEITHER FLOAT NOR STING.
SSTOP IT!
THE IRONIC THING IS...
...YOU WOULD'VE DONE A LOT BETTER IN THE RING.
GLOP
'CAUSE SOMETHING TELLS ME...
SPKAMM
UNNHH

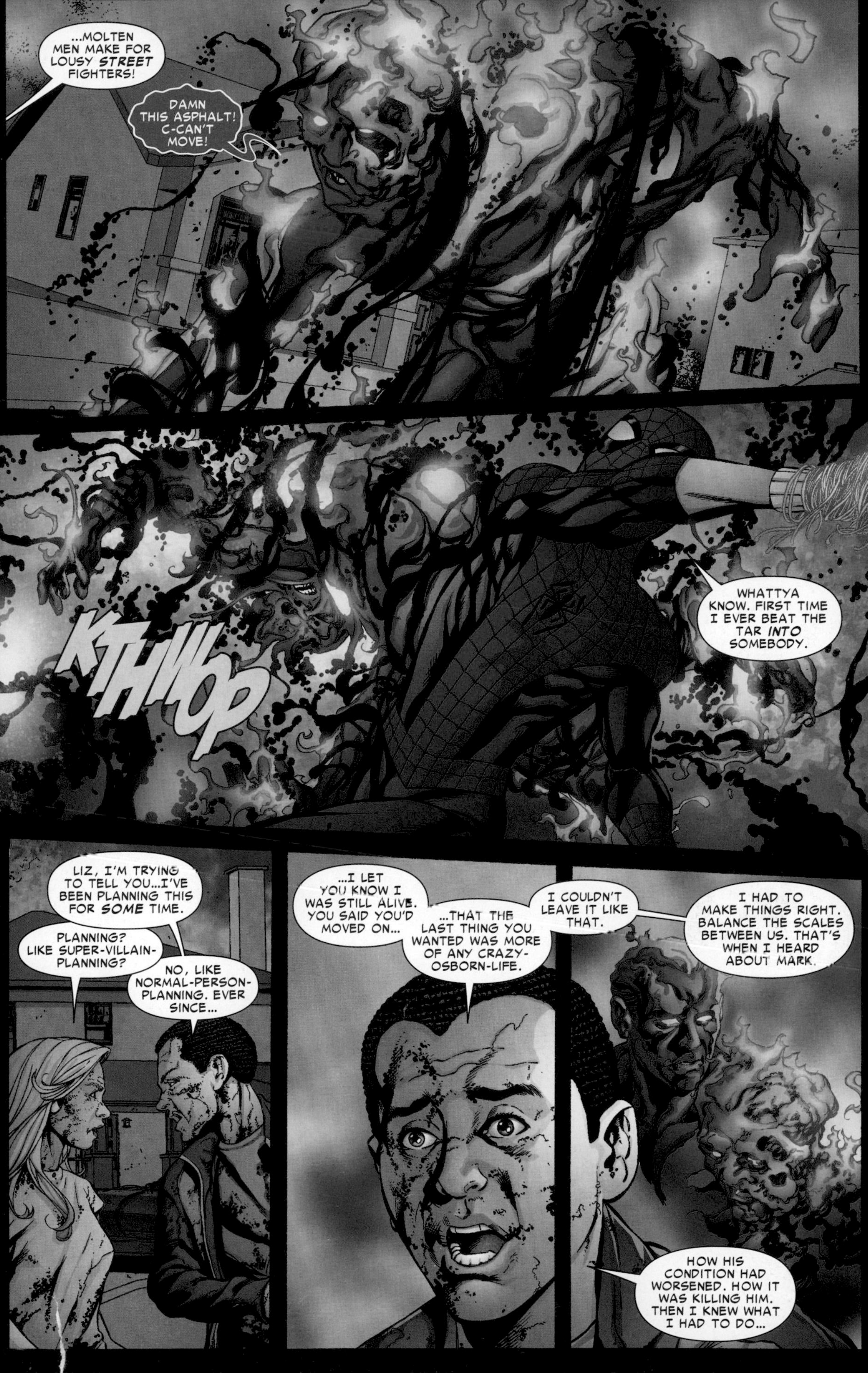
...MOLTEN MEN MAKE FOR LOUSY STREET FIGHTERS!
DAMN THIS ASPHALT! C-CAN'T MOVE!
KTHWOP
WHATTYA KNOW. FIRST TIME I EVER BEAT THE TAR INTO SOMEBODY.
LIZ, I'M TRYING TO TELL YOU...I'VE BEEN PLANNING THIS FOR SOME TIME.
PLANNING? LIKE SUPER-VILLAIN-PLANNING?
NO, LIKE NORMAL-PERSON-PLANNING. EVER SINCE...
...I LET YOU KNOW I WAS STILL ALIVE. YOU SAID YOU'D MOVED ON...
...THAT THE LAST THING YOU WANTED WAS MORE OF ANY CRAZY-OSBORN-LIFE.
I COULDN'T LEAVE IT LIKE THAT.
I HAD TO MAKE THINGS RIGHT. BALANCE THE SCALES BETWEEN US. THAT'S WHEN I HEARD ABOUT MARK.
HOW HIS CONDITION HAD WORSENED. HOW IT WAS KILLING HIM. THEN I KNEW WHAT I HAD TO DO...

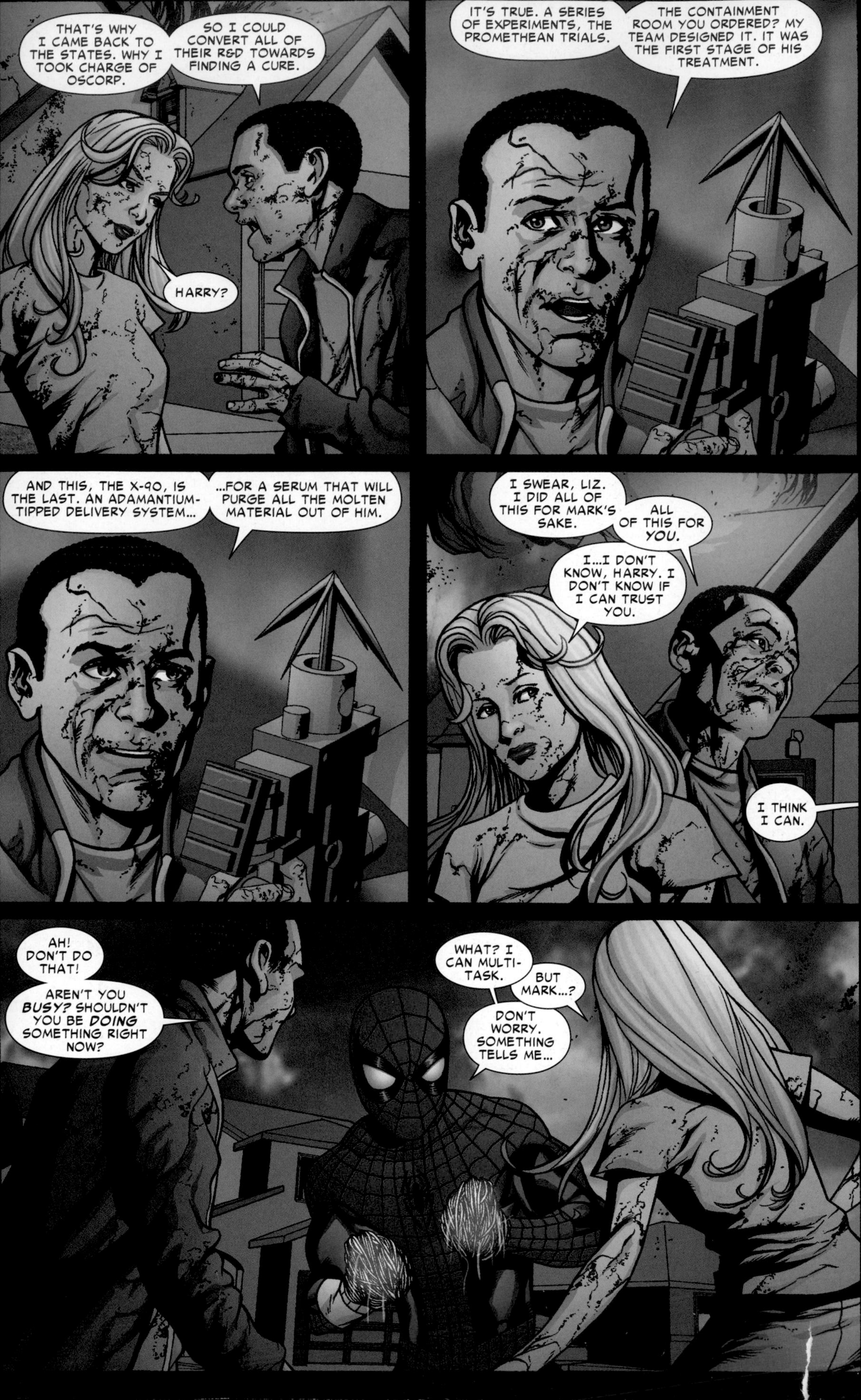
THAT'S WHY I CAME BACK TO THE STATES. WHY I TOOK CHARGE OF OSCORP.
SO I COULD CONVERT ALL OF THEIR R&D TOWARDS FINDING A CURE.
HARRY?
IT'S TRUE. A SERIES OF EXPERIMENTS, THE PROMETHEAN TRIALS.
THE CONTAINMENT ROOM YOU ORDERED? MY TEAM DESIGNED IT. IT WAS THE FIRST STAGE OF HIS TREATMENT.
AND THIS, THE X-90, IS THE LAST. AN ADAMANTIUM-TIPPED DELIVERY SYSTEM...
...FOR A SERUM THAT WILL PURGE ALL THE MOLTEN MATERIAL OUT OF HIM.
I SWEAR, LIZ. I DID ALL OF THIS FOR MARK'S SAKE.
ALL OF THIS FOR YOU.
I...I DON'T KNOW, HARRY. I DON'T KNOW IF I CAN TRUST YOU.
I THINK I CAN.
AH! DON'T DO THAT!
AREN'T YOU BUSY? SHOULDN'T YOU BE DOING SOMETHING RIGHT NOW?
WHAT? I CAN MULTI-TASK.
BUT MARK...?
DON'T WORRY. SOMETHING TELLS ME...

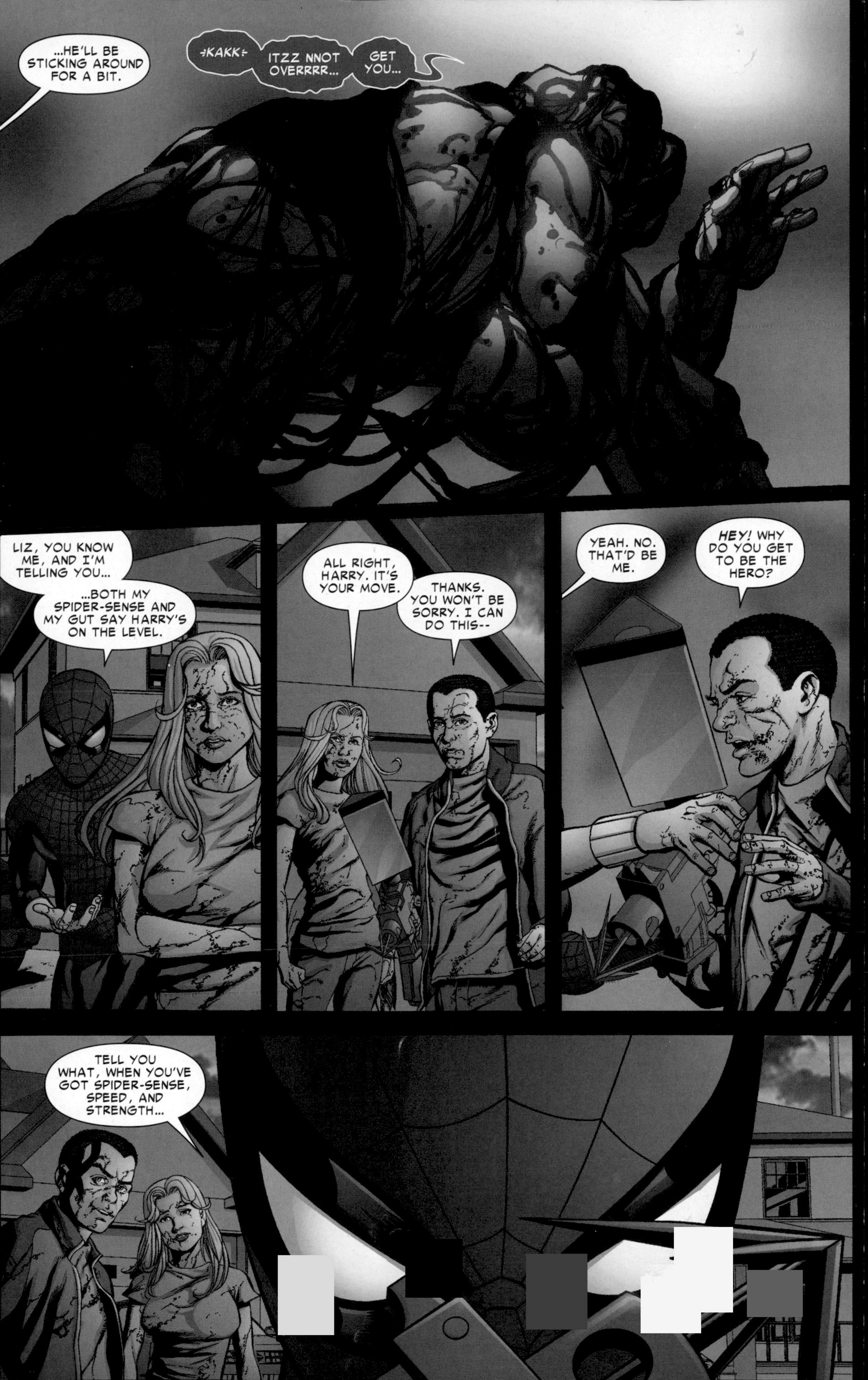
...HE'LL BE STICKING AROUND FOR A BIT.
-KAKK-
ITZZ NNOT OVERRRR...
GET YOU...
LIZ, YOU KNOW ME, AND I'M TELLING YOU...
...BOTH MY SPIDER-SENSE AND MY GUT SAY HARRY'S ON THE LEVEL.
ALL RIGHT, HARRY. IT'S YOUR MOVE.
THANKS. YOU WON'T BE SORRY. I CAN DO THIS--
YEAH. NO. THAT'D BE ME.
HEY! WHY DO YOU GET TO BE THE HERO?
TELL YOU WHAT, WHEN YOU'VE GOT SPIDER-SENSE, SPEED, AND STRENGTH...

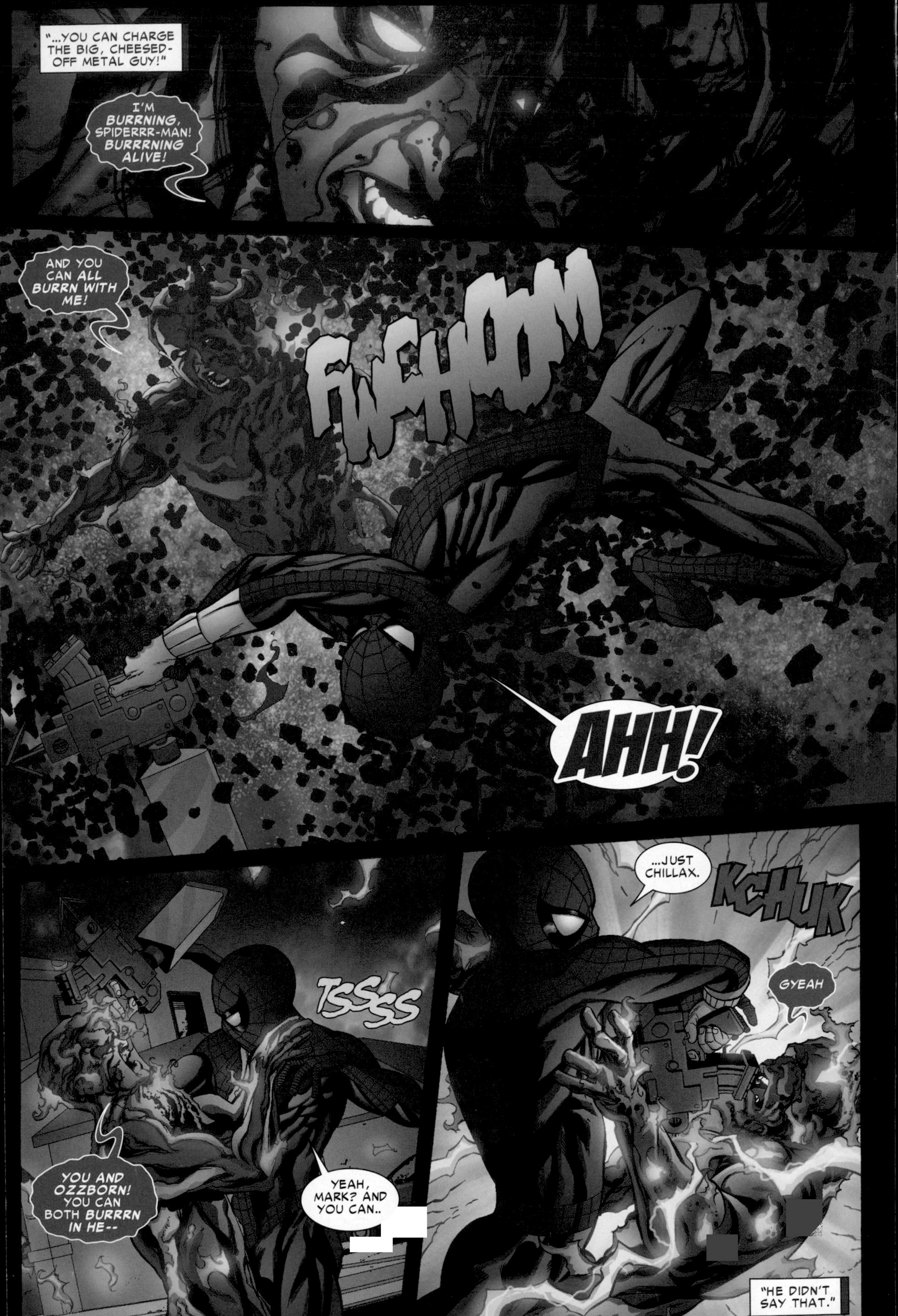
"...YOU CAN CHARGE THE BIG, CHEESED-OFF METAL GUY!"
I'M BURRNING, SPIDERRR-MAN! BURRRNING ALIVE!
AND YOU CAN ALL BURRN WITH ME!
FWOOM
AHH!
TSSSS
YOU AND OZZBORN! YOU CAN BOTH BURRRN IN HE--
YEAH, MARK? AND YOU CAN..
...JUST CHILLAX.
KCHUK
GYEAH
"HE DIDN'T SAY THAT."

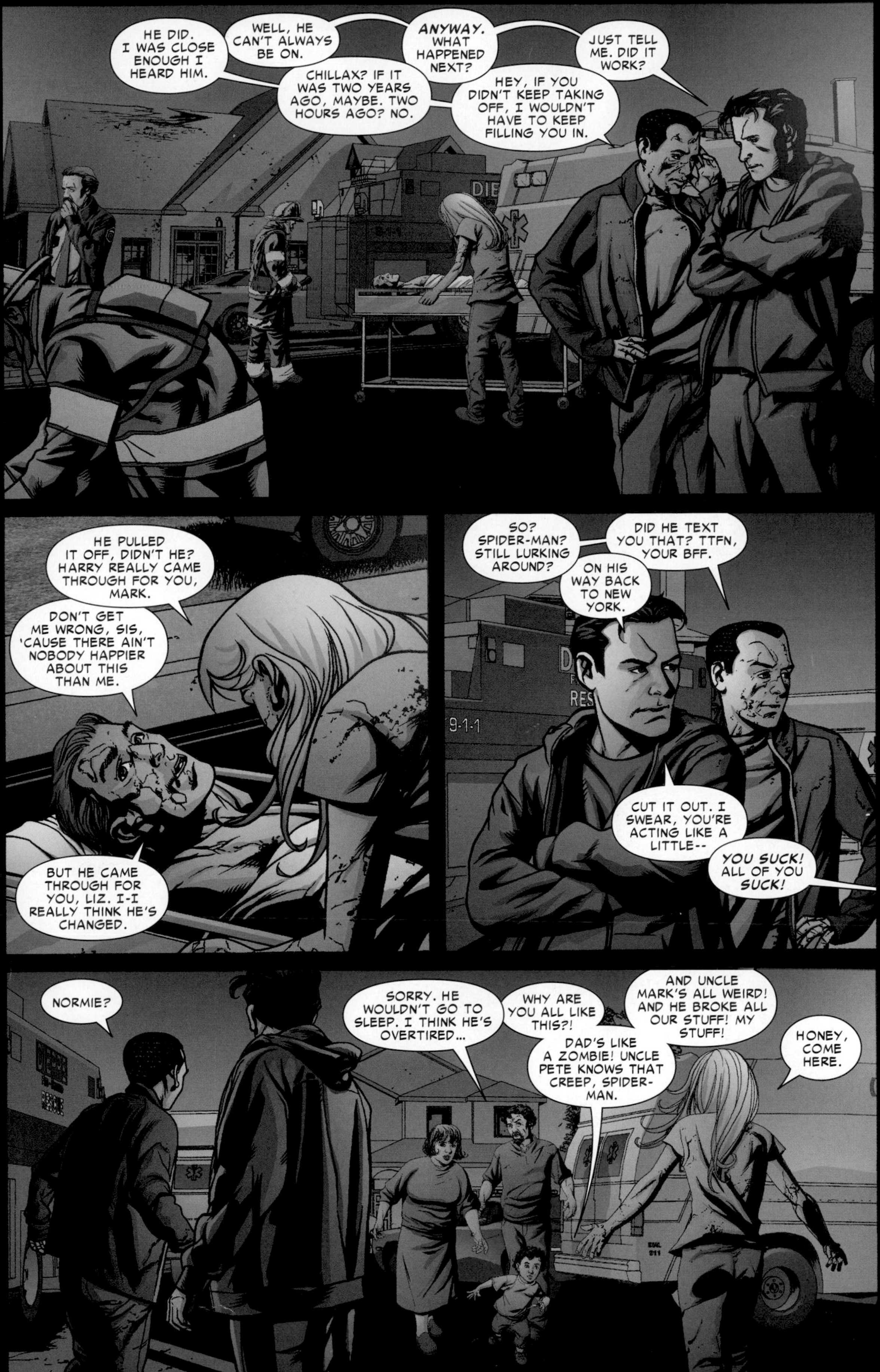
HE DID. I WAS CLOSE ENOUGH I HEARD HIM.
WELL, HE CAN'T ALWAYS BE ON.
CHILLAX? IF IT WAS TWO YEARS AGO, MAYBE. TWO HOURS AGO? NO.
ANYWAY. WHAT HAPPENED NEXT?
HEY, IF YOU DIDN'T KEEP TAKING OFF, I WOULDN'T HAVE TO KEEP FILLING YOU IN.
JUST TELL ME. DID IT WORK?
HE PULLED IT OFF, DIDN'T HE? HARRY REALLY CAME THROUGH FOR YOU, MARK.
DON'T GET ME WRONG, SIS, 'CAUSE THERE AIN'T NOBODY HAPPIER ABOUT THIS THAN ME.
BUT HE CAME THROUGH FOR YOU, LIZ. I-I REALLY THINK HE'S CHANGED.
SO? SPIDER-MAN? STILL LURKING AROUND?
DID HE TEXT YOU THAT? TTFN, YOUR BFF.
ON HIS WAY BACK TO NEW YORK.
9-1-1
CUT IT OUT. I SWEAR, YOU'RE ACTING LIKE A LITTLE--
YOU SUCK! ALL OF YOU SUCK!
NORMIE?
SORRY. HE WOULDN'T GO TO SLEEP. I THINK HE'S OVERTIRED...
WHY ARE YOU ALL LIKE THIS?!
AND UNCLE MARK'S ALL WEIRD! AND HE BROKE ALL OUR STUFF! MY STUFF!
DAD'S LIKE A ZOMBIE! UNCLE PETE KNOWS THAT CREEP, SPIDER-MAN.
HONEY, COME HERE.

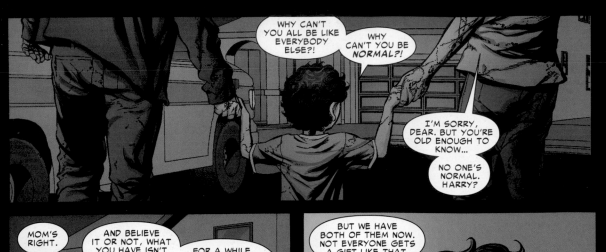

WHY CAN'T YOU ALL BE LIKE EVERYBODY ELSE?! WHY CAN'T YOU BE NORMAL?!

I'M SORRY, DEAR. BUT YOU'RE OLD ENOUGH TO KNOW...

NO ONE'S NORMAL. HARRY?

MOM'S RIGHT.

AND BELIEVE IT OR NOT, WHAT YOU HAVE ISN'T ALL THAT BAD.

FOR A WHILE WE THOUGHT DAD WAS GONE. AND THAT WE WERE GOING TO LOSE UNCLE MARK TOO.

BUT WE HAVE BOTH OF THEM NOW. NOT EVERYONE GETS A GIFT LIKE THAT.

REMEMBER THAT.

OKAY...

AND HARRY...THOSE SCALES?

CONSIDER THEM BALANCED.

LIZ, I...

WAIT.

BEFORE YOU CAME, YOU ASKED ABOUT SOMETHING. I TOLD YOU I LOST IT.

I DIDN'T. IT'S RIGHT HERE.

I HOPE... ...IT BRINGS YOU BETTER LUCK THIS TIME.

THANK YOU.

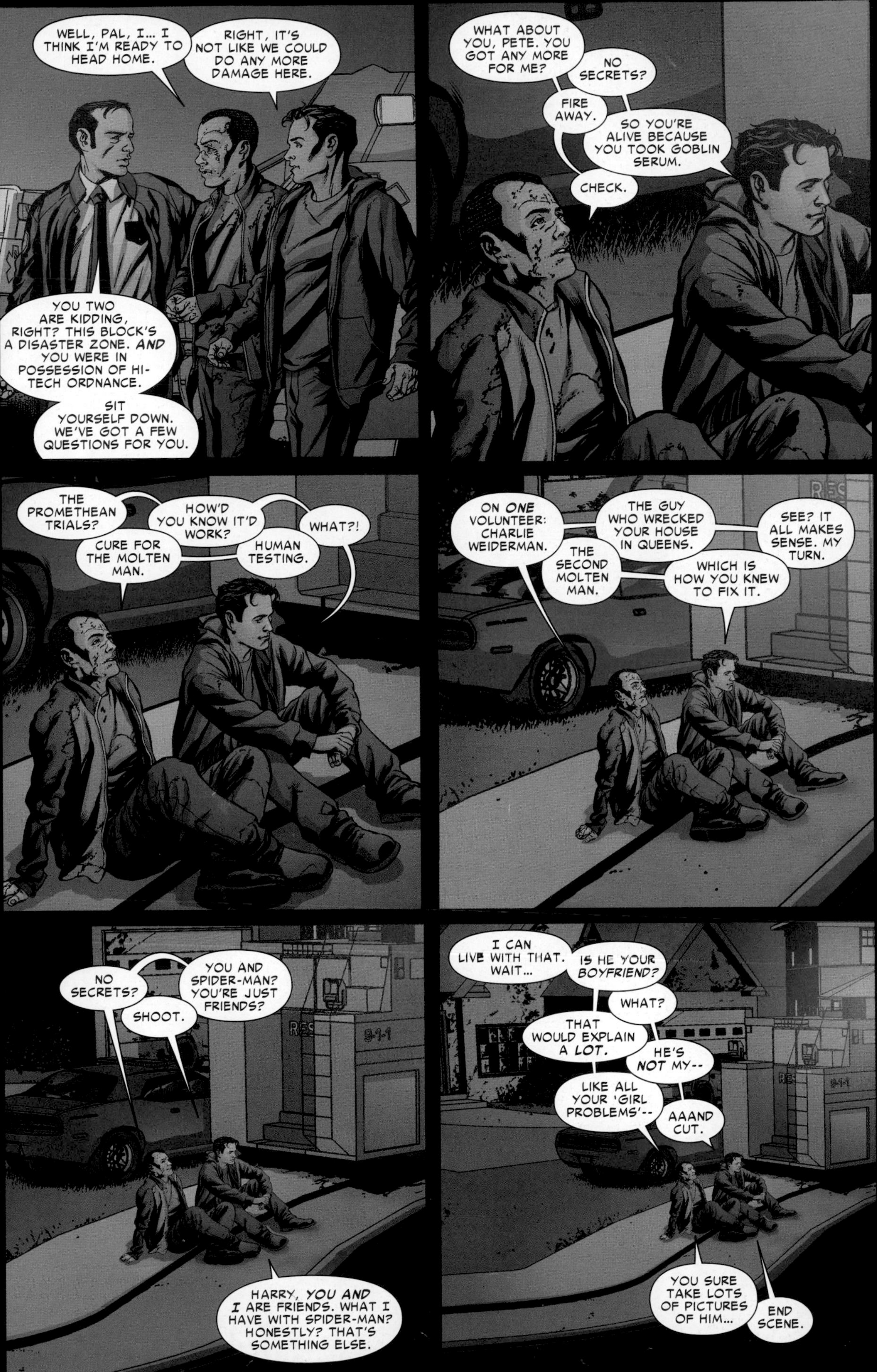
WELL, PAL, I... I THINK I'M READY TO HEAD HOME.
RIGHT, IT'S NOT LIKE WE COULD DO ANY MORE DAMAGE HERE.
YOU TWO ARE KIDDING, RIGHT? THIS BLOCK'S A DISASTER ZONE. AND YOU WERE IN POSSESSION OF HI-TECH ORDNANCE.
SIT YOURSELF DOWN. WE'VE GOT A FEW QUESTIONS FOR YOU.
WHAT ABOUT YOU, PETE. YOU GOT ANY MORE FOR ME?
NO SECRETS?
FIRE AWAY.
SO YOU'RE ALIVE BECAUSE YOU TOOK GOBLIN SERUM.
CHECK.
THE PROMETHEAN TRIALS?
HOW'D YOU KNOW IT'D WORK?
WHAT?!
CURE FOR THE MOLTEN MAN.
HUMAN TESTING.
ON ONE VOLUNTEER: CHARLIE WEIDERMAN.
THE GUY WHO WRECKED YOUR HOUSE IN QUEENS.
SEE? IT ALL MAKES SENSE. MY TURN.
THE SECOND MOLTEN MAN.
WHICH IS HOW YOU KNEW TO FIX IT.
NO SECRETS?
YOU AND SPIDER-MAN? YOU'RE JUST FRIENDS?
SHOOT.
HARRY, YOU AND I ARE FRIENDS. WHAT I HAVE WITH SPIDER-MAN? HONESTLY? THAT'S SOMETHING ELSE.
I CAN LIVE WITH THAT. WAIT...
IS HE YOUR BOYFRIEND?
WHAT?
THAT WOULD EXPLAIN A LOT.
HE'S NOT MY--
LIKE ALL YOUR 'GIRL PROBLEMS'--
AAAND CUT.
YOU SURE TAKE LOTS OF PICTURES OF HIM...
END SCENE.

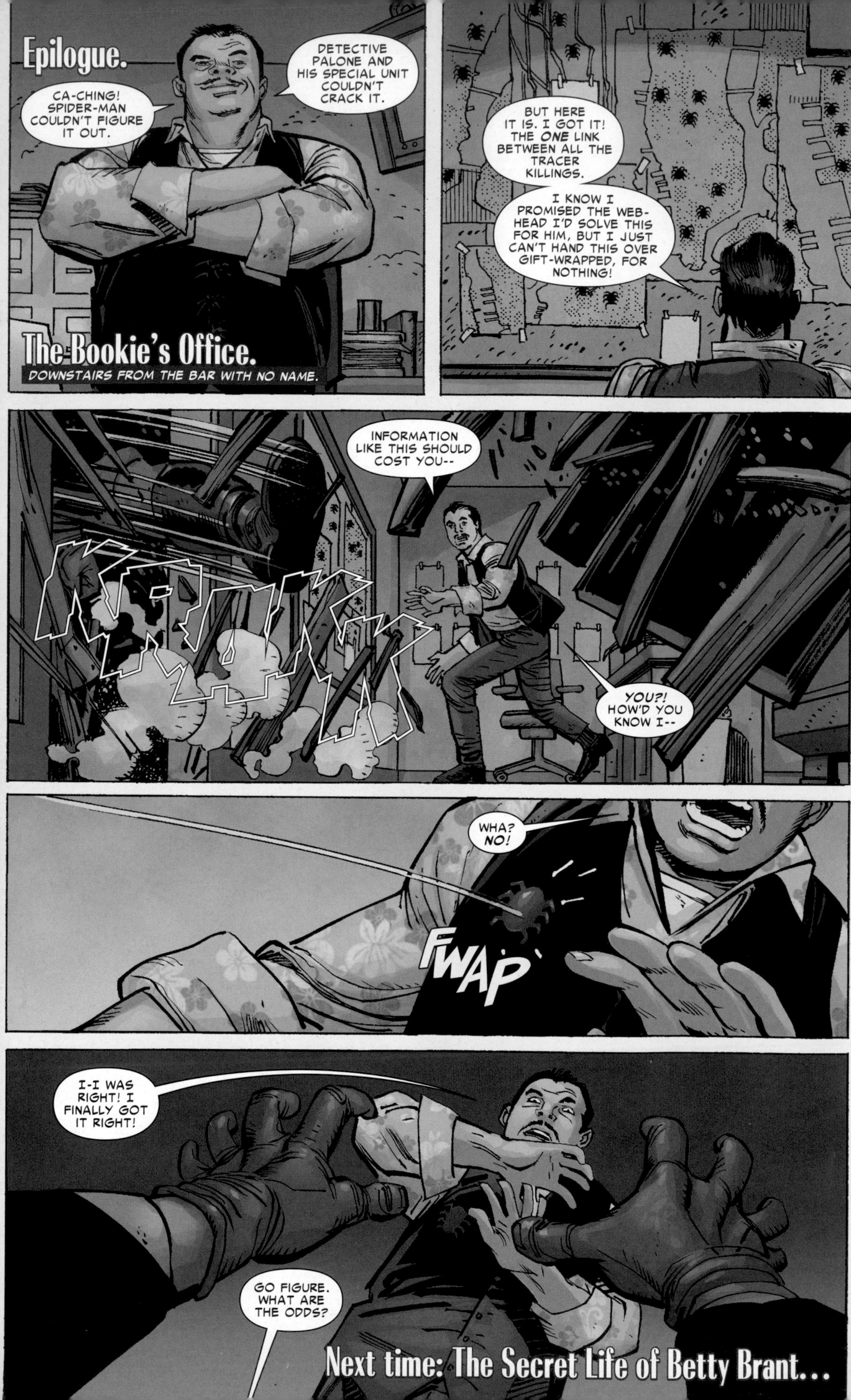
Epilogue.
CA-CHING! SPIDER-MAN COULDN'T FIGURE IT OUT.
DETECTIVE PALONE AND HIS SPECIAL UNIT COULDN'T CRACK IT.
The Bookie's Office.
DOWNSTAIRS FROM THE BAR WITH NO NAME.
BUT HERE IT IS. I GOT IT! THE ONE LINK BETWEEN ALL THE TRACER KILLINGS.
I KNOW I PROMISED THE WEB-HEAD I'D SOLVE THIS FOR HIM, BUT I JUST CAN'T HAND THIS OVER GIFT-WRAPPED, FOR NOTHING!
INFORMATION LIKE THIS SHOULD COST YOU--
KRAKK
YOU?! HOW'D YOU KNOW I--
WHA? NO!
FWAP
I-I WAS RIGHT! I FINALLY GOT IT RIGHT!
GO FIGURE. WHAT ARE THE ODDS?
Next time: The Secret Life of Betty Brant...

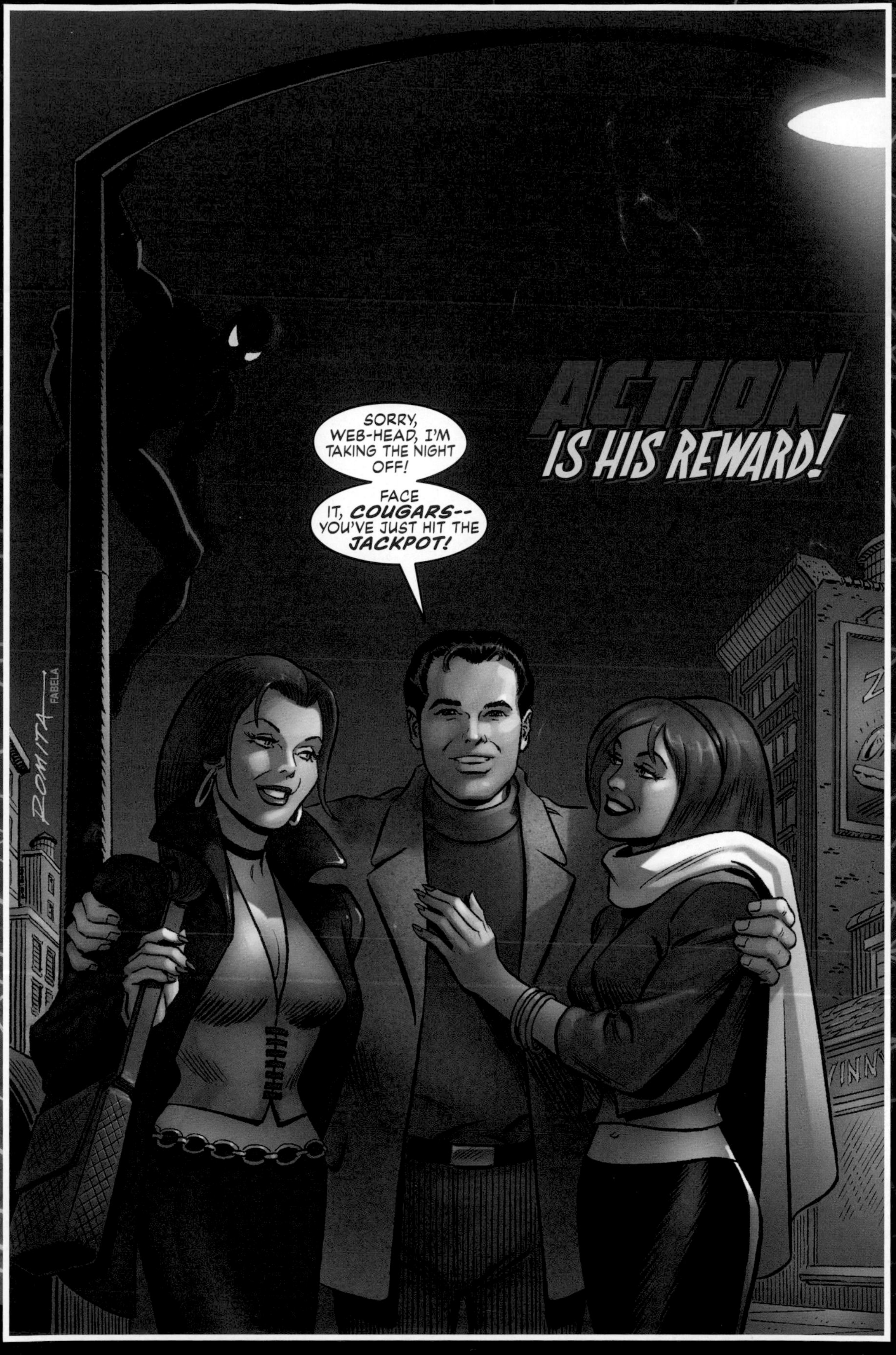
SORRY, WEB-HEAD, I'M TAKING THE NIGHT OFF!
FACE IT, COUGARS-- YOU'VE JUST HIT THE JACKPOT!
ACTION IS HIS REWARD!
ROMITA
FABELA

AMAZING SPIDER-MAN #583

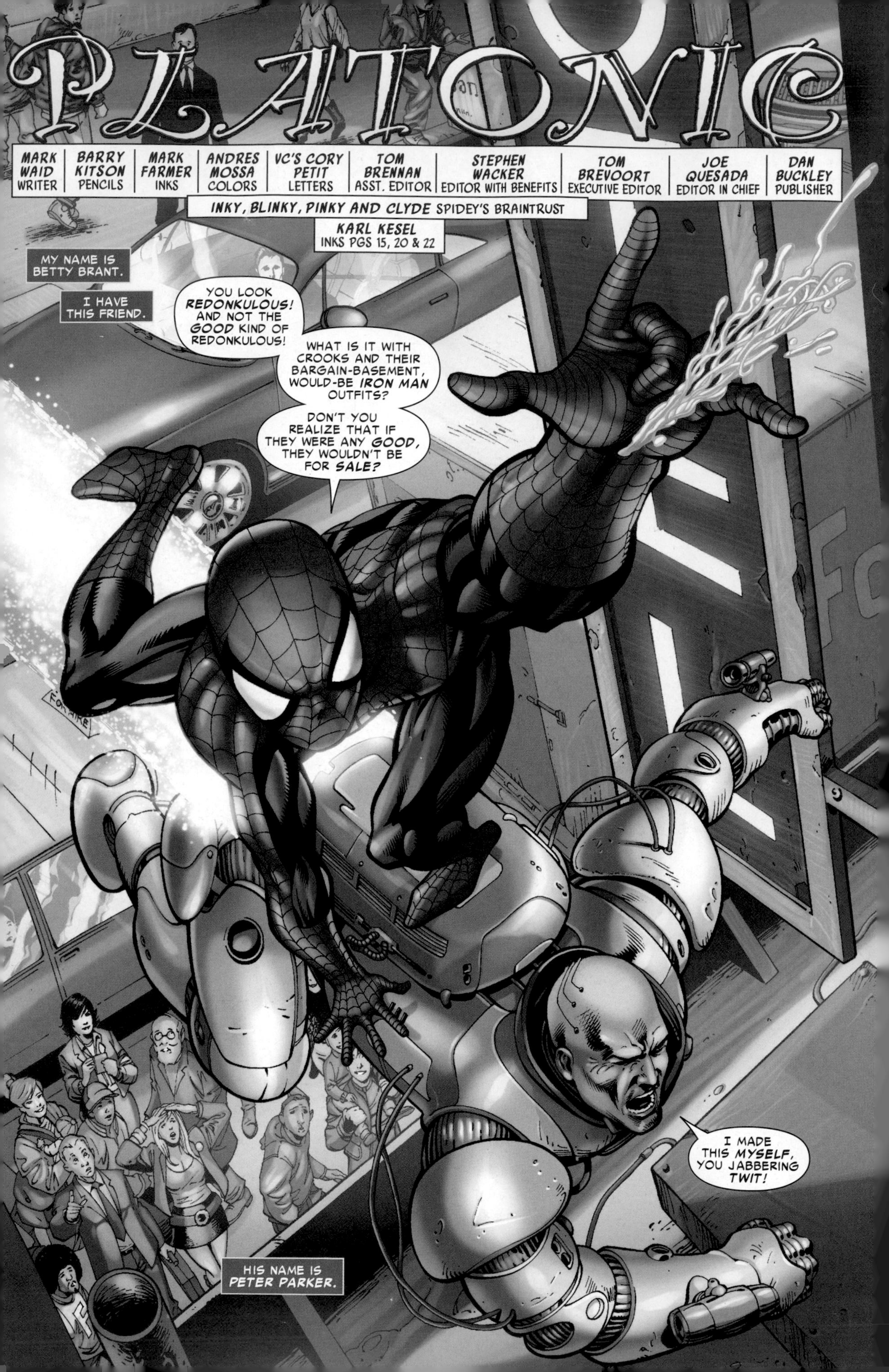
PLATONIC
MARK WAID WRITER
BARRY KITSON PENCILS
MARK FARMER INKS
ANDRES MOSSA COLORS
VC'S CORY PETIT LETTERS
TOM BRENNAN ASST. EDITOR
STEPHEN WACKER EDITOR WITH BENEFITS
TOM BREVOORT EXECUTIVE EDITOR
JOE QUESADA EDITOR IN CHIEF
DAN BUCKLEY PUBLISHER
INKY, BLINKY, PINKY AND CLYDE SPIDEY'S BRAINTRUST
KARL KESEL INKS PGS 15, 20 & 22
MY NAME IS BETTY BRANT.
I HAVE THIS FRIEND.
YOU LOOK REDONKULOUS! AND NOT THE GOOD KIND OF REDONKULOUS!
WHAT IS IT WITH CROOKS AND THEIR BARGAIN-BASEMENT, WOULD-BE IRON MAN OUTFITS?
DON'T YOU REALIZE THAT IF THEY WERE ANY GOOD, THEY WOULDN'T BE FOR SALE?
I MADE THIS MYSELF, YOU JABBERING TWIT!
HIS NAME IS PETER PARKER.

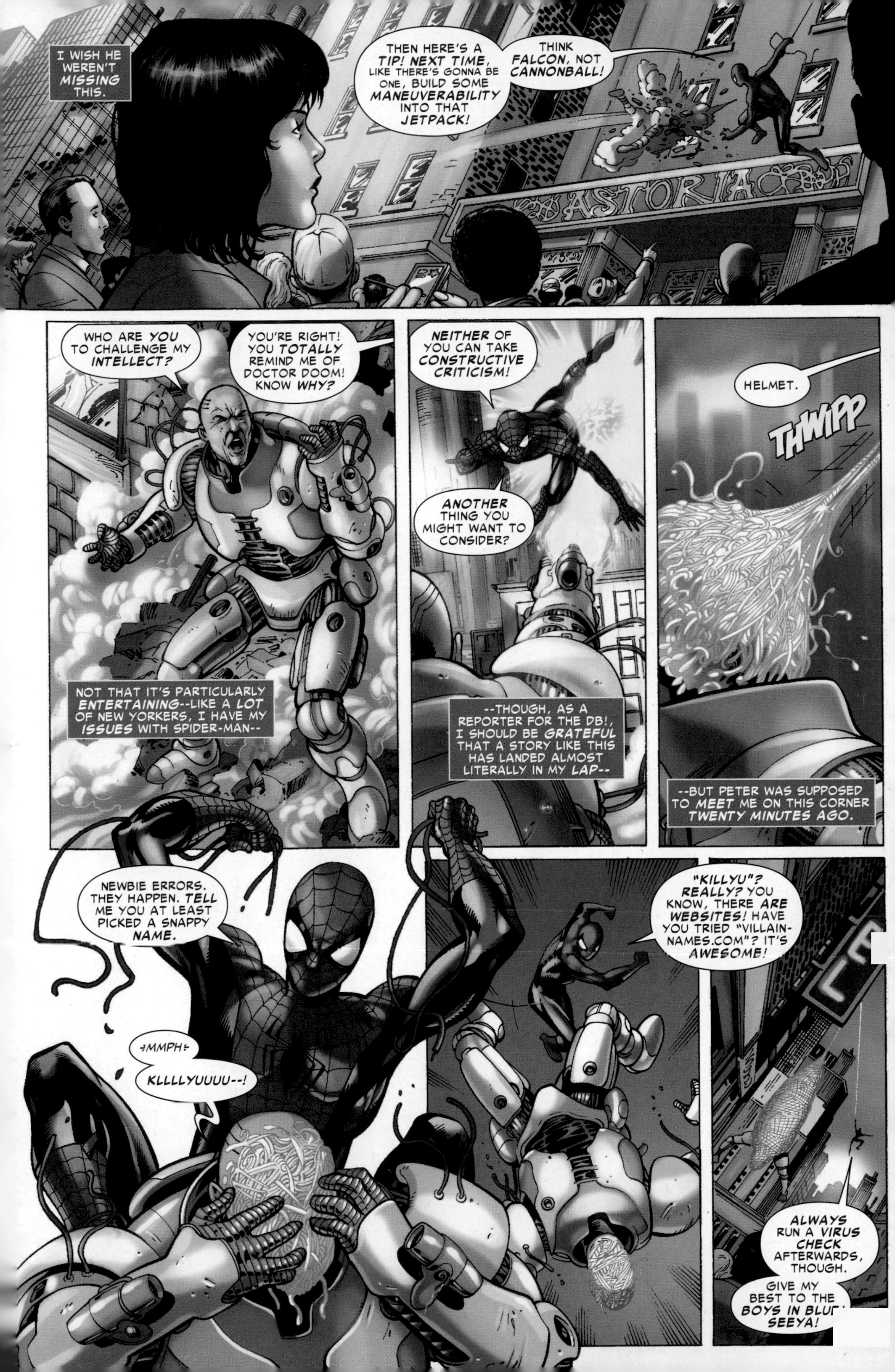

I WISH HE WEREN'T MISSING THIS.
THEN HERE'S A TIP! NEXT TIME, LIKE THERE'S GONNA BE ONE, BUILD SOME MANEUVERABILITY INTO THAT JETPACK!
THINK FALCON, NOT CANNONBALL!
ASTORIA
WHO ARE YOU TO CHALLENGE MY INTELLECT?
YOU'RE RIGHT! YOU TOTALLY REMIND ME OF DOCTOR DOOM! KNOW WHY?
NOT THAT IT'S PARTICULARLY ENTERTAINING--LIKE A LOT OF NEW YORKERS, I HAVE MY ISSUES WITH SPIDER-MAN--
NEITHER OF YOU CAN TAKE CONSTRUCTIVE CRITICISM!
ANOTHER THING YOU MIGHT WANT TO CONSIDER?
--THOUGH, AS A REPORTER FOR THE DB!, I SHOULD BE GRATEFUL THAT A STORY LIKE THIS HAS LANDED ALMOST LITERALLY IN MY LAP--
HELMET.
THWIPP
--BUT PETER WAS SUPPOSED TO MEET ME ON THIS CORNER TWENTY MINUTES AGO.
NEWBIE ERRORS. THEY HAPPEN. TELL ME YOU AT LEAST PICKED A SNAPPY NAME.
=MMPH=
KLLLLYUUUU--!
"KILLYU"? REALLY? YOU KNOW, THERE ARE WEBSITES! HAVE YOU TRIED "VILLAIN-NAMES.COM"? IT'S AWESOME!
ALWAYS RUN A VIRUS CHECK AFTERWARDS, THOUGH.
GIVE MY BEST TO THE BOYS IN BLU SEEYA!

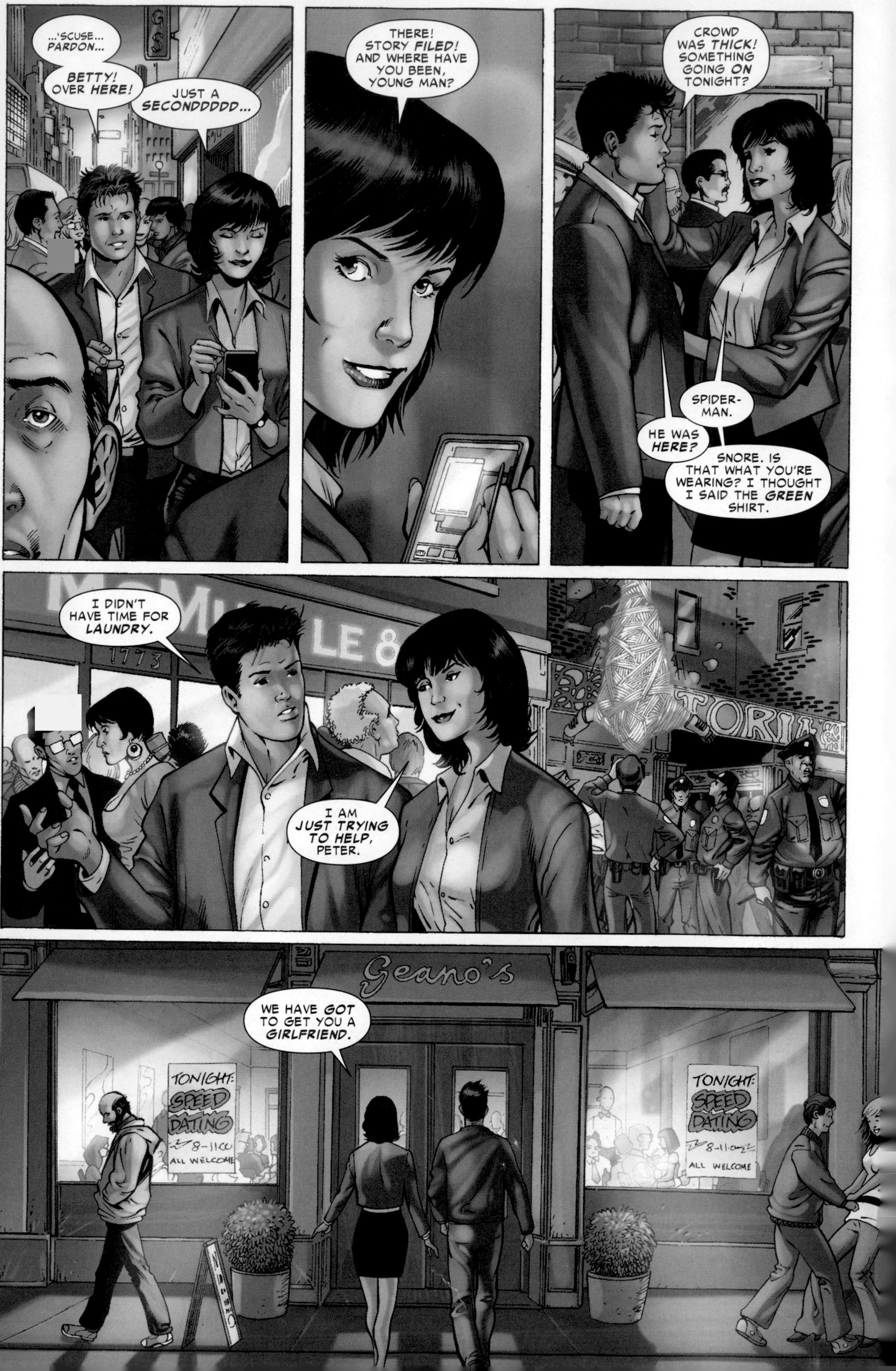
...'SCUSE... PARDON...
BETTY! OVER HERE!
JUST A SECONDDDDD...
THERE! STORY FILED! AND WHERE HAVE YOU BEEN, YOUNG MAN?
CROWD WAS THICK! SOMETHING GOING ON TONIGHT?
SPIDER-MAN.
HE WAS HERE?
SNORE. IS THAT WHAT YOU'RE WEARING? I THOUGHT I SAID THE GREEN SHIRT.
1773
I DIDN'T HAVE TIME FOR LAUNDRY.
I AM JUST TRYING TO HELP, PETER.
Geano's
WE HAVE GOT TO GET YOU A GIRLFRIEND.
TONIGHT: SPEED DATING
ALL WELCOME
TONIGHT: SPEED DATING
ALL WELCOME

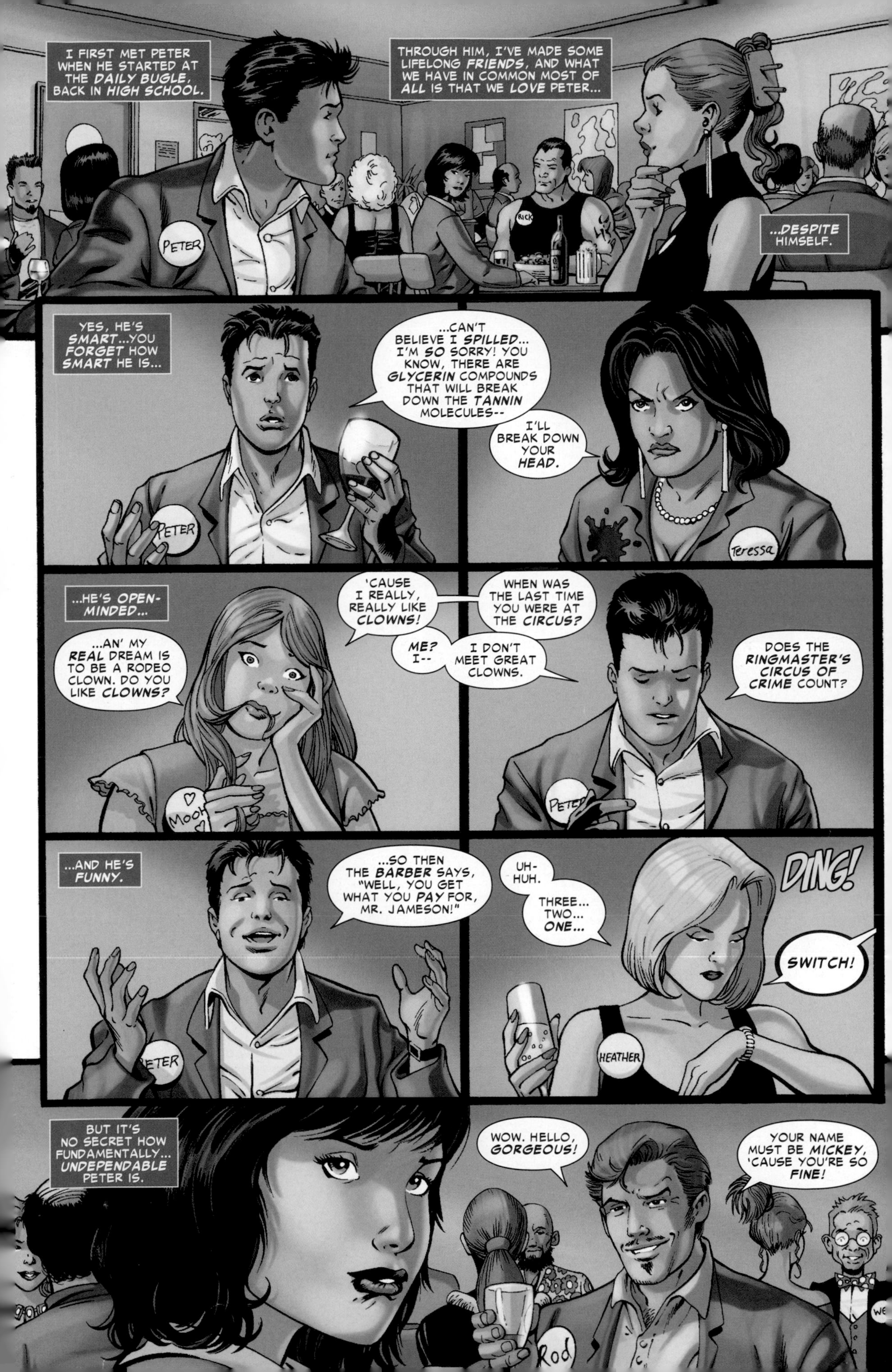
I FIRST MET PETER WHEN HE STARTED AT THE *DAILY BUGLE*, BACK IN *HIGH SCHOOL*.
THROUGH HIM, I'VE MADE SOME LIFELONG *FRIENDS*, AND WHAT WE HAVE IN COMMON MOST OF *ALL* IS THAT WE *LOVE* PETER...
...*DESPITE* HIMSELF.
PETER
RICK
YES, HE'S *SMART*...YOU *FORGET* HOW *SMART* HE IS...
...CAN'T BELIEVE I *SPILLED*... I'M *SO* SORRY! YOU KNOW, THERE ARE *GLYCERIN* COMPOUNDS THAT WILL BREAK DOWN THE *TANNIN* MOLECULES--
I'LL BREAK DOWN YOUR *HEAD*.
PETER
Teressa
...HE'S *OPEN-MINDED*...
...AN' MY *REAL* DREAM IS TO BE A RODEO CLOWN. DO YOU LIKE *CLOWNS?*
ME? I--
'CAUSE I REALLY, REALLY LIKE *CLOWNS!*
WHEN WAS THE LAST TIME YOU WERE AT THE *CIRCUS?*
I DON'T MEET GREAT CLOWNS.
DOES THE *RINGMASTER'S CIRCUS OF CRIME* COUNT?
...AND HE'S *FUNNY*.
...SO THEN THE *BARBER* SAYS, "WELL, YOU GET WHAT YOU *PAY* FOR, MR. JAMESON!"
UH-HUH.
THREE... TWO... *ONE*...
DING!
SWITCH!
HEATHER
BUT IT'S NO SECRET HOW FUNDAMENTALLY... *UNDEPENDABLE* PETER IS.
WOW. HELLO, *GORGEOUS!*
YOUR NAME MUST BE *MICKEY*, 'CAUSE YOU'RE SO *FINE!*
Rod

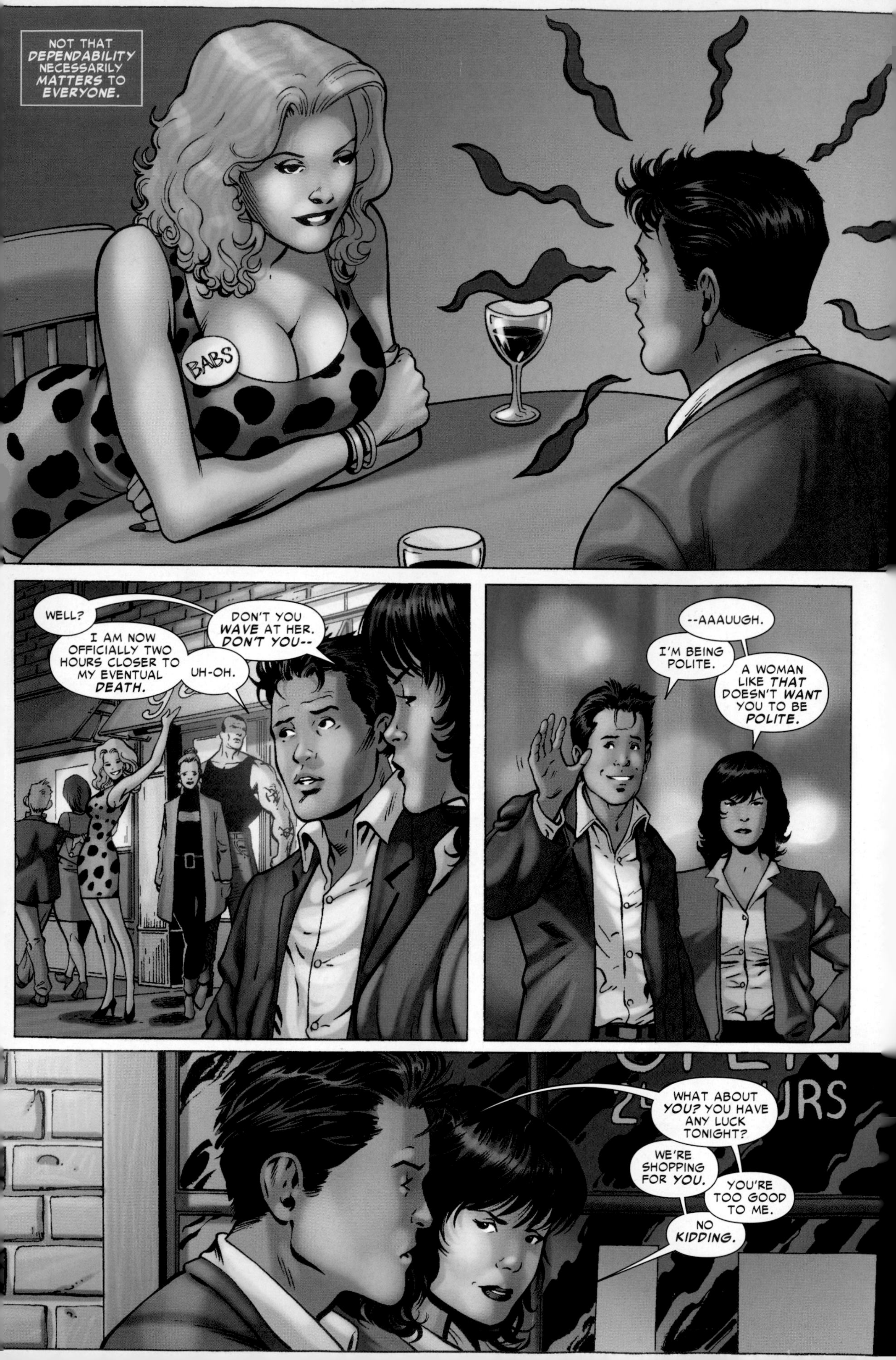
NOT THAT *DEPENDABILITY* NECESSARILY *MATTERS* TO *EVERYONE.*
BABS
WELL?
DON'T YOU *WAVE* AT HER. *DON'T YOU--*
I AM NOW OFFICIALLY TWO HOURS CLOSER TO MY EVENTUAL *DEATH.*
UH-OH.
--AAAUUGH.
I'M BEING POLITE.
A WOMAN LIKE *THAT* DOESN'T *WANT* YOU TO BE *POLITE.*
WHAT ABOUT *YOU?* YOU HAVE ANY LUCK TONIGHT?
WE'RE SHOPPING FOR *YOU.*
YOU'RE TOO GOOD TO ME.
NO *KIDDING.*

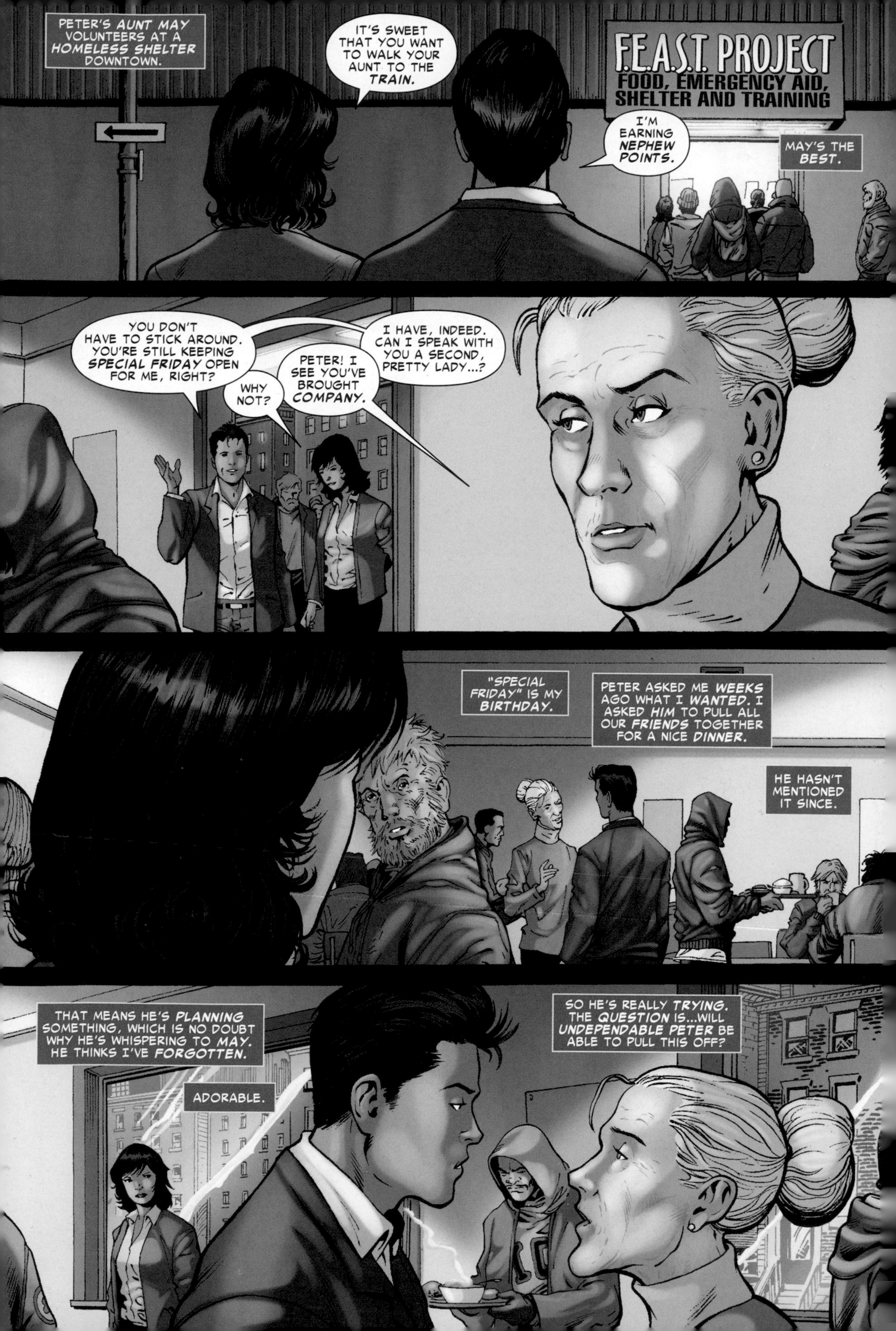

PETER'S AUNT MAY VOLUNTEERS AT A HOMELESS SHELTER DOWNTOWN.
IT'S SWEET THAT YOU WANT TO WALK YOUR AUNT TO THE TRAIN.
F.E.A.S.T. PROJECT
FOOD, EMERGENCY AID, SHELTER AND TRAINING
I'M EARNING NEPHEW POINTS.
MAY'S THE BEST.
YOU DON'T HAVE TO STICK AROUND. YOU'RE STILL KEEPING SPECIAL FRIDAY OPEN FOR ME, RIGHT?
WHY NOT?
PETER! I SEE YOU'VE BROUGHT COMPANY.
I HAVE, INDEED. CAN I SPEAK WITH YOU A SECOND, PRETTY LADY...?
"SPECIAL FRIDAY" IS MY BIRTHDAY.
PETER ASKED ME WEEKS AGO WHAT I WANTED. I ASKED HIM TO PULL ALL OUR FRIENDS TOGETHER FOR A NICE DINNER.
HE HASN'T MENTIONED IT SINCE.
THAT MEANS HE'S PLANNING SOMETHING, WHICH IS NO DOUBT WHY HE'S WHISPERING TO MAY. HE THINKS I'VE FORGOTTEN.
ADORABLE.
SO HE'S REALLY TRYING. THE QUESTION IS...WILL UNDEPENDABLE PETER BE ABLE TO PULL THIS OFF?

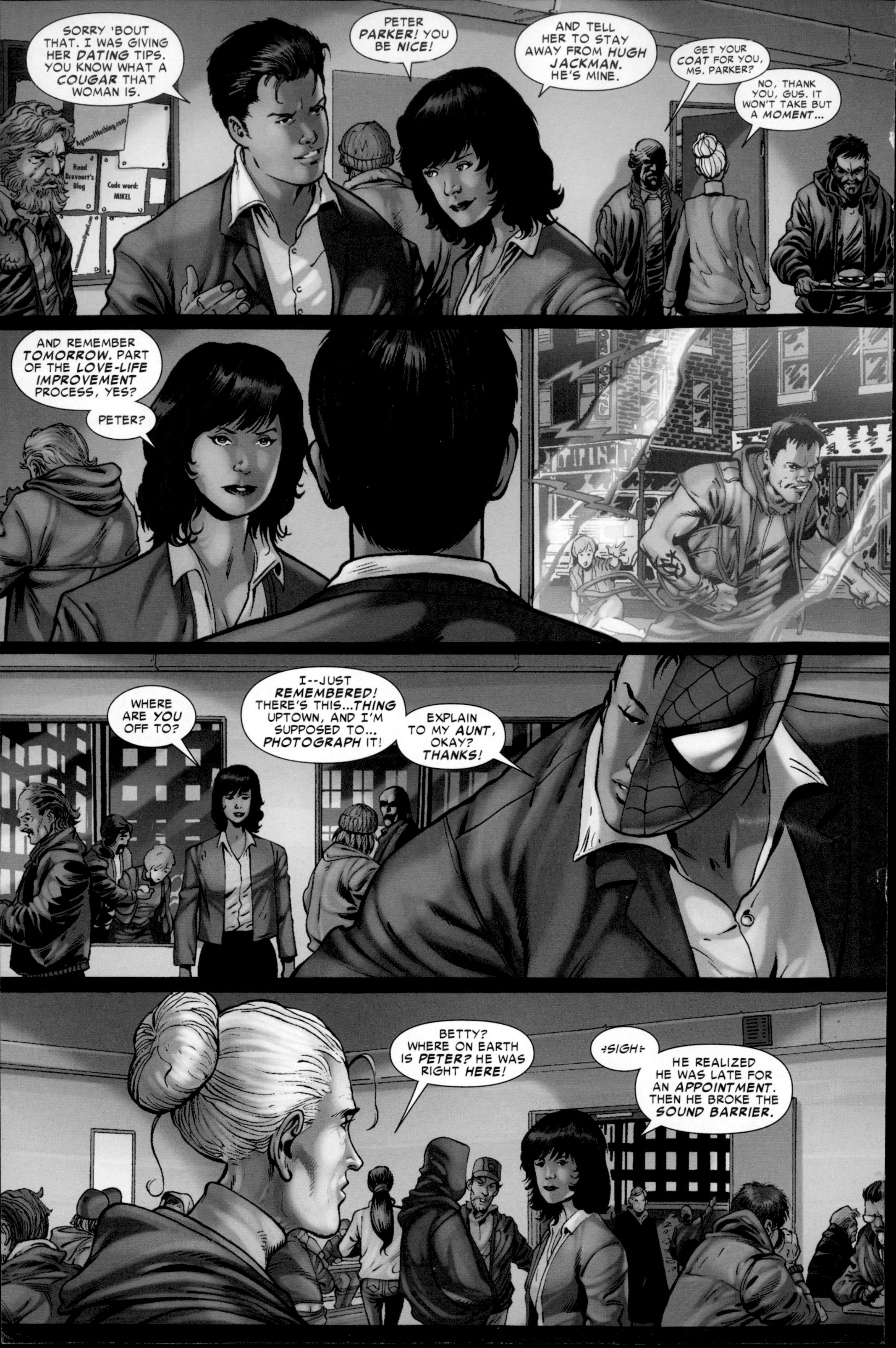
SORRY 'BOUT THAT. I WAS GIVING HER DATING TIPS. YOU KNOW WHAT A COUGAR THAT WOMAN IS.
PETER PARKER! YOU BE NICE!
AND TELL HER TO STAY AWAY FROM HUGH JACKMAN. HE'S MINE.
AgentofNothing.com
Read Brevoort's Blog
Code word: MIKEL
GET YOUR COAT FOR YOU, MS. PARKER?
NO, THANK YOU, GUS. IT WON'T TAKE BUT A MOMENT...
AND REMEMBER TOMORROW. PART OF THE LOVE-LIFE IMPROVEMENT PROCESS, YES?
PETER?
WHERE ARE YOU OFF TO?
I--JUST REMEMBERED! THERE'S THIS...THING UPTOWN, AND I'M SUPPOSED TO... PHOTOGRAPH IT!
EXPLAIN TO MY AUNT, OKAY? THANKS!
BETTY? WHERE ON EARTH IS PETER? HE WAS RIGHT HERE!
=SIGH=
HE REALIZED HE WAS LATE FOR AN APPOINTMENT. THEN HE BROKE THE SOUND BARRIER.

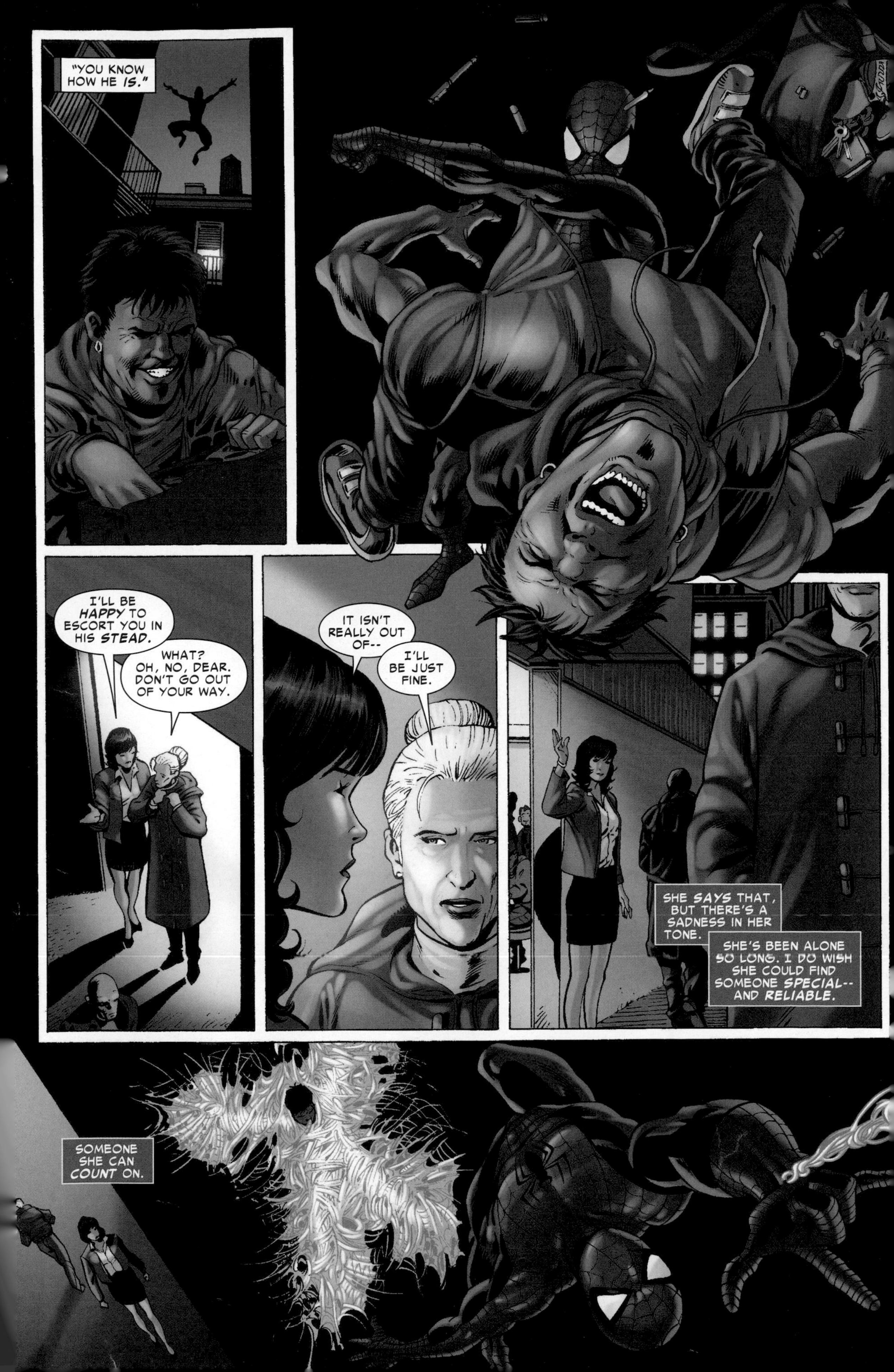
"YOU KNOW HOW HE IS."
I'LL BE HAPPY TO ESCORT YOU IN HIS STEAD.
WHAT? OH, NO, DEAR. DON'T GO OUT OF YOUR WAY.
IT ISN'T REALLY OUT OF--
I'LL BE JUST FINE.
SHE SAYS THAT, BUT THERE'S A SADNESS IN HER TONE.
SHE'S BEEN ALONE SO LONG. I DO WISH SHE COULD FIND SOMEONE SPECIAL-- AND RELIABLE.
SOMEONE SHE CAN COUNT ON.

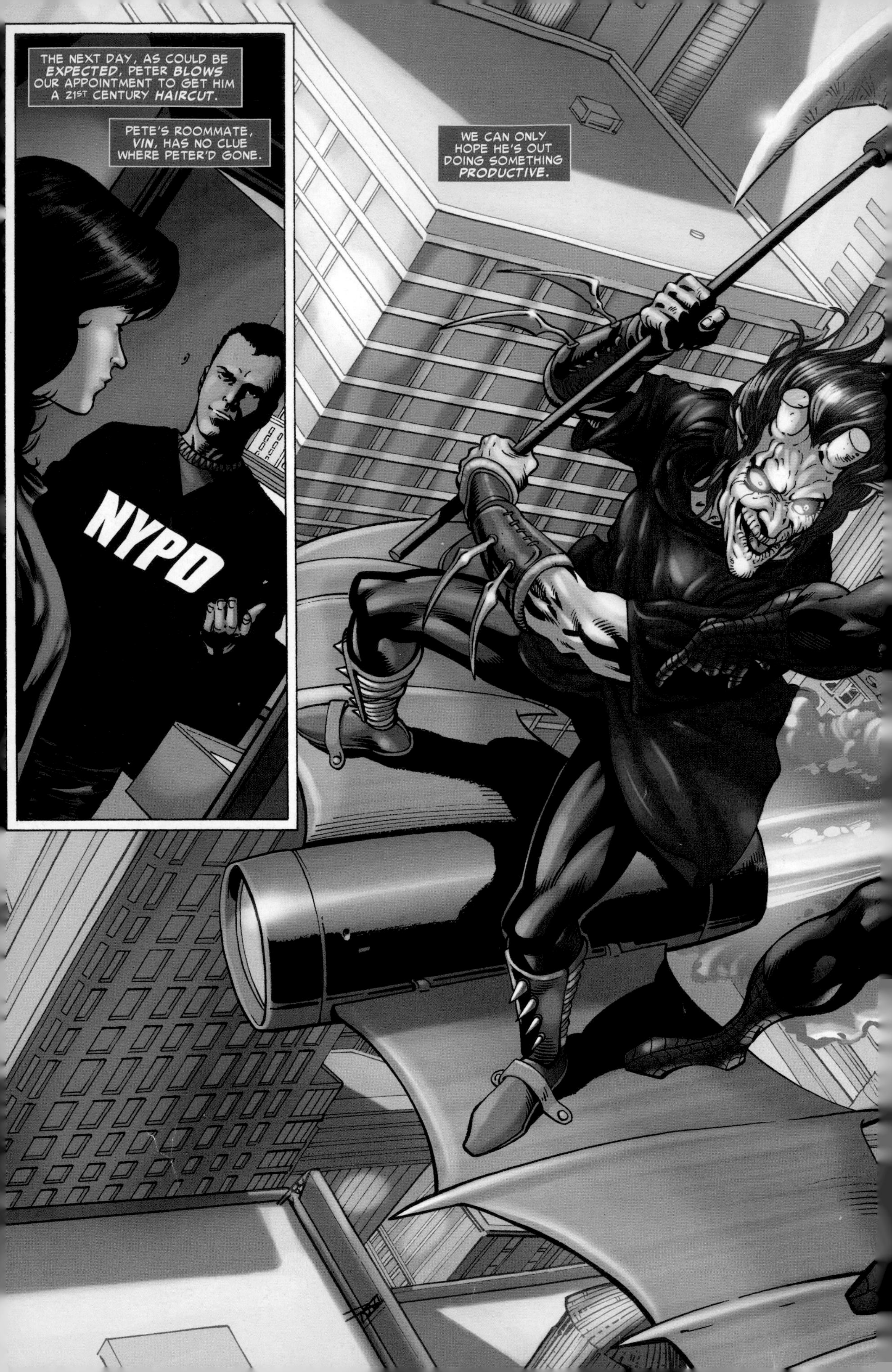
THE NEXT DAY, AS COULD BE EXPECTED, PETER BLOWS OUR APPOINTMENT TO GET HIM A 21ST CENTURY HAIRCUT.
PETE'S ROOMMATE, VIN, HAS NO CLUE WHERE PETER'D GONE.
NYPD
WE CAN ONLY HOPE HE'S OUT DOING SOMETHING PRODUCTIVE.

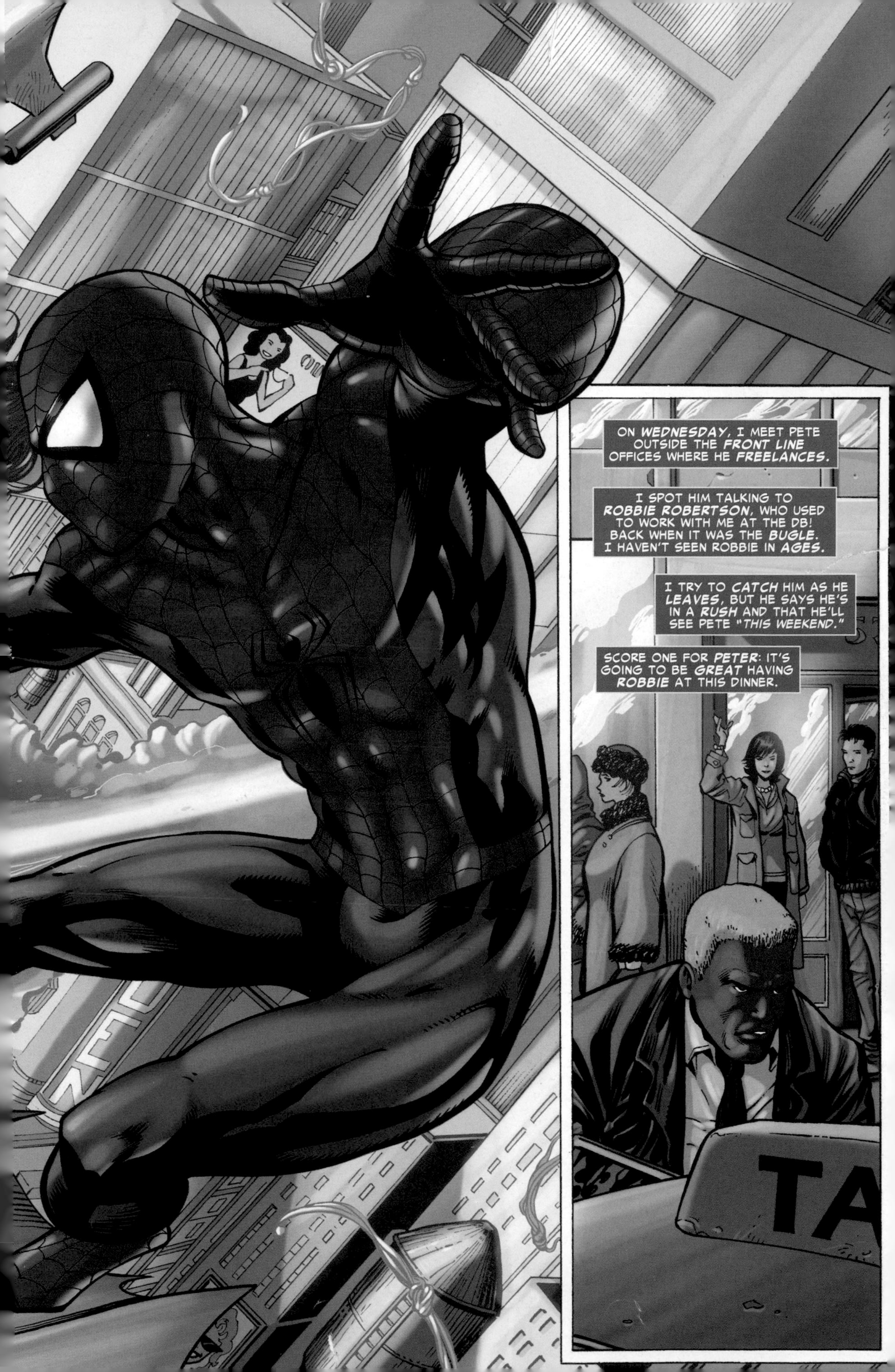
ON WEDNESDAY, I MEET PETE OUTSIDE THE FRONT LINE OFFICES WHERE HE FREELANCES.
I SPOT HIM TALKING TO ROBBIE ROBERTSON, WHO USED TO WORK WITH ME AT THE DB! BACK WHEN IT WAS THE BUGLE. I HAVEN'T SEEN ROBBIE IN AGES.
I TRY TO CATCH HIM AS HE LEAVES, BUT HE SAYS HE'S IN A RUSH AND THAT HE'LL SEE PETE "THIS WEEKEND."
SCORE ONE FOR PETER: IT'S GOING TO BE GREAT HAVING ROBBIE AT THIS DINNER.

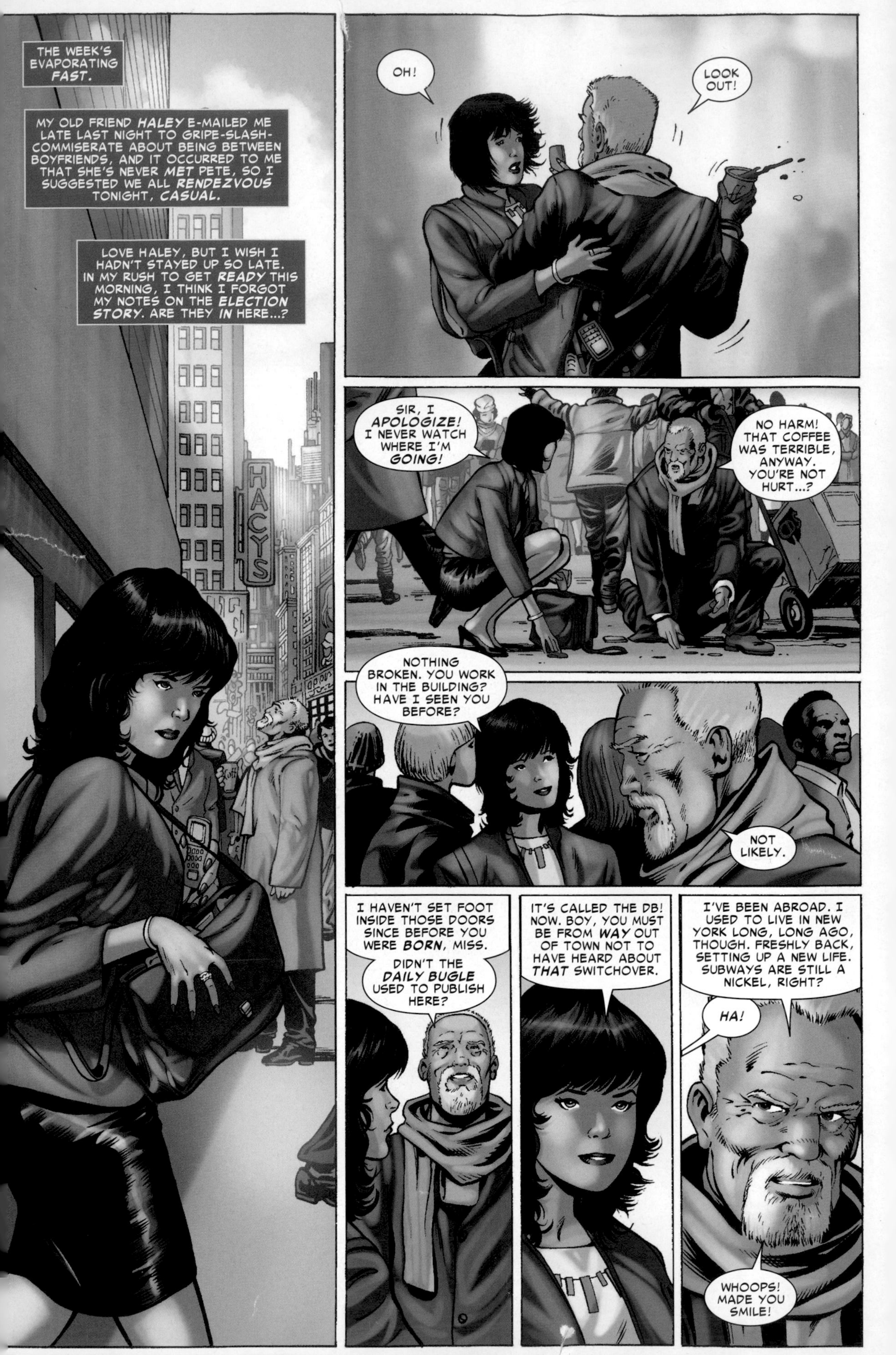
THE WEEK'S EVAPORATING *FAST*.
MY OLD FRIEND *HALEY* E-MAILED ME LATE LAST NIGHT TO GRIPE-SLASH-COMMISERATE ABOUT BEING BETWEEN BOYFRIENDS, AND IT OCCURRED TO ME THAT SHE'S NEVER *MET* PETE, SO I SUGGESTED WE ALL *RENDEZVOUS* TONIGHT, *CASUAL*.
LOVE HALEY, BUT I WISH I HADN'T STAYED UP SO LATE. IN MY RUSH TO GET *READY* THIS MORNING, I THINK I FORGOT MY NOTES ON THE *ELECTION STORY*. ARE THEY *IN* HERE...?
HACYS
OH!
LOOK OUT!
SIR, I *APOLOGIZE!* I NEVER WATCH WHERE I'M *GOING!*
NO HARM! THAT COFFEE WAS TERRIBLE, ANYWAY. YOU'RE NOT HURT...?
NOTHING BROKEN. YOU WORK IN THE BUILDING? HAVE I SEEN YOU BEFORE?
NOT LIKELY.
I HAVEN'T SET FOOT INSIDE THOSE DOORS SINCE BEFORE YOU WERE *BORN*, MISS.
DIDN'T THE *DAILY BUGLE* USED TO PUBLISH HERE?
IT'S CALLED THE DB! NOW. BOY, YOU MUST BE FROM *WAY* OUT OF TOWN NOT TO HAVE HEARD ABOUT *THAT* SWITCHOVER.
I'VE BEEN ABROAD. I USED TO LIVE IN NEW YORK LONG, LONG AGO, THOUGH. FRESHLY BACK, SETTING UP A NEW LIFE. SUBWAYS ARE STILL A NICKEL, RIGHT?
HA!
WHOOPS! MADE YOU SMILE!

WHAT A *STORY* THIS GUY IS, *WHOEVER* HE IS.

I DON'T MEAN *HEADLINE* MATERIAL. I MEAN, HE'S SO CLEARLY BEEN *AROUND* AND HAS SEEN A LOT. YOU CAN *TELL* WITH EVERY SENTENCE THAT COMES OUT OF HIS *MOUTH*.

I FIND MYSELF CHATTING WITH HIM FOR A SURPRISINGLY LONG TIME. THERE'S JUST SOMETHING VERY WARM AND LIKEABLE ABOUT HIM. SOME *INTEGRITY*.

AND WE *DEFINITELY* BOND ON THE SUBJECT OF HOW DIFFICULT IT IS TO *MEET* PEOPLE IN NEW YORK. SO IT *HITS* ME...

I SIMPLY *MUST* GET TO WORK, MISTER... I'M SORRY, WHAT'S YOUR NAME?

CALL ME "J."

JAY. LISTEN, JAY...

THERE'S SOMEONE I THINK YOU SHOULD *MEET*. HER NAME IS MAY PARKER.

MAY PARKER
718-555-C

GIVE HER A RING SOMETIME. TELL HER YOU'RE FRIENDS WITH ME.

I... ALL RIGHT.

DO IT.

I THINK YOU TWO MIGHT REALLY *HIT IT OFF*.

NEW YORK S
DRIVER LICEN
DOB: 08-09-39
J. JONAH JAMESON
39 STH ST.
NEW YORK, NY
SEX: M EYES: BROWN
441589
ISSUED

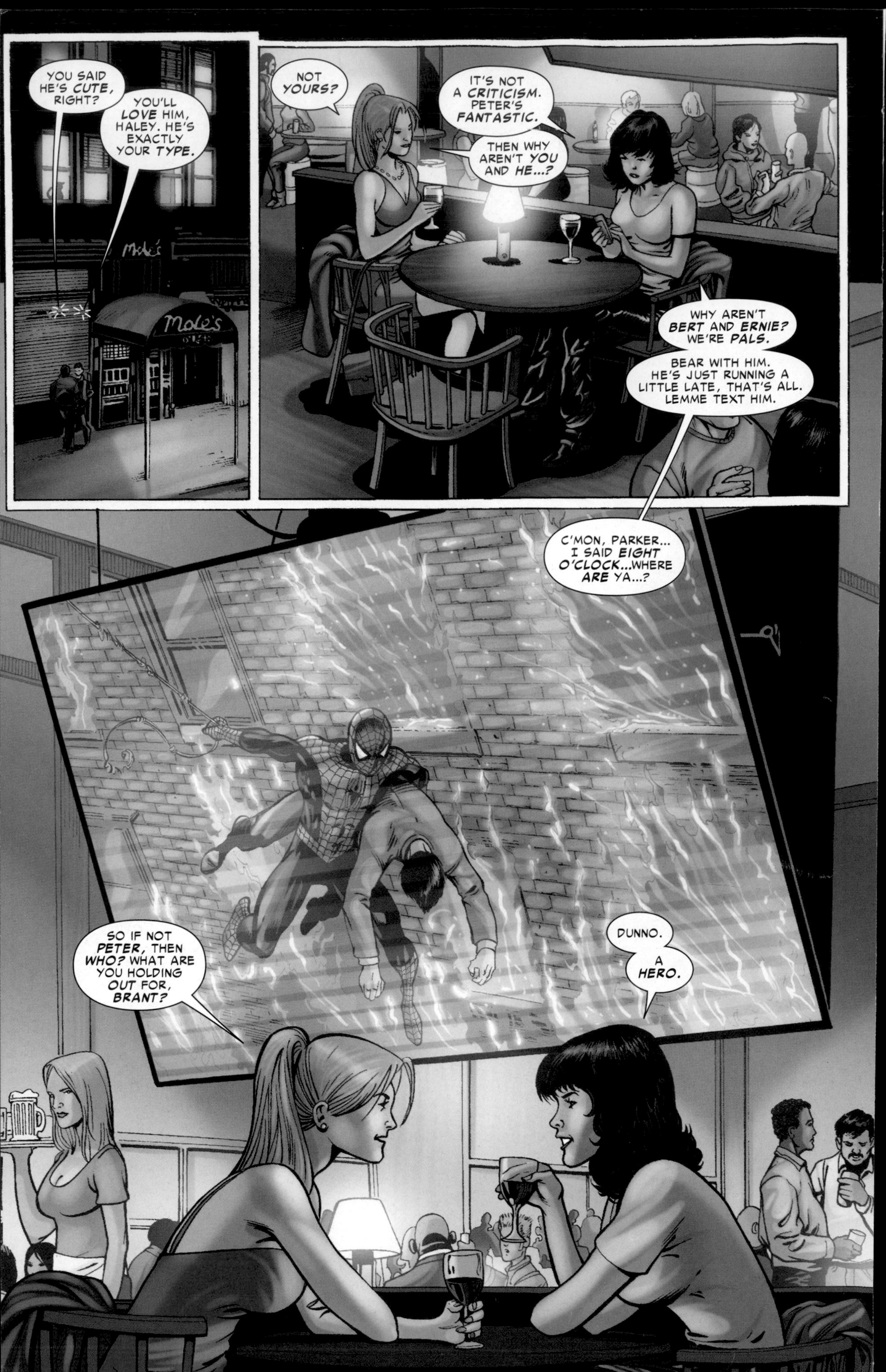
YOU SAID HE'S CUTE, RIGHT?
YOU'LL LOVE HIM, HALEY. HE'S EXACTLY YOUR TYPE.
Mole's
NOT YOURS?
IT'S NOT A CRITICISM. PETER'S FANTASTIC.
THEN WHY AREN'T YOU AND HE...?
WHY AREN'T BERT AND ERNIE? WE'RE PALS.
BEAR WITH HIM. HE'S JUST RUNNING A LITTLE LATE, THAT'S ALL. LEMME TEXT HIM.
C'MON, PARKER... I SAID EIGHT O'CLOCK...WHERE ARE YA...?
SO IF NOT PETER, THEN WHO? WHAT ARE YOU HOLDING OUT FOR, BRANT?
DUNNO.
A HERO.

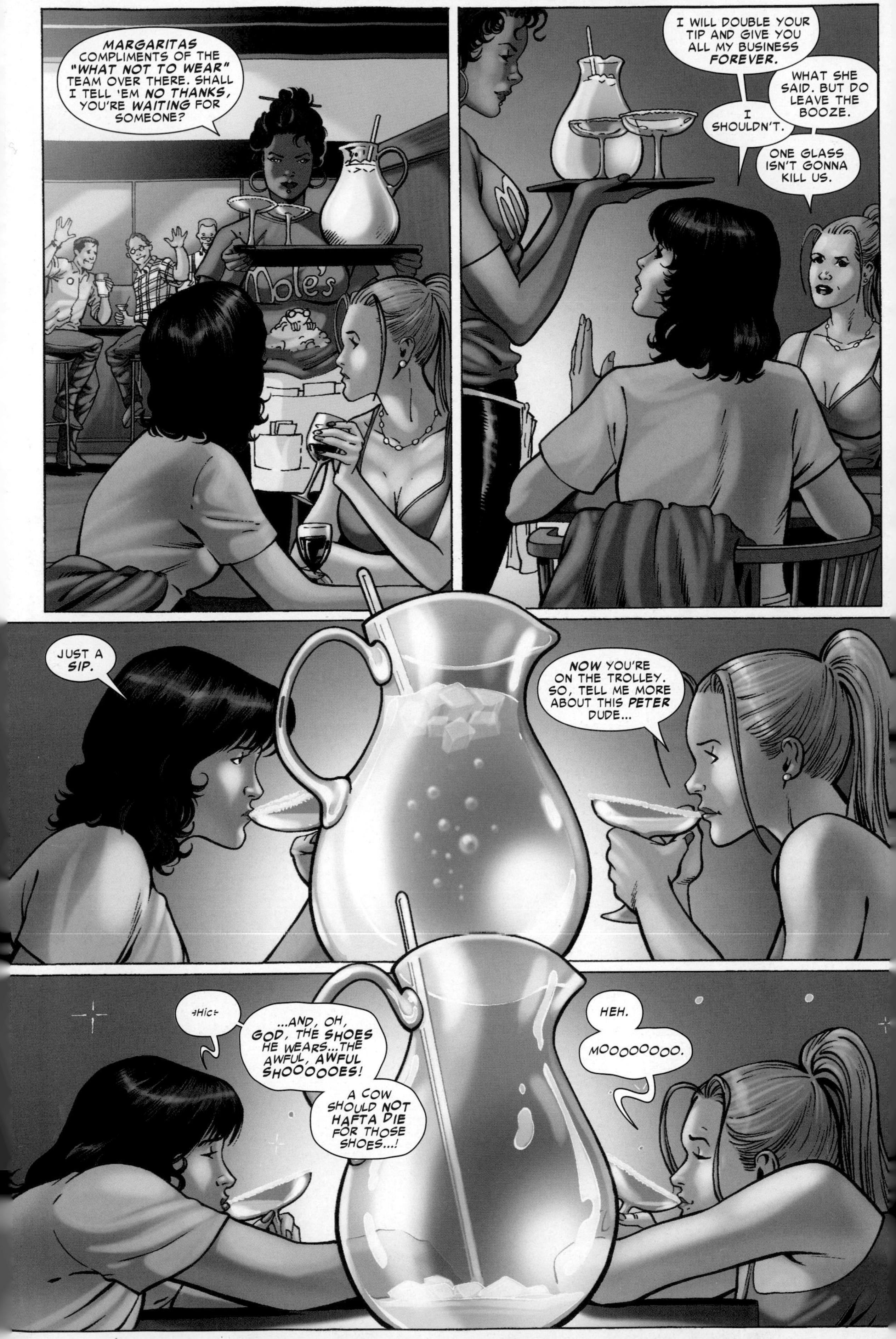
MARGARITAS COMPLIMENTS OF THE "WHAT NOT TO WEAR" TEAM OVER THERE. SHALL I TELL 'EM NO THANKS, YOU'RE WAITING FOR SOMEONE?
Mole's
I WILL DOUBLE YOUR TIP AND GIVE YOU ALL MY BUSINESS FOREVER.
I SHOULDN'T.
WHAT SHE SAID. BUT DO LEAVE THE BOOZE.
ONE GLASS ISN'T GONNA KILL US.
JUST A SIP.
NOW YOU'RE ON THE TROLLEY. SO, TELL ME MORE ABOUT THIS PETER DUDE...
HIC
...AND, OH, GOD, THE SHOES HE WEARS...THE AWFUL, AWFUL SHOOOOOES!
A COW SHOULD NOT HAFTA DIE FOR THOSE SHOES...!
HEH.
MOOOOOOOO.

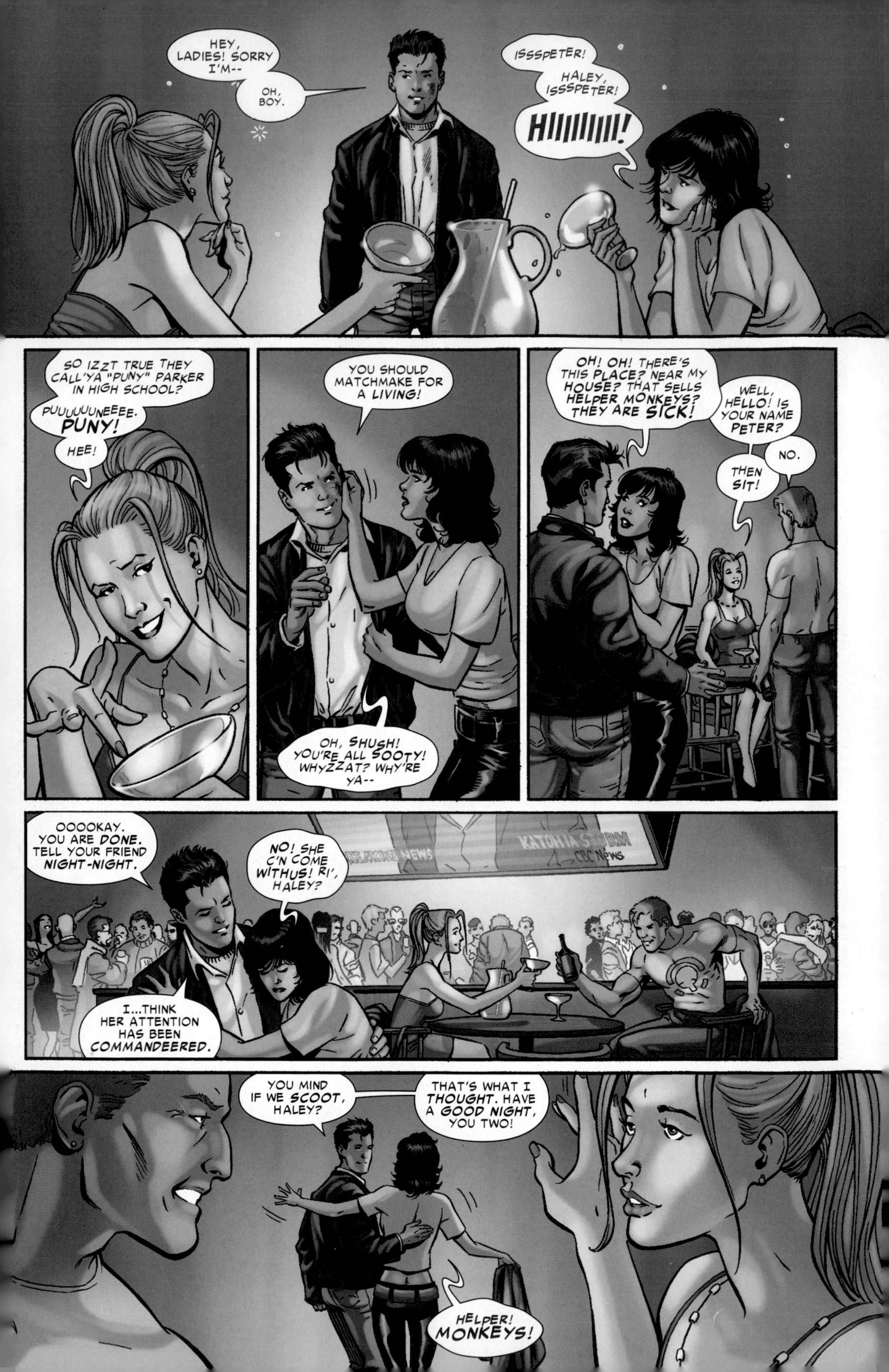

HEY, LADIES! SORRY I'M--
OH, BOY.
ISSSPETER!
HALEY, ISSSPETER!
HIIIIIIIII!
SO IZZT TRUE THEY CALL'YA "PUNY" PARKER IN HIGH SCHOOL?
PUUUUUUNEEEE. PUNY!
HEE!
YOU SHOULD MATCHMAKE FOR A LIVING!
OH, SHUSH! YOU'RE ALL SOOTY! WHYZZAT? WHY'RE YA--
OH! OH! THERE'S THIS PLACE? NEAR MY HOUSE? THAT SELLS HELPER MONKEYS? THEY ARE SICK!
WELL, HELLO! IS YOUR NAME PETER?
NO.
THEN SIT!
OOOOKAY. YOU ARE DONE. TELL YOUR FRIEND NIGHT-NIGHT.
NO! SHE C'N COME WITHUS! RI', HALEY?
I...THINK HER ATTENTION HAS BEEN COMMANDEERED.
YOU MIND IF WE SCOOT, HALEY?
THAT'S WHAT I THOUGHT. HAVE A GOOD NIGHT, YOU TWO!
HELPER! MONKEYS!

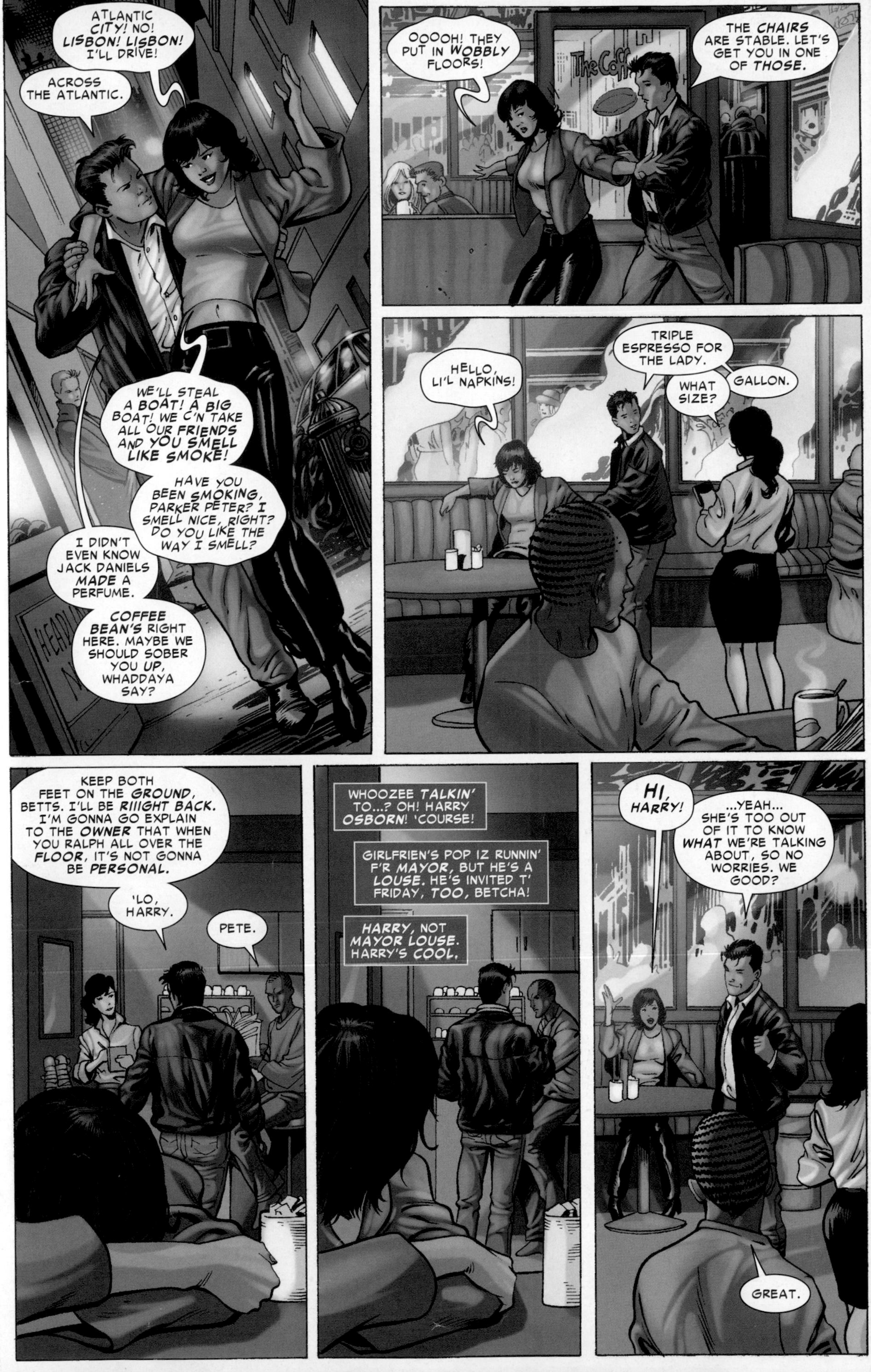

ATLANTIC CITY! NO! LISBON! LISBON! I'LL DRIVE!
ACROSS THE ATLANTIC.
WE'LL STEAL A BOAT! A BIG BOAT! WE C'N TAKE ALL OUR FRIENDS AND YOU SMELL LIKE SMOKE!
HAVE YOU BEEN SMOKING, PARKER PETER? I SMELL NICE, RIGHT? DO YOU LIKE THE WAY I SMELL?
I DIDN'T EVEN KNOW JACK DANIELS MADE A PERFUME.
COFFEE BEAN'S RIGHT HERE. MAYBE WE SHOULD SOBER YOU UP, WHADDAYA SAY?
OOOOH! THEY PUT IN WOBBLY FLOORS!
THE CHAIRS ARE STABLE. LET'S GET YOU IN ONE OF THOSE.
HELLO, LI'L NAPKINS!
TRIPLE ESPRESSO FOR THE LADY.
WHAT SIZE?
GALLON.
KEEP BOTH FEET ON THE GROUND, BETTS. I'LL BE RIIIGHT BACK. I'M GONNA GO EXPLAIN TO THE OWNER THAT WHEN YOU RALPH ALL OVER THE FLOOR, IT'S NOT GONNA BE PERSONAL.
'LO, HARRY.
PETE.
WHOOZEE TALKIN' TO...? OH! HARRY OSBORN! 'COURSE!
GIRLFRIEN'S POP IZ RUNNIN' F'R MAYOR, BUT HE'S A LOUSE. HE'S INVITED T' FRIDAY, TOO, BETCHA!
HARRY, NOT MAYOR LOUSE. HARRY'S COOL.
HI, HARRY!
...YEAH... SHE'S TOO OUT OF IT TO KNOW WHAT WE'RE TALKING ABOUT, SO NO WORRIES. WE GOOD?
GREAT.

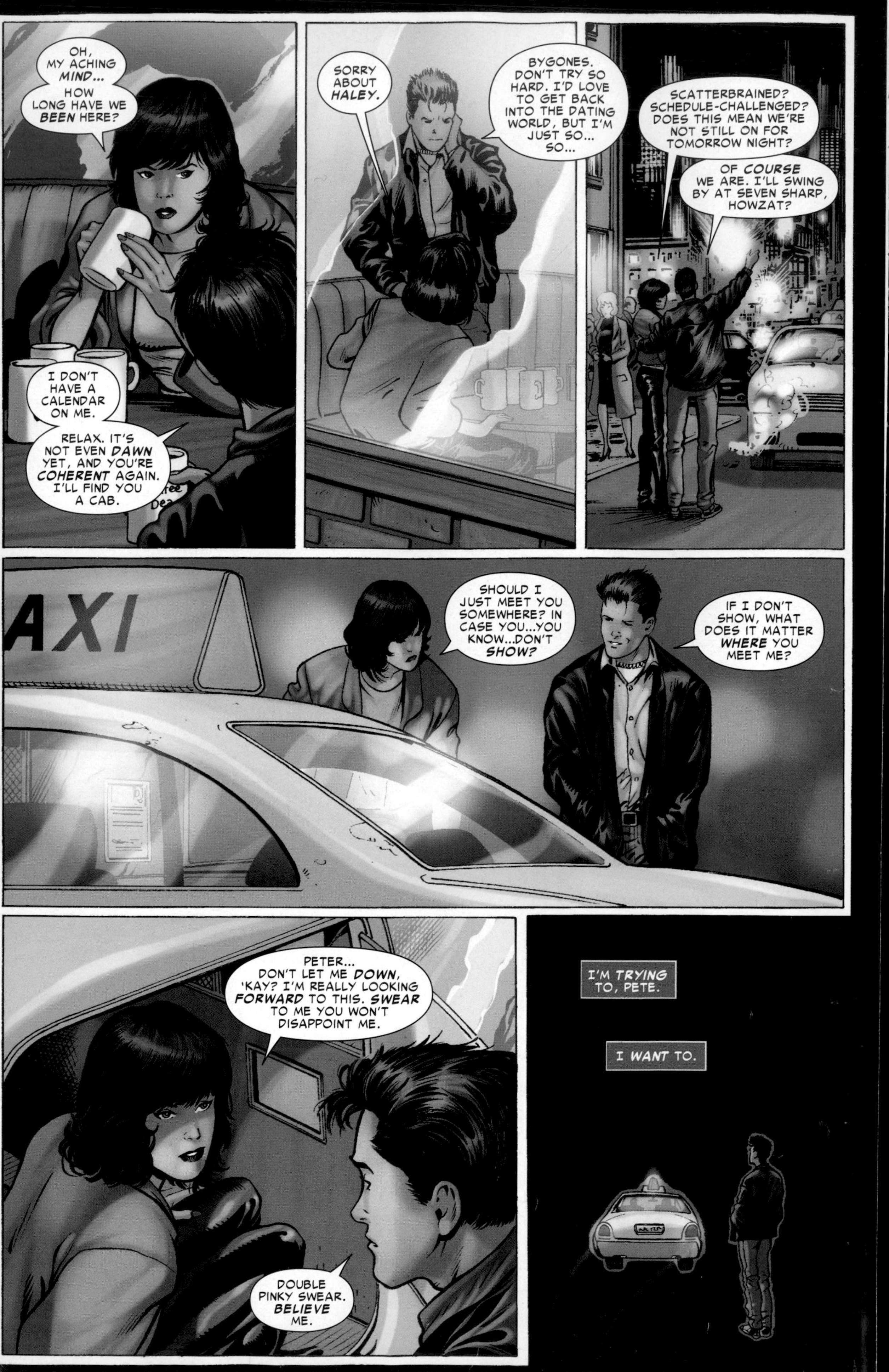

OH, MY ACHING MIND... HOW LONG HAVE WE BEEN HERE?
I DON'T HAVE A CALENDAR ON ME.
RELAX. IT'S NOT EVEN DAWN YET, AND YOU'RE COHERENT AGAIN. I'LL FIND YOU A CAB.
SORRY ABOUT HALEY.
BYGONES. DON'T TRY SO HARD. I'D LOVE TO GET BACK INTO THE DATING WORLD, BUT I'M JUST SO... SO...
SCATTERBRAINED? SCHEDULE-CHALLENGED? DOES THIS MEAN WE'RE NOT STILL ON FOR TOMORROW NIGHT?
OF COURSE WE ARE. I'LL SWING BY AT SEVEN SHARP, HOWZAT?
AXI
SHOULD I JUST MEET YOU SOMEWHERE? IN CASE YOU...YOU KNOW...DON'T SHOW?
IF I DON'T SHOW, WHAT DOES IT MATTER WHERE YOU MEET ME?
PETER... DON'T LET ME DOWN, 'KAY? I'M REALLY LOOKING FORWARD TO THIS. SWEAR TO ME YOU WON'T DISAPPOINT ME.
DOUBLE PINKY SWEAR. BELIEVE ME.
I'M TRYING TO, PETE.
I WANT TO.

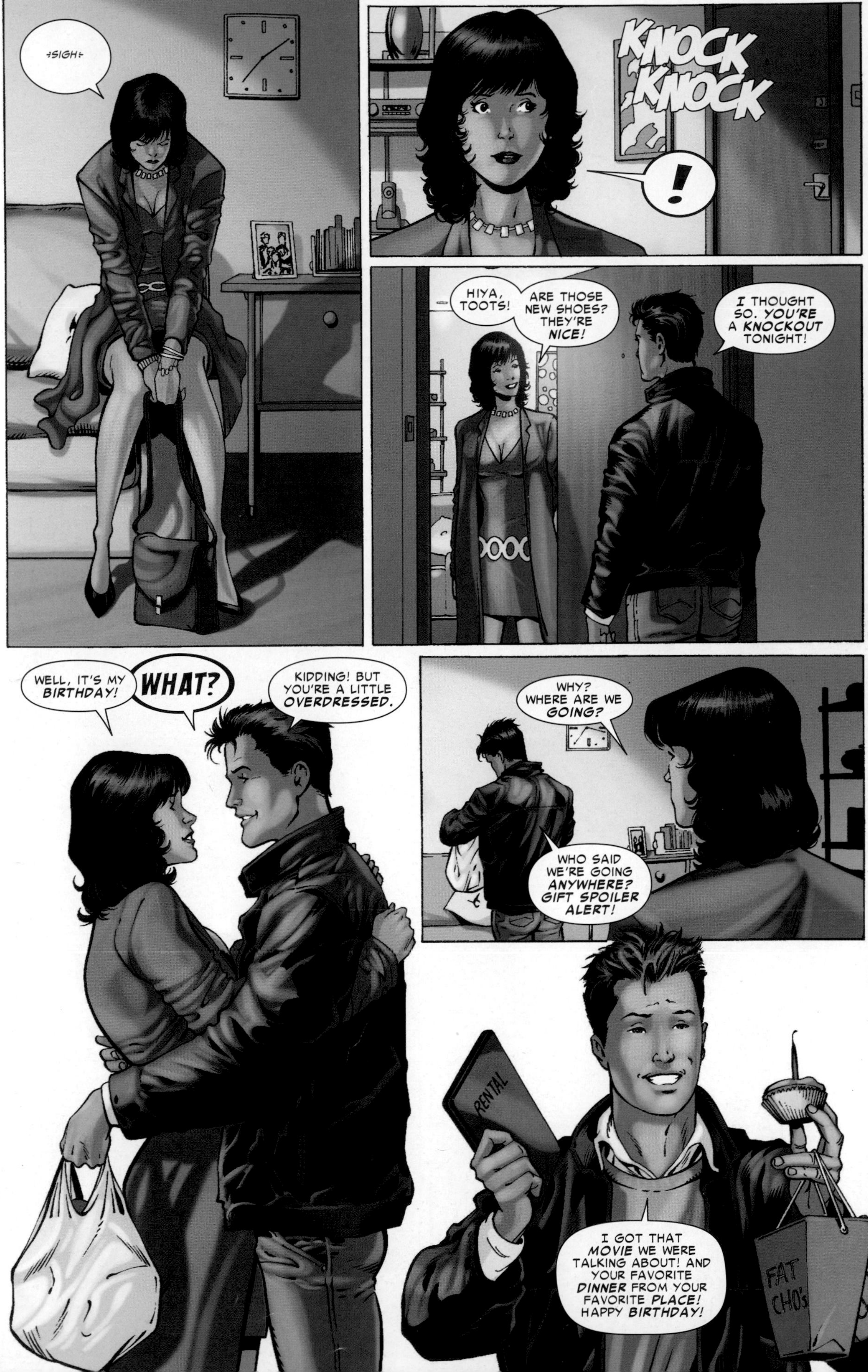

=SIGH=
KNOCK KNOCK
!
HIYA, TOOTS!
ARE THOSE NEW SHOES? THEY'RE NICE!
I THOUGHT SO. YOU'RE A KNOCKOUT TONIGHT!
WELL, IT'S MY BIRTHDAY!
WHAT?
KIDDING! BUT YOU'RE A LITTLE OVERDRESSED.
WHY? WHERE ARE WE GOING?
WHO SAID WE'RE GOING ANYWHERE? GIFT SPOILER ALERT!
RENTAL
I GOT THAT MOVIE WE WERE TALKING ABOUT! AND YOUR FAVORITE DINNER FROM YOUR FAVORITE PLACE! HAPPY BIRTHDAY!
FAT CHO's

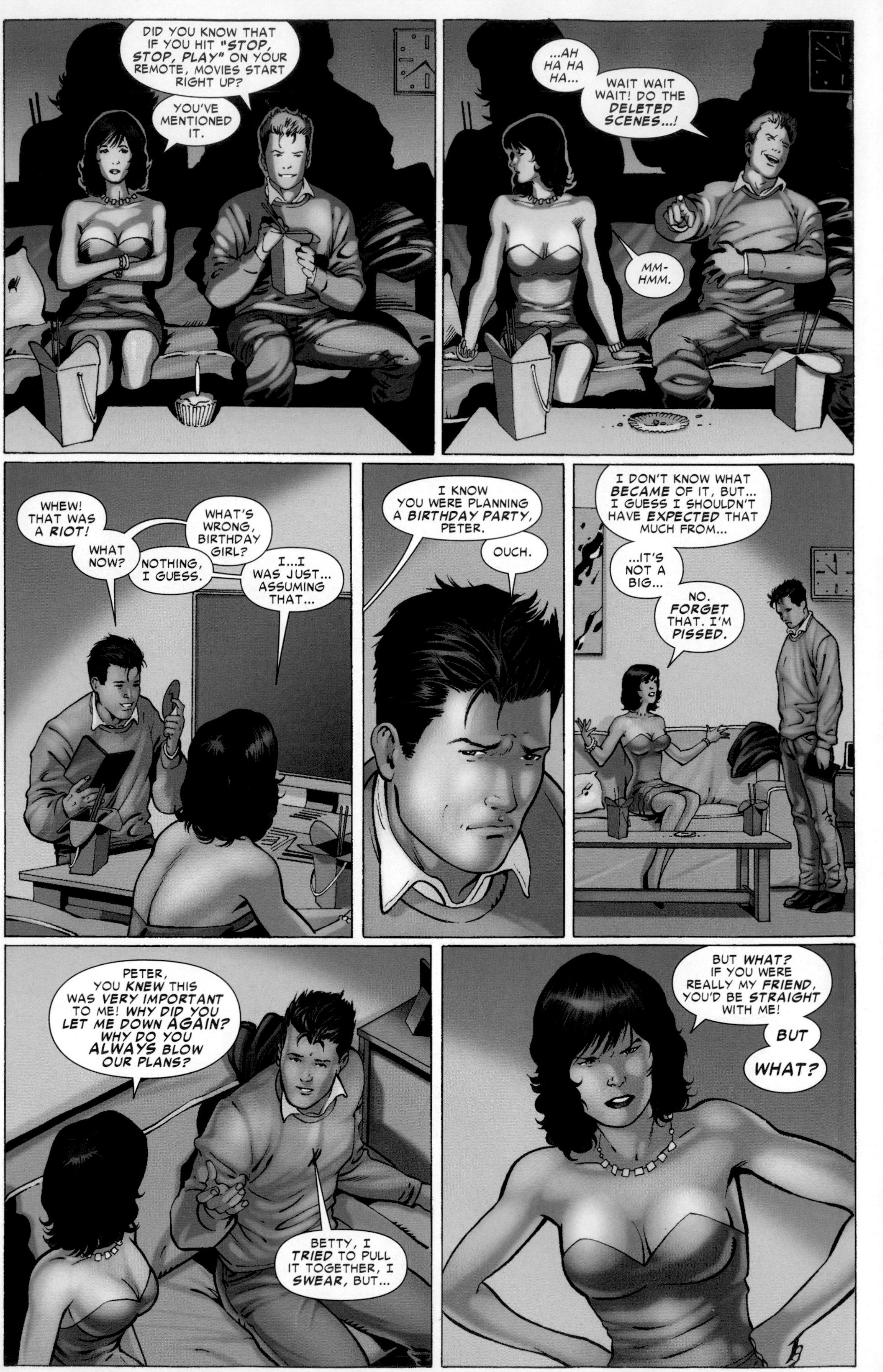
DID YOU KNOW THAT IF YOU HIT "STOP, STOP, PLAY" ON YOUR REMOTE, MOVIES START RIGHT UP?
YOU'VE MENTIONED IT.
...AH HA HA HA...
WAIT WAIT WAIT! DO THE DELETED SCENES...!
MM-HMM.
WHEW! THAT WAS A RIOT!
WHAT'S WRONG, BIRTHDAY GIRL?
WHAT NOW?
NOTHING, I GUESS.
I...I WAS JUST... ASSUMING THAT...
I KNOW YOU WERE PLANNING A BIRTHDAY PARTY, PETER.
OUCH.
I DON'T KNOW WHAT BECAME OF IT, BUT... I GUESS I SHOULDN'T HAVE EXPECTED THAT MUCH FROM...
...IT'S NOT A BIG...
NO. FORGET THAT. I'M PISSED.
PETER, YOU KNEW THIS WAS VERY IMPORTANT TO ME! WHY DID YOU LET ME DOWN AGAIN? WHY DO YOU ALWAYS BLOW OUR PLANS?
BETTY, I TRIED TO PULL IT TOGETHER, I SWEAR, BUT...
BUT WHAT? IF YOU WERE REALLY MY FRIEND, YOU'D BE STRAIGHT WITH ME!
BUT
WHAT?

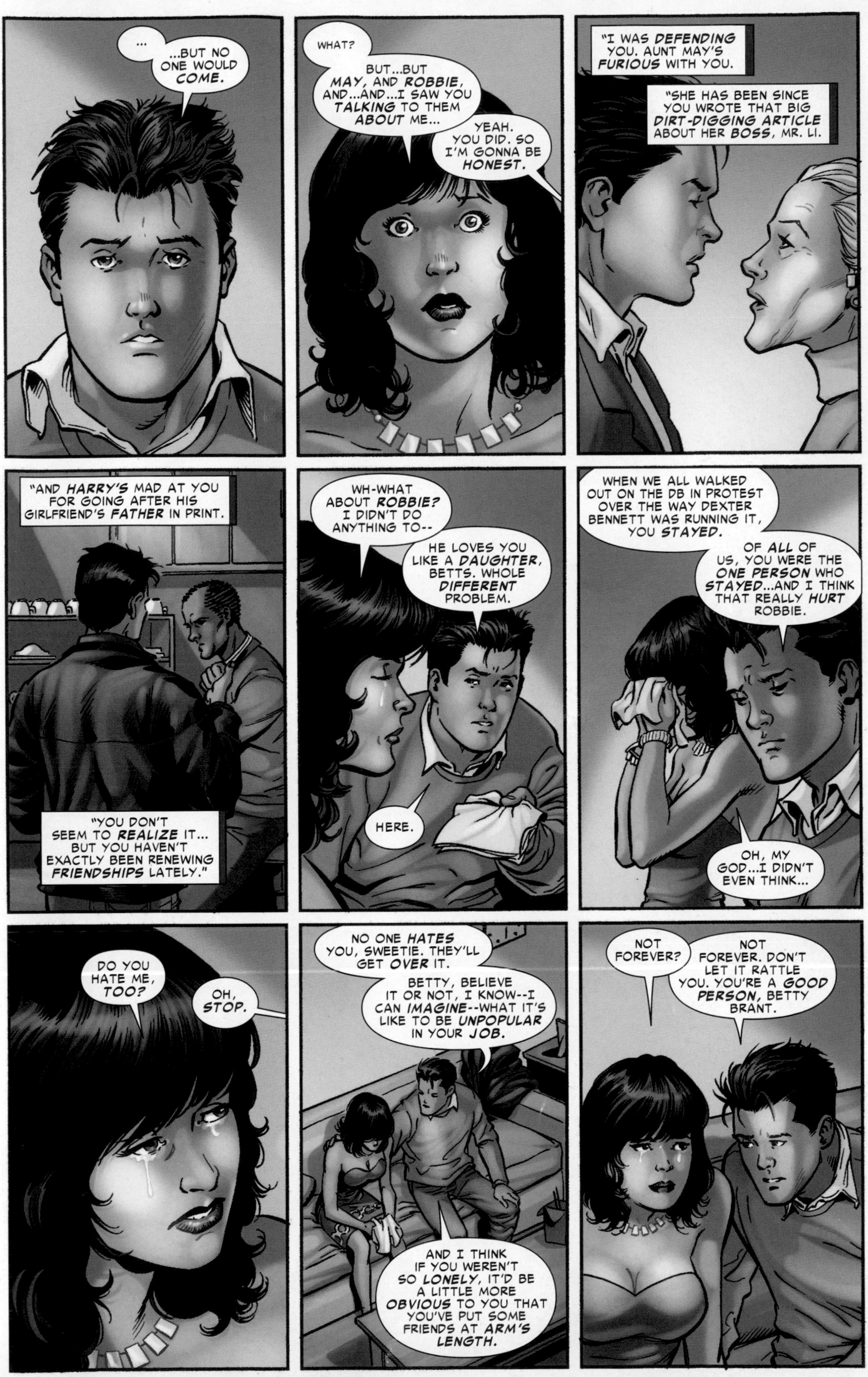
...
...BUT NO ONE WOULD COME.
WHAT?
BUT...BUT MAY, AND ROBBIE, AND...AND...I SAW YOU TALKING TO THEM ABOUT ME...
YEAH. YOU DID. SO I'M GONNA BE HONEST.
"I WAS DEFENDING YOU. AUNT MAY'S FURIOUS WITH YOU.
"SHE HAS BEEN SINCE YOU WROTE THAT BIG DIRT-DIGGING ARTICLE ABOUT HER BOSS, MR. LI.
"AND HARRY'S MAD AT YOU FOR GOING AFTER HIS GIRLFRIEND'S FATHER IN PRINT.
"YOU DON'T SEEM TO REALIZE IT... BUT YOU HAVEN'T EXACTLY BEEN RENEWING FRIENDSHIPS LATELY."
WH-WHAT ABOUT ROBBIE? I DIDN'T DO ANYTHING TO--
HE LOVES YOU LIKE A DAUGHTER, BETTS. WHOLE DIFFERENT PROBLEM.
HERE.
WHEN WE ALL WALKED OUT ON THE DB IN PROTEST OVER THE WAY DEXTER BENNETT WAS RUNNING IT, YOU STAYED.
OF ALL OF US, YOU WERE THE ONE PERSON WHO STAYED...AND I THINK THAT REALLY HURT ROBBIE.
OH, MY GOD...I DIDN'T EVEN THINK...
DO YOU HATE ME, TOO?
OH, STOP.
NO ONE HATES YOU, SWEETIE. THEY'LL GET OVER IT.
BETTY, BELIEVE IT OR NOT, I KNOW--I CAN IMAGINE--WHAT IT'S LIKE TO BE UNPOPULAR IN YOUR JOB.
AND I THINK IF YOU WEREN'T SO LONELY, IT'D BE A LITTLE MORE OBVIOUS TO YOU THAT YOU'VE PUT SOME FRIENDS AT ARM'S LENGTH.
NOT FOREVER?
NOT FOREVER. DON'T LET IT RATTLE YOU. YOU'RE A GOOD PERSON, BETTY BRANT.

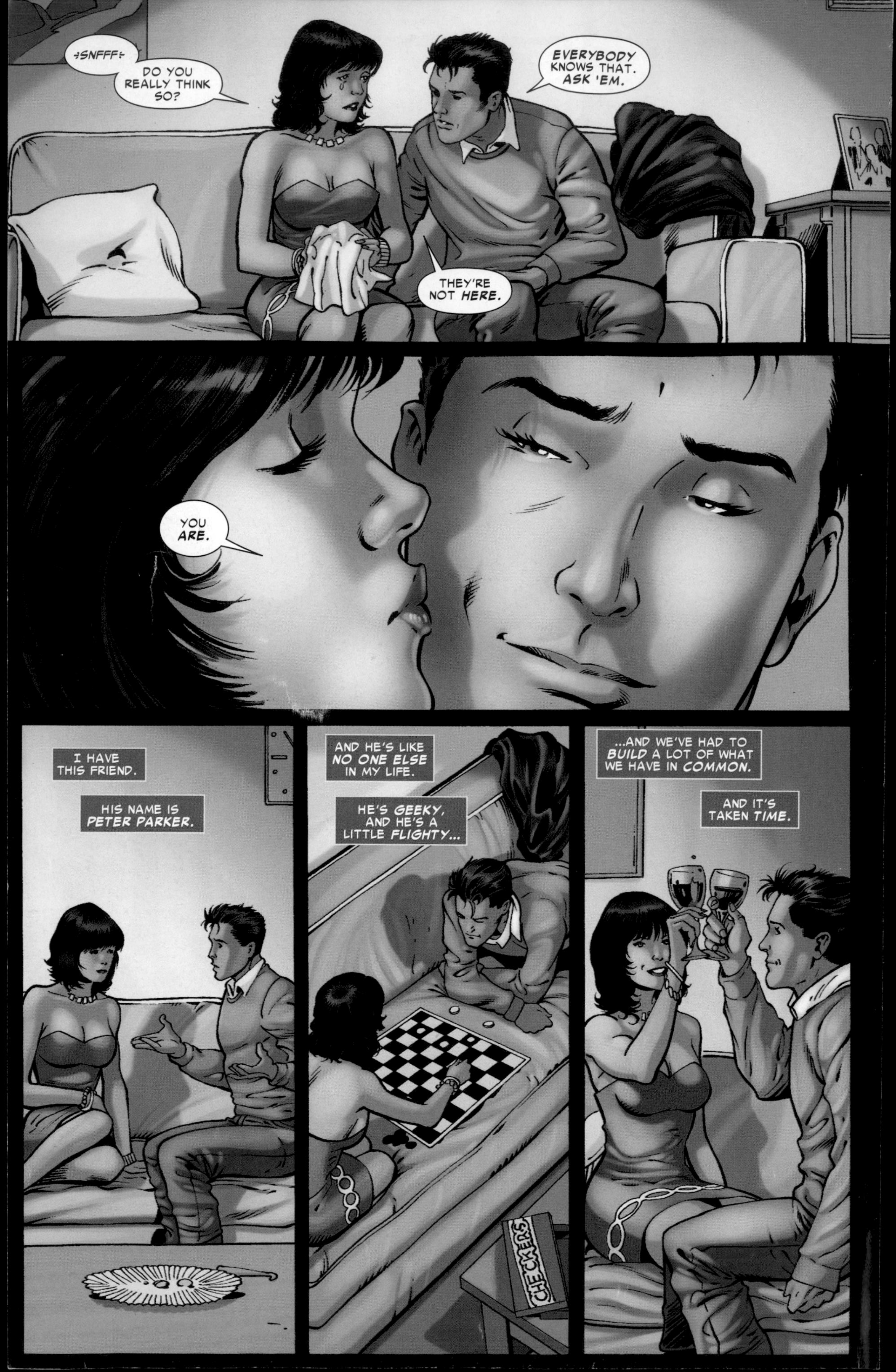

SNFFF
DO YOU REALLY THINK SO?
EVERYBODY KNOWS THAT. ASK 'EM.
THEY'RE NOT HERE.
YOU ARE.
I HAVE THIS FRIEND.
HIS NAME IS PETER PARKER.
AND HE'S LIKE NO ONE ELSE IN MY LIFE.
HE'S GEEKY, AND HE'S A LITTLE FLIGHTY...
CHECKERS
...AND WE'VE HAD TO BUILD A LOT OF WHAT WE HAVE IN COMMON.
AND IT'S TAKEN TIME.

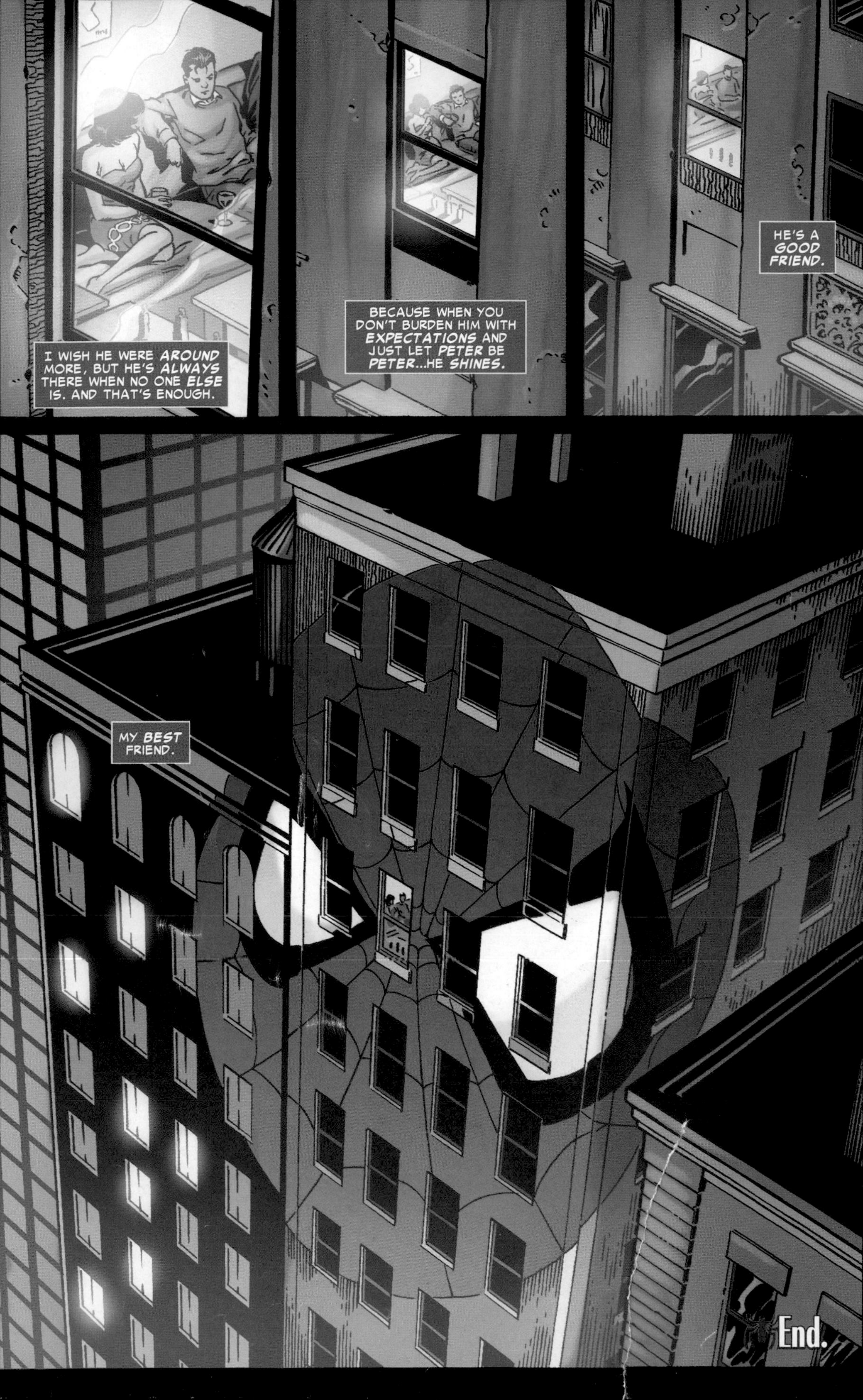
I WISH HE WERE AROUND MORE, BUT HE'S ALWAYS THERE WHEN NO ONE ELSE IS. AND THAT'S ENOUGH.
BECAUSE WHEN YOU DON'T BURDEN HIM WITH EXPECTATIONS AND JUST LET PETER BE PETER...HE SHINES.
HE'S A GOOD FRIEND.
MY BEST FRIEND.
End.

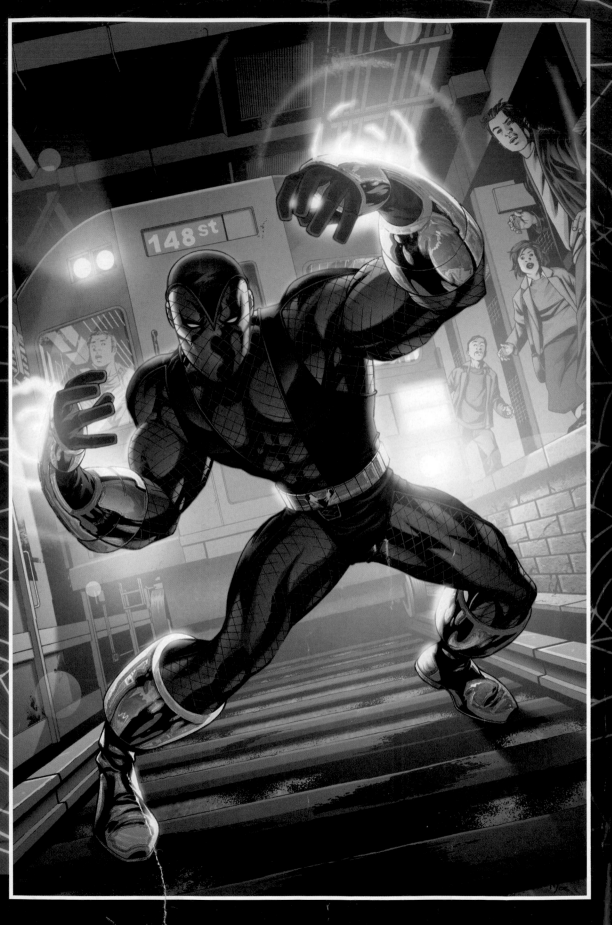

AMAZING SPIDER-MAN #579 VILLAIN VARIANT BY MIKE McKONE

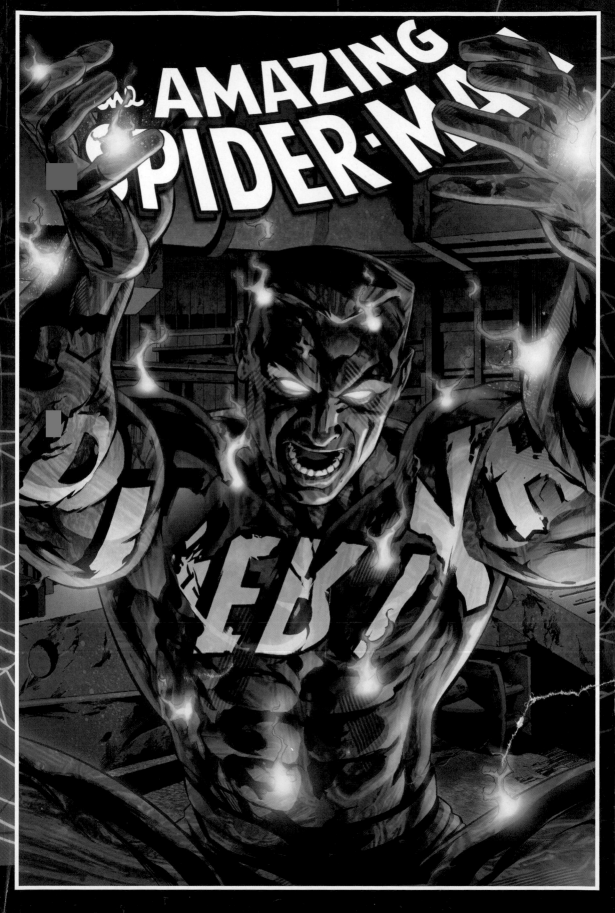

AMAZING SPIDER-MAN #581 VILLAIN VARIANT BY MIKE McKONE

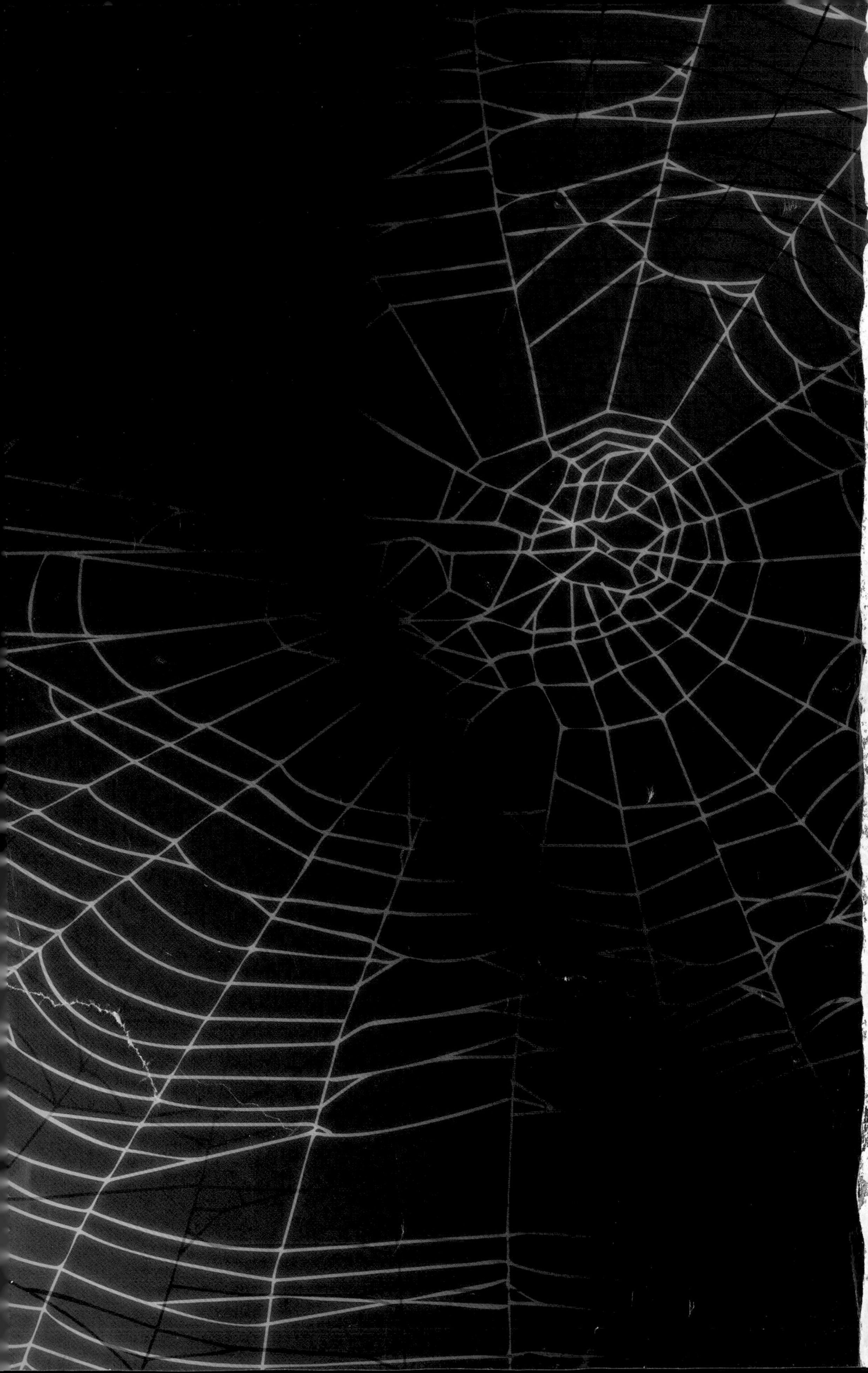